The Definitive Guide to Modernizing Applications on Google Cloud

The what, why, and how of application modernization on Google Cloud

Steve (Satish) Sangapu

Dheeraj Panyam

Jason Marston

BIRMINGHAM—MUMBAI

The Definitive Guide to Modernizing Applications on Google Cloud

Copyright © 2021 Packt Publishing

Group Product Manager: Rahul Nair

Publishing Product Manager: Rahul Nair

Senior Editor: Arun Nadar

Content Development Editor: Nihar Kapadia

Technical Editor: Shruthi Shetty

Copy Editor: Safis Editing

Project Coordinator: Ajesh Devavaram

Proofreader: Safis Editing

Indexer: Subalakshmi Govindhan

Production Designer: Alishon Mendonca

First published: December 2021

Production reference: 2121121

Published by Packt Publishing Ltd.

Livery Place

35 Livery Street

Birmingham

B3 2PB, UK.

ISBN 978-1-80020-979-4

www.packt.com

To the memory of my father, Ishwar, and my mother, Savithri, for their sacrifices and exemplifying that hard work has positive outcomes. To my wife, Sanju, for being my loving and supportive partner, and to my children, Riya and Risha, for keeping us on our toes.

– Steve (Satish) Sangapu

To my parents, who have encouraged me in writing this book, with their push for tenacity ringing in my ears.

– Dheeraj Panyam

Contributors

About the authors

Steve (Satish) Sangapu has been working with software since 2000. He specializes in migrating and modernizing applications from monoliths to containerized microservices as well as creating data engineering pipelines to mine vast amounts of structured and unstructured data.

He has extensive experience successfully leading large, cross-functional, geographically dispersed teams utilizing modern Agile development methodologies while collaborating effectively with product teams in creating high-performance, fault-tolerant, and high-availability systems.

He also holds seven patents from the United States Patent and Trademark Office and certifications from Carnegie Mellon Software Engineering Institute and Google Cloud.

I want to thank the people who have given me and the people around me love and support in different ways in my life.

Dheeraj Panyam has been working in the IT industry since 2000. His experience spans diverse domains (optical, telecom, retail, and healthcare) and covers all phases of the SDLC, including application development, production support, QA automation, and cloud architecture. He lives in India and collaborates with a Google Cloud consulting company, helping them design solutions and architecture set up on public cloud platforms.

He holds multiple Google Cloud certifications in addition to other certifications in networking and testing.(in new line)

Jason Marston is a Cloud Solution Architect based in England. He was recruited by Microsoft because of his OSS background. Jason has worked with Java since version 1 and has a long history with open source. He has over 30 years' of experience in developing software and now helps organizations migrate and modernize legacy applications to the cloud. Jason was an SME in the Worldwide Communities project at Microsoft and, as a part of the leadership team for those communities, helped many people solve their problems by adopting Java on Azure. In his spare time, Jason reads science fiction books and has two children who think he is a geek/nerd.

About the reviewer

Radhakrishnan (Krishna) Gopal is a cloud evangelist, seasoned technology professional, and mentor with over 22 years of industry experience in all major cloud hyperscalers, including AWS, Azure, and Google Cloud. He is currently helping organizations to drive business value through cloud adoption and innovation. He has worked in many facets of IT throughout his career and delivered high-quality, mission-critical, and innovative technology solutions leveraging multi-cloud, data, AI, and intelligent automation. He is a Google Cloud Certified Professional Cloud Architect, Google data engineer, Azure certified solutions architect expert, Azure data engineer, data science associate, AI engineer, and AWS Certified Solutions Architect Associate. He loves to explore new frontiers of technology and impart them in solutions to make his clients very successful.

Table of Contents

2

End-to-End Extensible Tooling for Cloud-Native Application Development

3

Cloud-Native Architecture Patterns and System Architecture Tenets

Section 2: Selecting the Right Google Cloud Services

4
Choosing the Right Compute Option

5
Choosing the Right Database and Storage

6
Implementing a Messaging and Scheduling System

7
Implementing Cloud-Native Security

Section 3: Rehosting and Replatforming the Application

8
Introducing the Legacy Application

9
The Initial Architecture on Google Compute Engine

10

Addressing Scalability and Availability

11

Re-Platforming the Data Layer

12

Designing the Interim Architecture

13

Refactoring to Microservices

Section 4: Refactoring the Application on Cloud-Native/PaaS and Serverless in Google Cloud

14

Refactoring the Frontend and Exposing REST Services

15

Handling Eventual Consistency with the Compensation Pattern

16

Orchestrating Your Application with Google Kubernetes Engine

17

Going Serverless with Google App Engine

18

Future Proofing Your App with Google Cloud Run

Appendix A

Choosing the Right Migration Strategy

Appendix B
Application Modernization Solutions

Other Books You May Enjoy

Index

Preface

75-80% of enterprise applications are legacy and stuck in the data center. How do we modernize these applications to transform them into modern cloud-native applications so that they can scale in a cloud environment without taking months or years to see the benefits?

This book introduces the services available on Google Cloud and showcases the steps involved in modernizing an example Java Spring Boot application from legacy status to the cloud by replatforming and rehosting with target deployments on IaaS, PaaS, and serverless options available on Google Cloud.

Who this book is for

Software developers and solution architects seeking to gain experience in how to modernize their applications, moving them to Google Cloud and transforming them into cloud-native applications, will benefit from this book.

What this book covers

Chapter 1, Cloud-Native Application Fundamentals, introduces the characteristics of cloud-native applications, including their benefits, along with the ever-popular Twelve-Factor App principles.

Chapter 2, End-to-End Extensible Tooling for Cloud-Native Application Development, introduces the development toolset and services available on Google Cloud to aid in building a modern cloud-native application.

Chapter 3, Cloud-Native Architecture Patterns and System Architecture Tenets, explains the different design patterns and best practices to address specific development challenges, client needs, and platform requirements.

Chapter 4, Choosing the Right Compute Option, introduces the various compute options available on Google Cloud from IaaS, PaaS, and containers to serverless options.

Chapter 5, Choosing the Right Database and Storage, introduces the various database and storage services available on Google Cloud.

Chapter 6, Implementing a Messaging and Scheduling System, explains the need for a messaging system for cloud-native applications, introducing the Pub/Sub service in Google Cloud and comparing it to other open source options.

Chapter 7, Implementing Cloud-Native Security, introduces identity and access management and how it can be used to secure applications deployed on Google Cloud.

Chapter 8, Introducing the Legacy Application, introduces the monolithic Java Spring Boot application along with the frontend and backend components that we will modernize at a later stage.

Chapter 9, The Initial Architecture on Google Compute Engine, explains how the sample legacy application can be rehosted on Google Compute Engine virtual machines.

Chapter 10, Addressing Scalability and Availability, addresses the scalability of the legacy application by utilizing **Managed Instance Groups (MIG)**, which is a collection of Google Compute Engine virtual machines.

Chapter 11, Re-platforming the Data Layer, showcases how to move the backend database from a self-hosted option on Google Compute Engine to a managed service on Google Cloud.

Chapter 12, Designing the Interim Architecture, focuses on understanding how infrastructure and software architecture needs to be changed to prepare for the move to microservices.

Chapter 13, Refactoring to Microservices, explains how we can package our application into separate microservices for the frontend and backend.

Chapter 14, Refactoring the Frontend and Exposing REST Services, explains how to break our monolithic legacy application into microservices for the frontend along with the backend REST APIs.

Chapter 15, Handling Eventual Consistency with the Compensation Pattern, explains how our legacy application can be designed to handle eventual consistency to allow loose coupling between the microservices.

Chapter 16, Orchestrating Your Application with Google Kubernetes Engine, explains the deployment of our legacy application to Google Kubernetes Engine. Now that we have all the individual microservices, we are ready to deploy to containerized platforms.

Chapter 17, Going Serverless with Google App Engine, explains how to deploy our containerized legacy application to Google App Engine.

Chapter 18, Future-Proofing Your App with Google Cloud Run, explains how to deploy our legacy application to Google Cloud Run, which is Google's latest serverless offering.

Appendix A, Choosing the Right Migration Strategy, explains the various migration options available when moving to Google Cloud.

Appendix B, Application Modernization Solutions, introduces Anthos, an application modernization platform.

To get the most out of this book

You will need to install the Google Cloud SDK that contains the gcloud CLI. You will also require familiarity with the Java Spring Boot framework and working knowledge of CLIs in general and the gcloud CLI specifically. You will need to have knowledge of basic DNS concepts such as setting up A records and CNAME records and understanding domains and sub-domains. Experience of working with domain registrars would be helpful. Familiarity with working YAML syntax will be useful to understand CloudBuild configuration files

Software/hardware covered in the book	OS requirements
gcloud CLI	Install the Google Cloud SDK specific to the OS installed on your machine. This comes packaged with the gcloud CLI.
Java 10 SDK	Windows, macOS, and Linux (any)

In addition, if you want to set up a custom domain for your application as mentioned in the chapters that refer to deployments on GCE, GAE, GKE, and Cloud Run, you will need to purchase a DNS domain from a domain registrar. App Engine and Cloud Run, however, come with predefined URLs provided by Google Cloud in case you do not want a custom domain.

If you are using the digital version of this book, we advise you to type the code yourself or access the code via the GitHub repository (link available in the next section). Doing so will help you avoid any potential errors related to the copying and pasting of code.

After reading the book, you should have a fair understanding of applying the right architecture pattern for your use case to transform a legacy application into a modern cloud-native application, and then use advanced application modernization technologies such as Anthos to create containerized applications that run on Kubernetes.

Download the example code files

You can download the example code files for this book from GitHub at https://
github.com/PacktPublishing/Modernizing-Applications-with-
Google-Cloud-Platform. In case there's an update to the code, it will be updated on
the existing GitHub repository.

We also have other code bundles from our rich catalog of books and videos available at
https://github.com/PacktPublishing/. Check them out!

Download the color images

We also provide a PDF file that has color images of the screenshots/diagrams used
in this book. You can download it here: https://static.packt-cdn.com/
downloads/9781800209794_ColorImages.pdf.

Conventions used

There are a number of text conventions used throughout this book.

Code in text: Indicates code words in text, database table names, folder names,
filenames, file extensions, pathnames, dummy URLs, user input, and Twitter handles.
Here is an example: "Developers can use the allUsers value to manage all of the users
of the application."

A block of code is set as follows:

```
<!DOCTYPE html>
<html th:fragment="layout (content)"
xmlns:th=http://www.thymeleaf.org
xmlns:sec="https://www.thymeleaf.org/thymeleaf-extras-
springsecurity3">
```

When we wish to draw your attention to a particular part of a code block, the relevant
lines or items are set in bold:

```
@Bean(name = "accountDataSource")
@ConfigurationProperties(prefix="spring.account-datasource")
public DataSource accountDataSource() {
return DataSourceBuilder.create().build();
}
```

Bold: Indicates a new term, an important word, or words that you see onscreen. For example, words in menus or dialog boxes appear in the text like this. Here is an example: "From the **Instances** page, click **CREATE INSTANCE**."

> **Tips or important notes**
> Appear like this.

Get in touch

Feedback from our readers is always welcome.

General feedback: If you have questions about any aspect of this book, mention the book title in the subject of your message and email us at customercare@packtpub.com.

Errata: Although we have taken every care to ensure the accuracy of our content, mistakes do happen. If you have found a mistake in this book, we would be grateful if you would report this to us. Please visit www.packtpub.com/support/errata, selecting your book, clicking on the Errata Submission Form link, and entering the details.

Piracy: If you come across any illegal copies of our works in any form on the Internet, we would be grateful if you would provide us with the location address or website name. Please contact us at copyright@packt.com with a link to the material.

If you are interested in becoming an author: If there is a topic that you have expertise in and you are interested in either writing or contributing to a book, please visit authors.packtpub.com.

Reviews

Please leave a review. Once you have read and used this book, why not leave a review on the site that you purchased it from? Potential readers can then see and use your unbiased opinion to make purchase decisions, we at Packt can understand what you think about our products, and our authors can see your feedback on their book. Thank you!

For more information about Packt, please visit packt.com.

Share Your Thoughts

Once you've read , we'd love to hear your thoughts! Scan the QR code below to go straight to the Amazon review page for this book and share your feedback.

`https://packt.link/r/1800209797`

Your review is important to us and the tech community and will help us make sure we're delivering excellent quality content.

Section 1: Cloud-Native Application Development and App Modernization in Google Cloud

On completion of *Section 1*, you will have gained an understanding of the cloud-native ecosystem, principles and benefits of cloud-native architecture as well as how to apply the 12-factor app principles on Google Cloud. In addition, you will get insights into the end-to-end tooling that goes into developing a cloud-native application on Google Cloud, along with a sample reference architecture. Finally, you will learn how to solve common challenges with cloud-native design patterns as well as hybrid and multi-cloud architecture recommendations.

This part of the book comprises the following chapters:

- *Chapter 1, Cloud-Native Application Fundamentals*
- *Chapter 2, End-to-End Extensible Tooling for Cloud-Native Application Development*
- *Chapter 3, Cloud-Native Architecture Patterns and System Architecture Tenets*

1
Cloud-Native Application Fundamentals

Cloud computing brought about a paradigm shift in the world of software engineering and changed how we build applications. The cloud ecosystem powers some of the most powerful, largest, and most innovative applications using the same set of universal principles. However, some of these principles go against the best practices in traditional application development but are crucial to the success of a cloud-native application.

In this chapter, we are going to explore these fundamentals and core principles to help you utilize the full potential of the cloud-native ecosystem. After finishing this chapter, you'll have a clear understanding of the following topics and how they are used in day-to-day development on the cloud:

- The cloud-native ecosystem
- Benefits of cloud-native architecture
- Principles of cloud-native architecture
- Applying the 12-factor app principles on Google Cloud

The cloud-native ecosystem

The cloud-native ecosystem is a combination of three very basic elements: the cloud platform, the architecture, and, of course, the cloud-native application. Let's break them down one by one.

The cloud platform is what makes cloud-native applications possible. For instance, the virtually unlimited computing and storage capabilities of a cloud platform give cloud-native applications the following characteristics:

- Scalability, a defining characteristic.
- The pay-per-use model makes the applications cost-effective.
- Managed services that make cloud-native applications not only versatile but also very developer-friendly.

There are ample reasons why the industry is choosing cloud-native architecture as the foundation for its applications. The architecture dictates how the software is engineered and with cloud-native architecture, developers have far more control. It enables developers to adopt DevOps, containers, automation, microservices, and more. Microservices, in particular, are one of the most important components of a cloud-native architecture and they are what give cloud-native applications the rest of their defining characteristics: *agility* and *resiliency*.

An application can be considered cloud-native when it can take advantage of the cloud platform, and in order to take full advantage, it usually needs to be built on a cloud-native architecture. Therefore, a cloud-native application should be the following:

- **Managed**: Use the cloud platform as an infrastructure (be dependent on it to do all the computing).
- **Scalable**: Quickly increase or decrease resources to match the demand.
- **Resilient**: A single bug or crash should not take down the application.
- **Loosely coupled**: Parts of the application should be isolated enough for them to be altered or removed without any downtime.

If the cloud-native ecosystem were a house, the cloud platform would be the underground foundation, the architecture would be the main pillars, and the cloud applications would be the rooms.

Benefits of cloud-native applications

Cloud-native applications have many benefits that make them superior to traditional applications in many ways. These benefits are why people build cloud-native applications, but not all the benefits are innate; they're not guaranteed automatically.

Simply rehosting to a cloud platform does not mean that the time to market will decrease or that the application will be more resilient. It's up to the developer to ensure that the characteristics of the cloud platform and architecture are carried over to the end user. So, before learning how to develop cloud-native applications, it's a good idea to learn what makes cloud-native applications so powerful and popular among businesses.

Increased speed of delivery

Simply building applications isn't enough – delivering the service to the market is just as important. Bringing a new service or product to the market before competitors has a huge advantage (first-mover advantage). Similarly, timely feature updates and bug fixes are incredibly important as well.

Cloud-native applications can be built in a very short time and are generally much faster at pushing updates as well. This is possible due to the way they are architected as well as because of the approach developers take. Let's take a look at some of the architectural benefits first.

Not monolithic

A decade ago, the trend was to make everything monolithic. Today, the trend is to break the monolith into microservices. This paradigm shift was driven by the need to be more agile and resilient and monoliths were neither. The solution? Use a loosely coupled architecture that is not affected by the limitations of monolithic architecture.

Unlike a monolith, the cloud-native architecture supports an application being built in pieces and then joined together. These pieces are called microservices and they are completely isolated from each other in their own environments called containers. They communicate with each other through APIs. The popular saying *breaking the monolith* refers to breaking down the web of a complex and interconnected code base into neatly organized microservices that are much easier to maintain.

A popular real-world example of breaking the monolith is Netflix. By the time it turned 1 in 2008, Netflix's monolithic architecture had already become a problematic mess that caused extremely long downtimes. So, after 3 years of refactoring, Netflix's engineers were able to break down their giant monolith into 500-700 microservices, reducing cost, time to market, and downtimes.

A microservices architecture also reduces the time to fix bugs as each microservice is monitored separately and buggy microservices can be quickly identified, replaced with an older version, or completely removed without any downtime.

Independent development of microservices

Another major advantage of microservices is that because they are independent, developers can work on different microservices at once. This gives developers the ability to build and update different parts of the application at once, without constantly worrying about app-breaking updates or having to shut down the entire server for a small bug fix. Although compatibility issues haven't been completely eliminated in cloud-native applications, they are far fewer and rarer.

Amazon's *two pizza policy* is a great example of the independent development of microservices. The policy states that a microservice is too big if the team working on it cannot be fed by two pizzas. Although not very scientific, it illustrates just how great microservices are for small, especially remote, teams.

Independent deployment of microservices

The loosely coupled design philosophy has given rise to a new breed of applications that are modular. As microservices are usually designed with functionality in mind, they can be thought of as modular features that can be changed, replaced, or completely taken out with minimum impact on the entire application. But they can also be introduced independently. When adding a new microservice to the main code base, no major refactoring is required, which significantly reduces the time to market.

Increased scalability

Scalability is one of the key characteristics of cloud-native applications. They are extremely scalable due to the vast (unlimited as far as most businesses are concerned) hardware capabilities of modern cloud platforms. However, cloud-native applications are not scalable in the same way as traditional applications.

Historically, businesses increased their capacity to serve concurrent users by *vertically scaling* or *scaling up*. This means that they went from 2 gigabytes of memory to 8 gigabytes and from a 1 GHz CPU to a 2.4 GHz one.

Cloud-native applications, on the other hand, scale up using a different approach: *horizontal scaling* or *scaling out*. Instead of increasing the raw computing and storage capabilities of each unit, cloud platforms increase the *number of units*. Instead of a single stick of 8 gigabytes, they have four sticks of 2 gigabytes.

Although vertical scaling is easier, horizontal scaling opens up far more possibilities in terms of how resources are allocated and how applications scale with the latter, providing much better scalability.

Additionally, cloud platforms provide a number of scalability benefits such as autoscaling and pay-per-use pricing schemes that make cloud-native applications much better investments.

Increased resiliency

Risks can never be completely eliminated, so instead of solely focusing on avoiding failures, cloud-native applications are architected to respond to failures – that is, to be resilient. The resiliency of a system refers to its ability to withstand failures and continue functioning.

Unlike monolithic architecture, where everything is interconnected and pinpointing errors takes time, a cloud-native architecture promotes isolation, which ensures that a single fault won't trigger a system-wide shutdown. Independent and fast deployments also ensure patches reach the end user in time.

The cloud platform, too, plays a role in making cloud applications more resilient compared to their traditional counterparts. For instance, an automated failsafe can take critical measures without human intervention. Additionally, the developer can adopt various practices and mechanisms such as canary development, automated testing, and **continuous integration and continuous delivery (CI/CD)** tools to not only mitigate failures but also respond to them quickly when they do happen.

Mixed technology stack and workforce

One of the things about the tech stack of cloud-native applications is its support for different programming languages *within the same application as well as various types of databases (such as a mix of SQL and NoSQL variants).* That's right, you do not need to write all the applications in the same language because of microservices.

The cloud platform will read and execute container images the same way, irrespective of the language, libraries, or dependencies used. This capability is often overlooked, but the functional value of this is incredible for a diverse workforce. The fact that a project is no longer limited to a single language is great news for teams that have members that are proficient in multiple because they can now work on different microservices without any issues, because remember, cloud development makes independent development very easy.

Continuous integration and delivery

CI/CD is a development model based on the DevOps philosophy of software engineering. Traditionally, the developers would write a piece of code, wait for it to be tested by the operations or QA team, and then use the feedback to make changes.

In hindsight, this was a counter-intuitive process that led to siloed teams and data and consequently, slower development, increased costs, and often more bugs. Instead of having the development and operations teams on different sides, the CI/CD model and DevOps, in general, remove this *the ball's in your court* mindset and aims to make this process of development and deployment concurrent and continuous.

The following are some of the practices that are part of the CI/CD model that you'll likely use:

- **Iterative development**: Instead of building everything at once, cloud developers opt for an iterative process that makes testing more manageable and also reduces the number of bugs on release.

  Not to mention, iterative development is faster and gives developers the flexibility to change priorities and pivot quickly (agility).

- **Automated testing**: Cloud developers depend on automated testing for fast feedback before the code is deployed to customers. If a change in code causes a failure, the test also doubles as a concurrent debugging aid that can identify what caused the failure.

  Most tests fall under one of five major categories: unit tests, integration tests, system tests, smoke tests, and performance tests. Each test serves a different purpose. That said, tests can be written by the developer to cover nearly all potential scenarios. Cloud platforms will also provide testing tools with existing tests and templates to make things easier and faster.

- **Continuous integration**: With every new code change, there is a possibility that something else will fail. To prevent this, developers use continuous integration to constantly monitor and validate the main code base after each change to avoid any major failures.

  There are different ways to implement CI, including setting up CI servers. These CI servers can be run on the cloud platform themselves or through an on-premises software such as Jenkins.

- **Continuous deployment**: CI acts as the stepping stone to the main actor in a CI/CD pipeline: continuous deployment (or delivery). Developers practice CD by automating the delivery process. After a change passes all of the tests, it is automatically deployed to the main (production) code base.

  CD helps make the feedback cycles shorter, saves time, reduces the release cycles, and increases overall reliability.

Increased automation

The cloud platform is built to promote automation and therefore a large part of the workflows and processes can be automated. Let's take a look at a few of them.

Environment creation and maintenance

To build your application, you need an infrastructure to build it on. Most cloud platforms give developers two options. They can either configure their own infrastructure and provision resources according to their exact requirements or let the cloud do it for them. Cloud solutions that offer the second option are called **managed services** and it is a big advantage.

In essence, automating environment creation and maintenance means you let the cloud do all the heavy lifting while you focus on your app. This results in benefits such as the following:

- Not having to worry about overprovisioning resources and paying for more than you will use

- Eliminating traditional server management and maintenance costs, which includes upgrades, patching, and licensing

- Getting a project up and running requires a smaller team

Additionally, environment automation also gives you autoscaling. Autoscaling is an operations pattern that automatically reduces or increases resources depending on traffic. Cloud-native applications are also built with autoscaling, so the change in resources does not affect it. More importantly, however, autoscaling significantly reduces cloud costs and ensures your customers always reach you irrespective of traffic.

Event generation

Event-based cloud automation refers to process automation on the cloud triggered by specific events. Developers can automate a number of responses, from simple scenarios such as sending emails and doing scheduled tasks to more complex workflows including orchestration with external applications, real-time file processing, and even using machine learning for analysis.

Analytics

Cloud platforms such as Google Cloud offer fully managed data analytics solutions that can monitor hundreds of metrics and analyze them using machine learning in real time. These tools can analyze your resource usage, traffic patterns, and more to provide valuable insights into how your application is performing.

Client needs include a variety of use cases, some of which are mentioned here:

- Analytics can be automated for warehouse and supply chain management demand forecasting and marketing analysis.

- Automating interactions with external business intelligence tools for easier control.

- Cloud platforms such as **Google Cloud** have decades of research and innovation in machine learning and AI that businesses can leverage for their day-to-day analytics.

- Cloud platforms also provide stream analytics, which is also a very powerful solution that automates real-time analytics and facilitates quick decision making.

To summarize, cloud-native app development and cloud computing, in general, has been one of the biggest technological developments in software engineering in the past decade. It offers significant improvements in terms of speed, resiliency, collaboration, and scalability over its monolithic counterparts. However, there is one similarity between cloud-native and monolithic applications – the importance of implementation. In order to enjoy the benefits of cloud-native app development to the fullest, developers must leverage cloud best practices and principles. In the next section, we'll take a look at some of the core principles of cloud-native architecture that must be remembered during app development.

Principles of cloud-native architecture

Cloud-native architecture is the design or approach of building and deploying applications that exist in the cloud to take advantage of the aforementioned cloud delivery models. These models, along with cloud-native architecture, result in scalability, flexibility, and resiliency over their traditional counterparts. Traditional counterparts tend to optimize for a fixed, high-cost infrastructure that requires considerable manual efforts to modify and doesn't allow the immediate scale of additional compute storage, memory, or network resources.

Cloud-native architecture also has five principles that will help you use the cloud-native ecosystem to its fullest while helping you navigate a new development platform. Let's take a look.

Principle 1 – lightweight microservices

Cloud-native architecture is fundamentally a different approach from traditional monolithic applications. Rather than the wholescale development and deployment of applications, cloud-native-architected applications are based on self-contained and independently deployable microservices. Microservices are at the heart of a cloud-native architecture and it is critical for a DevOps-focused pipeline because smaller teams are able to work on small portions of the application.

However, as microservices become more complex and larger, they lose their initial purpose of being agile and modular and become ineffective. Therefore, the first thing to remember when creating microservices is to keep them light and focused. The following are some additional factors to remember when working with microservices:

- **API-based architecture communication**: Microservices are completely isolated and packaged into their own portable environments called containers. But they do communicate through APIs, and so a cloud-native architecture uses API-based architecture communication.

- **Independent technology stack**: As we mentioned earlier, microservices can be written in different languages and since the microservices are independent of each other, this does not affect anything. So, it's a good idea to use this capability if different members of your development team are proficient in different languages to save time and effort.

- **Independently deployable**: Microservices do not need to be deployed at once or one at a time. They can be deployed continuously and concurrently, which is great for mass automated testing. The ideal use of this characteristic is to set up CI/CD pipelines to automate deployment and testing.

Principle 2 – leveraging automation

Cloud-native applications should be architected for automation. Both the architecture and the cloud platform (such as Google Cloud) are extremely automation-friendly, so it is very easy for developers to automate crucial but repetitive tasks involving repairing, scaling, deploying, monitoring, and so on:

- **Infrastructure setup and continual automation**: Creating, maintaining, and updating the infrastructure can be automated with tools such as Google Cloud Deployment Manager or Terraform, so if you do not have very specific resource or configuration requirements, automation is the way to go.

- **Development automation**: Google Cloud is full of development automation tools that boost productivity and help you focus on improving your app by taking care of more repetitive tasks. One of the most worthwhile investments on your end would be to set up a CI/CD pipeline using tools such as Google Cloud Build, Jenkins, or Spinnaker.

- **Monitoring and auto-heal**: Monitoring app performance and health is crucial, especially in the early stages of app development, but it's not feasible to be on the watch 24/7. That's why developers should integrate monitoring and logging systems in their applications right from the start. More importantly, machine learning can be used to analyze data streams in real time for faster decision making.

A cloud-native architecture is built to support automation at every step, so if a process can be automated, consider automating it.

Principle 3 – DevOps culture

The DevOps culture is a philosophy, a development method, and also a principle to abide by when working on a cloud-native project. Adopting DevOps not only boosts agility and your ability to work around problems, but there are also some important things to consider.

For instance, the use of small, independent teams to speed up development is all for nothing if the teams cannot work together. DevOps helps avoid this problem by reducing the friction between teams (especially between development and production teams) by introducing consistency in workflows, collaborative tools, and reducing the burden cross-functional teams traditionally put on each other.

Additionally, companies and teams that have implemented DevOps properly consistently outperform those who haven't. However, implementation isn't all about tools and platforms – it's equally about the people and the mindset. In order to promote the DevOps culture inside your team or company, you must promote innovation and the habit of refining and simplifying your cloud-native architecture.

Principle 4 – better to go managed

Managed services should almost always be chosen over manual operations. Modern managed solutions from cloud platforms are incredibly advanced and can reduce your responsibilities significantly. On top of the saved manpower and time, managed services will often result in cost savings by finding clever ways to reduce operational overhead.

Overall, when feasible, let the cloud do the heavy lifting because the benefits in cost and time savings will almost always outweigh any potential risks of letting the cloud manage things for you.

Principle 5 – innovate

Finally, it's important to always remember that cloud-native applications are very different from traditional application development in one way – they promote experimentation and innovation. First of all, cloud development won't punish developers the same way monoliths do if their experiments go wrong. There are so many protective measures in place that the chance of you damaging your code permanently is close to zero.

More importantly, though, cloud platforms give you the tools to innovate with. Integrate machine learning, conversational tech, IoT, and so much more. If you have a vision, chances are that you'll be able to make it a reality with cloud-native development.

Limitations of microservices

You might be thinking that microservices is the ultimate tool in modern software engineering, better than the monolith in every conceivable way – especially if your experience with microservices is limited or if you've recently learned about the wonders of microservices. However, you'll find that this is not the case.

Like everything else in life, microservices have their own sets of limitations, which means it's not the be-all and end-all that some people might make it out to be. In fact, it won't even be the obvious choice when building a modern application; in certain cases, you still might be better off with a monolith. Furthermore, in order to make the most of microservices, you need to understand the challenges of microservices and know when additional measures need to be undertaken to make up for where it's lacking.

Management of microservices

The value of change is subjective. While most of the changes introduced by microservices are positive in that they help simplify operations for the business, for some businesses, microservices can cause new complications to rise. In essence, the very things that make microservices so useful for modern applications can also make them less functional in certain scenarios – this will also be a theme in all of the limitations that we'll discuss, the first of which is managing microservices.

One of the main objectives behind using microservices is that it adds a degree of modularity, but to achieve that, we need to divide our application into lots of microservices, which, in the case of a growing application, can make mismanagement easier. Although there are additional tools and platforms available for easier microservices management (Google Cloud has one too), the point still stands – don't let your microservices get out of control.

Homogeneity of microservices

The mixed technological stack is a great feature of microservices, but ill-planned or irresponsible usage of this feature could mean that over time, you have microservices with multiple languages, databases, dependencies, and so on within the same project. While this may be convenient during initial application development, technologically complex and inconsistent microservices can become a major inconvenience when teams are switched or when a different developer starts working on a microservice with a language they aren't proficient in. Additionally, you may also have to use different tools to alter microservices within the same project.

Debugging and testing

The testing phase in a microservices architecture is almost always more complex than testing in a monolithic architecture as you are testing tens and hundreds of individual components that may or not be homogeneous in nature (meaning different technologies used).

Furthermore, in addition to testing microservices individually (known as unit tests), developers are also required to test the entire application together (known as integration tests) while taking into consideration interdependencies and APIs. These tests can be automated to a certain degree, but the tests need to be written manually by the developer.

Microservices Death Star

Even though microservices are designed to be isolated and independent of each other, there will be a point in application development (especially in larger projects) where inter-service dependencies are introduced. In fact, this isn't rare at all and there are numerous ways in which dependencies can emerge in an application. As development continues, this can get out of hand and result in an extremely complex architecture that is very interdependent and thus prone to implosion – hence called the microservices Death Star.

However, it's not all bad. As we said, a microservices Death Star is almost always a result of poor management and planning. Similar problems occur in monolithic architectures as well, but microservices provide the benefit of *visibility*, meaning you can see your architecture becoming interdependent and thus can take steps to control this before it's too late.

DevOps limitations

DevOps and cloud-native applications go hand in hand due to a myriad of reasons, but when paired with microservices, a DevOps implementation can face a few challenges. For instance, microservices development thrives on smaller, independent teams (leading to faster development). However, the large number of teams can make it difficult to unify the goals of the development teams with the operations teams and keep everyone on track – which is one of the main objectives of DevOps.

Fortunately, this can be avoided by planning ahead and making use of the numerous tools at your disposal for DevOps implementation (primarily automation). Remember, at the end of the day, DevOps is here to increase developmental efficiency while reducing time to market and the microservices architecture is an effective way of achieving these goals.

It's true that the microservices architecture won't always be the answer. Despite its limitations, a traditional monolithic application still might make sense in certain cases. For instance, if your application is relatively simple with little to no scope for expansion, the added complexity of the microservices architecture might not be worth it. And overall, regardless of your project, it's important to remember the limitations of microservices to prevent vulnerabilities and administrative headaches in the long run.

Applying the 12-factor app principles on Google Cloud

The 12-factor app is a set of 12 principles or best practices for building software-as-a-service applications. Written in 2011, 12-factor app is 12 important principles that can be followed to minimize the time and cost of designing scalable and robust cloud-native applications.

The 12 principles can be applied to any programming language and any combination of backing services (database, queue, memory cache, and so on), and is increasingly useful on any cloud vendor platform. However, to make these principles easier to follow as well as to help you apply them yourself, we'll discuss the principles in the context of Google Cloud and, more importantly, how you can apply the 12-factor app principles on Google Cloud

The 12 factors are as follows.

Code base

One code base tracked in revision control, many deploys.

Tracking code in a **version-controlled system** (**VCS**) such as Git or Mercurial has many benefits, such as the following:

- Enabling different teams to work together by keeping track of all the changes to the code.

- Providing developers with an intuitive way of resolving merge conflicts (and avoiding them to an extent).

- Allowing developers to quickly and easily roll back the code to a previous version.

- A single code base also helps simplify things when creating a CI/CD pipeline.

You can apply this principle to your process by using Google's Cloud Source Repositories, which helps you to collaborate with other members of your team as well as other developers while tracking and managing your code in a scalable, private, and feature-rich Git repository. It also integrates with other Google services, such as Cloud Build, App Engine, Cloud Logging, and more, which is quite handy.

Dependencies

Explicitly declare and isolate dependencies.

This principle translates into two best practices. First, developers should always declare any dependencies into version control explicitly. An explicit dependency declaration enables developers, especially those who are new to the project, to quickly get started without needing to set up too many things. It's also a good practice to keep track of changes made to dependencies.

The second practice suggested by this principle is to isolate an app by packaging it into a container. Containers are crucial to a microservices architecture as they are what keeps the app and its dependencies independent from the environment. As you package and isolate more and more dependencies, you can use the Container Registry tool to manage container images, perform vulnerability analysis, and grant access to users, among other things.

Config

Store config in the environment.

You might have only a handful of configurations for each environment when starting out, but as your application grows and develops, the number of configurations is going to increase significantly, which makes managing configurations for deployments a bit more complex.

To avoid this and ensure your application is architected to be as scalable as possible, you should store configuration in environment variables. **Environmental variables** (or **env vars**) can be easily switched between deploys and work with any programming language and framework. If you're already using Google Kubernetes to manage your microservices, you can also use ConfigMaps to attach various information, including configuration files, directly to the containers as well as the secrets manager service in Google Cloud to store sensitive information.

Backing services

Treat backing services as attached resources.

This principle states that developers should treat backing services (such as datastores, messaging systems, and SMTP services) as attached resources because we want these services to be loosely coupled to the deployments. This enables developers to seamlessly switch between third-party or local backing services without any changes to the code.

Build, release, run

Strictly separate build and run stages.

The software development process of creating a 12-factor app is divided into three stages: build, release, and run. Each stage creates a unique identification code that can be used to identify different stages of the development process with the main goal of creating an audit log.

So, at the first stage, a unique identification number is attached to the build. After that, we reach the release stage and the identification number of the build is attached to the configuration of the environment. Every release will have a unique ID in chronological order and since each change leads to a new release, these unique IDs can be used to track changes as well.

Processes

Execute the app as one or more stateless processes.

A 12-factor app completely avoids sticky sessions and instead uses stateless processes that can be created and destroyed without affecting the rest of the application. Developers can use backing services as a database or Google Cloud Storage to persist any data that may need to be reused.

Port binding

Export services via port binding.

Traditional web apps are written to run environments or servers such as Apache Tomcat, but since cloud-native applications are completely self-contained, they do not require such servers to listen to requests. Instead, they export HTTP as a service by binding to a port and listening to that port for requests.

When building apps on Google Cloud it's best to provide port numbers in the environment using *env vars* instead of hardcoding port numbers in your code to maintain portability in your apps.

Concurrency

Scale out via the process model.

12-factor apps are extremely scalable and to achieve the same level of scalability, it's recommended to divide your app into different types of processes and assign these processes to different types of works (background processes, web processes, worker processes, and so on).

App Engine, Compute Engine, Cloud Functions, and Kubernetes Engine all support concurrency, and thus it's highly recommended to follow this principle to make the most of your cloud-native application.

Disposability

Maximize robustness with fast startup and graceful shutdown.

A 12-factor app treats the cloud infrastructure, processes, and session data as disposable, and the application should be able to shut down and restart quickly and gracefully. This improves agility, scalability, performance, and user experience as processes can be moved between machines without any problems.

The level of disposability of your app depends on various factors, but you can do the following to make your app robust against startups and shutdowns:

- Use backing services as attached resources to decouple functionality.
- Limit the amount of layering in your container images.
- Use native features of Google Cloud to perform infrastructure tasks when possible.
- Leverage SIGTERM (stop) signals to perform graceful shutdowns.

Dev/prod parity

Keep development, staging, and production as similar as possible.

With traditional applications, development and operations teams had very different environments. The same cannot exist in cloud-native applications because speed is of the essence. Everything must be fast, smooth, and no time or effort should be spent on altering apps to suit different tools in different environments.

This becomes a little easier with cloud platforms that have a large ecosystem of auxiliary services. For instance, you can use Google Cloud's services for development, testing, staging, and production to maintain consistency across environments and also to speed up collaboration between teams.

Logs

Treat logs as event streams.

Logs are a great source of information about the performance and health of your apps. During development, developers will use logs as an important tool for monitoring the app's behavior. However, when your application is already running on public clouds, logs become unnecessary and come in the way of dynamic scaling.

Therefore, it's best practice to decouple logs from core logic instead of using other tools (such as the Cloud Logging agent) for the collection, processing, and analysis of tools.

Admin processes

Run admin/management tasks as one-off processes.

Admin processes should be decoupled from the core app to reduce maintenance and coordination. Google Cloud has many services built in to encourage this practice. For instance, you can use CronJobs in Google Kubernetes Engine to control the timing, execution, and frequency of admin processes using containers. Similarly, App Engine and Compute Engine have fully managed tools such as Cloud Tasks and Cloud Scheduler that help simplify admin processes.

The cloud-native platform (cloud vendor) and the cloud-native architecture have some very powerful benefits that developers must consider and leverage in order to utilize the full potential of cloud computing. To make this easier, developers can follow the framework of the 12-factor app until these principles and best practices become second nature.

Summary

Cloud-native app development is an extremely effective method for developing powerful applications that are based on relatively simple principles. However, despite the seemingly simple premise behind cloud-native app development, these applications, when scaled up, become increasingly complex and in order to maintain their core characteristics of resiliency, scalability, and agility, developers should follow the right principles, best practices, design patterns, and tools. The first part of this book (consisting of the first three chapters) goes through each of these factors in detail.

Now that you have a basic but strong understanding of how the cloud-native ecosystem works, the numerous benefits it offers over traditional app development, as well as its underlying principles, we can begin learning about the actual tools developers use to build cloud-native applications in the next chapter.

2

End-to-End Extensible Tooling for Cloud-Native Application Development

One of the best things about using a cloud platform such as **Google Cloud** is having access to hundreds of services that make software engineering significantly faster and easier. Google Cloud provides end-to-end tooling for cloud-native application development, which starts with cloud-native **integrated development environment (IDE)** tools that aid in maximizing development productivity code all the way to setting up monitoring and logging for your application. For cloud-native application development, Google Cloud offers a wide range of extensible services that allow developers to simplify their workflows.

In this chapter, we will understand what these services are and the benefits and roles of each service. We'll also explore how these services interconnect with the rest of the Google Cloud services used in the pipeline. Finally, we'll look at a sample cloud-native architecture pipeline to better understand how these services fit into the day-to-day workflows of a cloud-native developer.

In this chapter, we will cover the following topics:

- Moving past third-party services – the beauty of end-to-end tooling
- Google Cloud Code
- Google Cloud Build
- Google Container Registry
- Google Cloud Run
- Google Kubernetes Engine
- Operations suite

Moving past third-party services – the beauty of end-to-end tooling

Developers building applications on traditional architectures and on-premises infrastructure would often use the help of third-party services to accelerate productivity. Using third-party services meant that developers wouldn't need to reinvent the wheel every time, saving a lot of time and also simplifying their workflows. But third-party services always had challenges: integration nightmares, lack of technical support, compatibility with other services, and limited scope were some of the top complaints.

Enter cloud platforms!

Cloud vendors such as Google Cloud have already created a huge ecosystem of services, giving developers the ability to build applications from start to finish without ever leaving the ecosystem – end-to-end tooling. They have all of the convenience of third-party services and none of the problems.

The following are some of the core benefits of end-to-end tooling and why it's almost always worthwhile to learn how to use these services:

- **Simplified development and operations**: Development is simplified by offering easy integration to deploy to runtime environments on Google Cloud such as **Google Kubernetes Engine (GKE)**, Cloud Run, **Google Compute Engine (GCE) virtual machine (VM)**, and App Engine environments. Furthermore, these tools will automate a large part of the work required to build powerful CI/CD pipelines, allowing you to write, test, and deploy code faster.

- **Security and compliance across all artifacts**: Google Cloud services such as **Google Container Registry (GCR)** are packaged with features such as container vulnerability scanning and Binary Authorization installs important security features into your software delivery process and identifies vulnerabilities as soon as code is committed. With the help of these, you can set up automated real-time policy checks to gain tight control and ensure that only trusted artifacts are deployed.

- **Built on the same highly responsive infrastructure**: Making use of the end-to-end tooling means you no longer have to worry about performance differences between your tools and your server because they're powered by the same hardware, which is run and maintained by one of the biggest tech companies in the world.

- **Google's strong support for open source tooling**: Another worrisome thing about traditional third-party tools was the potential lack of support and updates. Though this was less likely with larger companies, it was still a valid concern. Alternatively, you're much more likely to receive continued support and updates on Google Cloud services. But if that isn't enough of a guarantee, many of the services we're going to use are open source, which further helps the case of long-term use and eliminates the risk of vendor lock-in.

- **Additional support for third-party services**: Even if you're never going to use external third-party services, you'll still likely want to be able to use them, just in case. For that extra peace of mind, some of the most popular tools among developers (GitLab, Jenkins, Terraform, Datadog, Prometheus, and so on) can be integrated easily with Google Cloud.

- **Consistent across workflows, teams, and projects**: In the first chapter, we mentioned the importance of consistency in DevOps. The end-to-end tooling will help increase consistency in development and operations teams, and between them as well. More importantly, the same best practices will apply everywhere, reducing the need for additional training and orientation.

Google Cloud Code

When building cloud-native applications, we use fully featured services known as cloud IDEs instead of traditional text editors to write code. Cloud IDEs serve a similar purpose as text editors but with exponentially more functionality – and Google has created a unified platform where you can manage multiple IDEs, write and debug your code, and also deploy it. Cloud Code currently supports three IDEs: VS Code, IntelliJ, and Cloud Shell.

Unlike some of the other Google Cloud offerings, Cloud Code can be used on other cloud platforms as well, although it works best on Google Cloud as it can be integrated with the rest of the Google Cloud ecosystem.

Features and benefits of Cloud Code

The following are some of the features and benefits of Google Cloud Code:

- **Simplifies Kubernetes development – local or remote**: Cloud Code provides a unified development environment that allows you to create and manage Kubernetes clusters within the IDE whether they are local clusters set up on your machine or on Google Cloud. Cloud Code uses popular tools such as Skaffold, Jib, and `kubectl` under the hood.

- **Debugs running Kubernetes applications**: Cloud Code provides an integrated development and debugging environment within your IDE that aids you in debugging your code by leveraging the built-in IDE debugging features.

- **Support for Cloud Run deployments**: Cloud Code now supports deploying your code directly to Cloud Run or Cloud Run for Anthos, which are both serverless offerings on Google Cloud, with a few clicks from your IDE.

- **Easy integration with Google Cloud APIs**: Chances are your application will interact with Google Cloud APIs such as Google Cloud Storage, Cloud SQL, or other managed services. With Cloud Code's library manager, you can configure these APIs from your project in the IDE and also view documentation for these services.

- **Access powerful IDE features**: Cloud Code brings most of the powerful features of your favorite IDEs in one place. The following table shows the VS Code, IntelliJ, and Cloud Shell features that are currently supported on Cloud Code:

Cloud Code Feature	VS Code	IntelliJ	Cloud Shell
Support for Java	✓	✓	✓
Support for Node.js, Go, Python, .NET Core	✓	✓ *	✓
Run-ready and debug-ready starter templates	✓	✓	✓
Support for multiple run configurations	✓	✓	✓
Continuously build and run applications	✓	✓	✓
Debugging support for your Kubernetes application under development	✓	✓	✓
Skaffold configuration editing support	✓	✓	✓
Advanced Kubernetes YAML support	✓	✓	✓
Kubernetes resource inspection and browsing	✓	✓	✓
Kubernetes cluster creation in GKE [Google], EKS [AWS] and AKS [Azure]	✓		✓ **
Log streaming and viewing	✓	✓	✓
Cloud Run support	✓	✓	✓
Cloud Build support for running apps	✓	✓	✓
Support for cloning and pushing repos to Cloud Source Repositories	✓	✓	✓
Google Cloud's operations suite snapshot based production debugging		✓	
Google Client Library Manager	✓	✓	✓
Google Cloud Storage Support		✓	
Google App Engine Support		✓	
Cloud Storage Browser support for viewing buckets and blobs		✓	

* Java is supported for all Cloud Code for IntelliJ functionality; Node.js, Go, Python for Kubernetes features

** Only GKE cluster creation is supported in Cloud Shell

Figure 2.1 – VS Code, IntelliJ, and Cloud Shell features supported on Cloud Code

The role of Cloud Code in the cloud-native app development pipeline

Like any other form of software development, creating apps in a cloud-native development process starts with writing code in the IDE of your choice. The role of Cloud Code as the first tool in the cloud-native app development pipeline is to provide the developer with everything they need to write, debug, and deploy their first (and subsequent) cloud applications.

Cloud Code comes with plugins for popular IDEs such as VS Code and IntelliJ, as well as sample templates, configurations, and workflows that will help your app get off the ground quickly.

After writing the code, you deploy it to either GKE or Cloud Run. Cloud Code has specific integrations for both, which makes the process easier. Furthermore, you can set up GCR to authenticate and push Docker artifacts automatically.

Google Cloud Build

Once you've written your code on Cloud Code, you'll need to execute it somewhere – Cloud Build does that for you. Cloud Build is a fully serverless CI/CD platform that imports your code (in any of the popular programming languages, including Java, Go, and Node.js) and executes a build to create artifacts. This is its basic function, but Cloud Build does a lot more. For instance, Cloud Build can be used to deploy your code to different environments including VMs, Kubernetes, and Firebase. You can also deploy a containerized application to Cloud Run or Kubernetes Engine.

The following are some of the additional features and benefits of using Google Cloud Build.

Features and benefits of Cloud Build

Here are some of the features and benefits of Google Cloud Build:

- **Extremely fast builds**: In addition to the standard machine type, Cloud Build provides two high-CPU VM types (`https://cloud.google.com/cloud-build/docs/api/reference/rest/v1/projects.builds#machinetype`) to run your builds so you get to choose them. To increase the speed of your build, select a VM with more powerful CPU specifications.

- **Build highly automated pipelines quickly**: Like every other tool that we're going to talk about in this chapter, Cloud Build is very automated-focused. You can use Cloud Build to automate deployments and go from pull requests to deploying in a few steps. For instance, Cloud Build supports automated triggers that you can set up to automatically build, test, or deploy source code when a change is pushed on Cloud Source Repositories, GitHub, or a Bitbucket repository.

- **Extensive support**: Cloud Build supports numerous other cloud services. For instance, you can automatically deploy to GKE, App Engine, Cloud Functions, and Firebase. Cloud Build also supports Spinnaker, which you can use to build complex pipelines.

The role of Cloud Build in the cloud-native app development pipeline

In *Chapter 1*, *Cloud-Native Application Fundamentals*, we learned how CI/CD pipelines can automate a large part of cloud-native app development and thus are crucial to set up early on. The role of Cloud Build is to create these pipelines to allow developers to continuously build, test, and deploy. Traditionally, developers would use build servers for CI/CD pipelines, but Cloud Build replaces those with a highly customizable, fully managed, serverless CI/CD platform that supports different deployment environments such as VMs, serverless, Kubernetes, or Firebase.

Google Container Registry

GCR is a fully secured container registry that allows you to store, manage, and secure your container images. GCR allows you to keep track of all your containerized workloads, whether they are running on App Engine, GKE, or Compute Engine.

It is a secure, private registry, which means you have full control over who can access, view, and download images. Another useful security feature of GCR is the automatic lockdown of container images. GCR can be integrated with Binary Authorization and used to define policies and prevent the deployment of risky images to GKE if the images conflict with the set policies.

Features and benefits of GCR

Here are some of the features and benefits of GCR:

- **Easy container image management**: GCR is a very handy tool for managing all of your container images in a single place. You can keep track of changes, control access, define multiple repositories, add container tags to images, and more.

- **Vulnerability scanning**: Vulnerability scanning is one of the most popular features of GCR and allows developers to scan your databases to identify any vulnerabilities in your container images. This is especially useful early in the software development life cycle. On set up, GCR will automatically scan any new images uploaded to the container registry and identify any accidental errors, loopholes that can be exploited, or potential malware.

- **Build triggers**: GCR also supports build triggers that allow you to automate and execute a large number of tasks. The main usage of build triggers in Cloud Build was to automatically start a build when a change was made to the source code. In GCR, build triggers are primarily used to build containers on code or audit changes.

The next-gen container registry – Artifact Registry

Google recently launched a new registry solution for managing container images and language packages called Artifact Registry. As of late 2020, it's still in beta with some key features (including vulnerability scanning) being added right now.

It shares many similarities with GCR, but it is built to be a step above GCR and will be replaced when it achieves **general availability (GA)**. Artifact Registry will have the following key features:

- **In-depth artifact management**: Along with all of the features of GCR, in terms of container management, Google Artifact Registry will also allow developers to manage all of their language packages (such as Maven and npm) in a single place. It will also integrate with existing CI/CD tools for continuous integration and management services such as cloud Identity and Access Management, among other Google services.

- **Multiple repositories for each project**: Developers will also be able to create multiple repositories under a single Google Cloud project that should help with image management. Furthermore, these repositories can be separated into regional and multi-regional repositories, each having its own set of images and packages.

The role of GCR in the cloud-native app development pipeline

GCR works in a similar way as other Docker registries – it stores and tracks Docker container images on a secure and easily manageable platform. In the pipeline, GCR comes into use after the code has been written inside Cloud Build. Once the build artifacts have been generated in Cloud Build, they are pushed into GCR.

After that, GCR serves as a one-stop platform for your team to manage container images, check them for vulnerabilities, control access, and automatically deploy images to private repositories.

Google Cloud Run

Cloud Run is one of the most powerful and versatile options for quickly creating containerized applications on serverless infrastructure. We will discuss Cloud Run in much greater detail in one of the upcoming chapters, but in a nutshell, Cloud Run is a fully managed serverless platform. This means that developers do not need to worry about resource requirements, provisioning, and configuration – the cloud does everything for you.

Cloud Run is also very scalable and will increase and decrease compute and storage according to the traffic.

Features and benefits of Cloud Run

Here are some of the features and benefits of Google Cloud Run:

- **Fully managed and serverless**: Setting up storage, compute requirements, and configurations can be overwhelming for new developers as under-provisioning would mean some customers won't be able to reach you, and overprovisioning would mean you'll be paying for more than what you use. This is where Cloud Run comes in with its auto-provisioning and automatic scaling, allowing you to let the cloud take care of the infrastructure while you focus on the code.

- **Open source**: Cloud Run is based on the open source Knative standard, which eliminates the possibility of vendor lock-in. More importantly, you can use Cloud Run to deploy your application fully managed on Cloud Run itself, on GKE, on-premises with Anthos, or on a completely different cloud platform.

- **Supports a wide range of languages**: Cloud Run supports all of the popular programming languages, including Go, Python, Java, Ruby, and Node.js. You can also use your own libraries and custom binaries.

The role of Google Cloud Run in the cloud-native app development pipeline

The role of Cloud Run is to actually deploy applications on the cloud. It is one of the many options available to developers for deploying containerized applications to the cloud but Cloud Run is a fully managed, serverless platform, which makes it one of the easiest and quickest.

Google Kubernetes Engine

Similar to Cloud Run, GKE is also a managed environment where you can run your applications, and like Cloud Run, we will dive deeper into the workings of GKE in subsequent chapters. But for now, we'll just understand GKE and how it fits into the cloud-native app development pipeline.

GKE provides developers with a managed environment where they can deploy and manage all of their containerized applications. Here, it is important to make a clear distinction between Cloud Run and GKE.

Both of these solutions help developers achieve the same goal – deploy and manage containerized applications – but Cloud Run is a fully managed service and will take care of a lot of things, making deployment faster and easier. Kubernetes, on the other hand, is an orchestration platform that provides far more flexibility and configuration options, allowing you to take control of everything.

Therefore, the platform you choose depends on how much control you want over the different aspects of container orchestration. Alternatively, you can use both for different purposes.

Features and benefits of GKE

Here are some of the features and benefits of GKE:

- **Prebuilt Kubernetes applications**: GKE has a library of enterprise-ready, open source applications with prebuilt deployment templates. Developers can use them to experiment and learn about the possibilities of GKE while still being able to use them for commercial purposes.

- **Cluster and pod autoscaling**: GKE has clusters of Docker containers that can be organized into pods (each pod containing multiple clusters). GKE has autoscaling for both clusters and pods and will change CPU and memory requests dynamically, depending on the requirements. Even though GKE isn't fully managed, autoscaling makes it much more developer-friendly.

- **Security**: GKE has a number of workload and network security features, including the GKE sandbox, which provides additional isolation between containerized workloads. GKE also supports Kubernetes Network Policy, which allows developers to restrict traffic with pod-level firewall rules and restrict clusters to a specific endpoint that only addresses within a specified range can access.

GKE and Cloud Run have a lot more interesting and powerful features and capabilities that will be discussed with real-world examples in the upcoming chapters.

The role of GKE in the cloud-native app development pipeline

GKE is a managed platform that gives developers a highly customizable and secure platform for deploying highly scalable applications. One of the reasons you might want to choose GKE over Cloud Run is for greater control over a more complex architecture with clusters and pods. GKE is built to speed up the development of powerful applications with auto-repair, auto-upgrade, release channels, and numerous equally powerful integrations, including native integration with GCR. GKE clusters are authorized to pull from private GCR registries in the same project without needing config.

Operations suite

Perhaps you already know this tool by its previous name – *Stackdriver*. Google recently rebranded its monitoring and logging cloud solution to the Cloud operations suite. The operations suite allows developers to monitor, track, analyze, and troubleshoot application performance.

The operations suite consists primarily of two separate tools: **Google Cloud Monitoring (GCM)** and **Google Cloud Logging (GCL)**. Other services in the operations suite include Cloud Trace, Cloud Debugger, and Cloud Profiler.

Let's take a look at the two main services separately.

Features of Google Cloud Monitoring

Google Cloud Monitoring (GCM) is a full-stack monitoring tool that helps you with critical information about your app, including performance metrics, uptime, health, and trends. It can also be integrated with popular tools such as Slack for easier notifications, discussions, and collaborative decision-making. Here are some of its key features:

- **Easy to get started with**: Developers can quickly begin tracking key metrics with GCM without having to go through complex setups. GCM offers powerful dashboards right out of the box that give users important insight into their resource usage and ongoing services.

- **Custom monitoring and alerts**: GCM is also highly customizable. You can create custom metrics that are tailored to your application's and your business's needs and also set up alerting policies to get notifications through email, SMS, Slack, and more when the application isn't behaving as you want it to.

- **Custom dashboards**: Dashboards become powerful data visualization tools when you can customize them to your liking. If you're using GKE, you can define relationships based on clusters, groups, projects, regions, accounts, and so on, to create targeted dashboards for easier tracking and monitoring. You can also integrate your log data and alerts into your dashboards.

Features of Google Cloud Logging

Logging and keeping track of changes is extremely important for effective cloud-native app development but becomes increasingly difficult as your app scales up. This is where GCL shines. GCL enables you to store, manage, and analyze your logs and data from different sources in real time. On top of that, it's a fully managed service, which reduces the number of things you need to do before getting started. Here are some of its key features:

- **Error reporting**: If used correctly, logging can double as a debugging aid and GCL certainly makes debugging easier in a number of ways. For instance, GCL has an error reporting feature that notifies you of production problems that may be hidden by automatically analyzing all of your log data.

- **Easy audit trails**: Audit trails are also crucial in any development process as they help maintain a chronological record of all the events. GCL helps create and manage audit logs that cannot be accessed or altered by any third party and, more importantly, can be customized to collect information according to your needs and not log any unnecessary resources.

- **Advanced stream analysis**: Real-time data analysis is a godsend in modern software development as it helps flag any issues during development before it's too late. GCL supports various forms of advanced analytics, including integration with BigQuery, GCM, as well as an in-built logs explorer.

The role of the Cloud operations suite in the cloud-native app development pipeline

Once your application is deployed on GKE or Cloud Run, you can use the Cloud operations suite to monitor, troubleshoot, and improve application performance on your Google Cloud environment. At this point in the development life cycle, the following services come into play:

- **GCM**: GCM sits at the core of the Cloud operations suite and provides performance, health, and availability information about the application along with a myriad of other useful metrics.

- **GCL**: GCL is a log management tool that helps you stay on top of your log data and analyze it in real time. It is a fully managed, secured, and highly scalable solution to data logging.

- **Cloud Debugger**: It's very likely that your app may not behave exactly the way you want it to. If it doesn't, you'll have to debug the problem. After identifying an issue, developers can use the Cloud Debugger tool to analyze the source code and find the source of any irregularities, without having to stop or even slow down the app.

- **Cloud Profiler**: The Cloud Profiler tool helps monitor and improve app performance by continuously tracking CPU performance as well as memory-intensive functions to visualize the call hierarchy and resources data, which developers can use to optimize the paths utilized by the code.

- **Cloud tracing**: Cloud Trace provides developers with another way to improve their app's performance and health, this time by identifying and eliminating production bottlenecks. Cloud Trace analyzes your application's latency data from your VMs, containers, and apps on Google App Engine.

The following is a sample cloud-native CI/CD pipeline diagram that connects all of the aforementioned services:

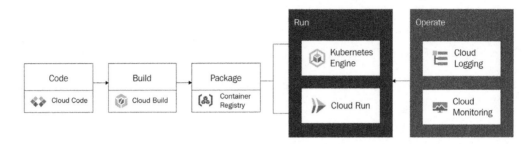

Figure 2.2 – CI/CD pipeline from writing code to deploying and monitoring on GKE or Cloud Run

The Cloud operations suite is a powerful set of services to assist the development team with monitoring, troubleshooting, and improving application performance and resiliency on your Google Cloud environment.

Summary

The CI/CD pipeline is central to all cloud-native applications and Google Cloud offers all of the tools required to build and maintain a powerful CI/CD pipeline directly in its ecosystem. The CI/CD pipeline significantly streamlines your development process throughout the application's life cycle by integrating various workflows associated with writing and debugging the code, executing the code on the multiple available environments, as well as monitoring and updating the application.

Now that you are aware of the key components that make up the CI/CD pipeline in all Google Cloud apps, we can move on to the third chapter of the first part of this book, where we will learn about the cloud-native design patterns, making it significantly easier for you to spot problems and implement solutions.

3
Cloud-Native Architecture Patterns and System Architecture Tenets

So far in the book, we've covered the fundamental principles of a cloud-native architecture as well as the tools in a cloud-native app development pipeline. This chapter is all about the operational best practices that you must adopt in order to create resilient, scalable, and secure cloud-native applications. As a developer, you are perhaps considering skipping this chapter as you're well aware of the design patterns involved in software development. But wait. The reason we've included this important chapter is that design patterns in cloud-native app development are different from traditional software development. More importantly, by the end of this chapter, you'll have a practical understanding of using different design patterns and best practices to address specific development challenges, client needs, and platform requirements.

This chapter is divided into three parts. The first part gives a brief overview of cloud-native patterns and their scope. The second part deals with the actual challenges solved by cloud-native patterns, and finally, the third part covers the actual architectural patterns that you can use to achieve your development goals.

In this chapter, we are going to cover the following topics:

- Cloud-native patterns
- Solving challenges with cloud-native patterns
- Cloud-native design patterns
- Hybrid and multi-cloud architecture recommendations

Cloud-native patterns

Like traditional design patterns, cloud-native patterns also help solve architectural problems by identifying common challenges of a development process and modifying workflows in a way that problem-solving becomes a part of the development process, thereby making app development significantly faster.

In order to create such patterns, first, a *problem* needs to be identified. Design patterns are usually created to solve recurring problems that can happen in any environment and while working on any project. The other part of design patterns is the *solution* to the problem. Due to the nature of the problems that design patterns solve, the solution needs to be broad enough to be applied to hundreds of different scenarios and still resolve the problem with equal effectiveness.

There is a third part in design patterns, but it isn't talked about enough and thus is often ignored – the *trade-offs*. Cloud-native patterns are a conscious design choice aimed at solving a wide range of problems, which means they are undoubtedly going to have limitations. Therefore, when applying a pattern, the developer needs to know the consequences of that design and decide whether it's going to affect the app negatively.

Furthermore, design patterns are also not just best practices or set-and-forget solutions. Some of them can be thought of as broad strategies to avoiding problems but the vast majority of cloud-native design patterns are methodological approaches to specific problems. They have a premise that contains the problems and a process to overcome them. We are calling them approaches here instead of workflows or processes because design patterns can be modified to an extent that they can be applied to different applications, different infrastructures, and different platforms.

The scope of cloud-native patterns

Design patterns are developed to solve recurring problems in app development. As technology progresses, new problems arise and so do design patterns. As a result, there is no defined number of design patterns. That said, cloud vendors and platforms recognize some common development challenges and best practices to avoid them and have packaged them into cloud design patterns to guide developers.

Since there are hundreds of cloud-native patterns available out there but a limited number of pages in this chapter, we are going to limit our discussion to a handful of the most powerful cloud-native patterns that are central to cloud-native app development. These core tenets will prove to be the most important for developers who are just starting out with the cloud and want to develop reliable, scalable, and secure applications.

In order to facilitate your understanding of these patterns and give you more context on why and when to use them, we'll also discuss the main challenges in cloud app development.

Solving challenges with cloud-native patterns

Picture this: you're an hour into creating your very own cloud-native application and you're face to face with your first major hurdle. It could be anything – a client request that you're not sure how to implement, misbehaving code, or any problem in any one of the dozens of spheres of app deployment: scaling, security, resilience, monitoring, and so on.

Now you can either stop development and focus on coming up with a solution for your problem or you can completely avoid this situation by taking a step back and plan your development process around cloud-native patterns.

You're almost certainly going to face challenges in any form of app development but that's fine because a solution for almost all of your problems already exists. But the goal isn't to use them to solve roadblocks but to completely avoid roadblocks in the first place. And the first step to do that is identifying the types of challenges you might face.

In this section, we'll look at some of the challenges that exist in modern cloud computing and how they can be overcome with cloud-native patterns.

Be proactive, not reactive

Design patterns are a forward-thinking engineering approach – it is not to be thought of as a failsafe but rather an active attempt at avoiding known problems before they arise. Thinking ahead saves time, effort, and money in the form of the following:

- Fewer errors
- Reduced downtime
- A more resilient and scalable application

To achieve any of this, you need to identify the main challenges that other developers face during cloud app development. There are hundreds of small issues that pop up at different stages of the development cycle, but a vast majority of these issues can be categorized into five main areas. The design patterns that we'll look at later in the chapter will also solve various challenges that fall under these categories.

Scaling and performance

The performance of your application is highly dependent on how it scales, and scalability is one of the main benefits of using a cloud-native architecture. Your application's performance refers to a wide range of metrics, such as latency and load times. These indicators are influenced by scalability (how much demand it can handle), availability (how often it fails), and overall responsiveness (how often the system kicks into action). For peak performance, developers adopt a wide range of design patterns, including very basic patterns such as autoscaling, autohealing, and load balancers to more specific patterns with very specific objectives such as **Command Query Responsibility Segregation** (**CQRS**) and event sourcing.

The performance of your app will also have a direct impact on running costs. **Google Cloud** uses a pay-per-use pricing system for most of its services and while using more resources may result in better performance, it's not the most efficient method. For one, Google Cloud does not allow for vertical scaling (running machine types cannot be changed for greater capacity, they can only be changed in quantity). Furthermore, there are numerous ways in which you can optimize your infrastructure and improve performance. For instance, using zones and clusters can decrease network latency. We'll talk about many other optimization tips throughout this book.

> **Tip**
>
> Thought bubble: In this context, the term clusters refers to a physical infrastructure unit within a data center. Zones refer to geographical locations – there are 28 regions and 85 zones. Being conscious of zones and clusters allows you to optimize your app for different parts of the world. As mentioned, decreased latency is one of the benefits but by using different zones in a region, you also ensure that if there is an outage or failure, your customers will still be able to use your service.

Deployments

Designing and implementing are two sides of the same coin and equally important – although, implementation is arguably more important, partly because implementation is underrated. The cloud-native architecture is all about speed and when working professionally, your customers will demand this speed in the form of more frequent deployments, reduced time-to-market, and a reduced update failure rate. Some common deployment challenges that you're likely going to face include automating and orchestrating different developmental and operational tasks, integrating different services and components together to complete the development pipeline (from *Chapter 2, End-to-End Extensible Tooling for Cloud-Native Application Development*), drafting and implementing policies, and more.

Thankfully, Google Cloud is architected around deployments and is full of tools, services, and design patterns that make deployment easier. We've already looked at two, very broad but also very important patterns for deployment, called **Continuous Integration/ Continuous Deployment (CI/CD)** pipelines and DevOps. In the next section, we'll look at more deployment patterns.

Resiliency and availability

Resiliency is one of the core tenets of the cloud-native architecture, along with scalability, agility, being serverless, and loose-coupling. In other words, cloud-native applications are architected to be resilient with the help of microservices. These loosely-coupled applications help isolate failures and ensure system-wide failures do not occur. However, while the apps themselves are isolated and inherently resilient (to some extent), the infrastructure needs to be properly configured and the right mechanisms (such as graceful shutdown/restart mechanisms, termination signals such as SIGTERM, audit trails, and so on) need to be put into place to improve disaster recovery and response times.

Resiliency and availability are similar concepts but they're not the same. While resiliency is concerned with unexpected failures, availability is concerned with uptime. It is measured in uptime and, ideally, we want around-the-clock availability. However, under real-world conditions, availability is affected by a number of factors, including infrastructure problems, high system loads, under provisioning, bad code, and more. Availability can be maximized using data stores, proper resource provisioning, monitoring, load leveling, and so on.

Monitoring

Monitoring is crucial to maximizing resiliency and maintaining security. However, compared to on-premises solutions, monitoring on a cloud-native architecture has different challenges, mostly because on the cloud, you're usually sharing resources on a public cloud where you do not have all the administrator rights and access. At first glance, this might seem like a big hindrance to management and monitoring. But this isn't a design flaw and cloud vendors provide a number of monitoring tools and services that can be combined with the wide range of monitoring patterns such as the anti-corruption layer, log sinks, audit trails, sidecar, partner services as single panes of glass, and so on.

Security

Cloud computing platforms such as Google Cloud are used to power some of the largest B2C operations in the world. Needless to say, security is a core aspect of cloud computing, and therefore, out of the box, it's much safer than on-premises solutions. However, without the proper implementation, these security protocols won't help much. Furthermore, individuals with malicious intents are always trying to find vulnerabilities and so developers must regularly update their policies and systems to ensure no security vulnerabilities arise between updates. Security patterns and approaches help mitigate problems related to confidentiality, compliance, availability, and system integrity.

Cloud-native design patterns

Now that you have a clearer understanding of the common challenges of cloud-native app development, we can take a deeper look at cloud-native design patterns. Remember, there are hundreds of design patterns out there and this book cannot possibly detail every single one of them. So instead, we'll be focusing on some of the popular design patterns and the ones that are most relevant to you.

Microservices

This might seem redundant now that we're in the third chapter, but microservices are more than just basic criteria of cloud-native applications – they often form the basis of the solutions to a surprisingly large number of problems faced in cloud-native app development. In addition to keeping your microservices very loosely coupled and isolated, developers can follow a range of microservices principles and best practices that will be crucial in avoiding problems such as system-wide downtime, slow updates, lack of agility, and slow response times to disaster and failures. Furthermore, it's highly recommended that these principles and best practices be followed strictly right from the start as it becomes more difficult to introduce them in the later stages of the developmental cycle.

With this in mind, the following is a list of powerful principles and best practices that, when followed, can help you avoid some common but annoying problems.

Separate database schemas for separate services

One of the ways microservices tend to lose their effectiveness is when developers do not create separate database schemas for each service, which results in services becoming less independent, prone to failures, and tightly coupled. To prevent this, each service should talk to a separate schema.

Services should communicate through their public APIs

Designing services to communicate directly with each other, through backdoors, or through any means other than their public APIs will also result in the architecture becoming more tightly coupled. Ensuring that services communicate solely through their public APIs also reduces administrative overhead and architectural ambiguity.

Ensuring backward compatibility through comprehensive testing and API versioning

One of the ways to ensure that no update causes consumer-facing failures is that developers can make use of API versioning along with testing the update for backward compatibility. Other ways to achieve safe deployments include staged roll-outs, blue/green deployments, and canary releasing (we'll learn more about this in the coming section).

Running standardized tests using a single command

Testing is non-negotiable. A high-performing cloud-native application requires a lot of testing, especially with regular updates. To make the testing process easier and quicker, it's highly recommended that developers create a standardized way to run tests on development workstations with a single command.

Setting up comprehensive monitoring

Even a thoroughly tested update can develop problems over time. More importantly, cloud-native applications can lose efficiency and performance without proper monitoring. This is why it's important to take the time to set up the proper monitoring solutions to keep a close eye on application performance, service health, system availability, and so on. The monitoring solution will also help immensely in debugging.

Setting service-level objectives (SLOs)

Setting expectations is important but setting goals is even more important. This is why it's recommended that developers set **Service-Level Objectives** (**SLOs**) early on. SLOs can bring more clarity in terms of application resilience and also help find limitations.

Performing disaster recovery tests regularly

Finally, it's equally important to push your application to its limits and beyond in a controlled environment. As such, developers should perform disaster recovery tests regularly. Developers can use techniques such as controlled failure injection to understand how the system would react during a failure.

These practices have emerged after a lot of research and are a proven way to improve cloud-native app development. That said, implementing these ideas can still be challenging, especially to new cloud developers. One way to counter these challenges is to share the workload with a team. At the end of the day, what's important is that you learn and improve – whether you do it alone or with a team does not matter.

Strangler applications

Creating a strangler application is especially useful for developers who already have a legacy monolithic application that they want to migrate to a microservice architecture. In the strangler process, a monolithic application is broken into microservices, starting from the core parts of the code and working your way up to other features:

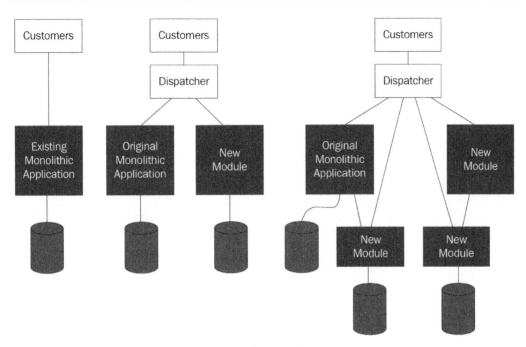

Figure: 3.1 – The strangler pattern

Over time, the monolith shrinks, and you incrementally develop a cloud-native application. Once most of the basic features have been ported from the monolith, developers can begin leveraging the cloud-native platform and its tools to add new functionality.

Decomposition patterns

Let's continue with the theme of migrating a monolith to a cloud-native application. There are a few ways in which you can break down an application into services, also known as decomposition patterns. For instance, you can decompose an application into services on the basis of business capability. By doing so, each resulting microservice will represent a specific app functionality, such as product catalog versus order management versus inventory management.

Alternatively, you can divide services on the basis of subdomains. Every business and its application can be classified into different subdomains that represent its core, supporting, and generic activities:

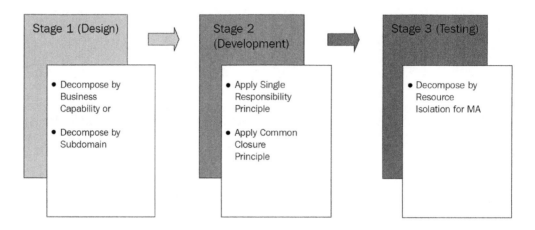

Microservice Decomposition Strategy
The process to define Microservice decomposition

Stage 1 (Design)	Stage 2 (Development)	Stage 3 (Testing)
• Decompose by Business Capability or • Decompose by Subdomain	• Apply Single Responsibility Principle • Apply Common Closure Principle	• Decompose by Resource Isolation for MA

Figure 3.2 – Decomposition strategy

Another option is to decompose each service by team. If you're working with a large team or have a number of developers working with you, you can assign one microservice to one team. This is ideal if you'd like to promote a more laissez-faire form of management where each team has complete control over and responsibility for their microservice.

Event-driven patterns

If the developer is using a traditional request/response protocol for communicating between microservices, the network becomes increasingly difficult as the app continues to scale. Therefore, cloud-native platforms support and promote the use of an event-driven architecture that includes a communication pattern that scales up easily and is capable of **Complex Event Processing (CEP)**.

The event-driven pattern works by using events to trigger certain actions – similar to the *If this, then that* principle. This is a very powerful design pattern as it helps remove the communication bottleneck and create complex chains of events and commands:

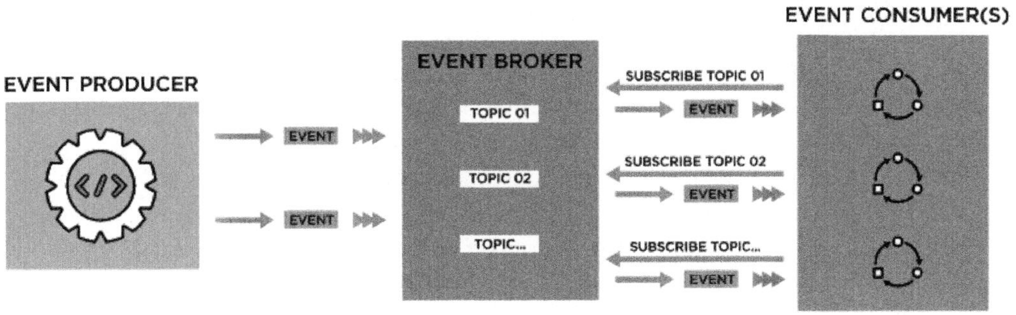

Figure 3.3 – Event-driven patterns

Next, we're going to discuss **Command Query Responsibility Segregation (CQRS)**.

Command Query Responsibility Segregation

CQRS is a data management design pattern that separates the write logic (commands) and read logic in a data store. But what's the point of separating the command part from the query part? Well, CQRS allows you to scale both read and write workloads independently, which results in benefits such as improved scalability and performance as well as greater flexibility and control.

The saga pattern

Since microservices are isolated from each other, they are also responsible for their own data. However, there are many scenarios where an app needs to reliably share data between different microservices. This is where sagas come in. The saga pattern is another important data management pattern, like CQRS, that helps overcome the isolated nature of data in microservices while still being loosely coupled. Sagas work by creating a sequence of local transactions, where each transaction is triggered by the previous. If, however, the microservice is unable to share its data and the local transaction fails, sagas also act as a failsafe and take a compensating action to undo any changes made by the preceding transactions.

Multiple service instances

Multiple service instances is a scalability pattern under which developers run multiple instances of a microservice. The premise behind multiple service instances is horizontal scaling. On Google Cloud applications scale by increasing the number of virtual machines, not by increasing the capacity of one machine. This concept is extended to microservices as well, where instead of provisioning more resources to one instance of a microservice, we just run multiple instances on different virtual (or physical) hosts. We will refer to this as horizontal autoscaling, which will be discuss in *Chapter 16, Orchestrating your Application with Google Kubernetes Engine*.

The benefits of the multiple service instances pattern include the rapid deployment of a microservice as well as far more efficient scalability.

Canary deployments

Canary deployments, also known as limited rollouts, are a deployment pattern that helps avoid major failures by releasing updates to a limited number of users or servers. The limited release gives developers the ability to test the update without affecting the entire user base with potential bugs or glitches. Furthermore, a failed canary deployment is far easier and quicker to recover from than an entire system failure.

Stateless services

The stateless services pattern is a data management design pattern with performance and cost benefits. The difference between stateless and stateful services is that the former does not permanently store information such as preferences, user profiles, workflows, and other session data. Every time a stateless application runs, it does so from scratch without any reference to the previous instance. Any information that the stateless application needs to run is stored on persistence data stores and is retrieved on startup each time. Stateless services help eliminate the additional overhead of maintaining state and also speed up the startup process. You'll be working with stateless applications if you decide to build your application on Kubernetes Engine and Cloud Run.

Immutable infrastructure

Immutable infrastructure is also a broader pattern that can be thought of as an infrastructure paradigm or strategy. The premise behind immutable infrastructure is to increase resiliency by never updating or modifying deployed servers. In order to change server preferences, a new server is deployed after the changes are applied to a common image. This improves reliability and resilience by avoiding problems such as configuration drift and snowflake servers that could arise on regularly updating a server. Immutable infrastructure also reduces the risk of failure and if there is a failure, it has a simple recovery process (using the version-controlled image history).

Anti-corruption layer

Let's, once again, assume that you're migrating a monolith to a cloud-native application. How do you ensure that the legacy monolith's domain model won't pollute the domain model of a new service? By implementing an anti-corruption layer between these two different systems. It won't completely separate the two systems but will act as a semi-permeable barrier that translates requests from the old system to the new system.

You'll also find anti-corruption layers useful later in the development cycle when you need to connect subdomains with different semantics. Using the same principle (a semi-permeable adapter layer), you'll be able to transfer data and requests from one domain to another without being limited by the different dependencies used in the other domain.

API composition

The API composition pattern helps to implement complex queries that join data from multiple services. By using an API composer, developers can invoke multiple services that own the data and perform an in-memory join of the results before aggregating results for the customer. This is a simple way to implement complex queries in a microservice architecture but in-memory joins become inefficient when working with larger datasets.

Event sourcing

You might find yourself in a position where you need to update the database and send messages to the consumer reliably. How do you do that? One of the most common ways of doing this is through event sourcing. The event sourcing pattern persists the state of the data or series of events. The application can then reconstruct an entity's state by using the append-only store as a system of record. Event sourcing improves scalability and performance and is also reliable as it provides a complete audit log of the changes made to a business entity.

The Retry pattern

A cloud-native application performs flawlessly when the dozens or hundreds of microservices in it never miss a beat. However, in the real world, it's very difficult to guarantee this. Errors such as Out Of Memory, timeouts, server errors, and so on are common culprits. Furthermore, even consumer-side problems can cause a microservice to be unable to complete its task.

Since in many cases, the error is often short-term and can be fixed after a delay, an error-handling design pattern known as the Retry pattern is adopted. The Retry pattern transparently retries failed elements over a network a given number of times. The goal of this pattern is to give faults a chance to self-correct and automatically retry.

Circuit breaker pattern

The Retry pattern works only when the fault is short-term and self-correcting. However, not all faults will meet these criteria and in many cases, the fault might not be fixed irrespective of the number of retries.

Unfortunately, in many cases, the failure of one microservice can lead to other microservices being unable to collect necessary information, causing them to fail and in turn, starting a snowball effect.

In such cases, it's important to not waste CPU resources in retrying. Accept that a microservice has failed, and tell the rest of the application to continue operations without the failed microservice (in highly decoupled systems).

This is a popular design pattern known as the circuit breaker and is often deployed alongside the Retry pattern.

The bulkhead pattern

The hulls of ships are designed as separate compartments to reduce the risk of sinking even when the hull is breached, by isolating water into a few compartments. A similar design called the bulkhead pattern can be implemented in cloud-native applications to reduce the risk of an entire application stack failure when one or two microservices fail.

The bulkhead pattern premise here is to partition the microservices based on their demand and availability metrics in such a way that resource exhaustion or failure isn't enough to bring down the system.

Using the cloud-native pattern judiciously

A cloud-native pattern is not a silver bullet. Simply adopting an organizational pattern will not make you five times as efficient nor will security resolve all security problems forever. Remember, design patterns aren't just a combination of a problem and a solution – they also come with complications and consequences.

There are hundreds of cloud-native patterns, each with its own set of trade-offs, and it's not realistic to be aware of all of them as you begin writing your first cloud-native application. The best thing you can do right now is to keep an open mind about the solutions and designs you implement and be open to experimentation. A key difference between cloud-native applications and traditional monolithic applications is that the former is more forgiving when it comes to experimentation (especially during the later stages of the development life cycle). Use this opportunity to find out more about the various design patterns so you can develop a powerful understanding of which pattern to use for different scenarios. Furthermore, there is a wealth of information and technical documentation available on most of Google Cloud's solutions and how their performance and productivity can be maximized.

Hybrid and multi-cloud architecture recommendations

In addition to the design patterns we have just discussed, there are a few recommendations that developers can adopt to improve their hybrid and multi-cloud architecture.

Going forward, we'll call these patterns as they do give developers potential solutions to the unique problems of cloud-native architecture despite not being strictly design patterns.

Distributed deployment patterns

The following patterns are to be deployed when your application is going to be running in an environment that suits it best, with the goal of testing all of its features and various characteristics.

The tiered hybrid pattern

The tiered hybrid pattern suggests migrating the frontend of the application to the cloud before the backend while the backend stays in its original computing environment. The main premise is that because frontend applications are usually stateless, they are often easier to migrate. Additionally, since frontend applications are updated frequently and are subject to varying levels of traffic, things such as CI/CD pipelines and auto-scaling enabled by the cloud helps in reducing workload through automation:

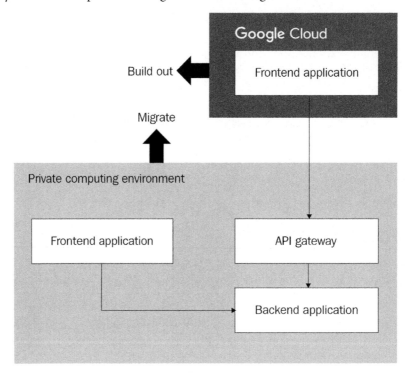

Figure 3.4 – The tiered hybrid pattern

However, going the tiered hybrid route isn't always recommended and it should be chosen on a case-by-case basis.

The partitioned multi-cloud pattern

In some cases, hosting your application on one cloud vendor (such as Google Cloud) may not be enough. For instance, developers may choose to host their application on two separate cloud platforms to test the differences and find out which is better for them. Additionally, developers may also come across region-based compliance issues on one platform that can be overcome by serving that region's traffic through a different platform:

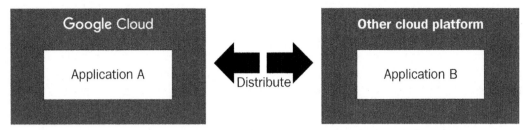

Figure 3.5 – The partitioned multi-cloud pattern

Whatever your reason may be, the partitioned multi-cloud pattern enables you to run the same application on two separate vendors.

The analytics hybrid and multi-cloud pattern

Many businesses prefer to host large silos of data on their private backend systems (on-premises) but want to move the processing and analysis workloads to the cloud – essentially feeding data to the cloud:

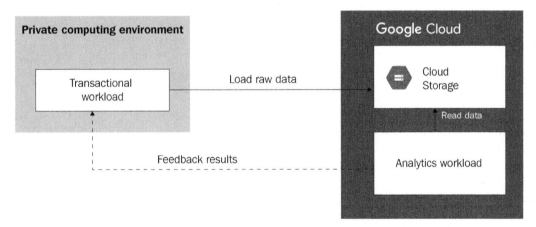

Figure 3.6 – The analytics hybrid and multi-cloud pattern

This is possible with the analytics hybrid and multi-cloud pattern. Furthermore, Google Cloud in particular is well suited to such an arrangement as Google Cloud does not have a charge/fee for ingress traffic coming into Google Cloud. Additionally, Google Cloud also offers numerous managed services that make ETL pipelines easier to create and maintain. Developers can also use Cloud Storage to build data lakes on the cloud.

Edge hybrid

Edge hybrid is a pattern for running workloads at the edge, which reduces latency and dependency on a fast internet connection. For many businesses, a fast and reliable internet connection isn't guaranteed. In these instances, a power outage in the on-premises facility shouldn't affect the end user's experience.

There are numerous other cases where a fast and stable connection isn't always present and here, an edge hybrid setup allows developers to run time-critical workloads in the edge-computing environment while non-critical workloads such as administration and monitoring can run (usually asynchronously) on Google Cloud:

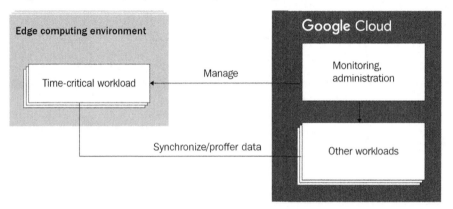

Figure 3.7 – The edge hybrid pattern

Additionally, as we mentioned in *Chapter 2, End-to-End Extensible Tooling for Cloud-Native Application Development*, Google Cloud has a range of services that can be used for such hybrid and multi-cloud setups including Anthos on bare metal, which provides a single-pane-of-glass-view that makes it easier to manage these partitions.

Redundant deployment patterns

The following patterns are for applications that will be deployed in different computing environments, with the goal of improving resilience in different scenarios.

The environment hybrid pattern

There are many cases where a business needs to (or simply prefers to) keep the production environment on-premises while moving other environments including various testing environments to the public cloud due to the following:

- Legal and compliance reasons
- Using third-party services that cannot be used on public clouds

- Simply preferring to keep the production environment in its existing data center:

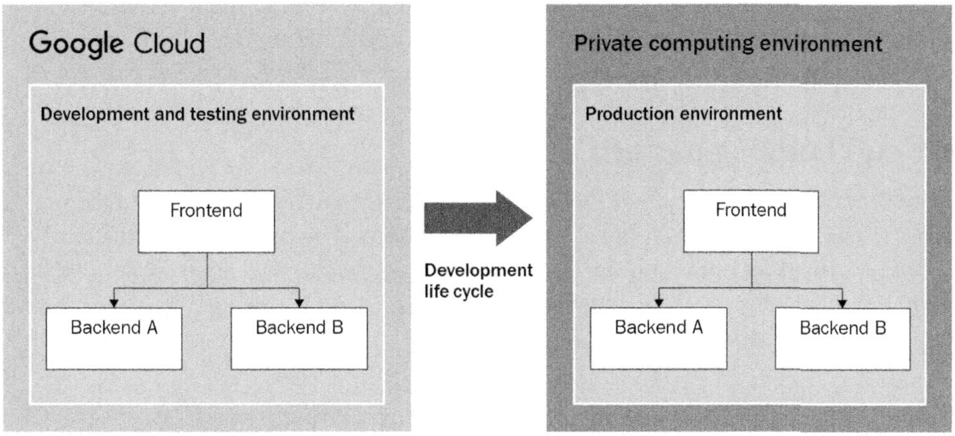

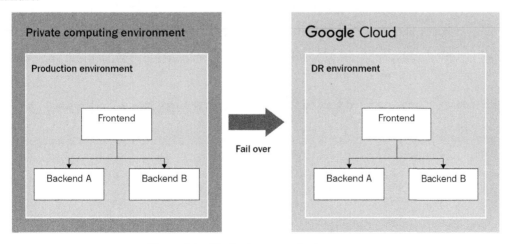

Figure 3.8 – The environment hybrid pattern

The environment hybrid pattern allows developers to easily create and tear down such partitions. This can also be used as an opportunity to get familiar with the cloud without risking the production environment.

Business continuity – hybrid and multi-cloud

Despite the increased resilience of cloud-native applications, disaster recovery plans are still crucial for cloud-native applications. One of the ways cloud-native applications can continue working in spite of major disasters is by replicating services and hosting them over geographically different data centers – eliminating the risk posed by single points of failure:

Figure 3.9 – The business continuity pattern

The business continuity pattern allows businesses to switch to a cloud-based disaster recovery environment that can take over in case of any disaster and ensure users still have access to the service. Additionally, the pay-per-use model ensures that businesses pay for storage and compute only when the VMs are running.

The cloud bursting pattern

The cloud bursting pattern allows developers to manage patchy traffic with high peaks (such as traffic on Black Friday and Cyber Monday) by using a separate cloud environment that kicks in when the base, on-premises production environment is overwhelmed with traffic. In theory, the cloud environment forms *an outer layer* that can contain temporary, albeit high-volume, traffic:

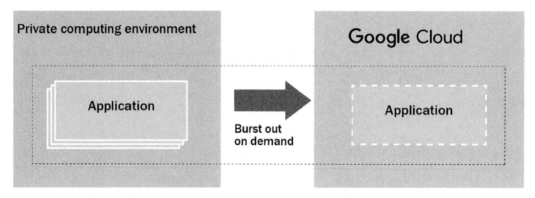

Figure 3.10 – The cloud bursting pattern

Cloud bursting is a great option as it allows developers to do the following:

- Use the same resources on the cloud and in on-premises environments.
- Not worry about overprovisioning resources.
- Ensure that the application has the capacity to serve customers in a timely manner without breaking the bank.

With this, we have completed learning about cloud-native architectural patterns.

Summary

Cloud-native design patterns were made to help you anticipate and prevent common challenges in cloud-native app development. By having a strong understanding of these patterns, you can save a significant amount of time and effort by avoiding problems that are often faced by new developers. In a way, these patterns can be thought of as shortcuts but as with all shortcuts, they must be taken with caution. Design patterns aren't meant to be perfect; they're meant to be quick and widely applicable. As a result, they often come with certain drawbacks that, depending on your project, may not affect you at all or create more problems down the line. Therefore, it's very important to not just understand what problem a pattern is solving but also at what cost.

Armed with this knowledge, you are now ready to make your first big decision – choosing the compute option. Google Cloud offers a wide range of compute options and in the next chapter, we will discuss these options and how you can choose the best place to run your application.

Section 2: Selecting the Right Google Cloud Services

On completion of *Section 2*, you will have gained hands-on experience in choosing the right Google Cloud services covering compute, databases and storage, and the other categories that make up a cloud-native application such as messaging system and cloud security.

This part of the book comprises the following chapters:

4

Choosing the Right Compute Option

In the first three chapters, we've tried to give you most of the information required to make better decisions when building cloud-native applications. Now, it's time to make your first decision: which cloud compute solution to use.

The **Google Cloud** offers a number of compute options—namely, Firebase, **Google Compute Engine (GCE)**, **Google App Engine (GAE)**, **Google Kubernetes Engine (GKE)**, Cloud Run, and an upcoming service called Workflows. In case you're thinking that so many choices will make your decision more difficult, don't worry—it won't. Each of these services is built for specific purposes but isn't too different from the others—all of them achieve similar goals with different approaches. One of the main differences between these services is the level of abstraction each service has.

In this chapter, we will go over each of these services, their advantages and disadvantages, use cases, and how to choose the right option for you. At the end of the chapter, you'll have a fundamental understanding of the various compute options offered by Google Cloud and be able to choose the right compute option for containerized, **virtual machine (VM)**-based, and other types of cloud-based applications.

We will cover the following topics:

- Five compute options… and Firebase
- How important is it to choose the right option?

Five compute options... and Firebase

There are five *main* platforms that you can use to create powerful cloud-native applications on Google Cloud: Cloud Functions, GAE, Cloud Run, GKE, and GCE. However, there is a sixth platform offered by Google that is also a viable compute option but is not fully a part of the Google Cloud ecosystem: Firebase.

Firebase

One of the reasons why Firebase isn't a major part of the Google Cloud is because it is a tool used to create mobile or **HyperText Markup Language** (**HTML**) applications, and thus does not need to fully support the powerful Google Cloud ecosystem. If you are not a mobile or HTML5 developer, you may skip Firebase and focus on the rest of the compute options discussed in this chapter.

However, if you are a mobile developer, then Firebase might be what you're looking for. It's a powerful platform for building mobile and web applications that can be scaled up in the same way as other Google Cloud-based applications, because your application are essentially running on the same infrastructure. More importantly, Firebase is one of the fastest ways to get your mobile or web application up and running as it provides developers with a fully managed backend, database hosting, storage options, and much more.

One of the main differences between Firebase and the rest of the compute options we'll discuss is that the latter actually do have compute capabilities, whereas Firebase only has storage, networking, and syncing capabilities.

Overall, as great as Firebase is, mobile and simple web applications are not the focus of this book. We want to guide developers to make use of the powerful features that the Google Cloud has to offer, and for such complex applications, we can choose from five different compute options.

Cloud Functions

At the base of our increasingly less abstract triangle of compute options is Cloud Functions. As the name suggests, Cloud Functions provides a scalable platform where developers can write and upload their independent functions, and the fully managed infrastructure does the initial provisioning, managing, and scaling (both up and down). Cloud Functions is event-driven and at the core of Cloud Functions sits Cloud **Publish/Subscribe (Pub/Sub)**, **Google Cloud Storage (GCS)**, HTTP, and **HTTP Secure (HTTPS)** requests.

Cloud Functions is an ideal compute option for developers who want a fully managed serverless platform to minimize server-side code. Cloud Functions enables developers to not worry about different runtime environments while still having additional capabilities such as powerful in-built monitoring, debugging, networking, and security features.

Furthermore, using Cloud Functions makes even more sense if your application already makes use of HTTPS requests or Cloud Pub/Sub or if you're planning to use the large library of Google's existing **application programming interfaces (APIs)**. Either way, Cloud Functions is a safe and reliable bet if you just want to work on the event logic while the cloud takes care of the rest. You can achieve a lot with Cloud Functions, including relatively simple tasks such as sending emails, analyzing data, uploading pictures or **Portable Document Format** files (**PDFs**), and even complex enterprise-level applications.

However, as you can imagine, this simplicity comes with some compromises and constraints. For Cloud Functions, this means that you are constrained to an event-driven architecture, which means that you must use events. You can also only use specific language runtimes. Furthermore, one of the great things about Cloud Functions is that your entire application is made up of functions, but as the application grows, managing and debugging all of these independent functions can become a bit tricky. Finally, your application may not be suitable to be broken down into independent functions in the first place or may be event-driven, in which case you should consider any of the other compute options, including the next one: GAE.

GAE

GAE was one of the first cloud services launched by Google (introduced in 2008). This service is older than the actual Google Cloud itself. In terms of abstraction, it sits just below Cloud Functions. GAE allows developers to move past event-driven architectures and the constraints of functions.

Some of the key features of GAE that make it a great compute option include being fully managed and providing fast auto-scaling. Despite being less abstract than Cloud Functions, GAE still takes care of enough things to make sure you, the developer, can focus on the code without worrying about the infrastructure. For instance, one of the features that will greatly facilitate application development for new developers is the zero-config deployment, which means the cloud will manage the backend infrastructure and all you have to do is write the code and execute it. As with GAE, it is billed on usage, which makes it ideal for users whose requirements are on the spiky side. When there isn't any usage, it scales down to zero (so do all of the other options, excluding GKE and GCE).

In terms of additional development control, GAE has powerful features such as versioning, traffic splitting, and granular diagnostic tools. The flexible environment in GAE also opens up more possibilities with custom language runtimes, libraries, and frameworks that can be imported to GAE in the form of Docker containers.

The pay-per-use pricing and great auto-scaling also make GAE a great option for projects that have seasonal demand or spiky loads, such as landing pages or marketing campaigns.

When using GAE as your compute option, developers will have the option of two distinct environments. Each GAE environment has its own uses and benefits. Let's take a closer look at each.

Standard versus flexible environments for GAE

Applications in GAE can run in two environments: standard and flexible. Each environment has subtle differences, and the ideal environment for your application depends on a number of factors.

The standard environment is based on container instances and provides developers with a stable environment for their application that will run reliably even under high and spiky loads. It can scale reliably and rapidly but is limited to certain versions of different programming languages, meaning you can still use popular programming languages but you must use specific versions, such as Python 2.7, 3.7, and 3.8, or Java 8, Java 11, and so on.

The standard environment is ideal if you are working with large amounts of data or cannot predict traffic reliably. The standard environment is also the most cost-effective as you are only billed on usage, and the platform can even scale down to zero.

> **Important note: First- and second-generation runtimes**
>
> If you choose the standard environment in GAE, you might come across first-generation and second-generation runtimes. First-generation runtimes include programming languages such as Python 2.7, Java 8, PHP 5.5, and Go 1.11, whereas second-generation runtimes include Python 3, Java 11, Node.js, PHP 7, Ruby, and Go 1.12+.
>
> As you might imagine, the first-generation runtimes are older and the second-generation ones have been significantly improved, with many capabilities. Therefore, it is strongly advised to base your application around one of the supported second-generation runtimes.

On the other hand, the flexible environment is based on Docker containers within GCE and offers developers more flexibility overall. In the flexible environment, developers can use any version of the supported languages (Python, Java, Node.js, Go, Ruby, PHP, and .NET) and custom runtimes. However, the biggest strength of the flexible environment is that you can customize the infrastructure with GCE's VMs and specify your own **central processing unit** (**CPU**) and memory requirements.

There are various other things that you can control in the flexible environment as well, but the gist is, if you're looking for a managed option and rapid scaling options, choose the standard environment. If not, then the flexible environment gives you more power and customizability.

As was the case with Cloud Functions, GAE has limitations as well, the biggest being its usage of HTTP/S requests. Where Cloud Functions was limited by its dependence on event-driven architecture and triggers, GAE is limited by web requests and responses. So, if you want something more concrete and open-ended, you can try using containers on Cloud Run. All of the remaining compute options support it as well.

Cloud Run

If you want to get started with containers while minimizing the amount of server-side coding, Cloud Run is your best bet. It is the fastest way to get containerized applications on a serverless platform as it does a lot of the heavy lifting for you.

Cloud Run uses stateless HTTPS containers that have all of the information required to run an application. As mentioned, these container images go live with zero infrastructure management or provisioning and will quickly auto-scale to effectively meet demand.

> **Tip: Stateless?**
>
> Cloud Run (and a few other Google Cloud services) uses containers that are stateless, which refers to their characteristic of not persisting information such as a session log, which allows the service to be started *from a clean slate* each time. This is important for applications on Cloud Run because it ensures that applications see the same initial state, irrespective of the environment they are deployed to. This improves consistency and allows operations and development teams to work together smoothly.

Another reason developers choose Cloud Run—and, particularly, containers—is that it significantly minimizes the risk of software not working in production, after passing all tests in the development environment. Containers achieve this by essentially packing the entire software along with all of the files (configuration, data, libraries, and so on) in a single ZIP file that Cloud Run executes from a repository.

> **Important note: Containers and cloud computing**
>
> *Container* is a common term that you'll hear a lot when working with cloud-native applications. If you don't know already, containerization is a logical packaging mechanism that decouples the environment from the infrastructure and adds it to the application, essentially wrapping all of the files required to run an application and packing it into a self-sufficient piece of software that runs consistently on different target environments.
>
> As you'll explore more capabilities of cloud computing, you'll find that the main concept of containers (loose coupling and isolation) works extremely well with modern requirements for faster, independent, and scalable development.

Cloud Run's containers are also a good idea if your aim is to improve portability and make testing and deploying updates quicker, especially if you do not have a team to manage the various aspects of cloud development such as monitoring health, provisioning, debugging, and so on. A final powerful benefit of writing applications on Cloud Run is that you can deploy them on GKE, or even an entirely different cloud platform, as long as it supports serverless container images.

But what about when you *don't* want to use Cloud Run? Well, there are a few cases where Cloud Run becomes less than ideal. For instance, if you're not planning on using containers, then you might want to reconsider the previous three options we've discussed because in Cloud Run as well as the upcoming compute options, all use containers.

GKE

If you have decided on using containers for your application and suspect that your application might quickly scale up to hundreds—or even thousands—of containers (which is entirely possible), then you would certainly be better off with GKE.

Kubernetes and GKE

GKE is a management platform based on an open source orchestration protocol of the same name (Kubernetes) that essentially groups together your containers for easier discovery, tracking, debugging, and overall management.

Kubernetes (the open source system) facilitates development by automating many aspects of container-based software development such as deployment, scaling, and how containers talk to each other.

With GKE, we're entering a different level of compute options in terms of abstraction that involve VMs, and most of the developers who decide to run their applications on GKE are already aware of Kubernetes and VMs. You can still use GKE as the platform for your first cloud-native application but it's targeted towards developers who want control of their applications (although it is one of the easiest ways to get started with containers and Kubernetes as an orchestration system).

Apart from the control aspect, you might also be interested in GKE if you're planning on running your application in multiple environments such as in separate development, testing, and production environments or on multi-cloud or hybrid cloud environments, and so on. Multiple environments also help if you want to run different instances in different geographical regions (due to language, legal, and political barriers, and other factors).

One thing to note is that GKE is architected to be used by a team (or multiple teams) of developers. It *can* be operated by a single developer but if you are just getting started, a fully managed option such as GAE or Cloud Functions might be a better starting point. Alternatively, if you already have different teams in charge of different aspects of cloud development such as debugging, monitoring, operations, security, and so on, then GKE is a fantastic option because it really facilitates team communication and the DevOps way of development (but you still need good communication to begin with). Speaking of DevOps, GKE is also one of the better options if you want to have **continuous integration/continuous deployment (CI/CD)** pipelines in your development. Finally, GKE supports network protocols other than HTTP/S, something not available in GAE or Cloud Functions.

Similar to Cloud Run, GKE is based around containers, and if your application isn't containerized, using GKE is out of the question. Also, GKE isn't the most cost-effective compute option available, although it is quite economical if your application has high utilization—that is, it can use all of the resources provisioned to your VMs (we'll talk about pricing later in this chapter).

Here is a table that summarizes the key differences between GAE, Cloud Run, and GKE:

GAE	Cloud Run	GKE
Unit of deployment is app. Very well integrated with native GCP services such as `memcache`, Datastore, and Cloud Trace. Based on `gvisor` container runtime. Supports traffic splitting out of the box	Unit of deployment is container. Serverless + Container model based on open source Knative. No upfront setup needed. Support exists. Supports traffic splitting across revisions out of the box	Unit of deployment is container. Need to set up load balancer and persistent storage, if necessary. Need to manipulate Kubernetes manifest files to achieve rolling updates, traffic splitting, and so on.
One of the oldest Google services. There is vendor lock-in, therefore hard to migrate applications written in GAE. Second-generation runtimes have better performance than first-generation runtime environments.	This is a relatively new service. Since it is based on open source Knative, the service offers very fast bootup times for the applications, and easier to migrate to on-premises or other cloud providers.	GKE is based on open source Kubernetes and applications can easily be ported to on-premises or other cloud providers.
Auto-scaling is based on CPU and memory parameters. With GAE flexible environment there always has to be one instance running.	HTTP stateless request-based scaling model. More cost-effective since metering starts only when requests are served.	Cluster Autoscaler and Horizontal POD Autoscaler (HPA) scaling types supported.
	Works well when multiple standalone public and private services are needed.	Container orchestrator with service endpoint that load-balances traffic directly between pods.

With this, we wrap up GKE and can move on to the next compute service: GCE.

GCE

Compared to the rest of the compute options we've discussed so far, GCE is in many ways in a different league (GKE and Cloud Run being somewhat similar). The core premise behind GCE is giving developers an entire computer (VM) to play around with. It has storage, compute, memory, and network capabilities as well as different **operating systems (OSes)** already built in, which can be customized to your needs (more CPU, memory, storage, and so on). We'll cover the different machine types and their specifications in the upcoming section.

But let's talk about VMs and general capabilities before we proceed any further. As we said, VMs are a computer (or, more precisely, a slice of a computer with all of the individual ingredients). VMs scale horizontally instead of vertically and are completely isolated from each other, which means you can do a lot of things without affecting any of your running instances.

> **Important note: Vertical versus horizontal scaling**
>
> There are two ways to scale: vertically and horizontally. Vertical scaling refers to increasing the compute, storage, network, and disk capabilities of the server. For example, one way to scale is to add more **random-access memory (RAM)** to your existing machine, or you could switch over to a more powerful CPU.
>
> Horizontal scaling is when we increase the number of machines. So, instead of going from 64 **gigabytes (GB)** of RAM and 2.4 **gigahertz (GHz)** CPU to 256 GB and a 4.8 GHz CPU, we would simply add multiple machines with 64 GB of RAM and 2.8 GHz CPU.
>
> Cloud vendors such as Google Cloud use horizontal scaling due to the numerous benefits it provides (isolation, resilience, flexibility, faster auto-scaling, and so on).

Although GCE is the least abstract compute option we have, it can still manage a lot of things. For instance, instead of using multiple instances on multiple VMs, you can simply use a single VM—or even a single container running on one VM—and let the cloud take care of most things, including starting the OS, running the container, and bringing updates. However, if you want to offload even more work to the cloud, you can use an API called **Managed Instance Groups (MIGs)**, which lets you manage multiple VMs as one.

MIGs in GCE

A MIG is a cluster of individual VMs that are managed as a single VM. The main purpose of using MIGs is automating things such as scalability, deployments, and updates.

By shifting applications (instances) on multiple VMs quickly, the cloud can do the following:

- Scale up and down.

- Minimize downtime in case one of the VMs crashes or shuts down.

- Monitor application health and verify each application is working as expected on every VM. If an application does not respond, the cloud auto-heals by creating a new instance of the app.

- Automatically deploy new versions using different rollout scenarios, such as canary deployments or rolling updates.

Other powerful features of MIGs include load balancing, support for stateful workloads, and multiple zone coverages (which can be used to reduce latency).

Tip: Reducing costs in GCE – preemptible VMs

One of the constraints of GCE is the VM-based billing. However, GCE does offer a more cost-effective solution to this: preemptible VMs. Preemptible VMs are short-lived instances that last up to 24 hours and can reduce the costs of GCE workloads (especially fault-tolerant workloads) by up to 80%.

Preemptible VMs are great options for batch jobs (you can start up as many preemptible VMs as you want) and they shut down gracefully, giving your app time to save its data. Most importantly, preemptible VMs cost significantly less than regular VMs and are easy to create and end.

GCE is an extremely versatile option for creating powerful (and even simple) container-based applications. It has a number of managed options as well, giving you the ability to take control over everything but never actually forcing your hand. It's also ideal for bringing existing systems or applications to the cloud (using a migration strategy as simple as lift and shift). On a similar note, GCE is also great for applications that require specific third-party solutions or a specific (or custom) OS or kernel, as it is most likely to be able to accommodate all of your licensing requirements. The powerful VMs are also ideal for large databases and other resource-intensive workloads. Finally, as with GKE, GCE also supports network protocols other than HTTP/S.

Limitations? Yes, they do exist. GCE (and GKE) are targeted toward teams of developers, and thus as a sole developer (or a small team), you may have to manage more things such as software updates. Finally, GCE is not ideal for rapid scaling. Adding a new VM can take up to 30 seconds, which is more than most users would wait around for. Therefore, if you're unsure about your traffic or are expecting traffic spikes, you can avoid this by overprovisioning and starting more VMs than you need (in anticipation of additional demand), but this isn't a great idea from a cost perspective.

Types of GCE machines

GCE has different categories of machine types with different use cases. Let's take a look at each one and what you should use them for.

General-purpose machine types

General-purpose machine types offer an ideal middle ground between price and performance. These value-for-money machine types can be further divided into four machine types. Here are their specifications:

- **E2 machine type**: Up to 32 **virtual CPUs** (**vCPUs**) and 128 GB of memory (maximum of 8 GB per vCPU). Available on both Intel and the second-generation AMD EPYC Rome platforms.

- **N2 machine type**: Up to 80 vCPUs with 8 GB of memory per vCPU (based on the Intel Cascade Lake CPU platforms)

- **N2D machine type**: Up to 224 vCPUs with 8 GB of memory per vCPU (based on second-generation AMD EPYC Rome platforms)

- **N1 machine type**: Up to 96 vCPUs with 6.5 GB of memory per vCPU (based on Intel Sandy Bridge, Ivy Bridge, Haswell, Broadwell, and Skylake CPU platforms)

These machine types can be used for a wide range of workloads, including everyday computing requirements such as web serving, streaming, back-office applications, development environments, and so on.

Memory-optimized machine types

Memory-optimized machine types are optimized for memory-intensive workloads and offer up to 12 **terabytes** (**TB**) of memory. These machine types are best suited for memory-intensive workloads such as in-memory analytics.

Compute-optimized machine types

Compute-optimized machine types are optimized for pure computing power. These machines are available only on Intel Scalable processors (Cascade Lake) and have the highest per-core performance of any machine type (up to 3.8 GHz). These machine types are best suited for compute-heavy workloads such as **high-performance computing (HPC)**, **electronic design automation (EDA)**, and applications that are more dependent on a single-core performance (for instance, gaming).

Shared-core machine types

Shared-core machine types are based on the E2 and N1 general-purpose machine types and timeshare one physical core. These are best suited for less demanding workloads.

GCE is one of the most powerful compute options available on the market today, capable of diverse workloads. It might seem the obvious option for intermediate and veteran developers but there's one last (and very important) factor still to be discussed: pricing.

Pricing

Perhaps you're still unsure of which compute option to go forward with, but maybe pricing would become the deciding factor.

Google Cloud's compute options can be roughly divided in two camps: the pay-per-use camp and then the VMs camp. Compute options such as GAE and Cloud Functions have usage-based billing, meaning you only pay for what you use. This reduces the risk of overprovisioning, but there are some services within these platforms that aren't billed on usage, but are instead of fixed costs.

On the other side, we have services such as GKE and GCE that use VMs, and thus the cost is dependent on how much CPU, memory, and disk your VMs have. That said, both of these compute options do offer managed services, which means that part of your bill could be usage-dependent (mentioned separately on your bill). Cloud Run offers a bit of both, and depending on how you configure it, the billing can be based on either usage or resources.

A common misconception is that pay-per-use is simply more cost-effective. However, this is only true if your application has spiky demand or you cannot predict the traffic. If your app gets consistent traffic with little variation, compute options such as GKE or GCE are just as economical, and sometimes even more economical.

Finally, the pricing model might seem overwhelming at first, but the pricing model at Google Cloud is still far simpler than what some of its enterprise-oriented competitors such as **Amazon Web Services (AWS)** and Azure have. Still, there are tools available that can help you estimate the cost of your project, such as the **Google Cloud Pricing Calculator**.

The upfront and long-term costs are one of the major things you need to consider when choosing the compute option, but not the only one. As a developer, there are a few more things you need to know before you are ready to make this decision, including the importance of this decision on your developmental life cycle and what it might mean to choose the wrong option. Let's take a look.

How important is it to choose the right option?

Is it possible to change compute options and, if so, what are the limitations to changing compute options later down in the development life cycle?

None of the compute options available on Google Cloud are inherently bad. They all achieve the same results but have a few key but subtle differences that make them ideal for different use cases. For instance, one of the key differentiating factors between the compute options is the level of control each gives the developer. Use the following diagram as a rule of thumb to understand the varying levels of control Google Cloud compute options provide:

Cloud Functions > GAE > Cloud Run > GKE > GCE

Figure 4.1 – Comparing Google Cloud compute options < Fully managed/More control >

One thing to remember is that the compute options on the left don't necessarily have fewer features, but a lot of the complex features are managed by the cloud. In other words, if you choose Firebase or Cloud Functions, you'll still have a powerful platform to build cloud-native applications on, as you would on GAE or GKE. The main difference is that most of the heavy lifting will be done for you.

Furthermore, if you're unsure about the level of control you'll actually need, don't worry —we'll cover exactly this, as well as the ideal compute options for different use cases and scenarios, in the next section.

Changing compute options

Since choosing a compute option is one of the first decisions cloud developers need to make, they often associate it with the foundation of the app, believing that like a foundation, once laid, it is very difficult to change. However, this isn't the case. It's ideal to choose compute options that fulfill all of your short- and long-term requirements but if your requirements change over time, you should know that going from one compute option to another isn't as difficult as you may imagine, and it largely depends on the two compute options you're working with. Just remember that going from GKE and GCE (and possibly Cloud Run, depending on your configuration) may require additional coding, particularly when reinforcing containerized applications into being non-containerized for platforms such as Cloud Functions and GAE (and again, possibly Cloud Run).

That said, it's still an important decision and you do want to spend some time considering all the options (just don't get stuck over the compute option).

Furthermore, it's usually a safer choice to start at a higher abstraction level (with services such as Cloud Functions or GAE) than at a lower abstraction level (with services such as GKE or GCE). There are two reasons for this. First of all, a higher abstraction level means the platform is more managed and you've got fewer things to do because the cloud does more. Secondly, moving down the abstraction chain is easier than moving up. If you start at Cloud Functions, you'll probably find it easier to move to Cloud Run since you're essentially getting more functionality for the increasing requirements of a growing application. Starting off at GKE means you'll have more things to set up, most of which you may not be able to use if you decide to use a less abstracted version, such as Cloud Functions or GAE.

Making a decision

As we mentioned at the start of this chapter, compute options *can* be changed. This isn't a permanent or even high-risk decision. Now, you do need to make this decision, and to help you with it, here are some additional factors that you can base your decision around as well as some questions to ask yourself.

How much thinking do I want to do?

The abstraction levels of these compute options aren't just there to help you understand the technologies each option is based around—they can also be used to make a decision as to which one to choose. For instance, Cloud Functions sits at the top of the abstraction chain and helps you create your own cloud-native application with the least amount of thinking (you only need to worry about your functions in an event-driven architecture).

Going down each level, developers are introduced with more powerful technologies that give you more control and functionality but also require you to spend more time deciding how you're going to set them up. For instance, with GCE, you'll have to decide on CPU, RAM, OS, load balancers, regions, firewall rules, and more.

What are my application's technical requirements?

Similarly, your application's technical requirements also play a big role. Even at the beginning of the development life cycle, you should have an idea about the technologies you'll need when building your application. Using these requirements as a foundation, you can choose which compute option to choose, since different compute options have different features.

Which pricing model suits me better?

Pricing is also a big factor in your decision, but arguably less complicated. Your main priority should be to decide which pricing model is ideal for your application: usage-based billing or resources-based. After you decide this, you can shortlist the applications depending on the type of pricing model they offer.

What is my team like?

Think about your team composition. Are you a solo developer? Do you have a small team, or are you managing the entire IT department? If you have a smaller team, it's probably a better idea to choose a compute option near the top of the abstraction chain because more items are managed for you, whereas if you have a group of well-managed teams with good communication, both GKE and GCE are powerful options with great versatility. Furthermore, these options are much better if you already have an existing app that you need to migrate and develop further on the cloud.

Think about your answers to these questions, and you should be able to find the right compute option for your application and get started on your cloud-native app in no time. In the next chapter, we'll learn more about the various database and storage options available in Google Cloud and how to choose the ideal solutions for your applications.

Summary

You should now be able to evaluate the different compute options offered by Google Cloud and objectively find the right service for different goals and requirements. This chapter was the first of many chapters where you'll learn about the different services and tools within the Google Cloud ecosystem and how you can best use them. In the next chapter, you'll learn how to make another important decision, as we'll learn more about the various database and storage options available in Google Cloud and how to find and choose the ideal solutions for your cloud-native applications.

5
Choosing the Right Database and Storage

Now that you've chosen your compute option, it's time to move on to the next decision: choosing the right database and storage for your cloud application.

Google Cloud's world of managed services is huge, and their library of database and storage options is very diverse as well. To put this in numbers, the Google Cloud ecosystem has well over 100 services and tools for nearly all aspects of cloud software development, and more than a dozen of these are dedicated solely to storage and databases. The goal behind such a large range of options is to give developers more customizability and agility. More importantly, developers are not required to choose a single service and stick with it—rather, they can choose multiple storage and database options together to meet their application's requirements; in fact, this is common practice.

To new developers who are diving straight into cloud computing, data storage might seem a secondary concern and far less important than, say, compute. However, data storage is an integral part of cloud computing and plays a big role in costs, agility, and security. In this chapter, we'll explore the different database and storage options available in **Google Cloud** and the ways in which you can use them. By the end of this chapter, we will have covered the following topics:

- Storage and database options on Google Cloud: the big three
- Additional storage and database options
- Security and flexibility

Storage and database options on Google Cloud – the big three

As we said, there are a lot of options available for database and storage. While we will talk about all of these services, this chapter will focus more on a few key services because as with compute options, Google Cloud offers fully managed platforms for storage that help new developers achieve more while doing less. Additionally, it's unlikely that most new cloud developers would need to use all of the services provided in Google Cloud. Most developers only need a few (or in some cases, only one) storage and database services to get things off the ground. These services, which we'll focus on first, are **Google Cloud Storage** (**GCS**), Google Cloud SQL, Google Firestore, Google Spanner, and Google Bigtable. Additionally, we'll also talk about Cloud FileStore, BigQuery, Memorystore, and Persistent Disk.

GCS – basics

Before we dive deeper, let's clear up some of the basics including concepts and terms that we'll use throughout the chapter, such as **structured** and **unstructured** data. Structured data comes in different formats and types, but the basic idea is that structured data can be organized into rows and columns. All of the major Google Cloud storage options (Cloud SQL, Cloud Datastore, Cloud Bigtable) support structured data except one: GCS. GCS stores a different form of data known as unstructured data, as it cannot structure your data into rows and tables. It will only store a sequence of bytes, exactly the way you store it. However, this isn't as big of a limitation as you might think it is.

In the real world, this means that you can still store data that has an internal structure with tables and rows such as a ZIP, **Joint Photographers Experts Group** (**JPEG**), or even a **comma-separated values** (**CSV**) file, the only difference being that GCS won't know of any internal structure and it will retrieve the exact same sequence of bytes that you uploaded—every time, reliably.

Another term you'll see in GCS is **object**. Because GCS stores data as unstructured— that is, without any information about their internal structure and only as a sequence of bytes—it calls them objects. In other words, objects are very much like files but because GCS does not have the traditional naming conventions and hierarchical structure most modern file formats have, it calls them objects.

These objects are stored in what is called a **bucket**. Think of a bucket as a container, but for your files and not your microservices. Developers create multiple buckets for different projects where they can then upload files (that will be stored as objects) and download them as well.

Here is a diagram that outlines some of the GCS options available on Google Cloud:

Google Cloud Storage Classes

STORAGE CLASS	CHARACTERISTICS	USE CASES	PRICE (PER GB PER MONTH)
Multi-Regional Storage	• 99.95% availability • Geo-redundant	Storing data that is frequently accessed ("hot" objects) around the world, such as serving website content, streaming videos, or gaming and mobile applications.	$0.026 (per GB per month)
Regional Storage	• 99.9% availability • Lower cost per GB stored • Data stored in a narrow geographic region	Storing data that is frequently accessed ("hot" objects) around the world, such as serving website content, streaming videos, or gaming and mobile applications.	$0.02 (per GB per month)
Storage Nearline	• 99.0% availability • Very low cost per GB stored • Data retrieval costs • Higher per-operation costs • 30-day minimum storage duration	Data you do not expect to access frequently (i.e. no more than once per month). Ideal for back-up and serving long-tail multimedia content.	$0.01 (per GB per month)
Storage Coldline	• 99.0% availability • Lowest cost per GB stored • Data retrieval costs • Higher per-operation costs • 90-day minimum storage duration	Data you expect to access infrequently (i.e. no more than once per year). Typically this is for disaster recovery, or data that is archived and may or may not be needed at some future time.	$0.0071 (per GB per month)

Figure 5.1 – GCS classes

Finally, Google Cloud also has **storage classes** that determine various characteristics of your buckets, including the cost. Storage classes are based on availability and access frequency (that is, how many times you'll access the stored objects). Additionally, storage classes can also be regional or multi-regional. The former is a good option if you're only serving a small region such as the US West Coast and will offer the best latency possible in that region. If your app's audience is more spread out, choose multi-regional buckets; these can cover numerous regions (and entire continents) and optimize objects and buckets depending on where it is accessed from to minimize latency.

GCS

GCS is an object storage platform and the default object storage option on Google Cloud. It does almost everything that most developers need from an object storage option and is a particularly good option for a new cloud developer, as it is a fully managed platform with some really handy features.

The highlights of GCS include unlimited storage: perhaps not a strict requirement for all of the readers of this book, but if you're creating enterprise-level applications or applications that are expected to scale really fast, on-premises disk storage just won't cut it. Additionally, unlimited storage comes with no minimum object size.

It also offers a wide range of object storage classes with different use cases and priorities. Storage classes also have different pricing so that you can configure your storage to be the most cost-effective. Additionally, GCS has a feature called **Object Lifecycle Management (OLM)** that allows you to define conditions for your data that, when met, will automatically move your data to a lower storage class to help reduce monthly bills.

Getting started with GCS

Developers can get started with GCS and begin storing their data in a few ways including using Cloud Console as well as the gsutil command-line tool (part of the Google Cloud **software development kit (SDK)**).

To start off, you first need to create a bucket, and one of the easiest ways to do that is to use Cloud Console and configure it. You can reach the configuration screen by clicking on **Storage** from the menu on the left and then clicking on **Create Bucket**.

Once on the configuration screen, you'll be asked to name your bucket and choose from one of the four available storage classes, outlined as follows:

- **Standard**: This is the storage class developers would need if their data is accessed frequently. It's a high-performance and high-frequency storage class (with 99.999999999% annual availability), and if your option is accessed more than a few times a month (or millions of times a week), this is the only option.

- **Nearline**: Nearline (and all of the remaining classes) are long-term storage options for data that is accessed less than a month. Using Nearline reduces the storage costs.

- **Coldline**: If your data will be accessed even less frequently, Coldline is great and will significantly reduce storage costs.

- **Archive**: The Archive storage class is ideal for cold data storage and **disaster recovery** (**DR**). It has a minimum storage duration of 365 days and also the lowest storage costs.

After you've chosen your storage class, you'll also need to choose the location type. You can either choose a single region and give users from that region the best performance or you can choose a multi-regional location that is a cluster of individual regions and provide optimal latency to a geographically spread-out user base.

Furthermore, you can customize other parameters such as access control. By default, all data on GCS is encrypted and is only accessible to users who have access to your project. GCS offers highly granular access control using **access control lists** (**ACLs**) that enable you to grant roles to different users, with each role having different permissions. Developers can grant the following roles:

- Readers
- Writers
- Owners

You can also make some **Quality of Life** (**QOL**) changes to your GCS by turning on features such as **Object Versioning**. Apart from creating multiple versions of an object, Object Versioning also means you do not run the risk of overwriting objects and losing older versions. Instead, with Object Versioning, your previous version simply gets archived (although this will consume additional storage). If you make a lot of changes to objects and don't want to lose any data, your monthly bills will certainly rise, and there is a way to counteract that as well: with OLM.

OLM is a feature that enables developers to define parameters for their data, and upon fulfillment, your data will automatically be migrated to a lower storage class, reducing your storage costs.

There is another way to keep storage costs under control and at the same time get rid of unnecessary files and keep your storage easily manageable: object lifecycles. As your application continues to grow and change, you'll continue collecting data, some of which may be rendered useless. At this point, you can use object lifecycles to define conditions to automatically delete certain files. There are a number of conditions you can set, including per-object age, fixed data cut-off, version history, and latest version.

Finally, this brings us to the question: what should I use GCS for? Well, quite frankly, GCS can be used to store any unstructured data, which for most users will be everything, as long as they don't need their storage platform to identify and leverage an internal structure, in which case we have a handful of other options now. However, if you don't need to make use of an internal structure to store data, GCS offers extremely reliable storage at very affordable costs and extreme scalability.

GCS is an incredibly diverse platform that will take care of most of your general storage needs. However, if you're looking for more specific capabilities, the following storage options should provide that. We'll start with Cloud SQL.

Cloud SQL

Cloud SQL is a fully managed relational database service that's hosted on **Google Compute Engine** (**GCE**). Using Cloud SQL, you can create **virtual machines** (**VMs**) (Cloud SQL instances) running a version of MySQL (or PostgreSQL) of your choice while carrying over all of the important capabilities of **Structured Query Language** (**SQL**), including the following:

- Rich query language
- Primary and secondary indexes
- **Atomicity, Consistency, Isolation, Durability** (**ACID**) transactions
- Relational integrity
- Stored procedures

If you already have experience with MySQL and are looking for a relational database, Cloud SQL is the perfect option because it pretty much is MySQL underneath. The only difference is that Google hosts MySQL on its servers and takes care of updates, **operating systems** (**OSes**), configurations, backups, and other administrative tasks. If you already have a MySQL database and are looking to migrate to Google Cloud fairly simple and straightforward options to migrate your existing database to Cloud SQL exist as well.

Additionally, Cloud SQL also doubles as a fully managed platform for managing your PostgreSQL relational database. Similar to MySQL, most of the features of PostgreSQL have made their way into Cloud SQL, with a few exceptions. For instance, Cloud SQL currently does not support certain features that require SUPERUSER privileges, custom background workers, and a few other parameters. Otherwise, a PostgreSQL instance on CloudSQL is very similar to a locally hosted PostgreSQL instance. CloudSQL supports a wide range of PostgreSQL extensions, procedural languages, and powerful custom machine types (up to 624 **gigabytes (GB)** of **random-access memory (RAM)**, 96 **central processing units (CPUs)**, and 30 **terabytes (TB)** of storage).

Cloud SQL is a relational database, meaning it can store highly structured data with a complete schema, and if these two things match your requirements, you can shortlist Cloud SQL to be your database. Relational databases are also generally very good at asking complex questions, and Cloud SQL in particular has great query capabilities. In fact, it is one of the most complex (and capable) options if you're going to be using a lot of queries. On the other hand, there are other options available if your requirements are not as complex.

Furthermore, if you used **Google App Engine (GAE)** in *Chapter 4, Choosing the Right Compute Option,* as your compute option, you can use Cloud SQL with GAE with support for a wide range of programming languages, such as the following:

- Java
- Python
- **PHP: Hypertext Preprocessor (PHP)**
- Node.js
- Go
- Ruby

Now that you have a good understanding of what Cloud SQL is capable of, let's see it in action.

Getting started with Cloud SQL

Getting started with Cloud SQL is really simple and straightforward, and as with GCS can be done either through Cloud Console or through the Cloud SDK. In order to create your first Cloud SQL instance, simply go to Cloud Console and select **SQL** from the left-hand menu. You can either choose a first-generation SQL instance or a second-generation one. We recommend choosing a second-generation instance as this provides better performance and tools such as automatic storage increase. After that, use a complete basic configuration including name, password, region, and zone (you can leave it at the default setting **Any** and Google will find the zone with the least latency).

There are additional configuration options that you can access by clicking on **Show Configuration Options** to change things such as MySQL version, instance size, high availability, and to toggle features such as auto-update. Note that Cloud SQL can spin up instances supporting three versions of MySQL, as follows:

- 8.0
- 5.7
- 5.6

By default, your Cloud SQL instances will have version 5.7 and multiple options for machine types (up to 416 GB of RAM and 30 TB of data storage). Additionally, don't worry about provisioning resources and selecting the machine type at the start as you can always scale up and down by changing the computing power (going from a single core to a four-core machine type, for instance) and disk performance (changing the memory capacity so you can do more or fewer tasks at once).

Click **Create**, and Google will spin up your new SQL instance (this may take up to 90 seconds).

With the instance ready, you can now click on **Detail** and further configure it, including connecting it with the compute option you chose in *Chapter 4, Choosing the Right Compute Option*. You can also connect your SQL instance to other services by authorizing **Internet Protocol** (**IP**) addresses. If you didn't customize your instance and change the settings, you can change them now (or anytime). You can also do numerous other things to make your SQL instance exactly the way you need it to be.

For instance, you can change access control by specifying which IP addresses have access to your instance or connecting over **Secure Sockets Layer** (**SSL**), which adds an additional layer of security to communication on an unsecured connection. You can also set up maintenance schedules and windows by specifying a day and time at which Google can do maintenance each week.

To reiterate, Cloud SQL is a great option if your application uses highly structured data and complex queries—in fact, it's one of the best options if this is your biggest priority. That said, it's still based on GCE, which means while it does offer a lot of control over VMs, it doesn't scale very fast, nor is it the most scalable option available out there—it's somewhere in the middle. The pricing structure is similar to GCE too, and the bulk of your monthly bills would go toward running those VMs.

Cloud Firestore (previously Datastore)

If you're aware of SQL, you'll know that it has always suffered from one drawback—it is not very extensible with predefined schemas, and the fast-paced nature of today's market, along with the constant possibility of viral marketing, means that extensibility may not be something you want to ignore.

As a result, an alternative to SQL databases was developed—NoSQL databases, and Google Cloud has one too, called Google Cloud Datastore. However, a second generation of Datastore is available now, called Firestore. Firestore is relatively new (although it was launched in beta in early 2018). Firestore is a document storage solution, which is a non-relational form of a database. One of the key differences between a relational database such as Cloud SQL and a non-relational database such as Firestore is that the latter, while much more scalable, has far weaker query capabilities. This is mostly due to the fact that document storage does not use rows and columns; instead, it uses documents with properties. It can still do simple scans and lookups by a single key and it can do these very fast, on a large scale, and consistently.

Firestore is fully managed and serverless, which is part of the reason why it's so scalable and flexible. Being serverless also means you get to avoid any maintenance scheduling or downtime, which you might not be able to do in Cloud SQL. Furthermore, it still carries some of the capabilities of SQL, such as ACID transactions and relational integrity.

Getting started with Cloud Firestore

To get started with Firestore, there are two basic terms you need to be aware of. The first is *entities*. An entity is where you actually store data and is Firestore's equivalent of a document. When you start with Cloud Firestore, the first thing you'll be asked to create is an entity that will become your collection of unique identifiers called keys (we'll talk about keys in a second). An entity also supports a wide range of data types (primitives), including the following:

- Booleans
- Strings

- Integers

- Floating-point numbers

- Dates or times

- Binary data

Keys are comparable to unique IDs that we find in tables; they both represent a unique identifier. However, unlike table IDs, in order to create a key, developers don't need to create a table and then a row, as the key takes on both roles. In real-world usage, this means that you can simply start storing things without creating tables and add additional columns without an `ALTER TABLE` statement.

Open up GCS and follow these steps to create our first entity:

1. To start, select **Firestore** from the left-hand menu.

2. At the **Start** screen, you'll be prompted to create your first entity.

3. Then, select a location (once selected, this cannot be changed for an entity).

Once that's done, you can begin storing data by creating the first entity of its kind. You can then add a property and click **Create** to create your first entity and begin storing data (leave the indexed box checked to allow you to see this data in searches). You'll note that you didn't have to create a schema to start storing data, and that's because Firestore does not require you to define a schema in advance, but you still want to think about what you'll store, how you'll retrieve it, and the overall data model.

Another thing you might have noticed is that you didn't have to do any operational tasks such as creating VMs. That's because Firestore is a fully managed, serverless database that does most operations for you, which means you don't have to specify instance and cluster sizes or wait for an instance to spin up.

There are two aspects to Cloud Firestore: **storage** and **operations**. We've already looked at storage, so let's talk about operations. Operations are what you can do with the stored data, and as we said in the beginning, Firestore isn't the most complex database available. Therefore, your options are limited to basic operations such as the following:

- `get`: Retrieve an entity by its key.

- `put`: Save/update an entity.

- `delete`: Delete an admin operation.

- `describe`: Retrieve information about admin operations.

- `list`: List pending admin operations along with their status.
- `cancel`: Cancel a running admin operation.

Finally, let's talk about pricing. Since there are no VMs in Firestore, Google determines the monthly bill on the basis of storage and operations. Storage costs are calculated on the basis of GB/dollar. Operation costs are determined by the number of operations each month. Operations are of three types, as outlined next, and each one has a different cost:

- Read
- Write
- Delete

Write operations cost the most, while delete operations are significantly cheaper.

Wrapping up, is Cloud Firestore for you? Well, if you're looking for an incredibly scalable database without the requirement of complex queries, Cloud Firestore is a great option. Even without the need for high scalability, Cloud Firestore is a decent option due to its reliability (zero maintenance) but won't be as cost-effective as some other options.

However, if neither of the options we've discussed so far is completely suitable for your project and you're looking for a middle ground, Cloud Spanner is worth checking out.

Cloud Spanner

We've just discussed two very different storage options, each having its drawbacks. SQL databases such as Cloud SQL have richer queries, while NoSQL databases such as Firestore have raw extensibility. There is a middle ground, in that both of these platforms offer a few MySQL capabilities such as full ACID semantics (Cloud SQL, of course, offers more capabilities), but the trade-offs have always been there. To get around these trade-offs and enjoy the benefits of both rich queries and impressive scalability, a third type of database was created: a NewSQL database, and on Google Cloud, it is known as Cloud Spanner.

Cloud Spanner was created due to Google's growing storage and relational semantics requirements, which ruled out both MySQL and Firestore (back then known as Megastore). The result was Cloud Spanner, a NewSQL database that has most of the SQL features of a relational database and unlimited scale for all intents and purposes (for the average business anyway). So, what is Cloud Spanner? Cloud Spanner is a fully managed relational database (NewSQL) with unlimited scalability and excellent reliability. Here are some of the highlights of Cloud Spanner:

- It offers the best of Firestore (scalability) and Cloud SQL (relational semantics).

- Like Firestore, it has very low downtime and maintenance periods, with 99.999% availability.

- Because Cloud Spanner uses instances, it can easily move data across different VMs by resizing data chunks in case of a failure (very rare, even on extremely high loads). Your application always stays online and remains up to date.

With the fundamental concepts clear, let's take a look at how to get started with Cloud Spanner.

Getting started with Cloud Spanner

When getting started with Cloud Spanner, one of the most important concepts you need to know is that of an **instance**. An instance can be thought of as a container that stores your data as well as the compute required for operations. The closest equivalent would be the VMs we used in Cloud SQL, although entities from Firestore are similar too (they just don't have compute capabilities). However, unlike VMs in Cloud SQL, Cloud Spanner instances can replicate automatically within the region you configure (instead of zones). This gives Cloud Spanner the flexibility to quickly move data across different instances in different zones to avoid any downtime in the case of a failure.

The next important concept to understand is that of a **node**. Nodes are responsible for replicating data across zones, as well as carrying out operations such as retrieving data. Multiple individual nodes make up an instance, and each node is replicated for zones that are in your region.

Finally, as with other relational databases, Cloud Spanner has databases and tables. To store your data on Cloud Spanner, you will first have to create an instance and a database. Let's take a look at how to do this, as follows:

1. Again, let's use Google Cloud Console to start Cloud Spanner.

2. When you begin, you'll be prompted to create an instance and will find a similar configuration screen to when we created VMs in Cloud SQL. You'll need to name your instance, give it a unique identifier, and choose between **Regional** and **Multi-regional** (this is the same as what we learned in the *GCS – basics* section).

3. Choose the number of nodes. If you have a node and one region, it gets replicated thrice (one in each zone). Remember—you'll be billed for each node (a total of three here), so keep your nodes at 1, especially if you're just testing out (and turn off the instance when you're done).

With your instance created, you'll now have the option to create a database. Click on the **Create database** button to proceed, and enter the details of your database by choosing a name and filling in a schema. You can leave the schema empty and proceed to create a table by entering a name and clicking on **Create**.

Tables in Cloud Spanner are similar to tables in other relational databases for the most part, and you can use a text editor as well as a schema-building tool to get started. However, differences do arise when you proceed further. For instance, Cloud Spanner doesn't have an INSERT SQL query unlike some other databases, but rather a separate **application programming interface** (**API**) to insert data using keys. We will not go into more detail about adding, querying data, altering schemas, and other advanced topics just yet. The goal of this section is to help you understand whether Cloud Spanner is the database for you. So, is it?

Cloud Spanner solves two major problems in two different databases, but it does so by using a lot of resources. As a result, it offers a highly structured relational database, full SQL capabilities, reliability (guarantee on uptime), as well as raw scalability. However, it all comes at a cost, and a relatively high one at that. Cloud Spanner does almost everything, but it is not a cost-effective option. But the truth is, the majority of storage options are enterprise-focused, and thus achieving cost-efficiency isn't their top priority—performance is. And on top of this performance hierarchy of storage options sits Cloud Bigtable.

Cloud Bigtable

So far, we've talked about a few options, each offering something unique but having some trade-offs. But what if the scale isn't something you wanted to trade for and none of the platforms we've discussed so far seemed as though it offered enough scale? What if you wanted truly massive scale? Well, there is an option for that as well, and it's called Cloud Bigtable.

Bigtable is a fully managed, highly scalable NoSQL database that's specifically architected for extremely large workloads (over a TB of structured data). It was first announced in a paper published by Google in 2006 that resulted in the open source community building many similar systems, including HBase by Hadoop. Due to the similarities, Cloud Bigtable can be integrated into the Hadoop ecosystem through the HBase API, with a surprising amount of functionality.

In a nutshell, Cloud Bigtable is the database you want to choose if you need to store over 1 TB of data, require consistent read and write latency within 10 **milliseconds (ms)**, or if you're already using HBase and want to migrate to Google Cloud in a simple and straightforward manner.

Getting started with Cloud Bigtable

As with the other options we've discussed so far, Cloud Bigtable also has some core concepts that are crucial to understanding how this platform works and making the most out of it. The first of these concepts is row keys. Since Cloud Bigtable is a non-relational NoSQL database, it uses keys to find data, similar to Firestore. However, in this case, these are called row keys. Row keys are extremely important because they are the only unique identifiers we have in Bigtable. Unlike SQL databases, there are no secondary indexes such as additional columns that you can use during lookups, so you must rely on row keys. Therefore, it's a good idea to carefully think about how you're going to structure your row keys and organize your data model to avoid overwriting data and inefficient queries.

The second major concept in Bigtable is the infrastructure hierarchy. At the highest level, we have an instance—inside an instance we can have multiple clusters, and inside each cluster there can be multiple nodes. An instance can be thought of as the main storage unit. However, because Bigtable is a fully managed platform, you do not need to spend any time provisioning resources and creating VMs yourself; you can spin up new instances with a few clicks.

Inside each instance are clusters. There can be up to four clusters in an instance, and inside the clusters, we have nodes. If you remember from the previous chapter, nodes in Spanner would replicate across different zones; however, in Bigtable, nodes replicate in the same zone to keep the latency at a minimum. You can configure how many nodes each cluster has (up to 30) to control the number of operations, throughput, and cost. Here's a statistic that puts the level of scale Bigtable has into perspective: *A 30-node cluster is capable of performing 300,000 operations per second with a throughput of 300 megabytes (MB) per second. To put that into perspective, 300 MB per second is about 25 TB per day, which would add up to about 9 petabytes (PB) in a year.*

With these concepts out of the way, we can create our first Bigtable instance. Follow the next steps to get started with Bigtable:

1. We'll once again use Cloud Console to start up Bigtable.

2. Once there, click on **Create instance** to configure your instance and cluster.

3. As before, enter the name, instance, and cluster ID, and then select a zone. The zone should ideally be close to any VMs that will access your database.

You'll also be asked to specify the number of nodes you want. Again, keep this at a minimum (which is 3 in this case) if you're doing a test, and don't forget to turn the instance off after you're done because, as with Cloud Spanner, Bigtable can get quite expensive—but is it worth it?

Well, it depends. Bigtable wasn't built for small applications. Even at its lowest configuration, it still has three nodes and is capable of 30,000 operations per second, which is more than what's needed for almost every small business out there. More importantly, unlike some of the other Google Cloud services, Bigtable pricing isn't based on usage. Even if you leave the three nodes unused, you'll still be billed the same amount because each node is reserved for sole use by your application.

So, what are the main takeaways? Well, Bigtable is fairly unstructured compared to databases such as Cloud SQL and isn't capable of richer queries (it only has row keys). But it provides extremely low latency, some of the highest throughput out of all databases, and it is extremely scalable. On the downside, it costs a lot and isn't really ideal for small-scale usage.

Wrapping up the big five

With the information presented so far, you should have a good idea of the capabilities of the five database/storage options that we've discussed so far, as well as the ideal use cases for them. That said, to make things a little bit easier, here is a decision tree that you can use to put all five of these options in perspective:

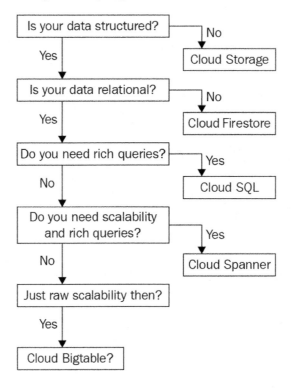

Figure 5.2 – Decision tree

These were the major cloud storage options that Google Cloud provides, and hopefully you found the one that fits your needs the best. However, if you didn't, don't worry—we've not yet exhausted our options. The Google Cloud ecosystem has numerous other cloud storage and database options that might be a better fit for you. Let's take a look.

Additional storage and database options

The Google Cloud ecosystem is huge, and it's not possible to cover every service in a single chapter. The five services that we've already covered make the biggest part of Google Cloud's storage and database services and are, in many ways, the pillars. However, there are some additional services that you'll find useful as your journey in cloud application development continues. Here are four such services.

BigQuery

Cloud BigQuery is a SQL relational database that is also used as a big data analytics platform. It's under the **Big Data** section of Cloud Console instead of the **Storage** section because its main purpose is to query extremely large datasets extremely quickly—terabytes of data within minutes.

The reason we didn't include BigQuery in our main list of database options was that most small businesses and developers who are just starting out won't be working with datasets that are measured in TB and PB. However, you might find BigQuery to be an extremely useful tool when you need to analyze large datasets such as public records and archives.

Filestore

Filestore is the opposite of a storage solution such as GCS that stores unstructured data with no internal hierarchy to manage it. Filestore is a fully managed file storage solution that works great for applications that need a filesystem interface. Instead of storing a sequence of bytes, Filestore is a great option for tasks such as media rendering, analytics, and shared content.

Persistent disks/local solid-state drive (SSD) (block storage)

Block storage can be thought of like physical hard drives that we use in our regular computers. They can be removed from a computer and plugged into another, and they would still have all of the data. Google offers a similar high-performance and high-availability service called Persistent Disk. Persistent disks can be added to your VM instances running on GCE or GKE. There are two types of persistent disks available, outlined as follows:

- Standard persistent disk: This is the low-cost version that uses **hard disk drives (HDDs)**.
- Local SSD: This is the high-performance option, with better speed and lower latency.

Persistent Disks is a great cost-efficient cloud storage option that gives developers incredible flexibility and control over their data.

MemoryStore

MemoryStore is a database option that uses memory instead of traditional HDDs and SSDs for storage. Since memory is considerably faster than any SSD available, MemoryStore is able to significantly reduce latency, which can be crucial in applications that need to show users real-time updates by the ms (competitive e-sports, bidding, stream analytics, and so on). MemoryStore can be integrated with Redis and Memcached for automating monitoring, updates, and failover protocols. As with other Google Cloud storage options, MemoryStore is scalable, with support for up to 5 TB clusters.

Security and flexibility

There is no definite pattern that you need to follow when choosing your storage and database options. Different database and storage options can be used together—and often are—to complete tasks that have different priorities; the cloud gives you that flexibility.

That said, some services are more flexible than others. For instance, GCS—despite supporting only unstructured data—can be used for a large number of tasks due to its low cost, high scalability, low latency, and reliability. The only task you shouldn't use GCS for is querying your data. Instead, you can use GCS with a relational database that is capable of rich queries, such as Cloud SQL or Cloud Spanner.

Finally, there is data security. While data storage in the cloud is still safer than most on-premises solutions, there are still steps you should take to ensure the safety of your data. For starters, all of the data stored in Google Cloud is encrypted by default. That said, developers can further improve security by bringing their own encryption keys using the in-built Cloud Key Management service that Google Cloud provides or an on-premises system. Furthermore, almost all the storage options we've discussed offer some form of failover protection to ensure your data isn't wiped out in the case of a failure.

Summary

Google Cloud has an expansive list of cloud and database solutions—we've covered most of them, and you should've been able to find the right service for you. However, remember that one of the benefits of using Google Cloud services is that most of them can be used in tandem with each other, which opens up numerous other possibilities.

We also briefly touched on cloud security, but we'll take a much closer look at this. In the final chapter of *Part 2* (*Chapter 7, Implementing Cloud Native Security*), we'll dive a lot deeper into the world of cloud security.

6
Implementing a Messaging and Scheduling System

The main idea behind microservices is to decouple the individual services and functions of an application by creating several *micro* applications that can be scaled more easily and are far more resilient. However, this entire arrangement breaks down completely if the microservices have no way of communicating with each other. Your microservices need to be able to communicate with each other and there are numerous ways this can be done. In this chapter, we'll explore these different ways and look at how **Google Cloud** services can be used to do this. We'll also cover services from other vendors and compare how they stack against each other.

In this chapter, we will cover the following topics:

- Understanding the requirements of a messaging system
- Introduction to asynchronous messaging
- Introduction to **Publish/Subscribe (Pub/Sub)**
- Introduction to Cloud Tasks
- Introduction to Cloud Scheduler

Understanding the requirements of a messaging system

Broadly, there are two ways messaging systems work—synchronously and asynchronously. We'll talk about these two types of systems in a minute, but first, let's understand the requirements of a cloud-native messaging system as this will help us narrow down the hundreds of ways a messaging system can be configured.

Requirement #1: Scalability

The first requirement is that it needs to be scalable. One of the main reasons you're choosing to create a cloud-native application is because you know your application's demand will grow, and when it does, you need to be able to quickly and efficiently scale. Take, for instance, the architecture depicted in *Figure 6.1*. Let's say we're building a simple e-commerce application that has four microservices taking care of some of the core functions of your e-commerce business. As soon as a payment is confirmed, a message is sent to the packaging microservice, which begins the packaging of the order. At the same time, a notification is also sent to the user. After the packaging is done, a message to ship the order is sent and along with it a notification to the end user, as well as acknowledgment notifications to the services.

This basic architecture is portrayed in the following figure:

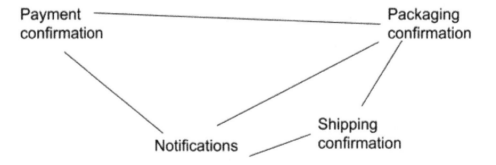

Figure 6.1 – Basic architecture

Now, let's assume that we want to scale up operations—in particular, shipping. To do so, we can add two more instances of the shipping microservice, along with a load balancer. However, this overly complicates things for us because we now need to keep track of which order is under which instance and, more crucially for an e-commerce business, whether an order is too far down the supply chain for it to still be canceled. Similar problems arise in this arrangement. Therefore, we need a messaging system that can be scaled up without making operations more complicated.

In addition to raw scalability, performance factors such as latency and availability are also important. When comparing the different messaging systems available on the market, you'll find that not all have the same latency or availability, even if they're using the same protocols and delivery patterns. That's partly because of underlying hardware, as well as optimization. In general, low latency is great but it's not a deal breaker for asynchronous messaging; availability plays a bigger factor and, depending on the task the messaging system has been optimized for, it may be more or less available. Therefore, when you're choosing your messaging system, be sure to take into consideration your latency and availability needs and whether or not the platform can deliver on those needs.

Requirement #2: Extensibility

If we want to add a new service to our growing e-commerce business—say, a monitoring system to track orders more accurately—we'll need to redo the entire messaging system and face a similar problem of overcomplication.

The following screenshot shows how the number of messages required can increase dramatically when adding new services:

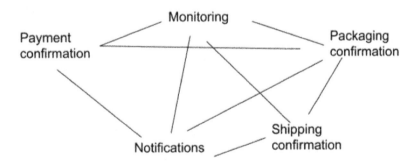

Figure 6.2 – Adding new services increases the number of messages

Each additional service will spawn an exponential number of new elements in our messaging system, limiting the agility of our application. Speaking of which, we have the next requirement: agility.

Requirement #3: Agility

We want the application to be agile, and this extends to the messaging system as well. We need to have the ability to add, remove, temporarily turn off, and exclusively test individual microservices in a system such as this because it is fundamentally not isolated. Everything is interconnected, and that means it's not very agile—nor very cloud native. In order to make any changes, we'll have to reconfigure the entire system to ensure the messages reach their intended destination.

Requirement #4: Resiliency

And, of course, there's the matter of resiliency. No matter how failproof our application is, risk can never be truly fully mitigated, and thus we need to think about how the messaging system can not only survive failures but also continue to work in spite of them. In our current configuration, the four microservices communicate directly and synchronously—that is, in real time. In its current state, there is no failover mechanism; worse still, if even one of the microservices failed, multiple others would fail too.

In essence, we need a messaging system that can scale quickly and meet the demands of a growing business. It should also be able to scale down to be cost-effective and needs to make expansion easier. The process to add new microservices into the messaging system should be straightforward. Similarly, developers should also have individual control over each element/factor in the system and be able to add, remove, test, or otherwise alter existing services without affecting the entire system. And finally, it needs to be resilient and capable of not losing critical information and instructions during a failure.

Are there other requirements? Yes, there are. In fact, these are just the basic qualities that make a messaging system more compatible with a cloud-native application. Different businesses have different goals, and it's possible that some businesses have more or fewer requirements.

Is there a messaging system that meets all of these requirements? There is. In fact, there are multiple messaging systems—but they're not interchangeable. We'll talk about the different messaging systems available—and when to use them—in greater detail in this chapter.

Introduction to asynchronous messaging

In our day-to-day life, the concept of communication is fairly straightforward and simple—we call a person and if they receive the call, we can communicate in real time. However, there's another form of communication that is equally important. In this other form, messages cannot be delivered instantly (in real time); rather, once a message is sent, it is stored and is only received when the receiver is able to access it—for instance, voicemails or text messages. If you send a friend a text message and their mobile phone is turned off, they'll still receive the message because the service you're using to send text messages stored it. The first type of messaging is known as synchronous (because it's in real time) and the second type is called asynchronous (because it's not in real time). In this chapter, we'll limit our discussion to asynchronous messaging as it has a greater number of business use cases.

Messaging products available (open source and cloud native) on the market

Even though most of us don't think about the details of what goes on behind the scenes when talking to our friends, as application developers you'll learn that messaging is more complicated than it seems. However, as with a lot of other things, cloud application development has made messaging a bit simpler to get started with and manage.

Over the years, multiple open source standards and platforms have emerged that have made it easier for developers to integrate powerful messaging systems into their apps. Google Cloud Platform has one too; in fact, it offers a variety of messaging services, and we'll discuss them in greater detail later in the chapter.

However, there is a common misconception that all of these platforms achieve the same objective and are thus interchangeable. This is not true. Most of these platforms—such as Kafka, **Amazon Simple Queue Service (Amazon SQS)**, Cloud Pub/Sub, RabbitMQ, and so on—are different services, each with its own set of benefits and limitations. Migration is possible; in fact, in some cases, it's as easy as a single click. However, we still want to try to make the right choice to begin with. Next, we are going to discuss some of the open source and cloud-native messaging products available on the market currently (other than the Google Cloud services).

Amazon SQS

Amazon SQS is a fully managed distributed queue system that allows applications to send, store, and receive messages. One of the main purposes of a service such as SQS is to store messages in applications that receive messages faster than they can process them. In this sense, SQS can be thought of as a central and temporary database in a distributed system that sends messages where they need to go *after* collecting them. Many other services that we'll talk about in this chapter also work on a similar principle as this makes them more resilient, practical, flexible, and scalable, at the cost of being asynchronous (which isn't a strict requirement for most workloads).

A basic architecture in a distributed messaging system such as Amazon SQS includes the components of your distributed system, the microservices/serverless application, the message queue, and the messages themselves. The process begins when one component (one of your microservices) in your distributed system sends a message that gets added to the queue. Now, SQS maintains multiple servers, and each message is distributed in multiple servers for reliability. After that, a different component in your distributed system receives the message and SQS sends it over. To ensure the message isn't sent to the same component multiple times, SQS has a visibility timeout period; once it passes, the second component deletes the message from the queue.

The following diagram portrays how SQS carries out this process:

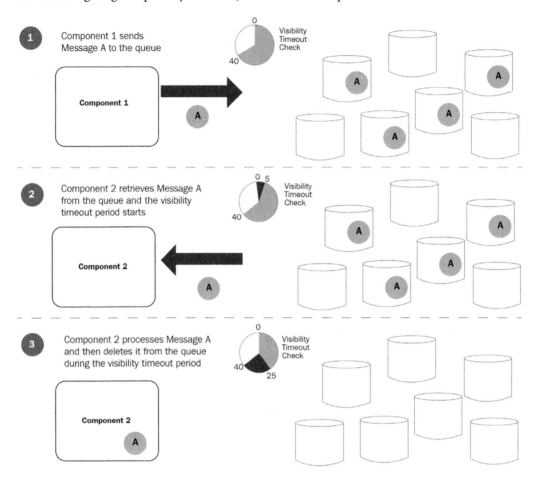

Figure 6.3 – Amazon SQS process

Although part of the **Amazon Web Services** (**AWS**) ecosystem, SQS can be used with any application by using a generic web services **application programming interface** (**API**), as long as the application is written in one of the languages supported by the AWS **software development kit** (**SDK**). SQS also has important features such as autoscaling (it's fully managed), storing messages across multiple zones to improve resilience, and Amazon's **server-side encryption** (**SSE**).

Kafka

Kafka is one of the most popular and powerful messaging systems on the market right now, used by 35% of the *Fortune 500* companies. Originally developed by LinkedIn, Kafka is an open source, distributed messaging system that works great in real-time streaming data architectures as it can provide latency of less than 10 **milliseconds (ms)**. Along with its high performance, Kafka is also a great option for projects that have high throughput as it can scale horizontally (like the cloud itself) and process millions of messages every second and trillions of messages in a day.

Additionally, Kafka isn't used as a messaging system by everyone. Due to its capabilities, Kafka can also be used as an application data log, an **Internet of Things (IoT)** activity tracker and monitor, a stream analysis tool, and more. It is also used for big data analysis as it can be integrated with Spark, Flink, Storm, Hadoop, and so on.

Like SQS, Kafka is a distributed messaging system, but unlike SQS, Kafka uses a Pub/Sub model along with the queuing model seen in SQS. The Pub/Sub messaging model allows messages to be sent to every subscriber but traditionally, these two distinct models were incompatible. To overcome this limitation and bring together the best of both worlds, Kafka uses a partitioned log model whereby a sequence of ordered messages is created and then broken down into different partitions for different subscribers. The Pub/Sub messaging model also gave Cloud Pub/Sub its name and is the model it is based upon.

Due to its scaling capabilities, Kafka is mostly used at the enterprise level, where hundreds of billions of messages (often over a trillion) need to be processed in a single day. It is also optimized for stream analysis, which means it's capable of processing a continuous flow of data from thousands of data sources—at the same time.

RabbitMQ

RabbitMQ is a message broker, which is another term for a middleware messaging system. RabbitMQ is very similar to Amazon SQS as both of them use a basic architecture that involves the same three components: the message, the application (microservices), and the message queue (also called the message broker). It was originally architected to support the **Advanced Message Queuing Protocol (AMQP)** but today supports other protocols, including the following:

- **HyperText Transfer Protocol (HTTP)**
- **Simple (or Streaming) Text-Oriented Messaging Protocol (STOMP)**
- **Message Queuing Telemetry Transport (MQTT)**

To an extent, RabbitMQ works like other message queuing systems under the same basic principle. However, RabbitMQ also has some additional capabilities, such as clustering and serving multiple clients under different protocols. As with SQS, messages are stored in different queues in RabbitMQ, but not just for safety reasons. Each consumer/client is given its own queue based on a different algorithm, called an exchange. There are four types of logic in an exchange, outlined as follows:

- Direct exchange

- Fan-out exchange

- Topic exchange

- Headers exchange

Each type of logic dictates how a message will be queued slightly differently. This exchange becomes an additional component in a RabbitMQ architecture, giving developers further control over how messages are sent—similar to a Pub/Sub architecture.

The following diagram shows the components of a RabbitMQ architecture:

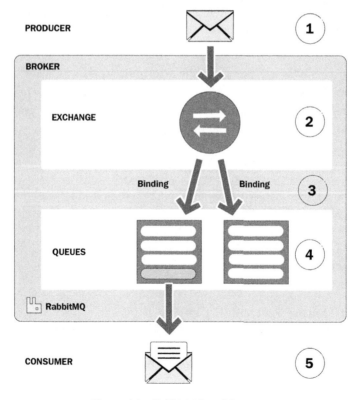

Figure 6.4 – RabbitMQ architecture

When looking at different messaging systems, you'll find many similarities (even more when you realize that different systems use different terms for the same thing (queue/log, queue/topics, message/record, and so on). In other words, while they may not be perfectly congruent (or interchangeable), they are comparable. For instance, both Kafka and RabbitMQ can be used as basic message queuing systems as both provide high throughput and reliability, but would you want to use Kafka as a basic messaging system? Probably not. Kafka is optimized for the real-time streaming, logging, and analyzing of data. On the other hand, RabbitMQ is optimized for easy integration within applications that need to run long-running processes reliably. Neither is objectively better or worse than the other; rather, it's more subjective—that is, dependent on your use case. In other words, Kafka or RabbitMQ might be better for one company but not necessarily for you.

NATS Streaming

Neural Autonomic Transport System (**NATS**) is a popular messaging system written in Go that is capable of handling millions of messages a second. It is based on a Pub/Sub model but is capable of queuing messages as well, although in a limited capacity. What it's not capable of, however, is persistence. If the receiver is online/active and doesn't receive the message, then it's not stored in *sent items*—it's gone. However, unlike multiple servers and partitions in the messaging systems we've talked about so far, the messaging queues in NATS aren't replicated but are sharded by nodes, meaning that if a node fails, the messages in those queues are gone with it. To overcome this limitation, NATS Streaming can be used to add features such as persistence and replay to existing NATS servers, making it more comparable to modern messaging systems such as Kafka and RabbitMQ.

Core NATS is a good option for businesses that require low-latency, synchronous communication, but if you require more than just a fire-and-forget system, you can use NATS Streaming for the additional reliability of storing messages on disk, along with a number of benefits such as the ability to replay historical messages and create durable subscriptions, among others.

At the beginning of the chapter, we mentioned that there are two major types of messaging systems: **synchronous** and **asynchronous**. Let's take a closer look at the two and understand why one may be better suited for your project than the other.

Advantages of asynchronous messaging

Most of the major messaging systems available on the market today are asynchronous (although many synchronous messaging systems also exist, such as core NATS). In case you're wondering why that is, asynchronous messaging systems offer capabilities and features that are more aligned with modern businesses and cloud-native applications. In this section, we'll look at some of the advantages of choosing asynchronous messaging over synchronous messaging.

At first, it might seem that synchronous is better because it's in real time and is thus far more accurate, and that's true. This is also part of the reason why so many IoT applications use NATS as their messaging system, as it allows them to process millions of messages with relative ease and accuracy. Furthermore, if a business's needs grow over time and they begin to require greater reliability and scalability, they can use **acknowledgments** (**acks**), sequence numbers, or NATS Streaming. However, by doing so, we begin to move into asynchronous messaging territory, where most of these capabilities are built in.

Microservices and loosely coupled communication

Go back to the first three chapters of this book, and remember that the fundamental principle of a cloud-native architecture is to create individual services that can scale and operate independently. Together, these services create extremely scalable, flexible, and resilient applications. However, in order for this architecture to work, independent and isolated services must have an efficient way to communicate that is also loosely coupled. The thing is, loose coupling in a microservices architecture isn't something you add when you need it; in a working architecture, it's already there. Loosely coupled communication is a prerequisite of a microservices architecture.

The following screenshot is a basic visual representation of these two distinct architectures but should help you understand the core premise of isolation in a microservices architecture:

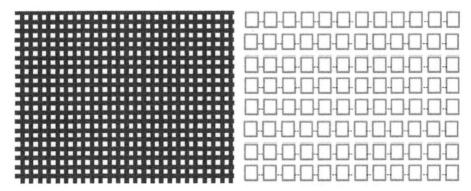

Figure 6.5 – Monolithic architecture versus microservices architecture

On the left side of *Figure 6.5* is a monolithic architecture, where each line denotes a line of code/a function—it's all interconnected, and changing one aspect of your application means changing the rest too. On the right side is a distributed system using a microservices architecture, where each square represents an individual microservice. These microservices are containerized and fully isolated—they already have all of the infrastructure and information they need to run inside their container. However, in order to create a full-fledged application, they *must* talk to each other. One of the most common ways of doing this is through **REpresentational State Transfer (REST)** APIs, and in *Figure 6.5*, each line connecting the microservices is an API. REST APIs are generally synchronous (although asynchronous operations are possible) and they are based on a request-response system whereby a response is required. This method of communication can be limiting in a lot of cases and may increase your compute requirements. An alternative way to communicate between microservices is asynchronous messaging, which uses a queuing or Pub-Sub pattern (decoupling of publisher from subscriber).

Let's take a look at some of the capabilities of asynchronous messaging and why it makes sense to use it over REST APIs.

The ability to handle failures using a built-in retry mechanism

One of the biggest limitations of synchronous messaging and one of the most important features of asynchronous messaging is the resilience that comes with data persistence. In a synchronous messaging system, messages are real-time or live, which means if the receiving application fails or goes offline even for a brief moment, the message is lost.

This problem is completely avoided in asynchronous messaging due to data persistence. When a message is sent it is written to the disk instead of the memory, and it stays there until the receiver has acknowledged the message. Both message queuing and Pub/Sub patterns use a central messaging component that stores and sends out messages after receiving them.

In essence, if the receiving component failed before/while receiving the message, the message is stored. When the component comes online, the message is sent again and again until the component acknowledges receiving the message or the maximum retention period is over (this can be specified by the developer in most platforms).

Implementation changes in subscribers do not impact publishers

The message format is consistent across publishers and subscribers, thus keeping their implementation agnostic from each other.

Scale-out latency

Volatile demand and traffic spikes are very common these days, and it's entirely possible that your application will find itself receiving more requests/messages than it can handle. If you are on a fully managed platform, like with most of Google Cloud's services, you have little to worry about as autoscaling will kick in and scale your application to handle additional requests. However, there is a latency involved in scaling up. **Virtual machine (VM)** instances take time to spin, and during this time, it's possible that your additional requests will fail to reach their intended destination as new containers spin up. In a synchronous system, these messages would be lost forever but in an asynchronous system, the message queue or broker acts as a buffer, storing messages that cannot be processed—better late than never, right?

For this reason, an asynchronous messaging system is also a great option for systems that receive more requests than they can process at a time—granted that speed is not a priority.

Programming language and execution environment abstraction

This decouples publishers from subscribers, paving the way for interoperability among different language implementations and programming environments across publishers and subscribers.

Now that you're well aware of the core concepts and the key idea behind asynchronous messaging, we can see how messaging systems work on Google Cloud starting with Pub/Sub—the model, not the Google Cloud service.

Introduction to Pub/Sub

We've mentioned Pub/Sub a few times so far in this chapter, referring to both the messaging pattern and also Google Cloud Pub/Sub, a fully managed messaging system. Let's dive a little deeper into this topic, starting with the pattern itself.

Pub/Sub is short for Publish/Subscribe, which refers to a type of messaging system similar to a messaging broker or a queuing system. However, unlike these systems, a Pub/Sub model has a different architecture. In a Pub/Sub model, messages from different sources or components (the publisher) are stored separately. Other components in the system that need to communicate with the publisher can subscribe to it and become a subscriber. As a result, whenever the publisher sends out a new message, all of its subscribers receive it.

The following screenshot provides an example of a Pub/Sub architecture:

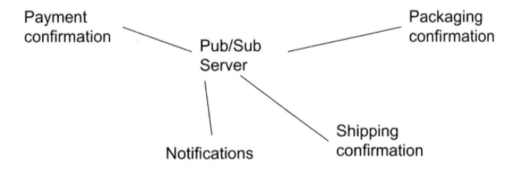

Figure 6.6 – Pub/Sub architecture

Implementing a Pub/Sub model for our previous example simplifies the entire arrangement significantly. Developers no longer need to worry about connecting the components with each other; rather, all components (or microservices) now speak to a single messaging system. For instance, in our example, the packaging confirmation is subscribed to the payment confirmation, the shipping confirmation is subscribed to the packaging confirmation, and all of our services (payment, packaging, and shipping) are now subscribed to the notifications service. This is the basic principle upon which Google Cloud Pub/Sub is based.

What is Cloud Pub/Sub?

As with many other Google Cloud services, Cloud Pub/Sub was built upon Google's existing internal systems as they realized that other businesses had growing messaging requirements similar to their own. It is a fully managed, asynchronous messaging service that can be used as a message broker (middleware) or for real-time analytics. Since Cloud Pub/Sub works on many of the same concepts we've discussed, you'll find many similarities between this service and others such as Kafka. At the end of this section, we'll also have a more in-depth comparison between Cloud Pub/Sub and Kafka.

Pub/Sub key features

Google Cloud Pub/Sub is a fully managed, serverless platform that has all of the features you're going to need to make a highly scalable and resilient messaging system. Let's take a look at some of its key features, as follows:

- **Serverless**

  As you have already learned, serverless is an extremely powerful feature that makes getting started with any cloud service almost effortless. This is true here as well. Even new developers can set up a messaging system for their application in Cloud Pub/Sub in less than 15 minutes. There is no planning required at your end; the cloud takes care of everything—no partitions or shards, but fully automatic scaling and provisioning.

- **Guarantees at-least-once delivery and exactly-once processing**

  The persistence and replication features built into Cloud Pub/Sub, along with additional retry mechanisms, ensure at-least-once delivery, no matter the scale of your application. At the same time, it ensures that processed messages are always removed from the queue and are never added back, ensuring the reliable transfer of information.

- **Global scale**

  Cloud Pub/Sub is built on the same infrastructure as other Google services, including YouTube. It has access to a lot of compute and storage—in other words, it's extremely scalable. But it's not just scalable—it also has high performance and high availability. Even if your application receives messages from different corners of the world, Cloud Pub/Sub will be able to manage messages consistently with low latency, making it a viable choice for businesses and applications with a global reach.

There are a few other benefits of using Cloud Pub/Sub as well.

Additional benefits

Here are some additional benefits of Cloud Pub/Sub:

- Cloud Pub/Sub's open APIs and client libraries allow you to integrate with other cloud platforms and deploy messages cross-cloud.

- Cloud Pub/Sub is **Health Insurance Portability and Accountability Act (HIPAA)**-compliant and comes with security features such as granular access control and end-to-end encryption.

- Cloud Pub/Sub supports out-of-the-box integrations with other cloud services such as Cloud Storage, Gmail update events, and Cloud Functions. It can also be integrated with third-party services such as Splunk, Datadog, Informatica, Kafka, and so on.

- Cloud Pub/Sub has features such as seek and replay, which allows you to rewind or fast-forward your backlog and reprocess or delete certain messages immediately. You can also use dead-letter topics to store unprocessed messages and investigate their failure later. Pub/Sub also offers message attribute-based filtering to further customize message streams.

Before we are ready to use Cloud Pub/Sub, we need to understand its key concepts.

Pub/Sub Concepts – topics and subscriptions

The basic architecture of Cloud Pub/Sub includes four main components: a producer, a message attribute, a topic, and a subscription.

Publishers

A publisher refers to an application or a microservice that is the source of our message. It both creates and sends a message to the topic.

Message attributes

Message attributes are optional pieces of information that the publisher may send along with the actual message to the topic and subscribers. A message attribute is a key-value pair. Developers can also use custom attributes when publishing messages.

> **Important note**
> If a message itself has no data then it must contain a message attribute (either a message attribute or non-empty data is required for a message to be published).

Topics

A topic is one of the two main core components of Cloud Pub/Sub (the other being subscriptions). It can be thought of as a category where multiple unique messages can be stored. When a producer publishes a message, a topic is automatically created inside Pub/Sub where the message is stored until it is ready to be sent to the subscriber via the subscription.

Subscriptions

A subscription is a component that lists all of the subscribers to a particular topic, and it also determines which application receives which message. It is the Cloud Pub/Sub equivalent of a queue or a message broker. For instance, a shipping confirmation service will send out different messages at different stages of shipping. Each message goes to a specific topic and has its own subscription. In order for the notifications service to get specific shipping updates, it must subscribe to the subscription associated with specific topics, as illustrated in the following diagram:

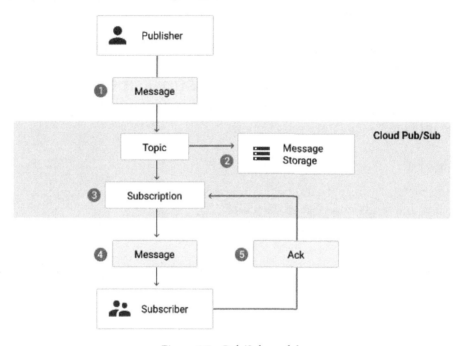

Figure 6.7 – Pub/Sub model

Figure 6.7 shows the basic architecture of the Pub/Sub model in action. The process starts when the publisher application creates a message, automatically creating a topic as well. The publisher then sends the message to the topic, and its job ends there. After that, the topic is responsible for storing and sending out messages to the correct subscription until the messages have been processed by the subscriber.

There are two ways in which a subscriber can receive messages from the subscription. First, the service can *push* the message to the subscriber, known as the push method. Second, the subscriber application can pull the message from Cloud Pub/Sub (that is, from the subscription itself). Finally, a pull subscription acknowledgment is in the form of receiving a HTTP 200 status, unlike with a pull model, where subscribers need to acknowledge them explicitly.

But what if a consumer application (subscriber) crashes or fails right before or while processing a message? Well, in this case, the application would not acknowledge the message within a specified period (which can be set by the developer). If this happens, Cloud Pub/Sub would put the message back into the queue and send the message again. This creates an automatic retry mechanism.

Pub/Sub model – fan-in and fan-out

Pub/Sub messaging systems can be configured in one of two ways: they can either have a fan-in design or a fan-out design. When multiple message sources or publishers send messages to a single consumer or subscriber, it is called a fan-in design. On the other hand, when a single publisher sends messages to multiple subscribers, it is known as a fan-out system.

Pull versus push types – differences and when to use each type

We already briefly mentioned pull and push types, and these are fairly simple to understand—to receive messages, subscribers can either pull messages or messages can be pushed to them. But how do you decide when to use which delivery model?

Well, a pull delivery model is ideal if your application needs higher efficiency and processes a large volume of messages per second. It's also the right choice if you cannot set up a public **HTTP Secure (HTTPS)** endpoint with a non-self-signed **Secure Sockets Layer (SSL)** certificate. On the other hand, a push delivery model is suitable for applications that have to be processed by a single Webhook, those that have App Engine Standard and Cloud Functions subscribers, and those that do not have Google Cloud dependencies.

Getting started with Cloud Pub/Sub

Let's try to use Cloud Pub/Sub like we did with the storage options in the previous chapter, by following these steps:

1. We'll use the Google Cloud Console, so go ahead and open it in your browser.
2. Open Cloud Pub/Sub, which should take a second if you haven't already enabled the Pub/Sub API.

3. Once loaded, Pub/Sub will ask you to create a topic before you can send your first message. The topic is just a name resource that acts as a category for your messages. Click on **Create Topic** on the top bar and choose a name.

4. After you create the topic, you'll need to install the client library out of the eight available options (Python, C++, C#, Go, Java, Node.js, PHP, and Ruby).

Once that's done, you're ready to write code and publish messages. As an example, if you choose the client library for Node.js, publishing a message would look something like this:

```
// Imports the Google Cloud client library
const {PubSub} = require('@google-cloud/pubsub');


// Creates a client; cache this for further use
const mypubSubClient = new PubSub();
async function publishMessage() {
    // Publishes the message as a string, e.g. "Hello, world!"
or JSON.stringify(someObject)
    const dataBuffer = Buffer.from(data);


    try {
        const messageId = await pubSubClient.topic(topicName).
publish(dataBuffer);
        console.log(`Message ${messageId} published.`);
    } catch (error) {
        console.error(`Received error while publishing: ${error.
message}`);
        process.exitCode = 1;
    }
}
```

You'll also need to receive messages if you want to create a proper messaging system, and to do that, you need to create a subscription. Back in the Google Cloud Console, you should have a **New Subscription** option to enable you to create a subscription under the topic you just created. Once again, enter the name of your subscription and choose the **Pull** type in this case. Now, you can write the code to start receiving messages as well. The code should look something like this:

```
const {PubSub} = require('@google-cloud/pubsub');
const pubSubClient = new PubSub();
```

```
function listenForMessages() {
const subscription = pubSubClient.
subscription(subscriptionName);
let messageCount = 0;
  const messageHandler = message => {
    console.log(`Received message ${message.id}:`);
    console.log(`\tData: ${message.data}`);
    console.log(`\tAttributes: ${message.attributes}`);
    messageCount += 1;
message.ack();
  };
  subscription.on('message', messageHandler);


  setTimeout(() => {
    subscription.removeListener('message', messageHandler);
    console.log(`${messageCount} message(s) received.`);
  }, timeout * 1000);
}
listenForMessages();
```

You'll notice that we also told Pub/Sub to acknowledge each received message within a specified timeframe and retry when a message isn't acknowledged.

Cloud Pub/Sub is the main messaging service that Google Cloud has to offer, but there are a few other scheduling services that work well with Pub/Sub and that can significantly increase functionality.

Introduction to Cloud Tasks

Cloud Pub/Sub is Google's main messaging system, but there are other services that can execute similar workflows but in a limited capacity. One such service is called Cloud Tasks, which is a fully managed cloud service that can be used to executive a large number of operations asynchronously. These operations are not limited to your main application, user, or services and can be performed outside a service-to-service request independently. We'll call these operations **tasks**.

Cloud Tasks works on a similar basic principle as a message queue, but instead of messages, tasks are added to the queue. However, both Cloud Tasks and Cloud Pub/Sub can be used as middleware in a simple messaging system since the tasks in Cloud Tasks are just a collection of a unique name, configuration, and an optional payload (information required to complete the operation, comparable to message attributes).

One of the main differences between Cloud Tasks and Cloud Pub/Sub is that the former is not a dedicated messaging solution, but rather a more general-purpose service for queuing operations. On the other hand, Cloud Pub/Sub is a dedicated messaging system, with the goal of decoupling the publisher from the subscriber. This means that both of these tools do different things better than the other. For instance, Cloud Pub/Sub has a maximum message size of 10 **megabytes** (**MB**) with no upper limit on maximum delivery rate, whereas the maximum task size allowed by Cloud Tasks is only 100 **kilobytes** (**KB**), with a maximum delivery rate of 500 **queries per second** (**QPS**). Similarly, Cloud Tasks has configurable retries, scheduled delivery, and can retain tasks for up to 30 days, whereas Cloud Pub/Sub only retains messages for 7 days and does not have the other two features.

In a nutshell, if you are looking for a fully managed, feature-rich, global messaging system with an incredible throughput, go with Pub/Sub. If you're looking for scheduling tasks, controlling traffic, task duplication (among other things), but with guaranteed delivery in a scalable and fully managed package, Cloud Tasks is better.

Introduction to Cloud Scheduler

Cloud Scheduler is another service in Google Cloud's arsenal that can be used for asynchronous communication within your application. However, it is more similar to Cloud Tasks than Cloud Pub/Sub. First of all, it is not a messaging system like Pub/Sub; instead, it can be defined as a powerful, fully managed platform to schedule all sorts of operations for your applications regularly. Cloud Scheduler is capable of handling a wide range of operations, including batch tasks and big data—in other words, it's a cron job scheduler.

Although not directly comparable with Cloud Pub/Sub, Cloud Scheduler can be used with Pub/Sub. Developers can create cron jobs using the platform for different types of targets, including Pub/Sub topics. Other types of Cloud Scheduler targets include HTTP/S endpoints and App Engine applications.

Cloud Scheduler is a powerful tool for automation with resilient features, including retry mechanisms and guaranteed at-least-once delivery. More importantly, Cloud Scheduler is an incredibly versatile tool that can be used outside of automating service-to-service requests. In fact, you can use Cloud Scheduler to automate almost anything in your application from a single place using HTTP endpoints.

Summary

The messaging system of an application is an integral part of any application, and you now have a deep understanding of how messaging systems work in a cloud-native architecture and the services you can use to fully utilize the cloud's potential. The messaging systems and concepts in a cloud-native application are different due to the inherent isolated nature of containerized applications. In order to maintain this isolation and enjoy the benefits of a cloud-native application, the messaging system used must also be loosely coupled and flexible. Thankfully, all cloud-native applications allow for their microservices to communicate with each other through APIs, without any additional service or platform.

However, while REST APIs are not a bad solution, they can be limiting in many scenarios, and managing hundreds of APIs can become more difficult and overall very inefficient as your application grows and evolves. To keep your messaging system clean and efficient, it's recommended to use an asynchronous messaging platform such as Cloud Pub/Sub.

Cloud Pub/Sub creates reliable and high-performance messaging based on the Pub/Sub pattern, and unlike some other message brokers (or middleware), Cloud Pub/Sub comes with additional features such as being globally scalable, having persistence and retry mechanisms, and benefiting from easy integrations with a wide range of other useful tools in the Google Cloud ecosystem, such as Cloud Tasks and Cloud Scheduler. In the upcoming chapters, we'll see these tools and services in action as we begin building our own application. However, before we do that, there's one more area of cloud-native application development that we need to cover—cloud-native security. In the next chapter, we'll talk about the various Cloud **Identity and Access Management (IAM)** concepts, Google Cloud Identity Platform, and the various security best practices that must be implemented in order to create a secure cloud-native application.

7
Implementing Cloud-Native Security

Unfortunately, there will always be actors with malicious intent who want to ruin your day as a developer – it doesn't matter if you're working on the cloud or not. As a developer, the responsibility to protect your users' data falls on you and even though the cloud is generally safer than most on-premises solutions, it's still vulnerable, especially when security systems aren't implemented correctly. When all the systems are implemented correctly along with Google Cloud's security best practices, you do not need to do anything else to ensure your app's and data's safety.

By the end of this chapter, you will have learned about the following:

- The principles and concepts of cloud security
- Cloud Identity and Access Management
- Concepts of IAM
- Cloud IAM on Google Cloud
- Components of Cloud IAM

- Limitations of Cloud IAM

- Introduction to Cloud Identity Platform and its features

- BeyondCorp (a new approach to enterprise security)

- Introduction to Cloud Identity-Aware Proxy (IAP)

The principles and concepts of cloud security

You may be tempted to skip ahead to the actual Google Cloud services and concepts, but we strongly recommend that you familiarize yourself with these principles first. Like the design patterns we learned about previously, these principles and policies are meant to prevent security vulnerabilities and guide your development around security best practices. It's also a relatively short section.

There are numerous design principles and methodologies that help secure an app. However, not all of them are equally relevant to cloud-native app development. In this chapter, we are going to cover three major principles listed below that cover most of what makes up cloud security.

Economy of Mechanism

This principle states that your application (microservices) needs to be small and simple enough that in case there is a security vulnerability or attack, it can be quickly identified and repaired.

To some extent, the Economy of Mechanism already exists in all cloud-native applications and is a feature. Its loosely coupled architecture, isolated microservices, and replication make it easier to identify and isolate problems relatively quickly. As you can imagine, this is much harder in a monolith.

However, this *feature* can be lost. For instance, if the developer isn't careful and doesn't follow best practices such as the 12 Factor App and Google Cloud guidelines, the application can become bloated. Additionally, adding more security systems than suggested can affect the user experience.

Defense in Depth

As we mentioned previously, no application is 100% impervious to attacks, so this should be accepted and planned for. Defenses *can* fail, which means your first line of defense cannot be your last. This is the premise behind another very popular security principle called Defense in Depth, which promotes having different *layers* of security, not necessarily separate security systems. The main objective of opting for such a multi-layered approach is to use different defenses to cover different threats and remove loopholes.

But here is a word of caution: a multi-layer strategy shouldn't bog down your security systems, nor overwhelm your personnel. Even if you stack more security systems and services, it's not going to guarantee 100% security, but what it might do is counter your Economy of Mechanism and make it harder to fix your vulnerabilities as you might have more services and systems to troubleshoot and debug.

Principle of Least Privilege

One of the most important questions while choosing your multi-layered defenses is what kind of threats would you be facing. So, what do you think is the most common reason for security breaches? It's not vulnerabilities in your firewall or lack of software updates. Brute-force attacks, then? No. The most common reason behind security breaches is the attacker having direct access to your application, usually with stolen or lost credentials.

Using difficult passwords and never sharing them with anyone else is one of the first things we learn when using the internet and as anticlimactic as it may be, basic access control is the most important aspect of cloud-native security.

This is also the premise behind the first principle – Principle of Least Privilege. This principle emphasizes two design policies. First, users do *not* have access *by default*. If a user wants access, the administrator must take active measures to grant that access instead of only being active to revoke access. Second, when access is granted, it must be minimal. If any additional access is required, it must be approved by the admin every time.

Due to the importance and relevance of access control for modern cloud security, a big part of this chapter will focus on Cloud Identity and Access Management.

Adding infrastructure security layers (revision)

Defense in Depth or layered security is a principle that Google takes very seriously. In this chapter, you'll see how Google's cloud infrastructure has multiple (five, to be exact) security layers, each targeting different threats, to create a comprehensive and cohesive security network that spans from the physical hardware to the topmost layer of operational security. This layered security can be applied in designing your cloud-native application by choosing the appropriate Google Cloud services available at each layer:

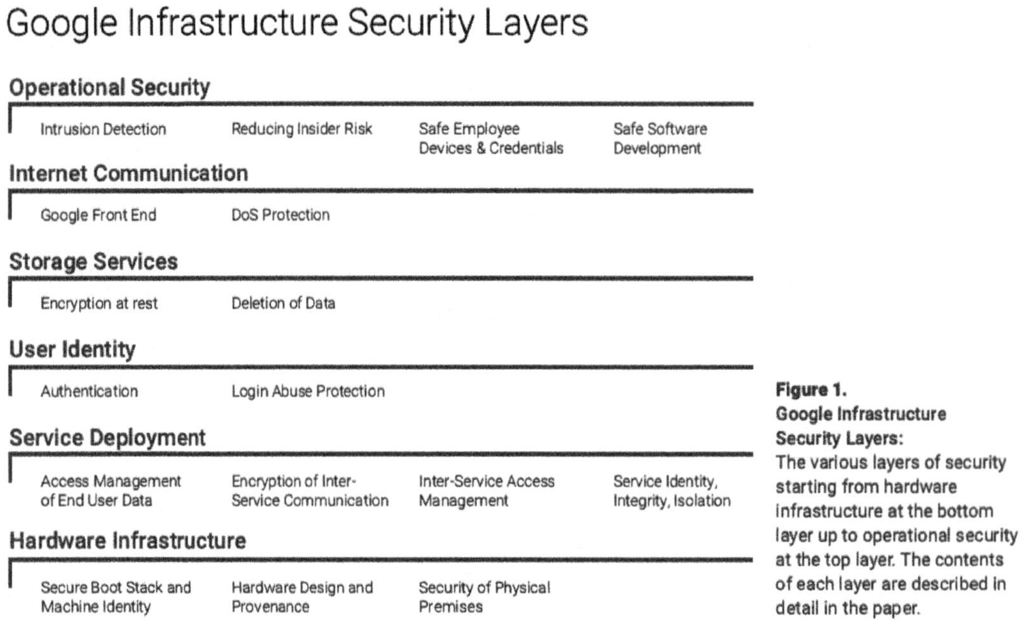

Google Infrastructure Security Layers

Operational Security

| Intrusion Detection | Reducing Insider Risk | Safe Employee Devices & Credentials | Safe Software Development |

Internet Communication

| Google Front End | DoS Protection |

Storage Services

| Encryption at rest | Deletion of Data |

User Identity

| Authentication | Login Abuse Protection |

Service Deployment

| Access Management of End User Data | Encryption of Inter-Service Communication | Inter-Service Access Management | Service Identity, Integrity, Isolation |

Hardware Infrastructure

| Secure Boot Stack and Machine Identity | Hardware Design and Provenance | Security of Physical Premises |

Figure 1.
Google Infrastructure Security Layers:
The various layers of security starting from hardware infrastructure at the bottom layer up to operational security at the top layer. The contents of each layer are described in detail in the paper.

Figure 7.1 – Infrastructure security layers

These layers will make more sense as you learn more about Google Cloud security services later in this chapter, but we wanted to introduce these concepts early on for two reasons:

- To help you understand why Google services function the way they do

- To help you understand the concept of layered security so that you can apply it to your cloud-native applications

As we mentioned previously, there are five main layers of security in the Google Cloud infrastructure. Let's start from the bottom – the security of the physical hardware.

Physical security

For users like you and your clients, physical security sits at the bottom of the security layers as this isn't something you have direct control over, nor is it something most of us have to be concerned with. Google maintains its own data centers around the globe and has some of the best IT security in the world. It's also good to know that numerous government agencies host their confidential data on Google's data centers (including the CIA).

That said, in certain migration strategies, you may be using Google's infrastructure alongside your on-premises hardware. In such cases, it's recommended that you use the security measures as Google. Some of these measures include the following:

- Multi-factor authentication and biometric identification systems

- Implementing machine identity and validating low-level components such as BIOS using cryptographic signatures that cannot be tampered with.

- Automating the process of updating hardware firmware to the latest security patches.

- Only allowing a limited number of employees into the premises.

Secure deployments

The next layer of security is concerned directly with your application and deploying it securely. Deploying an application on the cloud may seem simple but it's not basic. There can be thousands of instances of the same application running at a time and each instance needs to be equally secure.

To achieve this, Google employs a practice called multi-tenancy, which ensures the burden of trust isn't solely on the infrastructure but rather shared between different services. Google Cloud uses cryptographic authentication and authorization to connect the right services using their own unique identities. On the off chance that a fault does appear, isolation and sandboxing measures are put in place to ensure that other services continue undisturbed.

We'll explore identity management in far greater detail later in this chapter.

Secure storage

We discussed the different data storage services Google Cloud offers but, in addition to that, Google also has a central key management service that is used to encrypt and decrypt data across all data storage services. In addition to software encryption of files, Google also supports hardware encryption of its hard drives (which are also closely monitored).

Another important security aspect of data storage is data erasure and data recovery. When data has served its purpose, it needs to be deleted securely. Google Cloud offers automated/scheduled options for this. On the other hand, the *scheduled for deletion* acts as a recycling bin, ensuring that files aren't permanently deleted right away to prevent unintentional data erasure. Regular backups and versioning also help in this regard.

Secure communicating

We explored messaging in detail in, *Chapter 6, Implementing a Messaging and Scheduling System*, but an application doesn't communicate just within its services – it also needs to communicate with the wider world using the internet, which poses greater threats such as **Denial of Service (DoS)** attacks. Google has a service called Google Front End Service that uses the right security protocols and certificates to prevent DoS attacks and allow applications to safely and easily connect to the internet. Additionally, there are other measures (once again, Defense in Depth) that are used to prevent DoS attacks.

Secure internet communication is also dependent on proper identity management, which we will discuss later.

Operational security

Finally, there is the topmost layer of security – operational security. Most of the layers below focus on malicious external actors but threats can come from anywhere, including from inside the company, and this is what operational security focuses on. For instance, in addition to having unique identities that are authenticated multiple times, we also need to look for unusual activity from authorized accounts (we'll take a closer look at how Google does this in the *BeyondCorp (a new approach to enterprise security)* section).

Additionally, *smart* rules help developers include numerous variables in security policies, making them more effective against wider forms of intrusions and threats. But sometimes, developers make mistakes and vulnerabilities pass through the battery of tests into the live application. In such cases, constant automated vulnerability monitoring helps us find points of access that attackers can exploit.

How Google manages its infrastructure gives us powerful insights into how extremely scalable and resilient apps are maintained, and also statistics to put our minds at ease when it comes to cloud security. That said, most aspects will not apply to apps for SMBs or even enterprise-level applications. However, what does apply to every app, irrespective of its size and scope, is **Identity and Access Management (IAM)**. Let's take a closer look.

Cloud IAM

IAM is a combination of practices that allow you to give access and privileges to the right users. Different tools and platforms implement these controls in different fashions, which also affects the level of control. Perhaps you're thinking, how is IAM any different from access control? The answer is in the name – Identity *and* Access Management.

There are two main components to IAM: *identity*, which refers to a role given to users or systems, and *access*, which refers to privileges and rights. These components are closely interrelated and are thus often talked about as a single discipline. However, they are two different things. We'll go into the different components and concepts of IAM in the upcoming sections, but what you need to understand right now is that identity and access are two different security components that *can* be used as self-sufficient security controls. However, they are much more efficient when used in tandem. Additionally, when used together, IAM can provide better security by simply doing more, which is adding another layer of security of traditional access control.

As applications became larger and more complex, there was a need for better security. At the same time, cloud computing adoption grew, and an increasing number of applications were migrated to the cloud. As a result, every major cloud vendor launched their own Cloud IAM services that improved IAM in the same way the cloud improved applications – by making it more reliable and scalable.

Cloud IAM is popular for giving developers granular access control, but you may be wondering how it is any different from access control mechanisms in traditional IT systems. To answer this, let's take a look at the limitations of traditional access control that Cloud IAM can overcome.

Traditional access control versus Cloud IAM

When discussing the Principle of Least Privilege, we mentioned that lost or stolen credentials pose one of the biggest security threats to modern application security. To overcome this problem, access control systems were adopted. These systems try to prevent unauthorized access by removing the traditional credentials system of usernames and passwords with a system of entities and permissions. For instance, instead of giving users login credentials for different filesystems, users (as well as systems and administrators) are divided into different groups. Each group has access to different security clearances.

This is fairly simple and common. Most modern enterprises have both physical access controls (checking into the office building using an ID card) and network access control (who has access to company networks). However, traditional access control mechanisms had a few limitations that exposed applications to different risks.

One of the challenges with access control was that the groups and permissions needed to be regularly updated by the administrator, which means there was a risk for human error. Imagine that you had to let go of one of your developers a few months ago but the admins forgot to revoke their access. This is a big problem – the developer had access to your internal data for months. This sort of situation becomes more likely the bigger your team grows (or the more users your client has). Another problem emerged with the use of long-lived authentication tokens, which grant access to developers even after their access has been revoked but the local computer hasn't been refreshed and might not be for a while. Issues like these still exist in many traditional IT systems but can be overcome with cloud services such as Cloud IAM.

Concepts of IAM

The following are some of the basic concepts involved in an IAM system.

Entity

This is the simplest concept to understand – an entity can be a user, an administrator, or even a system. On its own, it's just a cog in a system with no authority or access (assuming that you are following the Principle of Least Privilege and have given no access by default).

For an entity to be able to access the network/application, it must be given an identity.

Identity

This is where people get confused – an identity is separate from an entity. An identity is a group of entities that all have the same privileges. Recall the concepts of messages and topics from the previous chapter; this is comparable to that. Just as messages are categorized into topics based on similar characteristics, entities are given identities.

Permissions

Permissions (such as read and write) are a part of the identity rather than a standalone concept in IAM. This means that entities cannot be granted permissions directly or individually. Instead, permissions must be granted to an identity, and then that identity must be given to an entity.

Policy

IAM can be manual. If your application requires a very high level of security, you may opt for an authentication system that generates a ticket, for instance, for every request. To approve this request, an admin must view the ticket personally and grant an identity manually. However, this sort of setup becomes less and less feasible as your application and user grows. There will be a point where you must automate at least some of the authentication and authorization – this is where policies come in.

Policies are like rules of engagement that your IAM system follows when creating and deleting identities, as well as granting and revoking access. In a nutshell, a policy is responsible for attaching identities to entities and controlling access to resources automatically.

Authentication and authorization

Let's imagine you've recently onboarded a new developer to help with the development of your new cloud-native application. You've also given them (the entity) an identity with developer privileges. Now, your developer logs into the system and requests access to the filesystem. This is where the IAM system verifies the identity of the entity. This process is known as authentication and there are numerous ways this can be done.

Once the system is sure that the entity that requested access is indeed a developer, it will verify whether the request that was made is in line with the permissions allowed to that developer, which in this case means that the system will check if developers are allowed to access the filesystem. If they are, the IAM system will grant the request. This process is known as authorization.

This might seem confusing – convoluted even if you're not used to working with security systems – but both authentication and authorization are critical to ensuring that the right people have the right access. For instance, without an authentication mechanism, any random or anonymous user could request access and while authorization ensures that that request would be denied, it can be used to spam or even overwhelm the system with requests. Additionally, it adds another layer of security that does more than just filter traffic – it also spreads the burden to two mechanisms instead of one.

Cloud IAM on Google Cloud Platform

Many cloud service providers have versions of IAM for their cloud applications. So far, whenever we've mentioned *Cloud IAM*, we were referring to IAM on the cloud in general but since the IAM service on Google Cloud Platform is called Cloud IAM, we will refer to that specifically whenever we use the term Cloud IAM.

Cloud IAM and traditional IAM are very similar in that they both allow developers to control access and manage identities from the same service, with the cloud service being much more flexible and scalable. Cloud IAM also has a wide range of additional features on top of the basic IAM functionality. We'll discuss these components in this chapter as well but first, let's take a look at the features of Cloud IAM, as well as the Cloud IAM life cycle.

Features of Cloud IAM

We will provide a brief explanation of the key features of Cloud IAM in the following subsections.

Comes at no additional cost

Since we're already using other Google Cloud services, it makes no sense to an IAM service other than Cloud IAM because Cloud IAM can be used at no additional cost. For instance, if you're already using Compute Engine, then you only pay for Compute Engine, and Cloud IAM is given to you for free. This all makes sense to your Cloud IAM because of its single access control interface, which means you can control permissions and users across all of the Google services from a single place.

Fine-grained control for enterprise-level applications

Most IAM services offer project-level access control, whereas Cloud IAM offers a much higher degree of granularity when it comes to creating your access control policy. There is a comprehensive hierarchy, starting from the organization itself down to individual resources such as buckets in Cloud Storage for virtual machines in Cloud Compute.

Automated access control

Like other Google Cloud services, Cloud IAM supports a high level of automation. Some of its automated features include an Access Control Recommender that helps you identify and remove unnecessary permissions and suggest better options, baked into other users in the organization and their access habits.

Context-aware access

Content-aware access is a powerful tool that brings Zero Trust security to many of Google Cloud's security services, including Cloud IAM. Contextual access takes into consideration various contextual factors, such as the user's identity, IP address, resources, and more, without needing a VPN.

Customizability

On one end of the spectrum, Cloud IAM gives developers the option to create very basic roles for users such as Owner, Editor, and Viewer. On the other end, developers can create custom roles for individual services, projects, and even resources.

Audit trail

To make compliance easier, Cloud IAM has an automatic, built-in audit trail that keeps track of all the operations without any additional setup or costs.

Components of Cloud IAM

Cloud IAM shares many of the core concepts as traditional IAM, but the naming structure is slightly different. The key components of Cloud IAM are explained in the following subsections.

Members

Instead of entities, in Cloud IAM, we have members. This is the same concept as entities, it's just that Google Cloud calls them members, which makes sense – that's exactly what they are:

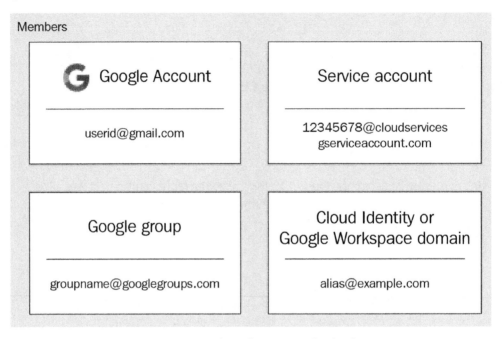

Figure 7.2 – Types of members in Google Cloud IAM

There are several types of members (the preceding screenshot shows some examples of each) and the following are brief explanations of them:

- **Google Accounts**:

    Google accounts can serve as identities and be used to verify and authenticate your administrators, developers, and other users of your application. Although this type of member is called a Google account, you don't necessarily have to use a gmail. com email address; other domains will work as well (additional verification may be required).

- **Service Accounts**:

    Remember that entities specifically included not only human users but also systems? This is very similar. Service accounts represent other systems and applications. In your case, this may be your microservices and VMs, although any resource/component can have a service account.

- **Google Groups**:

  Google groups consist of multiple Google accounts and service accounts and can be created by you to manage similar members and associated services in one place. When you create a Google group, you're also given a home page to manage your group, as well as a unique email address. Google groups are very useful when you want to grant, revoke, or otherwise change access to a large number of members, without having to change one at a time by simply updating the access policy that is attached to the group.

  Although groups are a type of member, you cannot attach a separate identity and they don't even have login credentials. They're only to be used to make permission management faster and easier.

- **Google Workspace Domain**:

  If you're working with a company that has a Google Workspace account, you can use it to manage permissions as well. The Workspace domain represents a virtual group that creates Google accounts for every user. They can be used similarly to Google groups and like Google groups, they do not create identities themselves; they can only be used to manage members that already have identities through permission policies.

- **Cloud Identity Domain**:

  Cloud Identity is an **Identity-as-a-Service** (**IDaaS**) platform from Google that creates Cloud Identity domains that act as virtual groups and serve a similar purpose as Workspace domain groups but without the explicit features of Google Workspace. We'll cover Cloud Identity in greater detail once we've looked at Cloud IAM.

All authenticated users

Developers can use the `allAuthenticatedUsers` value to manage all the Google accounts and service accounts that have already been authenticated, including users that aren't connected to a Google group or virtual group (Workspace, for instance).

All users

Developers can use the `allUsers` value to manage all of the users of the application – even those that haven't been authenticated, including anonymous visitors.

> **Important Note**
>
> Some Google services have authentication as a mandatory requirement, which means the `allUsers` value will not work with every service (or with every resource).

Resources

Cloud IAM can be used to manage *resources*. These resources include your virtual machines on Compute Engine, clusters on Kubernetes Engine, buckets on Cloud Storage, and other internal resources such as filesystems and assets. Cloud IAM allows you to grant specific members access to these resources by giving them the right role.

Cloud IAM is a platform for granular access control, but the extent of granularity differs from service to service, which means some Google services will have more in-depth control options than others. For instance, in Cloud Storage, you'll be able to grant the user a specific role to a specific bucket, or in Cloud Compute, you can grant the user a specific role to a specific VM. But this same level of granularity isn't available across the board and differs from resource to resource.

Permissions

We briefly touched upon permissions as a concept in the previous chapter, but now, let's look at how they work in practice. First of all, there is a general format in which permissions are expressed, which is `service.resource.verb`. When we place the actual service, resource, and action, we get the permission. In practice, a permission in Cloud PubSub that's instructing a subscription to consume a message would look like `pubsub.topics.publish`.

If a user wants to publish a message on Pub/Sub, then they must have the preceding permission attached to it; otherwise, their request would be automatically denied.

Roles

A role is a set of predefined permissions that can be given to a member. This means that when a role is given to a member, they also get all of the permissions that were attached to that role:

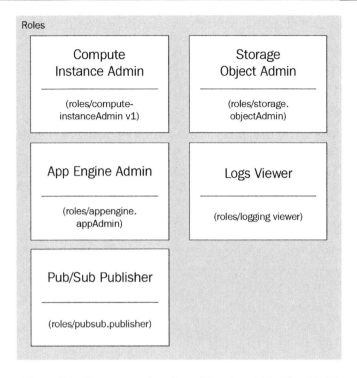

Figure 7.3 – Some examples of possible roles within Cloud IAM

Cloud IAM also has multiple types of roles, starting from the least granular, basic, to the most granular, custom. The preceding screenshot shows examples of what roles in different Google Cloud services look like. In the following subsections, we will briefly explain each type.

Basic roles

Basic roles refer to the three roles that are available in almost all of Google Cloud services: Owner, Editor, and Viewer. Although they are called *basic*, these roles contain thousands of permissions across the Google Cloud ecosystem that give members various kinds of access. Therefore, it's not recommended that you use basic roles. Instead, you should use either the predefined roles or custom roles to ensure members only have the permissions they need.

Predefined roles

Predefined roles offer greater granularity in that they have specific permissions for specific roles. Compared to basic roles, predefined roles contain far fewer permissions, which is ideal. For instance, the specific role of a Pub/Sub publisher looks something like `roles/pubsub.publisher` and will only allow the member to publish messages.

Custom roles

The most granular access controls can be exercised with custom roles, which allow you to create roles with the permissions you need.

Policy

This is the main component that encapsulates all of the other components (members, roles, and permissions) and determines how they all work together. Like the policies in traditional IAM, a Cloud IAM policy dictates which member gets which role, what permissions are granted with each role, when to reauthenticate and reauthorize, when to revoke access, and more.

The policy itself is an object that can be bound to a resource. It also contains a list of statements called bindings. A binding is responsible for attaching members to a role:

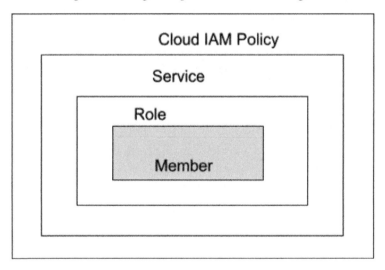

Figure 7.4 – Core structure of a Cloud IAM policy

The preceding diagram shows the basic structure of a Cloud IAM policy. Written in code, a policy looks something like this:

```
{
    "bindings": [
        {
            "role": "roles/storage.objectAdmin",
            "members": [
                "user:ali@example.com",
                "serviceAccount:my-other-app@appspot.gserviceaccount.
```

```
com",
            "group:admins@example.com",
            "domain:google.com"
        ]
    },
    {
        "role": "roles/storage.objectViewer",
        "members": [
            "user:maria@example.com"
        ]
    }
    ]
}
```

As you can see, the code is JSON key/value pairs to denote the configuration associated with the IAM policies.

Cloud IAM policies are also inherited, which means when a policy is applied, they follow a set hierarchy, as shown in the following diagram. For instance, if you apply a policy at the organizational level (which will be your root folder), then the policy statements (bindings) will apply at every level, up to the individual services. However, if you apply a policy at the project level (one of your applications), then it will apply to the services too, but it's not going to affect any of the folders:

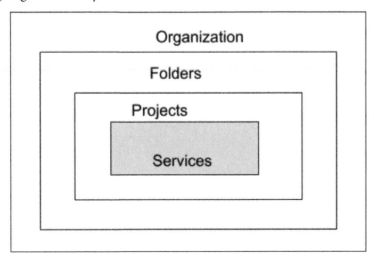

Figure 7.5 – Basic hierarchy of components in an IAM policy

This was the concept behind policies, but in practice, policies are used slightly differently (best practices) to ensure maximum security. For instance, in most of the apps you'll create, you'll attach a policy to a resource rather than the project. You can also do this the other way around, but it's not recommended because of the Principle of Least Privilege. If there *are* child resources, they will inherit the policy too.

Let's take a closer look at policy bindings and how they are used to get a better understanding of their real-world application.

IAM policy bindings

As we mentioned previously, policy bindings are a collection of statements that tell Cloud IAM who gets access to what. Each binding includes a member, a role, and a condition. Conditions are logic expressions that alter how a role is granted to a user, depending on contextual conditions. For instance, we can ensure that the policy only grants access to a developer between working hours.

Along with bindings, developers also need to specify the audit configuration and metadata for each policy. The following is a brief explanation of these fields:

- **AuditConfig**: Since Cloud IAM has a built-in audit trail, developers are asked to fill in the **AuditConfig** field.

- **Etags**: This is a type of metadata field that is used for concurrency control and policy updates. **Etags** are crucial for ensuring that policies don't overwrite each other.

- **Versions**: This is also a metadata field. Versions mention the schema version of the policy.

When you create any resource that supports IAM policies such as Compute Engine's virtual machines, Cloud Storage's buckets, or Cloud Pub/Sub's topics, Cloud IAM will automatically attach a default IAM policy to that resource. By default, most of these policies will be empty and won't give any access to users, but certain resources will give access to users by default. For instance, certain resources will bind the role of the Owner to you, the creator.

Limitations of Cloud IAM

So far, we've discussed the various features of Cloud, IAM as well as how it works, but before we wrap up Cloud IAM, let's take a look at what you cannot do with Cloud IAM.

Like any other cloud service, policies have limitations. For starters, each Google Cloud resource can only have one policy attached to it. It does not matter at what level in the hierarchy it is; the organization can have the number of policies as a Cloud Storage bucket, which is 1. You can, however, have different versions of a policy, but only one will be active at a time.

A single policy can only have up to 1,500 members (out of which 250 can be Google groups). This might seem like a major limitation at first but from a practical standpoint, 1,500 members *per* resource is more than most projects require. Furthermore, if you want more than 1,500 individual users, you can simply add them to a Google group because users in a Google group are counted as one member (the Google group itself). So, this means you can have 250 Google groups with hundreds of users each and it will still only count as 250 members.

Policies are also not applied instantly. If you make a change to a policy or create a new one, it can take up to 60 seconds for the change to be reflected. In some extreme cases, it can take up to 7 minutes for the change to be reflected.

Finally, at the time of writing this book, policy conditions aren't supported by all Google services to the same extent. This means that if you want to apply contextual conditions to your bindings, you may be limited in terms of the contextual factors you can use.

With this, we've come to the last section of this chapter. The Google Cloud ecosystem has a wide range of services dedicated to security. All of these services fit into the larger Cloud IAM suite of services, so they can be thought of as extensions of Cloud IAM.

Cloud Identity

Cloud Identity is Google Cloud's main service for identity management. It is an **IDaaS** solution that gives developers a unified platform to manage all of their members (users and groups). These users can even be your team members' personal Gmail accounts, which you can use to grant them access. This would not be possible without Cloud Identity.

In essence, it is an authentication tool that verifies the identities of users – it does not assign them the roles. It only checks if they are eligible for access and that authorization is still done by the IAM policy, as shown in the following diagram:

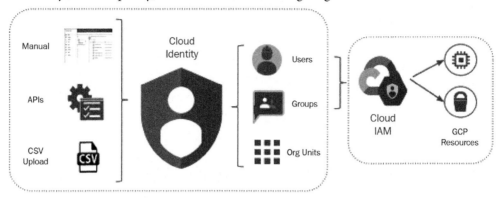

Figure 7.6 – Visualization of authentication and authorization within Cloud IAM

Cloud Identity is also, in a way, cross-platform as it allows you to use identities between Google Cloud and other cloud vendors that have their own identity services: AWS and Azure. However, this isn't something we will be discussing as we will be sticking to the Google Cloud ecosystem to create our first cloud-native application.

Features of Cloud Identity

Due to the importance of security, both Cloud IAM and Cloud Identity are free but Cloud Identity also has a premium addition with more features. You can use the free edition of Cloud Identity and still be able to create a secure app but you won't get certain advanced features. For instance, for device management, Cloud Identity Free has Basic Mobile Management, while Cloud Identity Premium has Advanced Mobile Management with additional features such as reporting, mobile audit, support for company-owned devices, and more.

> **Tip**
> Google Cloud has a free tool that can you use to compare different editions of Google Cloud services at `https://gsuite.google.com/compare-editions/`.

There are a few additional differences but since we only need the core features of Cloud Identity, let's focus on them for now. In the following subsections, you'll be given a brief explanation of the key features of Cloud Identity.

Multi-factor authentication

Cloud Identity supports different forms of **multi-factor authentication** (**MFA**) such as push notifications, Google Authenticator, and Titan security keys. Google's intelligence and threat signals also help in identifying and stopping phishing attacks.

Mobile device management

Device security is also a critical part of securing your app, and Cloud Identity gives you extensive mobile device management, especially if you're using the Premium edition. You can do a remote data wipe, deploy apps, enforce security policies (on the Premium edition), and more through the same platform that you use for managing app security.

Single sign-on

Single sign-on (**SSO**) is what it sounds like. With Cloud Identity, users only need to sign in once and they get access to thousands of business intelligence platforms such as Salesforce, SAP, Google Workspace, and more. SSO increases productivity and removes the need for unnecessary sign-ins without affecting security.

Quick onboarding

Cloud Identity has a digital workspace that uses SSO and allows you to quickly onboard new members and give them access to thousands of resources, such as pre-integrated SAML 2.0, **OpenID Connect** (**OIDC**), and custom and on-premises applications.

Automation

Cloud Identity features automated user provisioning, which reduces your administrative role into simple tasks such as creating, updating, and removing user profile information so that you can focus on more important tasks.

There are a few more useful features of Cloud Identity such as support for Microsoft **Active Directory** (**AD**), secure LDAP, and BeyondCorp, which we will talk about soon. Cloud Identity also has an automatic account takeover protection mechanism that detects anomalous logins and forces users to authenticate their identity through other means.

Setting up Cloud Identity

Cloud Identity is a must if you wish to use Cloud IAM because it does half the work for you (authentication). When you set up Cloud Identity, you can create a Cloud Identity account for your users, which will be used to authenticate them before Cloud IAM gives them access to Google Cloud resources.

Best of all, getting started with Cloud Identity is relatively easy as well. To begin, sign up for Cloud Identity using the Google Cloud Console. For this, we'll be using the free edition. You'll find **Identity** under **Identity & Organization**. To get there, click on the **Products & Services** menu and then **IAM & Admin**.

Once you've created your account, you can create your first user. To do so, you can use the **Setup** wizard, where you'll be prompted to enter the following details:

- Name
- Current email address
- Business name
- Country/region

Press **Next** to set up your Cloud Identity Domain. Here, you need to enter the domain of your company/product and verify your ownership either by creating or uploading a CNAME record. After this, you'll be at the **Create your Cloud Identity** page, where you'll be asked to set a username and password. Note that the email (username) you create here cannot be the same as the one you created earlier (on the **About Me** page).

To finish, go back to the Cloud Console, where you'll have to accept the Cloud Identity Agreement and that's it. You'll be redirected to the **Identity** page, where you'll have your first identity ready for use.

Cloud Identity Platform

Cloud Identity Platform is another authentication service in the Google Cloud ecosystem but whereas Cloud Identity was an IDaaS platform, Cloud Identity Platform is a **Customer Identity and Access Management** (**CIAM**) system, which means it can also be used to manage the identities of customers and business partners, along with developers and other team members.

Identity Platform is a self-sufficient service in that it has identity and access management capabilities built in and does not need to be used in tandem with Cloud IAM or Cloud Identity, although it can be. It has powerful and flexible authentication features that give users the option to sign up and sign in. You can also use it with the most popular app (Android, iOS, and the web) and admin SDKs (Node.js, Java, Python, and so on).

Features of Cloud Identity Platform

Let's take a brief look at what can be done with Identity Platform.

Multi-tenancy

Multi-tenancy is a powerful feature that's becoming more and more popular in modern cloud-native applications, especially at the enterprise level. In a nutshell, multi-tenancy creates silos of users and configurations. These silos can be used for different groups of users such as different customers, different departments, and more.

Multiple authentication methods

Identity Platform supports multiple authentication protocols such as SAML, OIDC, username/password, social media logins, a mobile device as an authenticator, and even custom authentication protocols. These authentication protocols are different from MFA, which is something Cloud Identity also supports.

Highly scalable

If your app is going to be used by a lot of people and all they need to be verified, Cloud Identity is a great option due to its extreme scalability. It also has a 99.95% SLA, ensuring you don't suffer from unexpected downtime.

BeyondCorp (a new approach to enterprise security)

BeyondCorp can be thought of as a new approach to enterprise security. Despite being a relatively new standard in the world of the security domain, BeyondCorp has become very popular and widely adopted. It is based on the Zero Trust model and aims to remove the need for a VPN by securing the individual users themselves, allowing users to access resources from anywhere in the world securely.

BeyondCorp takes a different and very interesting approach to security. Where traditional security platforms try to keep everyone out of the business assets by creating a plethora of firewalls and defenses and only giving access to those who have been authenticated, BeyondCorp removes the need of having an inside and an outside (with a firewall in-between). Instead, it sees every request (for access), regardless of it was made by a member or not, and grants access based on several contextual factors and conditions. This Zero Trust model means it doesn't trust any user from the get-go. For instance, if a user sends another request for access after their identity has already been authenticated and their previous requests were approved, BeyondCorp will still analyze the request and if the context of the request has been changed (for example, the request is being sent after working hours), access will be denied.

In a nutshell, BeyondCorp shifts the focus from securing only the assets and information to ensuring a secure connection with the user before any access is granted. And it does all of this without a VPN.

BeyondCorp's capabilities are supported by Cloud IAM and Identity Platform as well but the easiest way to get started with BeyondCorp is to use Identity-Aware Proxy.

Cloud Identity-Aware Proxy (IAP)

Cloud Identity-Aware Proxy or Cloud IAP is one of the platforms that can be used to deploy BeyondCorp to business infrastructure. While Cloud Identity does support BeyondCorp as well, Cloud IAP is built with the Zero Trust model and is a service designed specifically for securing user connections without creating a **virtual private network** (**VPN**).

IAP works by eliminating the need for a network-level firewall by substituting network access controls for application-level access controls. This is done through an authorization layer for applications accessed by HTTPS. IAP extends Cloud IAM functionality by ensuring that resources can only be accessed by members with the correct roles. This is where the term *proxy* comes in. The users aren't accessing the roles directly; they are given the role of an authorized user through IAM, thus giving access to only secure users without the need for a VPN.

Summary

In this chapter, we've covered Google Cloud's suite of IAM services and how they can be used to create effective boundaries for access and ensure that individuals who need to stay out, stay out. Cloud IAM sits at the core of these services and does everything an IAM platform needs to do. However, with changing requirements such as remote working, developers may need to expand on their security capabilities. For this, we have new solutions and methods such as context-based conditions and BeyondCorp.

With this chapter, we've reached the end of the first part of this book. So far, we've learned about the various concepts and components involved in cloud-native infrastructure. We've also taken an in-depth look at the various services in the Google Cloud ecosystem and how we can use them together and leverage their strengths to create the app we want.

The upcoming chapters mark the start of the second part of this book, where we will begin creating our very own application. In the next chapter, in particular, we'll talk about a legacy application that we will migrate to the cloud and transform into a truly cloud-native application.

Section 3: Rehosting and Replatforming the Application

On completion of *Section 3*, you will have gained hands-on experience in rehosting, replatforming, and refactoring the application using GCE while using the legacy application introduced in chapter 8. Furthermore, we will address scalability and availability while designing the interim architecture.

This part of the book comprises the following chapters:

- *Chapter 8, Introducing the Legacy Application*
- *Chapter 9, The Initial Architecture on Google Compute Engine*
- *Chapter 10, Addressing Scalability and Availability*
- *Chapter 11, Re-Platforming the Data Layer*
- *Chapter 12, Designing the Interim Architecture*
- *Chapter 13, Refactoring to Microservices*

8
Introducing the Legacy Application

In this chapter, we will apply different modernization strategies to an existing legacy application, and use the services provided by **Google Cloud** to incrementally move from legacy to cloud-native.

This chapter introduces the example application we will be modernizing. We will examine the architecture of the application from an infrastructure and software perspective, and then review important parts of the implementation. This application will be used throughout the book, so it is important that we gain a firm understanding of the application. Once the application has been reviewed, *Appendix B* presents the modernization strategies that will be used so that we understand how and when to apply them.

In this chapter, we will cover the following:

- The infrastructure architecture
- The software architecture
- The software implementation – configuration
- The software implementation – layers
- Modernization strategies

Technical requirements

You are required to have a working knowledge of Java Spring Boot, Thymeleaf, Bootstrap, and jQuery to understand this chapter.

The infrastructure architecture

Our application is a traditional Java application that runs on **Tomcat**. It uses **MySQL** to store the relational data and **Redis** to store the user sessions. As this is an enterprise application, security, availability, and scalability are all important factors. For this reason, we have placed the data tier into a separate subnet protected by a firewall; likewise, the presentation and application tiers are placed in another subnet, also protected by a firewall. The firewalls are configured so that only the Tomcat servers can connect to the data servers, and only HTTP(S) traffic from the internet is allowed into the Tomcat servers. Finally, a load balancer has been placed in front of the Tomcat servers to support our scalability and availability needs.

The following diagram captures the overall architecture of the infrastructure that houses the legacy application being introduced:

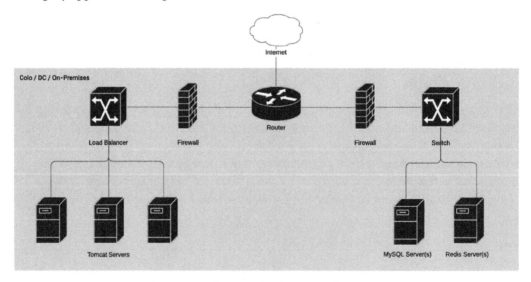

Figure 8.1 – Legacy infrastructure architecture

The infrastructure architecture depicted in the preceding figure is a very common one for legacy applications as it addresses the basic needs for security, scalability, and availability. A key drawback of this kind of architecture, however, is the lack of elasticity. The number of servers provisioned is generally determined by the peak workload. However, if the workload is not constant, this can result in the utilization of the servers being very low outside of these peaks. This means that we are paying for resources that are not being used most of the time. The other problem is that if the peak usage is higher than expected, then the application may fail, or users can experience poor performance. We will address these issues through the chapters. Now that we have discussed the infrastructure architecture, lets look at the software architecture for the application.

The software architecture

Our legacy Java web application uses the following main frameworks:

- **Spring Boot**
- **Thymeleaf**
- **Bootstrap**
- **jQuery**

Spring Boot

Spring Boot is an opinionated framework built on top of the Spring Framework. In this case, opinionated means that Spring Boot makes a lot of decisions on how to handle things such as security and persistence. This means it is also auto-configuring, so the configuration we need to provide is minimal, and mostly only needed when we are overriding the default decisions made by Spring Boot.

In our application, we are using the following Spring Boot capabilities:

- **Persistence**: Spring Data JPA
- **Sessions**: Spring Session Data Redis
- **Security**: Spring Security
- **Email**: Spring mail with Thymeleaf templates
- **Validation**: Spring validation
- **Presentation**: Spring **Model View Controller** (**MVC**) with Thymeleaf templates

The opinions and auto-configuration provided by Spring Boot mean that the developer can focus more on solving the business problems and less on technical issues. Because of this, it is a very popular framework for enterprise applications.

Thymeleaf

Thymeleaf is a template engine that is very well suited to creating HTML5 web pages and emails. It completely replaces **Jakarta Server Pages (JSP)** and **Jakarta Server Faces (JSF)**. It is designed based on the concept of natural templates so if the template is opened directly in a web browser, it can still render as a web page.

Thymeleaf also integrates very well with Spring Boot and we have used the Spring standard dialect of Thymeleaf along with the Spring Security integration to enable features such as guards. Guards allow us to place conditions on parts of a page for rendering; so, for instance, we can add options to menus that are only available to someone with the administrator role.

Bootstrap

Bootstrap is a framework for simplifying and standardizing web page design using Cascading Style Sheets. It is a responsive framework, meaning that the styles are designed so that the pages render well across a range of devices and window sizes. This means we don't have to design separate web pages for desktop, tablet, and mobile users, but instead design one page that responds to its environment.

jQuery

jQuery is a JavaScript framework that simplifies working with the **Document Object Model (DOM)**. In our application, we have not used JQuery directly. This is because it is already integrated with Bootstrap and Bootstrap extensions that we are using such as Bootstrap Validator. jQuery is the glue that allows the frameworks and extensions to work together seamlessly. Now that a high level of the architecture has been covered, let's understand the details.

Explaining the software architecture

For our application, we have combined **Domain-Driven Design (DDD)** and MVC so our legacy application has layers or tiers.

As we followed these approaches, we have the following categories of classes:

- **Controller**: Processes the requests from the browser, invokes the appropriate **service**, and passes the result to the appropriate view (Thymeleaf template).

- **Bean**: Encapsulates the information sent to and received from a web page. This is also known as the ViewModel.

- **Service** (domain service): Orchestrates the transaction by obtaining an **aggregate** from the repository, invoking the appropriate business logic on the aggregate and updating the repository.

- **Repository**: The abstraction of the relational database that handles **Object Relational Mapping** (**ORM**). Thanks to Spring Data JPA, this is an interface and Spring Boot provides the implementation.

- **Aggregate**: An object that is a group of domain objects that can be treated as a single item and has an identity. The grouping is usually based on transaction boundaries so what changes together stays together. These aggregate objects are composed of the aggregate itself, entity objects, and `ValueObject` instances. The business logic is implemented in the aggregate and may be delegated to other objects within the aggregate.

- **Entity**: Like the aggregate in that it has an identity and can contain other entity objects or `ValueObject` instances, but it is owned by the aggregate and does not exist without the aggregate.

- **ValueObject**: An object that represents a specific value and has no identity; two `ValueObject` instances with the same value can be considered as the same object and are completely interchangeable.

- **Specification**: An object that encapsulates query logic on the repository. This allows consumers of the repository to add query logic without having to make changes to the repository itself.

We will now examine the application flow starting from the frontend. The user interface is presented in a web browser using HTML5, CSS3, Bootstrap, and jQuery. Client-side logic is restricted to validation and presentation logic; there is no business logic in the page. Interaction with the application is done either by submitting a form or following a link, following the standard request/response structure. Once an action has taken place, the **Controller** mapped to the URL is invoked. The Controller then takes the input from the web page (encapsulated as a **bean**) and passes that information to the appropriate **service**. The **service** then typically follows a pattern of retrieving the correct **aggregate** from the **repository**, invoking a business method on the **aggregate**, updating the **repository**, and returning the result. The result is then populated into a **bean** by the **Controller** and passed to the correct view (Thymeleaf template), which is then rendered and sent to the web browser.

The following diagram shows a simplified view of the software architecture for our example application:

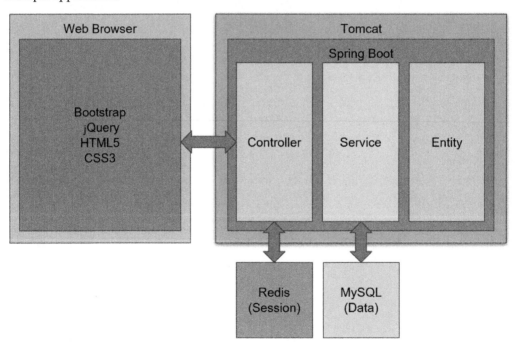

Figure 8.2 – Legacy software architecture (simplified)

Now that the software architecture has been explained, let's implement it.

Implementing the software

Now would be a good time to visit the GitHub repository for this book and review the code for the sample application. This can be found at `https://github.com/PacktPublishing/Modernizing-Applications-with-Google-Cloud-Platform`. The following sections of this chapter examine key aspects of the implementation to ensure we understand how the architecture for the example application has been implemented.

Spring Boot configuration

We discussed earlier that Spring Boot is an opinionated auto-configuring framework, so what does this mean in practice? Simply put, we make sure the appropriate dependencies are available and enable the features we are interested in. This sets up a sane set of defaults that works for most situations (but not all).

In our example application, the dependencies are managed by Gradle, so in our `build.gradle` file, we have the following configuration in the dependencies section:

build.gradle

```
implementation 'org.springframework.boot:spring-boot-starter-web'

implementation 'org.springframework.boot:spring-boot-starter-data-jpa'

implementation 'org.springframework.boot:spring-boot-starter-security'

implementation 'org.springframework.boot:spring-boot-starter-validation'

implementation 'org.springframework.boot:spring-boot-starter-thymeleaf'

implementation 'org.springframework.boot:spring-boot-starter-mail'

implementation 'org.springframework.session:spring-session-data-redis'

implementation 'redis.clients:jedis'

implementation 'org.apache.commons:commons-pool2'
```

Notice that in the preceding `build.gradle` file, we have not specified the versions for these dependencies. This is because the versions of the dependencies are handled by the Spring Boot Dependency Management plugin, which is configured as follows:

build.gradle

```
plugins {
    id 'org.springframework.boot' version "2.0.5.RELEASE"
    id "io.spring.dependency-management" version "1.0.8.RELEASE"
}
apply plugin: 'io.spring.dependency-management'
```

In the preceding configuration, we have specified the version of the Spring Boot Framework we wish to work with, along with the version of the Spring Boot Dependency Management plugin, then applied the plugin to enable automatic resolution of the dependency versions. This can be overridden by specifying a specific version of a dependency in the dependencies section.

Now we have the dependencies managed, we can enable the features we need by creating configuration classes. In our example application, the main one is the `ServletApplication` class, as follows:

ServletApplication.java

```
@SpringBootApplication
@EnableScheduling
@EnableAsync
@EnableSpringConfigured
@EnableRedisHttpSession
public class ServletApplication extends
SpringBootServletInitializer {
    public static void main(final String[] args) {
        SpringApplication.run(ServletApplication.class, args);
    }
}
```

The preceding annotations enable the following:

- Our application to be configured by annotations (@EnableSpringConfigured)
- Our application as a standalone Spring Boot application (@ SpringBootApplication)
- Scheduled tasks, which we will use for cleaning up expired tokens (@ EnableScheduling)
- Asynchronous tasks, which we will use to send emails without having to wait in our user interface (@EnableAsync)
- Sessions as a service using Redis cache, which makes our application stateless while acting like a traditional stateful Java web application (@ EnableRedisHttpSession)

The parts of the configuration not handled by annotations are as follows:

- Enabling the application to run inside of a servlet container instead of being standalone and having an embedded servlet container by extending the SpringBootServletInitializer class
- Providing the entry point for the application to run standalone with an embedded servlet container by providing a public static void main method that invokes the static public static ConfigurableApplicationContext run method of the SpringApplication class.

Additional configuration is generally done by replacing the default Spring beans with the ones that provide the features we want, as in the TaskConfig class as follows:

TaskConfig.java

```java
@Configuration
public class TaskConfig {
    @Bean
    public TaskScheduler taskScheduler() {
        final ThreadPoolTaskScheduler scheduler =
                new ThreadPoolTaskScheduler();
        scheduler.setPoolSize(20);
        scheduler.setThreadNamePrefix("scheduler-");
        scheduler.setWaitForTasksToCompleteOnShutdown(true);

        return scheduler;
```

```
        }

    }
```

The preceding code configures `ThreadPoolTaskScheduler`, which replaces the default scheduler. This is needed when running inside a servlet container such as Tomcat as it allows Tomcat to manage the tasks and shut down cleanly rather than hanging and refusing to shut down.

In our application, we have enabled the common features in the `ServletApplication` class, and more specialized configuration is done in specific classes such as `TaskConfig`, `SecurityConfig`, `PersistanceConfig`, or `LocalisationConfig`.

Now that the implementation has been discussed, let's understand the layers of the application.

Understanding the layers of the application

Now we understand how Spring Boot is configured we will look at the layers of our example application. The following sections illustrate the general patterns applied in each layer and how we have implemented them.

The presentation layer

Thymeleaf is designed to be as unobtrusive as possible, so instead of embedding Java in tags like in JSP or using tag-based expression languages, we declare XML namespaces that add attributes to HTML tags and make the Thymeleaf expression language very unobtrusive. This also means that the templates created with Thymeleaf can be opened locally in a web browser and render correctly. The following fragment shows how we add core Thymeleaf to a template as well as the security extras, which provides attributes for accessing the security context. The `th` namespace enables the `th:fragment` attribute, which we use in `layout.html` to specify that this particular template is a layout that can be used by other templates:

layout.html

```
<!DOCTYPE html>
<html th:fragment="layout (content)" xmlns:th="http://www.
thymeleaf.org" xmlns:sec="https://www.thymeleaf.org/thymeleaf-
extras-springsecurity3">
```

The next part of our layout template we will examine is the inclusion of the stylesheets and JavaScript frameworks that all our templates will use.

For stylesheets, we are using the following:

- Bootstrap (`bootstrap.min.css`).

- A custom sheet for this application (`@{/app.css}`). The `@{}` syntax tells the templating engine to append `/app.css` to the context root of the application.

For the JavaScript frameworks, we are using the following:

- jQuery (`jquery-3.4.1.js`)

- Bootstrap (`bootstrap.min.js`)

- Bootstrap Validator (`validator.min.js`)

Now, let's discuss how the layout references these stylesheets:

layout.html

```
<link rel="stylesheet" type="text/css" href="https://cdnjs.
cloudflare.com/ajax/libs/twitter-bootstrap/3.3.7/css/bootstrap.
min.css" />
```

```
<link rel="stylesheet" type="text/css" th:href="@{/app.
css}"/>
```

```
<script src="https://code.jquery.com/jquery-3.4.1.js"></script>
```

```
<script src="https://maxcdn.bootstrapcdn.com/bootstrap/3.3.7/
js/bootstrap.min.js"></script>
```

```
<script src="https://cdnjs.cloudflare.com/ajax/libs/1000hz-
bootstrap-validator/0.11.9/validator.min.js"></script>
```

The last part of the layout template we will examine is the division, which will be replaced with the content of the individual page templates. We simply declare a division with the `th:replace` attribute. The value of the `"${content}"` attribute matches the layout defined in the `th:fragment` attribute of the (`"layout (content)"`) HTML tag:

layout.html

```
<div th:replace="${content}"></div>
```

Finally, we examine how individual pages use the layout described previously. The key parts are the th:replace attribute on the HTML tag and the first division found under the body. The value of ~{layout.html :: layout(~{::div})} instructs the template engine to render layout.html, replacing the first layout element marked with the th:replace attribute with the top-level division found on the individual page. All pages follow this same structure and only the content within the container division is different:

```html
<!DOCTYPE html>
<html th:replace="~{layout.html :: layout(~{::div})}"
xmlns:th="http://www.thymeleaf.org" xmlns:sec="https://www.
thymeleaf.org/thymeleaf-extras-springsecurity3">
    <body>
        <div class="container">
            . . .
        </div>
    </body>
</html>
```

Now that layout.html has been addressed, let's get to the specific controller layer.

The controller layer

Our controllers are organized into two basic types of methods. These methods match the **HTTP GET** and **HTTP POST** requests.

The standard pattern for the GET requests, as seen in the following snippet, is to create a ModelAndView object, setting the Model to a bean representing the information to be sent to and/or returned from the page, and setting the View to the Thymeleaf template that will be used to render our web page. Finally, we return our ModelAndView object and Spring MVC uses it to render the web page:

UserPasswordChangeController.java

```java
@GetMapping("/user/password/change")
public ModelAndView getUserPasswordChange() {
    final ModelAndView model = new ModelAndView();
    . . .
    model.addObject("changePasswordBean",
            new ChangePasswordBean());
```

```
    model.setViewName("user/password/change");
    return model;
}
```

With POST requests, our bean is passed into the method as a @ModelAttribute parameter. Spring MVC also exposes additional information such as the logged-in user when we annotate a User parameter with @AuthenticationPrincipal. The information provided by our method's parameters is used to invoke the appropriate method on a Domain Service. In the following example, we get the user identifier from the User object and the new password from the ChangePasswordBean object, passing them into the changePassword method of the UserService object referenced in the userService variable. On completion of the changePassword method, we then set the view to the appropriate Thymeleaf template and return the ModelAndView object, passing control to Spring MVC to render our web page:

UserPasswordChangeController.java

```
@PostMapping("/user/password/change")
public ModelAndView postUserPasswordChange(
        @AuthenticationPrincipal final User user,
        @ModelAttribute("changePasswordBean")
        @NotNull @Valid final
        ChangePasswordBean changePasswordBean,
        final WebRequest request) {
    final ModelAndView model = new ModelAndView();
    ...
    final User updatedUser =
            userService.changePassword(user.getId(),
            new Password(changePasswordBean.getPassword()));
    ...
    model.setViewName("confirmation");
    return model;
}
```

Now that the controller layer has been addressed, let's get to the specific domain layer.

The domain layer

Our domain layer is made up primarily of `Service` objects, `Repository` objects, `Aggregate` objects, `Entity` objects, and `ValueObject` instances. `Entity` objects and `ValueObject` instances are owned by `Aggregate` objects.

Service objects

In the following example service, we have the `public User changePassword` method, which receives an `EntityId ValueObject` instance, and a `Password ValueObject` instance. `EntityId` is used to find the user in the `UserRepository` object. If the user is not found, we throw an `IllegalArgumentException` exception as we are trying to change the password for a user that does not exist. If the user is found, we invoke the `changePassword` business logic method of that instance, update the user in `UserRepository`, and return the updated user:

UserServiceImpl.java

```java
@Override
public User changePassword(
        @NotNull @Valid EntityId id,
        @NotNull @Valid Password password) {
    final Optional<User> optional = userRepository.
findById(id);
    if(optional.isPresent()) {
        final User user = optional.get();
        user.changePassword(password);
        return userRepository.save(user);
    }
    throw new IllegalArgumentException("Invalid UserId");
}
```

Now that the domain layer has been addressed, let's get to the specific repository and specification objects.

Repository and specification objects

In the following example repository, we have extended the `JpaRepository` interface, specifying that the class to be persisted is a user aggregate, and the identity is an `EntityId ValueObject`. We have also declared a `findByEmail` method to enable retrieving a user from the repository by their `EmailAddress`.

If you have reviewed the code base, you may be wondering, where is the implementation for this repository? The answer is that the implementation is provided by Spring Boot, specifically Spring Data JPA. We don't have to write over and over boilerplate persistence code, as that is handled for us by Spring Data JPA. This even applies to simple finder methods such as the `findByEmail` method we declared in our interface:

UserRepository.java

```
@Repository
@Validated
public interface UserRepository extends JpaRepository<User,
EntityId> {
    Optional<User> findByEmail(final EmailAddress email);
}
```

So, what do we do when we want to find an aggregate in our repository and this cannot be accomplished by a simple finder? Another scenario could be that the repository has been provided to us and is used by multiple teams, so modifications to the repository interface are discouraged. In these situations, we use the specification pattern.

In the following example Specification, we build a `Predicate` object, which defines the rule for determining whether a `ResetToken` in the repository has expired:

ResetTokenSpecification.java

```
public class ResetTokenSpecification {
    public static class ResetTokenIsExpired
            implements Specification<ResetToken> {
        private static final long serialVersionUID = 1L;
        public Predicate toPredicate(
                final Root<ResetToken> root,
                final CriteriaQuery<?> query, final
CriteriaBuilder builder) {
            final ZonedDateTime current = ZonedDateTime.
ofInstant(Instant.now(), ZoneId.of("UTC"));
            return builder.lessThanOrEqualTo(
                root.<ZonedDateTime>get("expiryDate"), current);
        }
    }
}
```

Our specification is used as follows:

ResetTokenServiceImpl.java

```
@Override
public List<ResetToken> findExpiredTokens() {
    return resetTokenRepository.findAll(
            new ResetTokenSpecification.ResetTokenIsExpired()
    );
}
```

As we can see from the preceding example, the separation of complex logic, to find specific items in a `Repository`, into `Specification` classes allows for much greater flexibility and prevents the `Repository` from becoming overly complicated.

Aggregate, Entity, and ValueObject instances

These objects are the ones that implement the business logic and state of our application. `Aggregate` objects and the `Entity` and `ValueObject` instances they own are stored in the data store abstracted by the `Repository` interfaces. To standardize and simplify the development of these classes, we have created the framework illustrated in *Figure 8.3*:

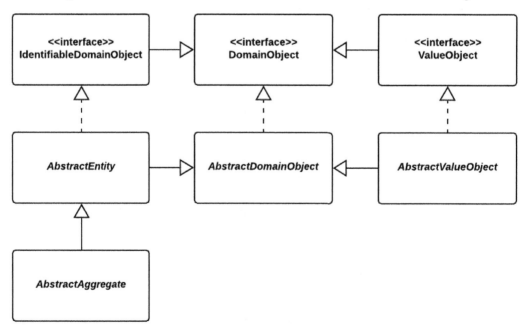

Figure 8.3 – Framework domain class diagram

At the root of our framework is the `DomainObject` interface, which simply extends the `Serializable` interface as our objects will be persisted. We then have the `AbstractDomainObject` class, which implements the `DomainObject` interface and provides default implementations for the `equals`, `hashCode`, and `toString` methods. This means we only need to consider these behaviors when we want to change the behavior, such as excluding an association from consideration as it is a two-way association.

Our `ValueObject` interface extends the `DomainObject` interface. Our `AbstractValueObject` class implements the `ValueObject` interface and extends the `AbstractDomainObject` class. All `ValueObject` implementations extend the `AbstractValueObject` class.

Our `IdentifiableDomainObject` interface extends the `DomainObject` interface, adding the `getId` method, which exposes the identity of our `IdentifableDomainObject`. Our `AbstractEntity` class implements the `IdentifiableDomainobject` interface and extends the `AbstractDomainObject` class. The behavior added to our `AbstractEntity` class is to handle the generation of and access to the identity of the object. This is done by adding a member variable called `id`, of type `EntityId`, and annotating it with the JPA annotations.

Finally, our `AbstractAggregate` class extends the `AbstractEntity` class, adding the `getVersion` method and `version` member variable. This variable is used to handle optimistic locking in the data store. If the value of the version variable is different in memory to what it is in the data store, then the data store has been updated since we retrieved the `Aggregate` from it.

With this framework in place, we can now focus, when building our `Aggregate`, `Entity`, and `ValueObject` classes, purely on what is unique to those classes, rather than repeating common details.

Validation and defensive programming

You may have noticed that our code is somewhat simple in respect to validation. This is because we are using **JSR-303/349**. No layer trusts its client. Instead of having lots of `if` statements to check for null parameters and validate the values of the parameters are correct according to our rule, we instead use annotations. In the preceding code fragments, the parameters to our methods are annotated with `@NotNull` and `@Valid`, which instructs Spring Boot to validate the parameters. `@NotNull` means the parameter must not be null, and `@Valid` means the object passed in must be valid according to the annotations specified against its member variables.

Our `Password` class, for example, has an instance variable annotated with `@NotEmpty` and `@StrongPassword`. `@NotEmpty` means the variable cannot be null or blanks, and `@StrongPassword` is a custom annotation that enforces the rules for a strong password:

```
@NotEmpty
@StrongPassword
private String password;
```

Validation on our `Controller`, `Service`, and `Repository` objects is enabled with the `@Validated` annotation on either the interface or implementation class.

This approach means we are validating all information passed between layers and so missing validation on one layer will be picked up in the next, and we can be happy that our objects are valid all the way from the user interface to the data store.

Summary

In this chapter, we introduced the example legacy application that we will be modernizing as we progress through the book.

We looked at the infrastructure architecture, which is a typical *n*-tier design, segregating the data and application tiers with firewalls to lock down traffic to only what is specified as necessary for the application to function. We examined the software architecture of the application, noting that we are combining DDD and MVC architectural patterns to have a well-structured and layered application architecture. We also saw how the software architecture makes use of frameworks such as Spring Boot to simplify and standardize our application and minimize *plumbing* code.

We then reviewed the application code base to understand how dependencies are managed, how to enable Spring Boot Framework components such as JPA `Repository` management, and how to override the default decisions and functionality provided by the Spring Boot Framework components. We then examined each of the major component types in our application, from Thymeleaf templates to generate HTML pages through to `Repository` classes to manage our ORM.

Appendix B will examine six strategies for application modernization, referred to as the 6Rs. We concluded that three of the six strategies were appropriate for modernizing our example application. These strategies are to rehost, replatform, and refactor.

To rehost is to move and improve with no changes to the application and minimal changes to the infrastructure architecture.

To replatform is to replace virtual machines with *as a Service* offerings from Google Cloud such as Google Cloud SQL and Google Kubernetes Engine.

To refactor is to iteratively and incrementally pull out capabilities from the monolithic legacy application, making them microservices that are packaged in containers.

In the next chapter, we will take the first steps in our modernization journey. We will apply the rehost strategy to create the first version of our architecture in Google Cloud and check the functionality works as expected.

9
The Initial Architecture on Google Compute Engine

We will now take our first step toward modernizing our application by moving it to the cloud. In this chapter, we will not be making any changes to the application itself, but instead we will be looking at the absolute minimum infrastructure architecture needed to run the application on **Google Cloud**. Once we have our initial architecture, we will then go step by step through implementing the architecture on Google Cloud using the Google Cloud Console.

In this chapter, we will cover the following:

- The initial infrastructure design
- Creating the modernization project
- Implementing the network

- Implementing the **Virtual Machines** (**VMs**)
- Importing the data

Technical requirements

In order to follow along and implement the steps in this book, you will need to have the following:

- An internet domain where you are the owner and can manage the **Domain Name Service** (**DNS**) records
- A Google Cloud account (a free trial account is fine)
- To have signed up to **Cloud Identity** (the free tier is fine) from the Google Cloud Console (using your internet domain)
- To have set up an **organization** to be the root of your structure in Google Cloud

The initial infrastructure design

Our starting point will be the legacy infrastructure architecture illustrated in *Figure 9.1*:

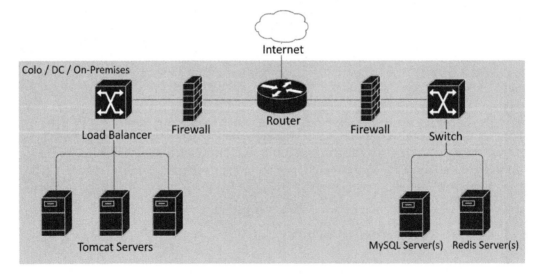

Figure 9.1 – Legacy infrastructure architecture

The key elements from this architecture that we need to consider for our initial rehosting are as follows:

- The network
- The network security
- The VMs

Before we begin to design our infrastructure architecture, there are a few Google Cloud terms that we need to define as they are key to understanding how Google Cloud is organized, and where we will place our resources. A resource in Google Cloud is classified as a *global resource*, *regional resource*, or *zonal resource*:

- **Global resource**: A resource that is not restricted to a specific *region* or *zone* within a region but is hosted in multiple locations worldwide.

- **Region**: A geographic location where we can host our Google Cloud resources. Examples of this are `US-WEST1` and `EUROPE-WEST1`. A list of available regions and zones can be found at `https://cloud.google.com/compute/docs/regions-zones#available`. Choosing which *region* to use is often based on proximity to our users or applicable regulations such as the **General Data Protection Regulation (GDPR)**.

- **Zone**: A specific location within a *region*. Each *region* has more than one *zone*, and each *zone* is physically separate from the others in the *region*. This separation is to provide isolated failure domains for each *zone*. Examples of *zone* names are `EUROPE-WEST1-C` and `EUROPE-WEST1-D`. The convention for naming zones is `<region>-<zone>`. In our example, we have zones C and D in region `EUROPE-WEST1`.

- **Regional resource**: A resource that is available only to other resources in the same *region*. An example of this is a static public IP address that can be assigned to any of the VMs in the same region as the address.

- **Zonal resource**: A resource that is available only to other resources in the same *zone*. An example of this is a *disk*. These can only be accessed by a VM in the same *zone*.

Now we understand *global*, *regional*, and *zonal* resources, we can begin to map out our infrastructure architecture.

Designing our network

In Google Cloud, our network is provided by a **Virtual Private Cloud** (**VPC**). This is a virtualized version of a physical network. A VPC is a **global resource** meaning it is not associated with a specific region or zone. When we create a project in Google Cloud a default VPC is provisioned for us automatically. This VPC has a *subnet* automatically provisioned for every Google Cloud *region* available. A *subnet* is a **regional resource** so cannot be in more than one *region* but is available to every *zone* in its *region*. In a production scenario we would not use the default VPC, but instead specify and configure a VPC based exactly on what we need in terms of *zones* and IP address ranges. For the purposes of our modernization journey, we will use the default VPC.

Our next step is to decide which *region* we will be using. As I am based in the UK, I chose `europe-west2` as that *region* is hosted in the UK. Choose a *region* that is close to you in order to minimize latency. Finally, we pick a *zone* to place our VMs in (remember that VMs are an example of a **zonal resource**). In this case we have chosen `europe-west2-c`.

These choices mean we have the following start to our infrastructure architecture, shown in the following figure depicting the initial infrastructure architecture (network):

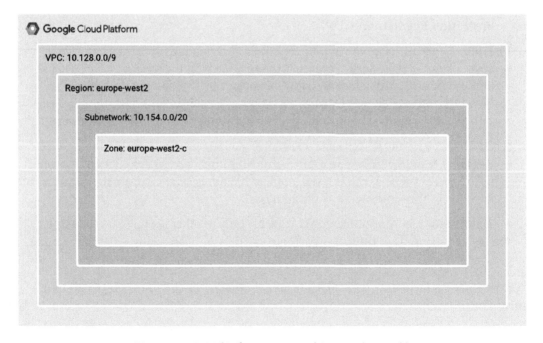

Figure 9.2 – Initial infrastructure architecture (network)

Now we have made our decisions on which *region* and *zone* we will be working in; we can continue onward and consider what VMs we will provision. From *Figure 9.1*, we can identify that we will need a minimum of three VMs. At this point, we are not considering concerns such as availability, we are just looking at the minimum to get our functionality running in Google Cloud..

The VMs we will need are as follows:

- A VM to run a Tomcat server

- A VM to host MySQL as our persistent data store

- A VM to host Redis to handle our application sessions

Adding these VMs to our infrastructure architecture gives us the following:

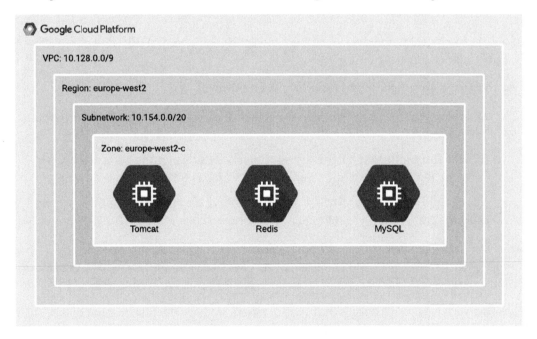

Figure 9.3 – Initial infrastructure architecture (VMs)

As this is development rather than production, we will initially give all the VMs public IP addresses. In production, this would be a serious security issue and must not be done. We are keeping things simple to focus on the actual modernization tasks and we have no private or confidential data at risk. For serious development, we would use either a VPN to access the VMs or create a Bastion host for the same purpose.

Now we have our network and VMs identified and added to our architecture. What next?

Designing our network security

Although we are giving every VM a public IP address, we will still need to implement some network security. The focus here will be on the network security for the application rather than our administration of the VMs. We will be making use of *Google Cloud firewall rules*.

This is a global service provided by Google Cloud and allows us to filter traffic based on the following:

- IP address ranges
- Network tags
- Service accounts
- Protocols and ports

Rules can be applied to ingress (incoming) and egress (outgoing) traffic, and either allow or deny traffic that matches the given rule.

Our rules from our legacy application state the following:

- All inbound traffic from the internet is blocked except for HTTP(S) traffic to the Tomcat servers.
- All inbound traffic to the Redis server is blocked except for the Tomcat servers using the Redis server on the standard port, which is 6379.
- All inbound traffic to the MySQL server is blocked except for the Tomcat servers using the MySQL server on the standard port, which is 3306.

As we are working in a learning sandbox, we will leave the default rule provided by Google Cloud in place that allows ingress to all VMs from any address to SSH. Again, we cannot stress enough that this is not recommended for production environments.

Now that we have taken firewalls into consideration, we have the final version of our initial infrastructure architecture laid out, which we will continue to build on in the rest of this book. The following diagram depicts that initial infrastructure and network architecture:

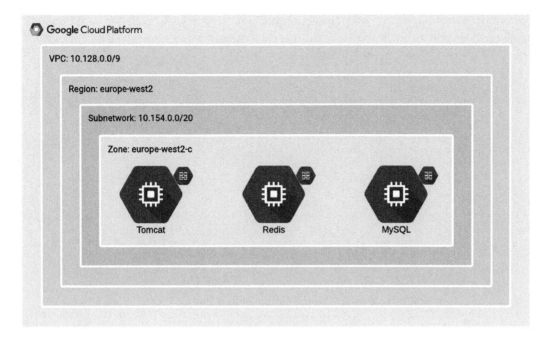

Figure 9.4 – Initial infrastructure architecture

Now that an initial network architecture has been created, let's plan to create the modernization Google Cloud project.

Creating the modernization project

Before we start building out our architecture in Google Cloud we need to set up the structure for our account. At the root of the structure, we have the **organization** we created when we set up **Cloud Identity** for **Identity and Access Management (IAM)**. An account can have only one *organization*. The *organization* can contain *folders* and/or *projects*. A *folder* can contain *folders* or *projects*. This provides us with a tree structure for organizing our resources, called the resource hierarchy.

The purpose of our **resource hierarchy** is to do the following:

- Provide an ownership hierarchy, often reflecting the structure of the enterprise and cost centers.

- Provide a structure for inheriting access control and policies.

For our *organization*, we will keep things simple and create a *folder* called `modernization` and within that *folder* a *project* called `BankingApplication`. Our *resource hierarchy* will then look like this:

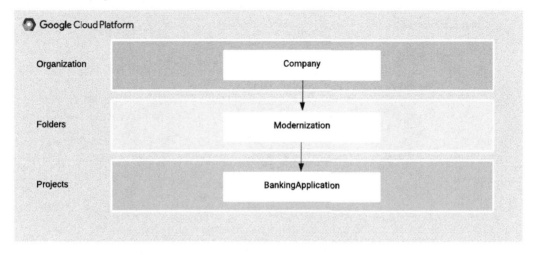

Figure 9.5 – Initial resource hierarchy

A more realistic *resource hierarchy* for an enterprise may look like this:

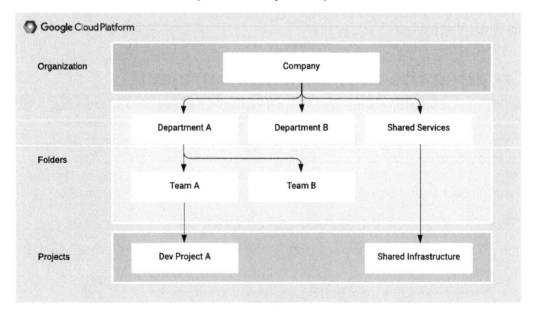

Figure 9.6 – Example resource hierarchy

Now we have defined our *resource hierarchy*, we will create it in Google Cloud using the following steps:

1. From the Google Cloud Console at `https://console.cloud.google.com`, click the navigation menu button in the top left of the window:

Figure 9.7 – Navigation menu button

2. In the navigation menu, select **IAM & admin | Manage Resources**:

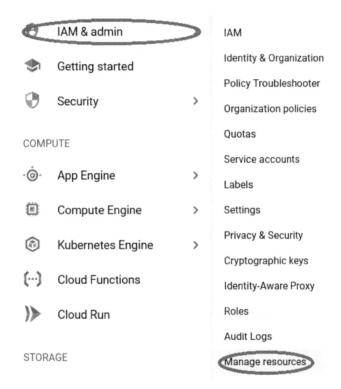

Figure 9.8 – IAM & admin menu

3. You will now see the **resource hierarchy**. Click the **Create Folder** button at the top of the window:

Figure 9.9 – Create folder button

4. You will now see the **New Folder** form. Enter the name you want to give to your folder, ensure the **Location** field is set to your *organization*, and click **Create**:

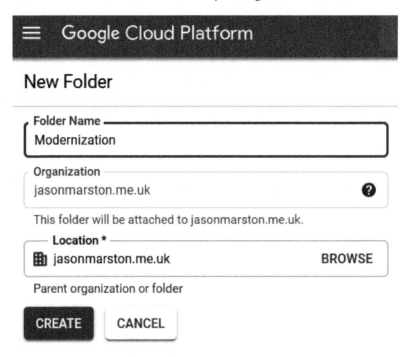

Figure 9.10 – New folder form

5. Your *folder* has now been created and you have been returned to the **Manage Resources** page. Click **CREATE PROJECT**:

Figure 9.11 – CREATE PROJECT button

6. You will now see the **New Project** form. Enter the name you want to give to your *project*, ensure **Location** is set to the *folder* you created in the previous step, and click **Create**:

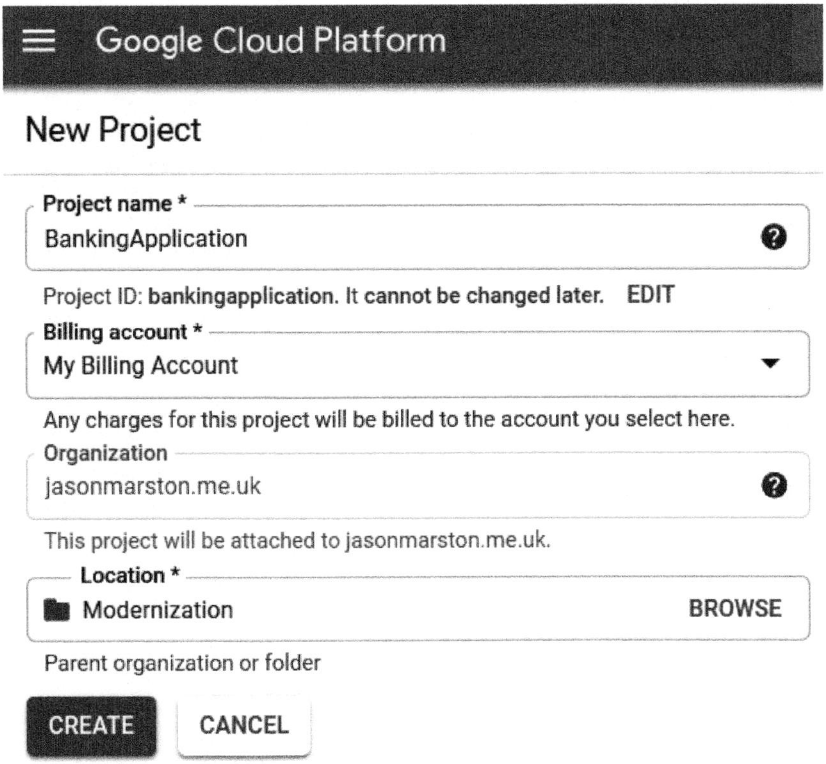

Figure 9.12 – New Project form

Now that we have established our **resource hierarchy** and created our **project**, we can begin implementing our infrastructure architecture.

Implementing the network

We described earlier in this chapter how when a project is created, a default VPC is automatically created for us. This means we can simply reuse that VPC for our modernization work. What remains to be done is implementing the firewall rules we defined previously. To recap, the rules are as follows:

- All inbound traffic from the internet is blocked except for HTTP(S) traffic to the Tomcat servers.

- All inbound traffic to the Redis server is blocked except for the Tomcat servers using the Redis server on the standard port, which is 6379.

- All inbound traffic to the MySQL server is blocked except for the Tomcat servers using the MySQL server on the standard port, which is 3306.

We will now implement these firewall rules using the following steps:

1. In the navigation menu, select **VPC network | Firewall rules**:

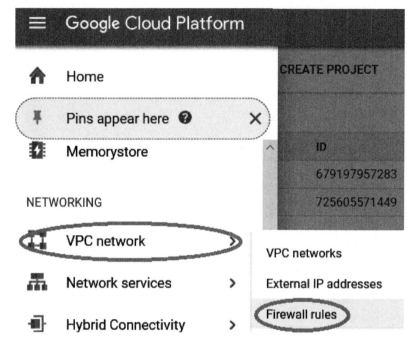

Figure 9.13 – VPC network menu

2. Ensure that at the top of the window, your *project* is selected:

Figure 9.14 – Project selection dropdown

You will now see the default rules that are allocated to our project:

Name	Type	Targets	Filters	Protocols / ports	Action	Priority	Network ^
default-allow-icmp	Ingress	Apply to all	IP ranges: 0.0.0.0/0	icmp	Allow	65534	default
default-allow-internal	Ingress	Apply to all	IP ranges: 10.128.0.0/9	tcp:0-65535 udp:0-65535 icmp	Allow	65534	default
default-allow-rdp	Ingress	Apply to all	IP ranges: 0.0.0.0/0	tcp:3389	Allow	65534	default
default-allow-ssh	Ingress	Apply to all	IP ranges: 0.0.0.0/0	tcp:22	Allow	65534	default

Figure 9.15 – Default firewall rules

3. The first rule we will implement is to allow incoming traffic on ports 80 and 443 to our Tomcat servers. Click **CREATE FIREWALL RULE**:

Figure 9.16 – CREATE FIREWALL RULE button

4. You will now see the **Create a firewall rule** form. Enter the following and click **Create**:

a) **Name**: A unique name for your firewall rule. In this case, we'll use allow-http-https.

b) **Network: default(in new line L-regular)**

c) **Priority:** 1000

d) **Direction of traffic: Ingress**

e) **Action on match: Allow**

f) **Targets: Specified target tags**

g) **Target tags:** web

h) **Source filter: IP ranges**

i) **Source IP ranges:** 0.0.0.0/0

j) **Protocols and ports: Specified protocols and ports**

k) Select **tcp** and enter 80 and 443:

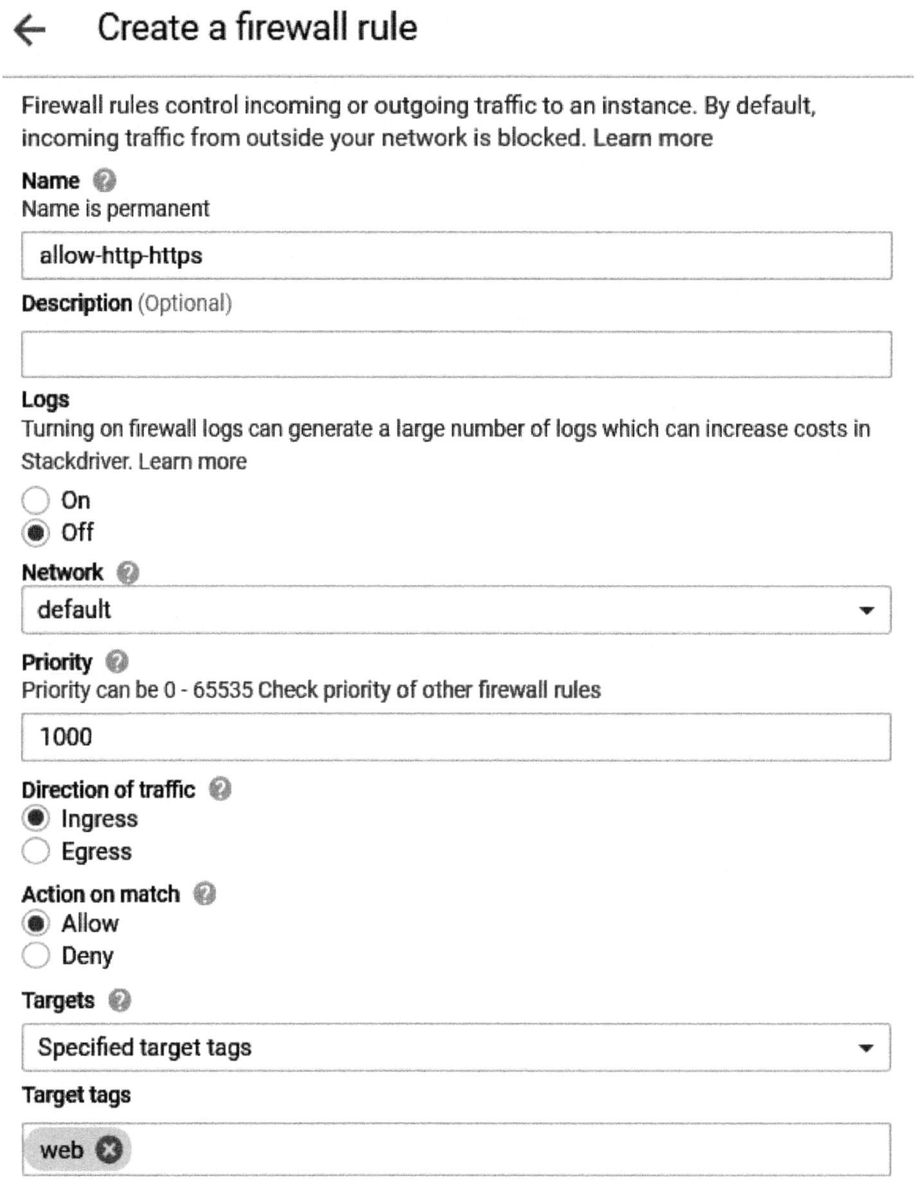

← **Create a firewall rule**

Firewall rules control incoming or outgoing traffic to an instance. By default, incoming traffic from outside your network is blocked. Learn more

Name ⓘ
Name is permanent

> allow-http-https

Description (Optional)

>

Logs
Turning on firewall logs can generate a large number of logs which can increase costs in Stackdriver. Learn more

○ On
◉ Off

Network ⓘ

> default ▼

Priority ⓘ
Priority can be 0 - 65535 Check priority of other firewall rules

> 1000

Direction of traffic ⓘ
◉ Ingress
○ Egress

Action on match ⓘ
◉ Allow
○ Deny

Targets ⓘ

> Specified target tags ▼

Target tags

> web ✕

Figure 9.17 – Create a firewall rule form

5. Repeat the preceding process with the following details to create the rule to allow the Tomcat server to communicate with the Redis server:

   a) **Name**: `allow-redis`

   b) **Network: default**

   c) **Direction of traffic: Ingress**

   d) **Action on match: Allow**

   e) **Targets: Specified target tags**

   f) **Target tags**: `redis`

   g) **Source filter: Source tags**

   h) **Source tag: web**

   i) **Protocols and ports: Specified protocols and ports**

   j) Select **tcp** and enter `6379`

6. Repeat the preceding process with the following details to create the rule to allow the Tomcat server to communicate with the MySQL server:

   a) **Name**: `allow-mysql`

   b) **Network: default**

   c) **Direction of traffic: Ingress**

   d) **Action on match: Allow**

   e) **Targets: Specified target tags**

   f) **Target tags**: `mysql`

   g) **Source filter: Source tags**

   h) **Source tag: web**

   i) **Protocols and ports: Specified protocols and ports**

   j) Select **tcp** and enter `3306`

7. Finally, we delete the rule that allows all internal traffic on all ports. Select the
    default-allow-internal rule and click **DELETE**:

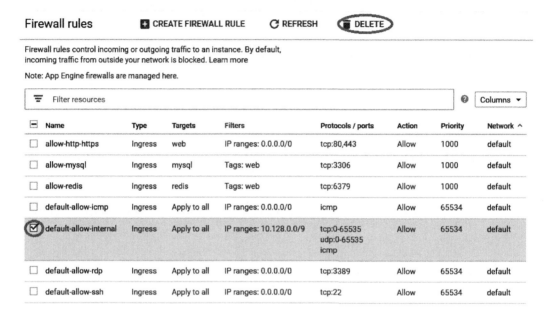

Figure 9.18 – Delete firewall rule

8. Click **DELETE** to confirm you want to delete the **default-allow-internal** firewall
    rule:

Delete a firewall rule

Are you sure you want to delete firewall rule "default-allow-internal"?

CANCEL

Figure 9.19 – Confirm the deletion of the firewall rule

Let's summarize what we have just done:

- We decided to use the default VPC that was automatically created when we created
  our project.

- We created a firewall rule to allow inbound HTTP(S) traffic to our Tomcat server.

- We created a firewall rule to allow inbound Redis traffic to our Redis server from
  our Tomcat server.

- We created a firewall rule to allow inbound MySQL traffic to our MySQL server from our Tomcat server.

- We deleted the default firewall rule that allowed all inbound traffic for all internal IP addresses.

In the next section, we will implement our VMs, applying the tags we referenced in our firewall rules to enable the required communications for our application.

Implementing the VMs

Now we get to the core of this chapter: implementing our VMs. We will build these up manually and create them using the Google Cloud Console. A later chapter will cover automation and creating a CI/CD pipeline in order to enable DevOps.

We will start at the backend of the solution and move forward. There are two backend services in our solution, *sessions* and *persistence*. As we must choose one or the other, we will start with persistence, meaning our MySQL database.

As we want to make as few changes as possible, and not have to install software if we can avoid it, we will make use of the Google Cloud Marketplace. Specifically, we will use the *MySQL certified by Bitnami* image from the Marketplace.

This VM image comes with MySQL preinstalled and is set up to minimize costs for a development environment. It is well suited for the purpose of learning about modernization.

We will create and configure the MySQL VM using the following steps:

1. In the navigation menu, select **Marketplace**:

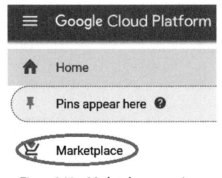

Figure 9.20 – Marketplace menu item

2. In the search field on the **Marketplace** page, enter `MySQL Certified by Bitnami` and hit *Enter*:

Explore, launch, and manage solutions in just a few clicks

Marketplace lets you quickly deploy software on Google Cloud Platform

Q   MySQL Certified by bitnami

Figure 9.21 – Marketplace search

3. Select **MySQL Certified by Bitnami** from the list:

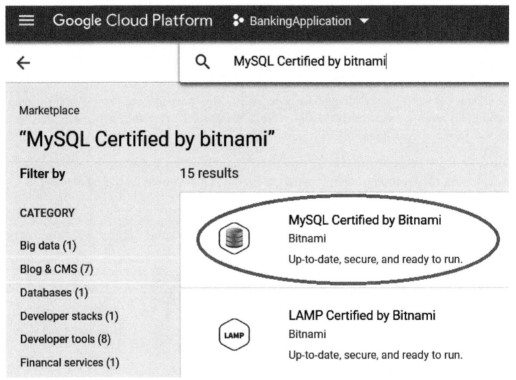

Figure 9.22 – MySQL in the Marketplace search results

4. Click **LAUNCH ON COMPUTE ENGINE**:

Figure 9.23 – Launch the Bitnami image on Compute Engine

5.   Enter mysql for **Deployment name**, and select **europe-west2-c** for **Zone**:

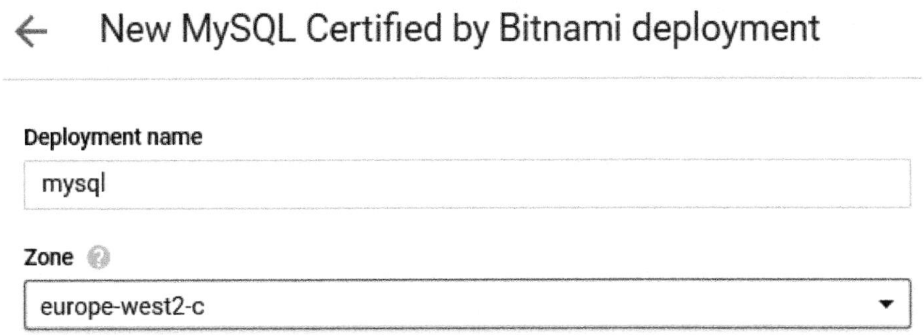

← New MySQL Certified by Bitnami deployment

Deployment name

mysql

Zone

europe-west2-c

Figure 9.24 – Name and zone for MySQL VM

6.   Tick the **I accept the GCP Marketplace Terms of Service** box and click **Deploy**:

Figure 9.25 – Deploy the MySQL VM

7. This deployment will take a few minutes to finish. Make a note of the key information given by the deployment, specifically, the **Admin user** and **Admin password values**:

Figure 9.26 – Admin user and admin password

8. Once the VM has finished provisioning, we use SSH to perform administration tasks in the VM. Click **SSH**:

Get started with MySQL Certified by Bitnami

Figure 9.27 – SSH button for access to the VM

9. Now we need to ensure all the software is up to date, as changes may have been released since the image was placed on the marketplace. Let's do this by entering the following command:

```
sudo apt-get -y update
```

Next, we will change the password we recorded in the previous *step 7*. To do this we need to log in to the MySQL server from our SSH session following the steps:

1. Enter the following command:

```
mysql -u root -p
```

2. When prompted, enter the password we recorded previously. Enter the following commands to change the password (where `<yournewpassword>` is the password you have chosen):

```
alter user '''root''@''localhost' 'localhost'' identified
by ''<yournewpassword>'';
flush privileges;
quit
```

Log in again using the command from *step 1* and your new password to ensure this has worked. At this point, we have an empty MySQL server ready to configure as needed for our application.

3. We will now create our empty database and the user our application will utilize to access the database, and grant our user authority over the database, by entering the following commands in our MySQL session:

```
create database banking;
create user ''bankinguser''@''%'' identified with mysql_
native_password by ''<newpassword>'';
grant all on banking.* to ''bankinguser''@''%'';
```

With the preceding commands we did the following:

a) Created the database.

b) Created our user with the name `bankinguser`, allowed access from any host using the `%` location, and set `<newpassword>` as the password. In production, we would lock down the location more precisely. Please be sure to record the password.

c) Granted our user all authorizations on the banking database. In production, we would not need all authorizations, but as we are in development, our application will create the database artifacts (schemas, tables, and others) as needed.

The final step in setting up this server is to apply our firewall rule. We will do this by adding the `mysql` tag to the VM. As we used the marketplace image for the MySQL server, a tag has already been added, but it is important to understand how to add network tags to our servers, hence we will do this, even though if we had used the tag provided by the marketplace, we would not have needed to do this.

To apply the mysql tag, follow the steps:

1. In the navigation menu, select **Compute Engine**:

Figure 9.28 – Compute Engine menu item

2. Click **mysql-vm** on the **VM Instances** page to open the **VM instance details** page:

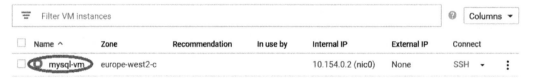

Figure 9.29 – VM instances page

3. Click **EDIT**:

Figure 9.30 – Edit VM instance button

4. Scroll down to the **Network tags** section and enter mysql:

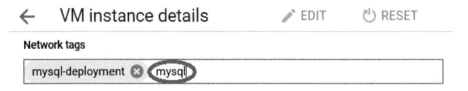

Figure 9.31 – Network tags

5. Scroll to the bottom of the page and click **Save**.

That completes the provisioning and configuration of our MySQL VM. We have prepared the database for our application and applied the `mysql` tag to allow for communication between the Tomcat server and the MySQL server.

Now we will create our Redis VM. The steps already explained previously will not be repeated in detail for this VM:

1. Using the marketplace, provision a VM using the **Redis certified by Bitnami** deployment. Enter `redis` for **Deployment name** and select **europe-west2-c** for **Zone**. Remember to make a record of the username and password.

2. Apply the `redis` tag to the network tags section of the **VM instance details** page.

3. Once the VM has deployed and started, connect to it via SSH and enter the following commands, where \<CURRENTPASS\> is the password we recorded earlier, and \<NEWPASS\> is the password we have chosen:

```
sudo apt-get -y update
redis-cli -h redis-vm
AUTH <CURRENTPASS>
CONFIG SET requirepass <NEWPASS>
AUTH <NEWPASS>
```

Finally, we will create our Tomcat VM. The steps already explained will not be repeated in detail for this VM:

1. Using the marketplace, provision a VM using the **Tomcat certified by Bitnami** deployment. Enter `tomcat` for **Deployment name** and select **europe-west2-c** for **Zone**. Remember to make a record of the username and password.

2. Apply the **web** tag to the network tags section of the VM instance details page.

3. In the **VM instances details** page, change **Virtual Machine** to use a static public IP address by clicking **Create IP address**:

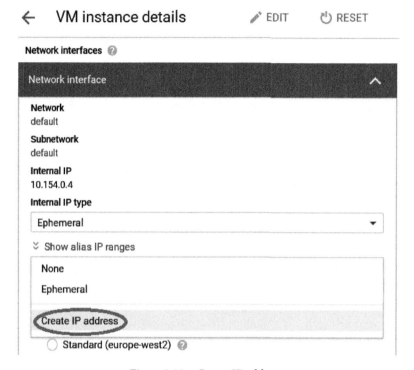

Figure 9.32 – Create IP address

4. Provide a name for the IP address and click **RESERVE**:

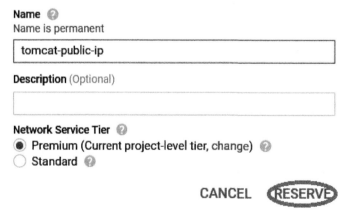

Figure 9.33 – Reserve a static IP address

5. On the VM instance details page, save your changes by clicking **Save**.

6. Add records to your domain using the IP address. We used www.banking. jasonmarston.me.uk with the address 35.189.84.60, and banking. jasonmarston.me.uk with the same address. Note that how this is done will depend on your provider. (It may take a few minutes for the changes to propagate.)

7. In the Tomcat VM, set up the **SSL certificate** for these hosts using the Bitnami HTTPS configuration tool, which obtains certificates from Let's Encrypt. Enter the following command and responses to set this up. Note that we have removed most of the informational text and just focused on the questions and responses (replace the domain names with the one you used):

```
sudo /opt/bitnami/bncert-tool

Domain list []: www.banking.jasonmarston.me.uk banking.
jasonmarston.me.uk

Enable HTTP to HTTPS redirection [Y/n]: ny

Enable non-www to www redirection [Y/n]: n

Enable www to non-www redirection [y/N]: ny

Do you agree to these changes? [Y/n]: y

E-mail address []: jason@jasonmarston.me.uk

Do you agree to the Let's Encrypt Subscriber Agreement?
[Y/n]: y

Press [Enter] to continue:
```

8. Configure the application by connecting to the Tomcat VM via SSH and add the following content to the end of the /opt/bitnami/tomcat/bin/setenv. sh file. We will start with the MySQL configuration details, such as hostname, username, and administration:

```
# MySQL Configuration

export BANKING_DATASOURCE_DDL_AUTO="update"

export BANKING_DATASOURCE_DIALECT="org.hibernate.dialect.
MySQL5Dialect"

export BANKING_DATASOURCE_PASSWORD="<YOUR_MYSQL_
PASSWORD>"

export BANKING_DATASOURCE_URL="jdbc:mysql://
mysql-vm.europe-west2-c:3306/
banking?useSSL=false&allowPublicKeyRetrieval=true"

export BANKING_DATASOURCE_USERNAME="bankinguser"


# Hostname for use in emails
```

```
export BANKING_HOST_NAME="<YOUR_FULLY_QUALIFIED_DOMAIN_
NAME>"
```

```
# Administration user configuration
```
```
export BANKING_INITIAL_ADMIN_CONTEXT_PATH="/"
```
```
export BANKING_INITIAL_ADMIN_EMAIL="<YOUR_EMAIL_ADDRESS>"
```
```
export BANKING_INITUAL_ADMIN_PASSWORD="<YOUR_INITIAL_
PASSWORD>"
```

We will continue with the configuration for logging, email, environment, and Redis:

```
# Logging configuration
```
```
export BANKING_LOGGING_LEVEL="WARN"
```

```
# Email Configuration
```
```
export BANKING_MAIL_AUTH="true"
```
```
export BANKING_MAIL_FROM="noreply@<YOUR_DOMAIN>"
```
```
export BANKING_MAIL_HOST="<YOUR_SMTP_SERVER>"
```
```
export BANKING_MAIL_PASSWORD="<YOUR_SMTP_PASSWORD>"
```
```
export BANKING_MAIL_PORT="<YOUR_SMTP_PORT>"
```
```
export BANKING_MAIL_SOCKET_FACTORY="javax.net.ssl.
SSLSocketFactory"
```
```
export BANKING_MAIL_STARTTLS="false"
```
```
export BANKING_MAIL_USERNAME="<YOUR_SMTP_USERNAME>"
```

```
# Environment configuration
```
```
export BANKING_PROFILES_ACTIVE="DEV"
```

```
# Redis configuration
```
```
export BANKING_REDIS_HOST="redis-vm.europe-west2-c"
```
```
export BANKING_REDIS_PORT="6379"
```
```
export BANKING_REDIS_PASSWORD="<YOUR_REDIS_PASSWORD>"
```

The preceding configuration does the following:

a) Informs the application that we are using MySQL as the relational database, and how to connect to it

b) Sets the logging level to **WARN** (we can change this to **INFO** or **DEBUG** if we need more detailed logging)

c) Provides the details of our initial administration user for the application

d) Provides the information needed to send emails from the application

e) Specifies that this is a development environment

f) Provides the details on how to connect to Redis

We are now ready to deploy and test the application.

9. Download the `ROOT.war` file from `https://github.com/`
    `PacktPublishing/Modernizing-Applications-with-Google-`
    `Cloud-Platform/tree/master/Chapter%2009`.

10. From your SSH session, upload the `ROOT.war` file:

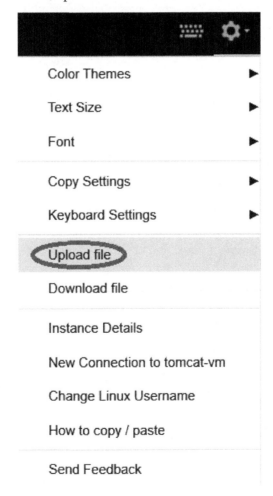

Figure 9.34 – Upload file

11. Select ROOT.war from your local drive:

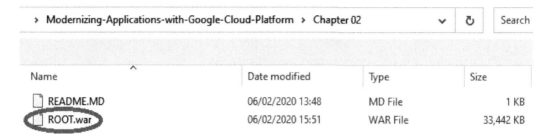

Figure 9.35 – The local ROOT.war file

12. Once the file has uploaded, delete all the default applications deployed to Tomcat:

```
sudo rm -rf /opt/bitnami/tomcat/webapps/*
```

13. Copy ROOT.war from your home directory in the Tomcat VM to the webapps directory:

```
sudo cp ~/ROOT.war /opt/bitnami/tomcat/webapps
```

14. Make sure the .war file is owned by tomcat:

```
sudo chown tomcat:tomcat /opt/bitnami/tomcat/webapps/
ROOT.war
```

Now you have deployed the application and, in a few minutes, you can test it using the fully qualified domain name you set up earlier. In my case, the custom domain I set up was www.banking.jasonmarston.me.uk.

Once that is completed, we need to ensure the database is updated appropriately.

Importing the data

The goal now is to create an applicable table in the database and the rows associated with that table. The necessary files are provided in the repository:

```
sudo mysqldump –add-drop-table -u root -p banking > banking.sql
```

Copy the file to the destination server:

```
mysql -u root -p banking < banking.sql
```

Then follow the earlier steps to make sure that bankinguser exists and has the correct permissions.

Summary

In this chapter, we looked at the infrastructure architecture of our legacy application and designed a simple initial infrastructure architecture for moving the application into the Google cloud. We decided that there would be no changes to the application code base, and we would only be changing the infrastructure. The infrastructure architecture did not address concerns such as scalability or availability, but instead focused on hosting our functionality and on network security between the layers of our application.

We then created our organizational structure and the project we will be working on throughout this book. Next, we implemented the firewall rules and the three VMs using the Marketplace. Then, we introduced persistence with a MySQL VM, sessions storage using the Redis VM, and an application web server with the Tomcat VM. Finally, we deployed our application and performed a basic test to see if we could access it.

In the next chapter, we will continue to refine our infrastructure architecture. Specifically, we will start to address concerns such as scalability and availability by making use of Google Cloud features such as **zones** and **load balancers**.

10
Addressing Scalability and Availability

We have taken our first steps into the cloud with our initial infrastructure architecture, implementing virtual machines and a virtual private cloud. We will now extend that architecture and address scalability and availability concerns.

In this chapter, we will cover the following topics:

- Designing for scalability and availability
- Using instance templates
- Using managed instance groups
- Using an HTTP(S) load balancer

Technical Requirements

In this chapter, we will set up our three-tier web application to autoscale and ensure its availability to protect against zonal failures by using a **regional managed instance group**. Our frontend Tomcat application is stateless and hence works well with managed instance groups.

Designing for scalability and availability

Our starting point will be the initial infrastructure architecture illustrated in the following screenshot:

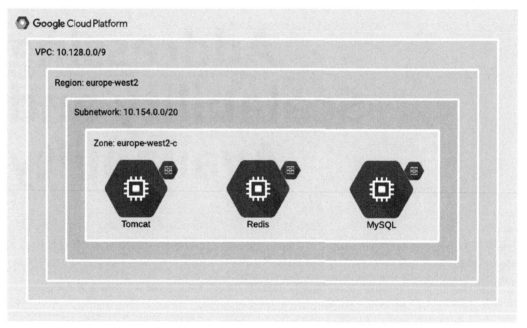

Figure 10.1 – Initial infrastructure architecture

In order to address scalability and availability, we will need to make use of both a **managed instance group** and an **HTTP(S) load balancer**.

A managed instance group is a collection of identical virtual machines that are managed as a single entity, and which enables the following:

- Autoscaling (horizontal)
- Auto healing:
  - VM-based
  - Application-based
- Automatic updating
- Regional (as opposed to zonal) deployment
- Load balancing (in conjunction with HTTP(S) load balancers)

A **regional managed instance group** allows us to spread our virtual machines across more than one zone in a region. This protects us from the failure of a single zone. If we deployed all our virtual machines in a single zone and that zone failed, then our entire application would fail. By spreading the virtual machines across multiple zones, we instead have a reduction in capacity, rather than a complete outage. When this is combined with autoscaling and auto healing, our regional managed instance group can return to full health without human intervention.

So, how many virtual machines do we need in a regional managed instance group to protect against failure? The advice from Google is N plus two, where N is the minimum number of virtual machines you want to ensure are running. Where does the plus two come from? Simply put, if one virtual machine is out of service for maintenance reasons and then another one fails, we still have N virtual machines running. However, if we just had one, then we would end up with less than N. For the purposes of learning, in our case, N will be one, so we need a total of three virtual machines in a regional managed instance group.

We will focus only on the scalability and availability of the Tomcat virtual machines as they are stateless, although a managed instance group supports both stateless and stateful workloads. We will be re-platforming the Redis and MySQL virtual machines in the next chapter.

Our first step will be to create a regional managed instance group for our Tomcat virtual machines, as illustrated in the following screenshot:

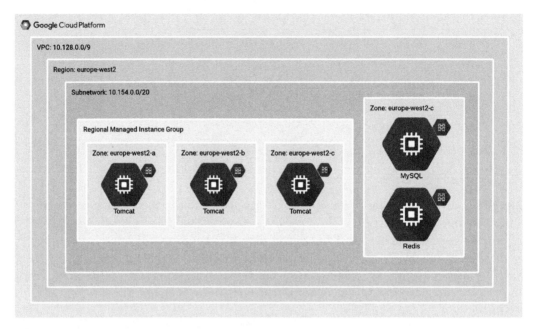

Figure 10.2 – Infrastructure architecture: regional managed instance group

Now that we have a regional managed instance group in place, we need to be able to route traffic to any of the instances in a way that means the client only deals with one endpoint and is unaware of the group. This is where the HTTP(S) load balancer comes in.

The final update to our infrastructure architecture is to add in this HTTP(S) load balancer, as shown in the following screenshot:

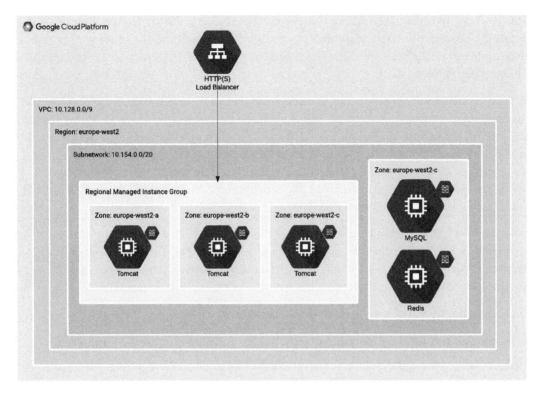

Figure 10.3 – Infrastructure architecture: HTTP(S) load balancer

Now we have all the parts in place to provide availability and scalability for our application. Remember that in the next chapter, we will address the scalability and availability of the database (MySQL) and session (Redis) aspects. In this chapter, we are only concerned with the scalability and availability of the infrastructure running the application logic.

Now that we have a regional managed instance group, let's walk through how to use instance templates.

Using instance templates

We discussed earlier that a managed instance group is a collection of identical virtual machines. This collection can be autoscaled, meaning that instances can be added and removed from the collection automatically based on the workload. How then do we ensure the instances are all identical, have all the software installed, and have the configuration applied?

This is where an **instance template** comes into the picture. An instance template is a definition of a machine type, boot disk image, start up scripts, and the other properties that can be set on a virtual machine. It is used to create virtual machine instances with identical configurations.

We can create an instance template in many ways, but for our purposes, we will create the instance template from our existing Tomcat virtual machine. This means we don't have to concern ourselves with the installation and configuration of software on the first boot, but are taking all the configuration we have already provided in our Tomcat virtual machine and placing it in an instance template. This means that new virtual machines based on the instance template will become available much quicker than if we had to install and configure all the software at boot time.

Before we create our instance template, we will need to make a change to our Tomcat virtual machine. In the previous chapter, we assigned an external static IP address to our Tomcat virtual machine. Two virtual machines cannot have the same external static IP address, so we will need to change back to using an external ephemeral IP address.

Let's make the change to our Tomcat virtual machine:

1. On the **VM instance details** page, click **Edit** and open the **Network Interface** section. Change **External IP** back to **Ephemeral**.

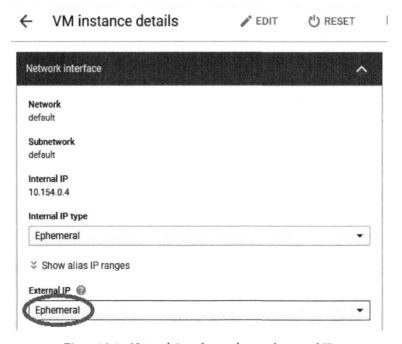

Figure 10.4 – Network interface: ephemeral external IP

2. Scroll to the bottom of the page and click **Save**.

3. We need to create an image to use when creating the instance template. From the **Navigation** menu, select **Compute Engine | Images**.

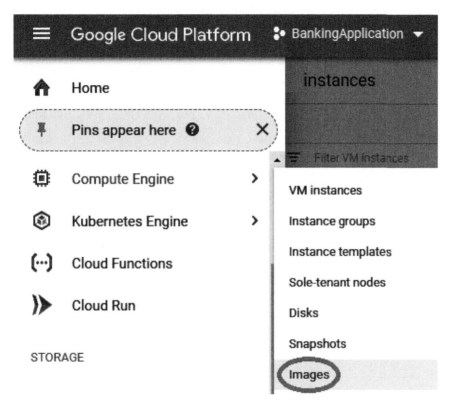

Figure 10.5 – Images menu option

4. At the top of the **Images** page, click **CREATE IMAGE.**

Figure 10.6 – CREATE IMAGE

5. On the **Create an image** page, enter the following information and click **Create**:

- **Name**: `tomcat-image`.
- **Source**: Select **Disk**.

- **Source disk**: Select **tomcat-vm**.
- **Location**: Select **Regional** and then **europe-west2**.

← **Create an image**

Name ❓
Name is permanent

> tomcat-image

Source ❓

> Disk ▼

Source disk ❓

> tomcat-vm ▼

Location ❓
○ Multi-regional
◉ Regional

> europe-west2 (London) (default) ▼

Family (Optional) ❓

Description (Optional)

Labels ❓ (Optional)

> **+ Add label**

Encryption
Data is encrypted automatically. Select an encryption key management solution.
◉ Google-managed key
  No configuration required
○ Customer-managed key
  Manage via Google Cloud Key Management Service
○ Customer-supplied key
  Manage outside of Google Cloud

Your free trial credit will be used for this image. GCP Free Tier ↗

[Create] [Cancel]

Figure 10.7 – Create an image page

6. This will take a few minutes, so please be patient.

Now we are ready to create our **instance template**. For this activity, we will be using **Cloud Shell** and the gcloud command. gcloud is a command-line interface that interacts with **Google Cloud** to perform tasks. It is more powerful than using the console and provides additional capabilities. Cloud Shell is a Linux shell environment hosted by Google Cloud.. You don't need to manage this or create a virtual machine. Cloud Shell comes with common tools such as gcloud already installed.

To create our instance template, go to the Google Cloud console:

1. Click the *Cloud Shell* icon at the top right of the page.

Figure 10.8 – Opening Cloud Shell

2. At the bottom of the window, Cloud Shell will open (this may take a few minutes the first time).

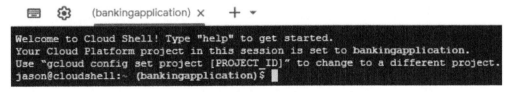

Figure 10.9 – Cloud Shell

3. Enter the following command:

```
gcloud compute instance-templates create tomcat-
template --source-instance=tomcat-vm --source-instance-
zone=europe-west2-c --configure-disk=device-name=tomcat-
vm-tmpl-boot-disk,instantiate-from=custom-image,custom-
image=projects/bankingapplication/global/images/
tomcat-image,auto-delete=true
```

The preceding command uses gcloud to create an instance template using the Tomcat virtual machine in the euope-west2-c zone as the source for the configuration. The --configure-disk parameter instructs the template to be created using the custom image we created from the Tomcat virtual machine.

4. You will see output like the following:

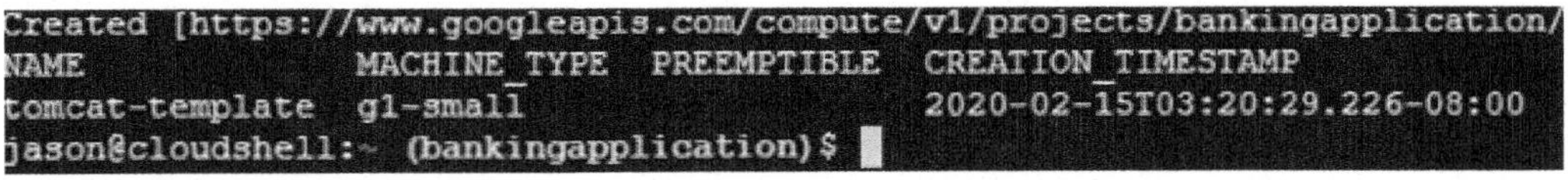

```
Created [https://www.googleapis.com/compute/v1/projects/bankingapplication/
NAME              MACHINE_TYPE  PREEMPTIBLE  CREATION_TIMESTAMP
tomcat-template   g1-small                   2020-02-15T03:20:29.226-08:00
jason@cloudshell:~ (bankingapplication)$
```

Figure 10.10 – Creating an instance template: result

Our instance template has now been created and is ready to be used with a managed instance group.

Using managed instance groups

As we discussed earlier, a managed instance group is used to create and manage a collection of identical virtual machines, and we will be using one for availability and scalability purposes.

To create our regional managed instance group, follow these steps:

1. From the cloud console navigation menu, select **Compute Engine | Instance groups**.

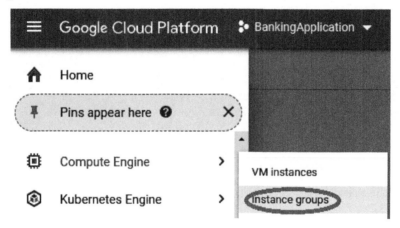

Figure 10.11 – Navigation menu: Instance groups

2. On the **Instance groups** page, click **Create instance group**.

Compute Engine
Instance groups

Instance groups let you organize VM instances or use them in a load-balancing backend service. You can group existing instances or create a group based on an instance template. Learn more

Figure 10.12 – Create instance group

3. Enter the following information as shown in *Figure 10.13*:

    -   **Name**: tomcat-group.

    -   **Location**: Select **Multiple zones**.

    -   **Region**: Select **europe-west2**.

    -   **Instance template**: **tomcat-template**.

    -   **Minimum number of instances**: 3.

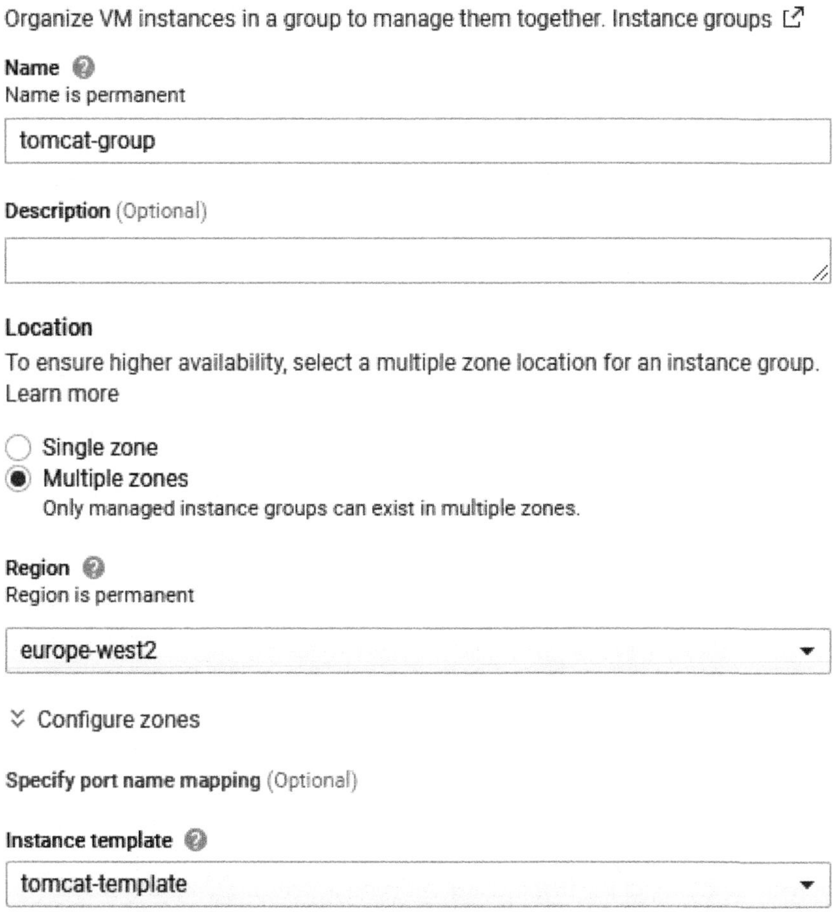

Organize VM instances in a group to manage them together. Instance groups ⬀

Name ❓
Name is permanent

tomcat-group

Description (Optional)

Location

To ensure higher availability, select a multiple zone location for an instance group.
Learn more

○ Single zone
◉ Multiple zones
    Only managed instance groups can exist in multiple zones.

Region ❓
Region is permanent

europe-west2   ▼

⪨ Configure zones

Specify port name mapping (Optional)

Instance template ❓

tomcat-template   ▼

Figure 10.13 – Creating an instance group

4. At the bottom of the page, click **Create**.

    In a few minutes, our instance group will have been created and the instances
    started.

5.   Once the instance group has been created, you will see the **Instance groups** page updated as follows:

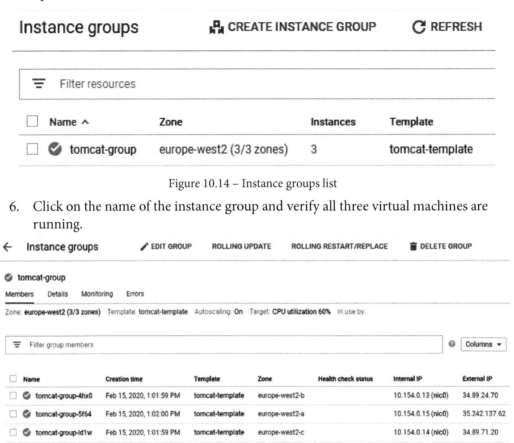

Figure 10.14 – Instance groups list

6.   Click on the name of the instance group and verify all three virtual machines are running.

Figure 10.15 – Instance group members

> **Important Note**
>
> The instance group depends on the Redis and MySQL virtual machines for correct operation. If they are not already running, start them, and once they are up, restart the instance group. This can be done by clicking **Rolling Restart/ Replace** at the top of the **Instance groups** page and clicking **Restart** on the **Restart/replace instances** page.

We can now test whether each of the virtual machines in our regional managed instance group is working correctly by using a web browser to access their external IP addresses. We will lock this down in the next section so that only the HTTP(S) load balancer can access the virtual machines on ports 80 and 443.

Using an HTTP(S) load balancer

Now we are getting to the final stage of our **rehosting** architecture changes. The HTTP(S) load balancer brings it all together. We have created our regional managed instance group from our instance template and used the existing configuration and drive from our Tomcat virtual machine to create that instance template. For the regional managed instance group, we accepted the defaults on which **zones** it uses (all **zones** in the **region** by default), and the default on the autoscale rules, but specified the minimum number of virtual machines as three. Remember the rule of thumb, $N + 2$. To ensure we have at least one server running, we need to have a target of three, so that one could go down for maintenance and one could go down due to failure, but one would still be running.

So, what is left to do? Well, we need to create an HTTP(S) load balancer, defining the backend configuration, host and path rules, and frontend configuration. The backend configuration will include a health check, which is used to decide whether a virtual machine is able to respond to requests. Once we have this in place and have tested it to make sure it is working, we will then update our firewall rules to restrict HTTP(S) traffic to the Tomcat virtual machines to come from the HTTP(S) load balancer.

To create the HTTP(S) load balancer, perform the following steps:

1. From the navigation menu, select **Network services | Load balancing**.

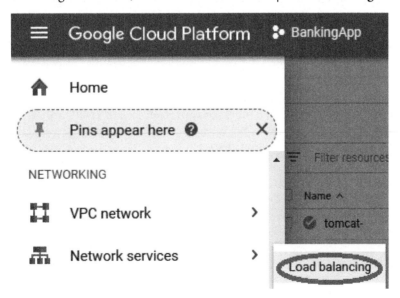

Figure 10.16 – Navigation menu: Load balancing

2. On the **Load balancing** page, click **Create load balancer**.

Network Services
Load balancing

Load balancers distribute incoming network traffic across multiple
VM instances to help your application scale. Learn more

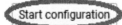

Figure 10.17 – Create load balancer

3. Click **Start configuration**.

HTTP(S) Load Balancing

Layer 7 load balancing for HTTP and HTTPS applications Learn more

Configure
HTTP LB
HTTPS LB (includes HTTP/2 LB)

Options
Internet-facing or internal
Single or multi-region

Figure 10.18 – Start configuration

Leave the selection as the default (**From Internet to my VMs**) and click **Continue**.

←   Create a load balancer

Please answer a few questions to help us select the right load balancing type for
your application

Internet facing or internal only

Do you want to load balance traffic from the Internet to your VMs or only between
VMs in your network?

◉ From Internet to my VMs
◯ Only between my VMs

Figure 10.19 – Create a load balancer: Continue

4. Enter a name for the load balancer (we used `tomcat-loadbalancer`) and click **Backend configuration**.

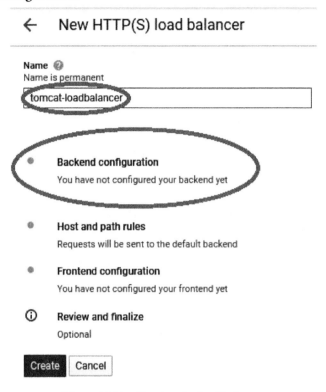

Figure 10.20 – Naming the load balancer

5. Select **Create or select backend services & backend buckets | Backend services | Create a backend service**.

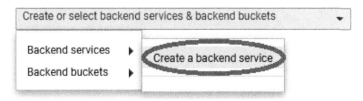

Figure 10.21 – Create a backend service

6.   Enter the following information in the form provided as shown in *Figure 10.22*:

- **Name**: `tomcat-backend`.

- **Backend type**: Select **Instance group**.

- **Protocol**: Select **HTTPS**.

- **Named port**: `https`.

- **Instance group**: Select **tomcat-group (europe-west2, multi-zone)**.

- **Port numbers**: `443`.

Figure 10.22 – New backend

7. Click **Done**.

8. In the **Health check** field, select **Create a health check**.

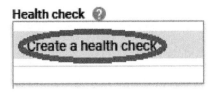

Figure 10.23 – Creating a health check

9. Enter the following information as shown in *Figure 10.24*:

- **Name**: tomcat-healthcheck.

- **Protocol**: Select **HTTPS**.

- **Port**: 443.

- **Request path**: /login.

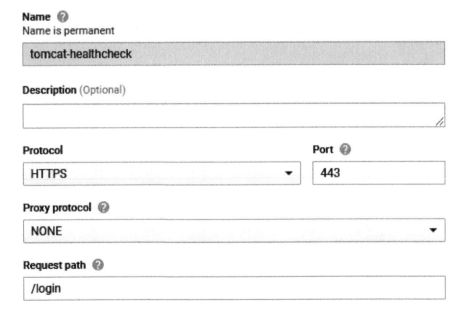

Figure 10.24 – Health check form

10. Click **Save** and continue.

11. We will accept the default host and path rules so you can either click to review or move to the next step.

12. Click **Frontend configuration** and enter the following information:

- **Name**: `tomcat-frontend`.
- **Protocol**: Select **HTTPS (includes HTTP/2)**.

Frontend configuration

Specify an IP address, port and protocol. This IP address is the frontend IP for your clients requests. For SSL, a certificate must also be assigned.

Figure 10.25 – Frontend name and protocol

13. In the **IP address** field, select **Create IP address**.

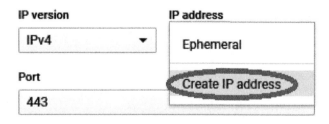

Figure 10.26 – Create IP address

14. Create the new external static IP address by entering a name and clicking **Reserve**.

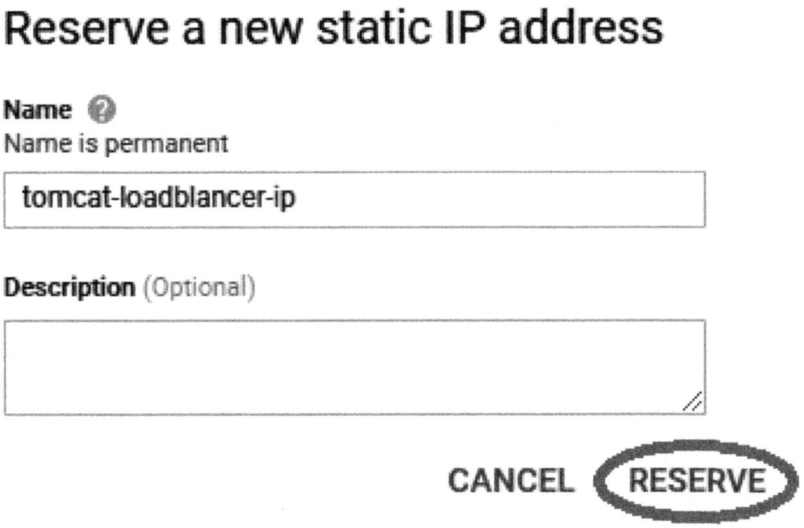

Reserve a new static IP address

Name ❓
Name is permanent

tomcat-loadblancer-ip

Description (Optional)

CANCEL   RESERVE

Figure 10.27 – Reserve a new static IP address

15. In the **Certificate** field, select **Create a new certificate**.

Figure 10.28 – Create a new certificate

16. Enter the following:

- **Name:** `tomcat-loadbalancer-certificate`.
- **Create mode:** Select **Create Google-managed certificate**.

- **Domains**: (replace these with your domain names)

  - www.banking.jasonmarston.me.uk

  - banking.jasonmarston.me.uk

Create a new certificate

Name ⑦
Name is permanent

> tomcat-loadbalancer-certificate

Add a description

Create mode

○ **Upload my certificate**
Use your own public key certificate, certificate chain and private key

⦿ **Create Google-managed certificate**
Google will automatically provision an SSL certificate once you finish your LB configuration and point DNS of all domains specified to the IP associated with the Load Balancer

Domains

www.banking.jasonmarston.me.uk	✕
banking.jasonmarston.me.uk	✕

> www.example.com

> ⓘ The managed SSL certificates feature is not covered by Cloud SLA. Learn more

Figure 10.29 – Create a new certificate form

17. Click **Create**.

18. Review the configuration and click **Done**.

Figure 10.30 – New Frontend IP and port

19. Click **Create**.

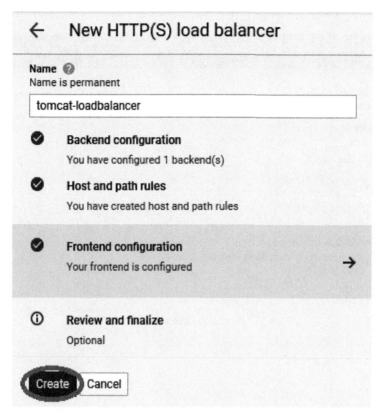

Figure 10.31 – Creating a new HTTP(S) load balancer

You will now be taken to the **Load balancers** list, as seen here:

Load balancers   Backends   Frontends

Filter by name or protocol

Name	Protocol ∧	Region	Backends	
tomcat-loadbalancer	HTTPS	Global	1 backend service (1 instance group, 0 network endpoint groups)	⋮

To edit load balancing resources like forwarding rules and target proxies, go to the advanced menu.

Figure 10.32 – Load balancers

20. Click on the load balancer name to see the status of the provisioning.

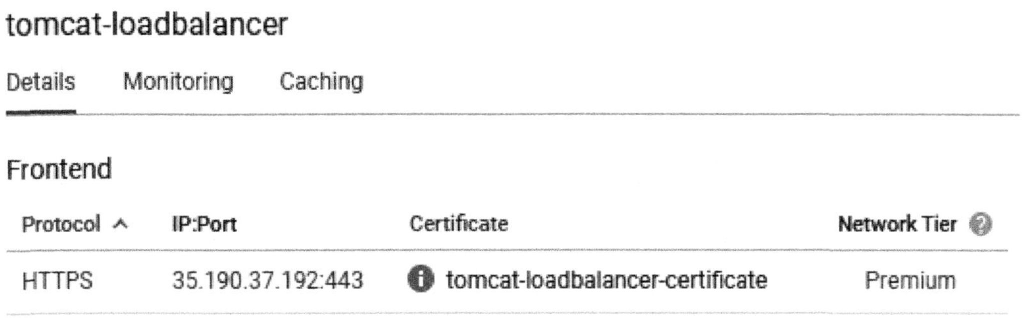

tomcat-loadbalancer

Details   Monitoring   Caching

Frontend

Protocol ∧	IP:Port	Certificate	Network Tier ❓
HTTPS	35.190.37.192:443	❶ tomcat-loadbalancer-certificate	Premium

Figure 10.33 – Load balancer provisioning status

See the information icon next to the certificate name? This indicates that there is processing being undertaken on provisioning your certificate. We can hover over the icon to see the status of the certificate provisioning.

> **Important Note**
>
> We will need to make a copy of the IP address reserved in this process and update our DNS, so the hostnames listed resolve to this address. If we do not do this, the certificate generation will fail.

The creation of the HTTP(S) load balancer will take a while. In our experience, this is usually a few minutes. What takes a lot longer is the creation of the Google-managed SSL certificate. The documentation says it can take up to an hour and it can indeed take that long. This is a good point to take a break, have a coffee, or just stretch your legs.

Once the information icon changes to a tick icon, the site will be ready to use. We can test this with our web browser by using the hostnames we provided earlier.

The last step is to lock down the back door into our Tomcat virtual machines that allows direct connections to the individual machines via HTTP(S) without going through the HTTP(S) load balancer. We already have a firewall rule in place for HTTP(S) access to our Tomcat virtual machines, so we just need to update the source IP ranges: `130.211.0.0/22` and `35.191.0.0/60`, to replace `0.0.0.0/0`. These two address ranges are the ranges used by the Google Cloud load balancing service and are the only ranges load balancing will come from.

Summary

In this chapter, we refined our infrastructure architecture to address scalability and availability concerns. We updated it to make use of a **regional managed instance group** to control a collection of identical virtual machine instances. These instances were spread across multiple availability zones to address availability. The regional managed instance group also has autoscaling capabilities and so addresses scalability. Finally, we updated our infrastructure architecture to incorporate an **HTTP(S) load balancer** to distribute traffic evenly across all the instances.

We implemented this architecture by creating an image from our Tomcat virtual machine. Then, we used the image along with the virtual machine configuration to create an instance template. After that, using the instance template, we created a regional managed instance group. Finally, we created our HTTP(S) load balancer using the regional managed instance group as the backend.

In the next chapter, we will begin the process of replacing capabilities hosted on virtual machines with capabilities provided by Google Cloud. In this case, we will migrate our MySQL database onto Google Cloud SQL.

11

Re-Platforming the Data Layer

At this point, we have a fully working solution that addresses scalability and availability in the application layer by using a **Regional Managed Instance Group** and an **HTTP(S) Load Balancer**. In this chapter, we will be looking at the data layer in our application and seeing how we can improve our architecture to address scalability and availability while reducing the administrative overhead of managing virtual machines. The two areas in the data layer we will cover are session handling and persistent relational data. We will do this by examining the services provided by Google Cloud in this area: Cloud Memorystore for handling sessions, then Cloud SQL (with Cloud SQL Proxy), and Cloud Spanner for relational data. Finally, we will take a brief look at importing data into our relational systems.

In this chapter, we will cover the following:

- Designing for scalability and availability
- Using Cloud Memorystore
- Using Cloud SQL
- Using Cloud SQL Proxy
- Using Cloud Spanner
- Importing data into Cloud SQL

Designing for scalability and availability

In this section, we will address scalability and availability in our architecture. Scalability is about being able to adjust an application to handle increased or decreased workloads so we do not run out of resources, and at the same time using only the resources we need. Availability is about ensuring an application is available when needed and making sure we do not have unexpected outages. Once completed, we will be able to design infrastructure using Google Cloud services to address these concerns.

Our starting point will be the High Availability(**HA**) infrastructure architecture illustrated in the following diagram:

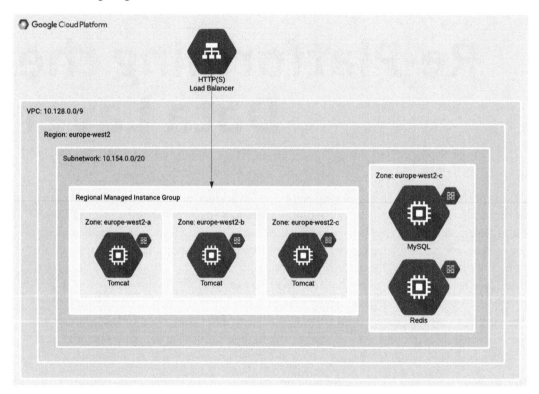

Figure 11.1 – HA infrastructure architecture

To add availability and scalability to our data layer, we will replace the MySQL and Redis virtual machines with services provided by Google Cloud that provide these capabilities. We are moving away from virtual machines because creating and managing a high-availability database cluster is complex and time-consuming. The services we will be using are the following:

- **Cloud Memorystore**: Fully managed, highly available, and scalable Redis as a Service
- **Cloud SQL**: Fully managed, highly available, and scalable Database as a Service that supports MySQL, PostgreSQL, and MS SQL

We could have used **Cloud Spanner** rather than Cloud SQL. Cloud Spanner is a globally distributed and strongly consistent database service. As we do not need this level of service for our application, we have chosen to use Cloud SQL. We will, however, examine how to use Cloud Spanner so that we can make use of it if our needs change later.

The change to our architecture is simply to replace the data layer virtual machines with Cloud Memorystore and Cloud SQL as illustrated in the following diagram:

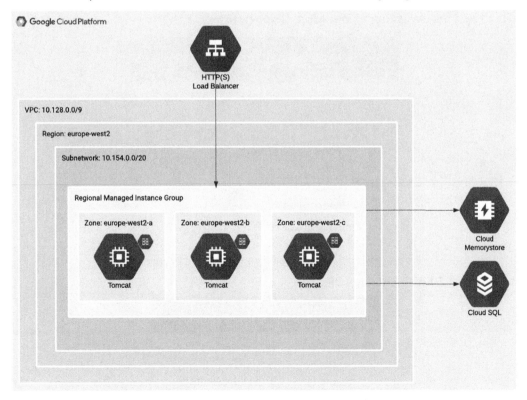

Figure 11.2 – Updated infrastructure architecture – data services

We have now updated our architecture to modernize the data layer, addressing the scalability and availability concerns in that layer. In the following sections, we will learn how to use Cloud Memorystore and Cloud SQL to implement this updated architecture.

Using Cloud Memorystore

As we learned in the *Designing for scalability and availability* section, Cloud Memorystore is fully managed, highly available, and scalable Redis as a Service. We will be using this to handle user sessions for our application. To use Cloud Memorystore with our application, we will need to perform two activities. The first activity is to provision an instance of Cloud Memorystore, the second activity is to update our Regional Managed Instance Group to use this instance.

Provisioning a Cloud Memorystore instance

We will now provision our Cloud Memorystore instance by performing the following steps:

1.   From the navigation menu, select **Memorystore**:

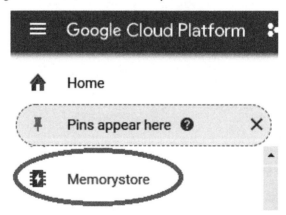

Figure 11.3 – Navigation menu: Memorystore

2.   Click **CREATE INSTANCE**:

Figure 11.4 – CREATE INSTANCE

3.   On the **Create a Redis instance** page, provide an **Instance ID** and **Display name**:

← **Create a Redis instance**

Cloud Memorystore for Redis is a fully managed Redis service for the Google Cloud Platform. Learn more

Name your instance

The instance ID is a permanent and unique identifier. The display name is optional and for display purposes only.

Instance ID *

redis-service

Use lowercase letters, numbers, and hyphens. Start with a letter.

Display name

Redis Service

Figure 11.5 – Instance ID and Display name

4. Select the **Tier** and **Region**. As this is not a production system, we have selected **Basic**. **Region** needs to match the region of the VMs that will connect to it:

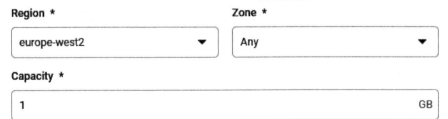

Set instance properties

Tier *
Determines availability, cost, and performance.

◉ Basic
   Lower cost. Does not provide high availability.

○ Standard
   Includes a failover replica in a separate zone for high availability.

Location
Your instance must be in the same region as the VMs that will connect to it. For better performance, choose the same zone within that region. Learn more

Region *   **Zone** *

europe-west2   ▼   Any   ▼

Capacity *

1   GB

Provision up to 300 GB of space

Figure 11.6 – Instance properties

5. At the bottom of the page, click **Create**.

6. The instance will now be created. This is a long-running process so will take several minutes to complete. Once completed, you will see a tick icon next to **Instance ID** as follows:

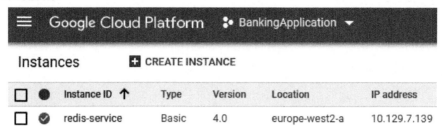

Figure 11.7 – Successful creation of an instance

Make a note of the IP address as we will use that in the next section.

As Cloud Memorystore has configuration by a client turned off for security reasons, we need to update the configuration via the portal. The specific configuration that we will change is to enable **Keyspace Event Notifications**. This informs a client (our application) when the session has expired, as shown in the following screenshot:

Configurations

Customize the behavior of your instance based on Redis configuration parameters. Learn more

Configuration	Value
notify-keyspace-events ▼	EA

Figure 11.8 – Enable notifications

In this section, we learned how to provision and configure a Cloud Memorystore instance. In the next section, we will learn how to update our application and Regional Managed Instance Group to use this new instance.

Updating the Regional Managed Instance Group

We will now update our Regional Managed Instance Group to use the new Cloud Memorystore instance by performing the following steps:

1. Log in to our Tomcat virtual machine (this is the virtual machine we used to create the instance template used in our Regional Managed Instance Group).

2. Install the telnet client by entering the following command:

```
sudo apt-get -y install telnet
```

3. Test the connectivity to the Cloud Memorystore instance by entering the following command:

```
telnet <redis-service_ip_address> 6379
```

4. When you are connected, enter the following command in telnet:

```
PING
```

5. You will receive the following response:

```
PONG
```

6. Exit the telnet client by entering the following command:

```
QUIT
```

7. Update the environment variables set up previously, editing the file as follows:

```
export BANKING_REDIS_HOST="<redis-service_ip_address>"
export BANKING_REDIS_PASSWORD=""
```

8. Shut down the Tomcat virtual machine.

9. Create an image of the Tomcat virtual machine.

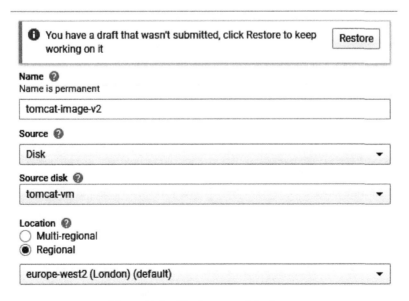

Figure 11.9 – Version two of the image

10. Using Cloud Shell, create a new instance template from the image and the virtual machine configuration by entering the following command:

```
gcloud compute instance-templates create tomcat-
template-v2 --source-instance=tomcat-vm --source-
instance-zone=europe-west2-c --configure-disk=device-
name=tomcat-vm-tmpl-boot-disk,instantiate-from=custom-
image,custom-image=projects/bankingapplication/global/
images/tomcat-image-v2,auto-delete=true
```

11. Navigate to our Regional Managed Instance Group and click **ROLLING UPDATE**:

➜ tomcat-group

Figure 11.10 – ROLLING UPDATE

12. Select the new instance template:

← **Update tomcat-group**

A rolling update is a gradual update of the instances in the instance group to the target configuration of templates. Learn more

Current configuration

tomcat-template : 3 instances

New configuration
Select 1-2 template(s), using the target size to specify percentage or number of instances per template

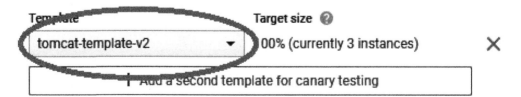

Figure 11.11 – ROLLING UPDATE – Template

13. Click **Update**.

14. Wait for the rolling update to complete. This is a long-running process and will take several minutes. Eventually, you will see the new virtual machines using the new instance template:

	Name	Creation time	Template
☐ ✅	tomcat-group-3t2c	Feb 24, 2020, 5:10:33 PM	tomcat-template-v2
☐ ✅	tomcat-group-8rvm	Feb 24, 2020, 5:10:32 PM	tomcat-template-v2
☐ ✅	tomcat-group-dvx5	Feb 24, 2020, 5:10:32 PM	tomcat-template-v2

Figure 11.12 – Updated Regional Managed Instance Group

You can now test the application is working with the updated configuration by accessing it using a web browser.

Now we have updated our solution to use Cloud Memorystore for session handling, we can move on to using Cloud SQL to handle our relational data.

Using Cloud SQL

To start using Cloud SQL, we will now provision an instance by performing the following steps:

1. From the navigation menu, select **SQL**:

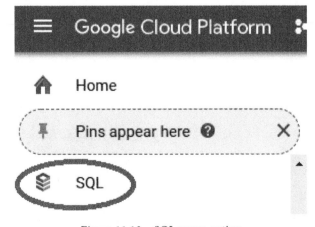

Figure 11.13 – SQL menu option

2. From the **Cloud SQL Instances** page, click **CREATE INSTANCE**:

Cloud SQL

Cloud SQL Instances

Cloud SQL instances are fully managed, relational MySQL, PostgreSQL, and SQL Server databases. Google handles replication, patch management, and database management to ensure availability and performance. Learn more

To get started with Cloud SQL, you can create a new instance or use Cloud SQL to migrate your SQL database to Google Cloud.

CREATE INSTANCE   MIGRATE DATA

Figure 11.14 – CREATE INSTANCE

3. From the **Create an instance** page, click **Choose MySQL**:

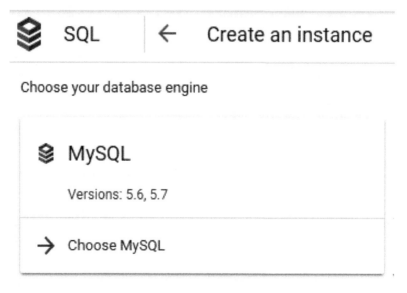

Figure 11.15 – Choose MySQL

4. Provide an **Instance ID** and **Root password**, select the **Region**, and click **Show configuration options**:

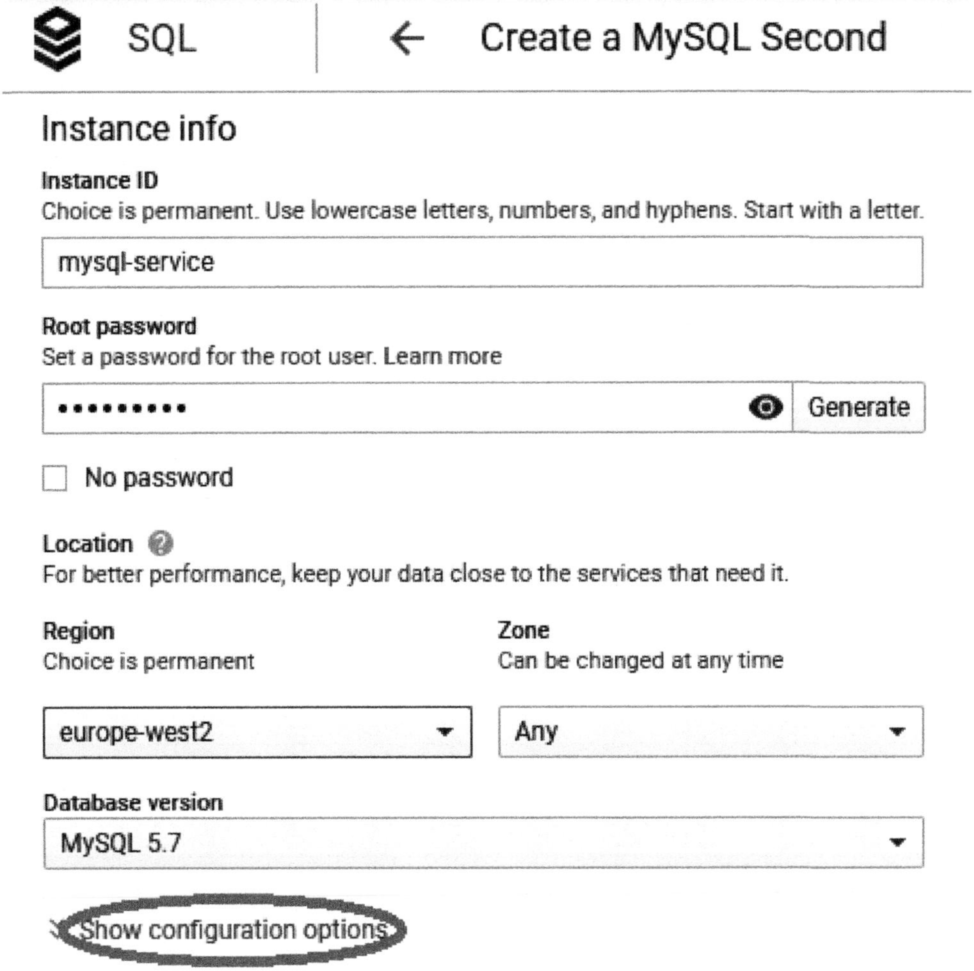

Figure 11.16 – Show configuration options

5. In the **Connectivity** section, select **Private IP** and unselect **Public IP**:

Configuration options

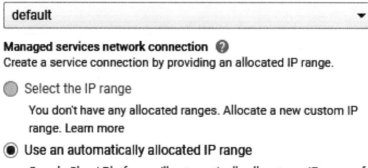

1   Connectivity   ⌃

Choose how you would like to connect to your database instance.

For extra security, consider using the Cloud SQL proxy to connect to your instances after creation. Learn more

☑ Private IP

Private IP connectivity requires additional APIs and permissions. You may need to contact your organization's administrator for help enabling or using this feature. Currently, Private IP cannot be disabled once it has been enabled.

Associated networking
Select a network to create a private connection

default ▼

Managed services network connection ❓
Create a service connection by providing an allocated IP range.

◯ Select the IP range

You don't have any allocated ranges. Allocate a new custom IP range. Learn more

◉ Use an automatically allocated IP range

Google Cloud Platform will automatically allocate an IP range of prefix-length 20 and use the name **google-managed-services-default**.

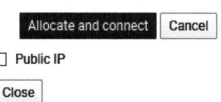

☐ Public IP

Close

Figure 11.17 – Cloud SQL network settings

6. In the **Flags** section, click **Add item**:

Figure 11.18 – Add item to flags

7. Enter sql_mode in the **Database flags** field and select **sql_mode**:

Figure 11.19 – sql_mode

8. Enter the following in the **sql_mode** field: ONLY_FULL_GROUP_BY, STRICT_TRANS_TABLES, ALLOW_INVALID_DATES, ERROR_FOR_DIVISION_BY_ZERO, NO_AUTO_CREATE_USER, and NO_ENGINE_SUBSTITUTION:

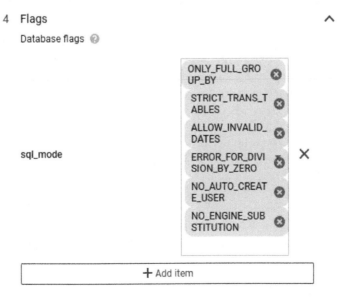

Figure 11.20 – SQL modes

> **Important Note**
>
> The **sql_mode** settings changed with the latest version of MySQL. The preceding settings apply all the same mode settings except those dealing with dates. We are replacing NO_ZERO_IN_DATE, and NO_ZERO_DATE with ALLOW_INVALID_DATES. This is because the **Hibernate** auto-creation of tables is not yet compatible with the latest MySQL sql_mode settings.

Follow these steps to create a user account:

1. At the bottom of the page, click **Create**.

2. Your instance will now be created. This is a long-running process so will take a few minutes. Once completed, you will see your new instance, as shown in the following screenshot:

≡ Filter tree

	Instance ID ❷ ↑	Type	Public IP address	Private IP address
☐	✓ mysql-instance	MySQL 5.7		10.55.0.3

Figure 11.21 – Newly created SQL instance

3. Next, we need to create the user for our banking application. Click the instance ID:

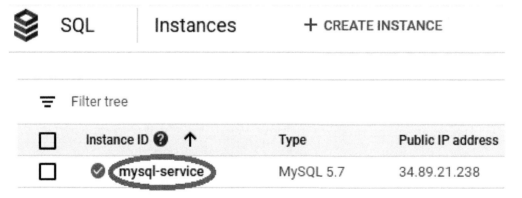

Figure 11.22 – Configure SQL instance

4. On the overview page, click **Users**:

Figure 11.23 – Users menu option

5. Click **Create user account**:

Users

All instances > mysql-service

 **mysql-service**

MySQL Second Generation master

MySQL user accounts

User accounts enable users and applications to connect to your Cloud SQL instance. Learn more

Figure 11.24 – Create user account

6. Enter the **User name** and **Password** we are using to access our database and click **CREATE**:

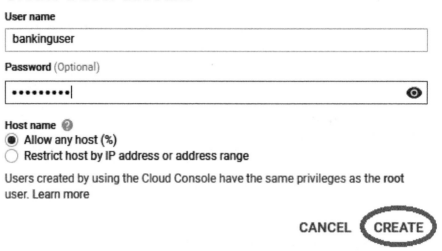

Figure 11.25 – User details

> **Important Note**
>
> We have left **Host name** as **Allow any host** as we don't know what host names will eventually access this database. This is due to hosts being created and destroyed in our **Managed Instance Group** when autoscaling occurs.

Now we have the instance and a database user for our application, we will create our database and grant the user the required authority by performing the following steps:

1. From our Tomcat virtual machine, enter the following command:

```
mysql -h <instance_private_ip> -u root -p
```

2. Enter the root user password when prompted, as shown here:

```
Enter password:
```

3. Create the banking database by entering the following command:

```
create database banking;
```

4. You will see a response showing the database has been created as follows:

```
Query OK, 1 row affected (0.01 sec)
```

5. Grant the `bankinguser` account the required authority to the banking database:

```
grant all on banking.* to 'bankinguser'@'%';
```

6. You will see a response showing the user has been granted authority as follows:

```
Query OK, 0 rows affected (0.01 sec)
```

7. You can now exit the `mysql` client by entering the following command:

```
exit
```

Our Cloud SQL instance is now configured. The database has been created, and our user has been granted authority to the database. We are now ready to update our application to use this instance via Cloud SQL Proxy.

Using Cloud SQL Proxy

Before getting started on updating our application to use Cloud SQL Proxy to connect to our Cloud SQL instance, it is important to understand why we use it.

Cloud SQL Proxy provides us with access to Cloud SQL instances without having to whitelist IP addresses or configure SSL. This means we get secure connections without complex configuration and easier connection management as Cloud SQL Proxy handles authentication with Cloud SQL. Because we don't need whitelisting or other such network security measures when using Cloud SQL Proxy, it uses a service account to authenticate with the Cloud SQL instance. Finally, Cloud SQL Proxy handles the failover from the primary to the standby Cloud SQL instance if the primary Cloud SQL instance becomes unresponsive.

Let's get started with installing and configuring Cloud SQL Auth Proxy by performing the following steps:

1. In our Tomcat virtual machine, enter the following command to download the Cloud SQL Auth `Proxy` binary:

```
wget https://dl.google.com/cloudsql/cloud_sql_proxy.
linux.amd64 -O cloud_sql_proxy
```

2. Make the `Proxy` binary executable by entering the following command:

```
chmod +x cloud_sql_proxy
```

3. Now we need to set up the `gcloud` tool on our virtual machine. Enter the following command to initialize `gcloud`:

```
gcloud init
```

4. You will get the following prompt. Enter *1* to use the virtual machine's service account:

```
Welcome! This command will take you through the
configuration of gcloud.


Your current configuration has been set to: [default]


You can skip diagnostics next time by using the following
flag:
   gcloud init --skip-diagnostics


Network diagnostic detects and fixes local network
connection issues.
Checking network connection...done.
Reachability Check passed.
Network diagnostic passed (1/1 checks passed).


Choose the account you would like to use to perform
operations for
this configuration:
 [1] 63100814425-compute@developer.gserviceaccount.com
 [2] Log in with a new account
Please enter your numeric choice:
```

5. At the next prompt, enter the project ID – we used `bankingapplication`:

```
You are logged in as: [63100814425-compute@developer.
gserviceaccount.com].
WARNING: Listing available projects failed: HttpError
accessing <https://cloudresourcemanager.googleapis.com/
v1/projects?filter=lifecycleState%3AACTIVE&alt=json&page-
Size=201>: response: <{'status': '403', 'content-length':
'138', 'x-xss-protection': '0', 'x-content-type-op-
tions': 'nosniff', 'transfer-encoding': 'chunked',
'vary': 'Origin, X-Origin, Referer', 'server': 'ESF',
```

```
'server-timing': 'gfet4t7; dur=94', '-content-encod-
ing': 'gzip', 'cache-control': 'private', 'date': 'Sat,
29 Feb 2020 14:07:27 GMT', 'x-frame-options': 'SAMEORI-
GIN', 'content-type': 'application/json; charset=UTF-8',
'www-authenticate': 'Bearer realm="https://accounts.
google.com/", error="insufficient_scope", scope="https://
www.googleapis.com/auth/cloud-platform https://www.goog-
leapis.com/auth/cloud-platform.read-only https://www.
googleapis.com/auth/cloudplatformprojects https://www.
googleapis.com/auth/cloudplatformprojects.readonly"'}>,
content <{
   "error": {
     "code": 403,
     "message": "Request had insufficient authentication
scopes.",
     "status": "PERMISSION_DENIED"
   }
}
>
Enter project id you would like to use:
```

Next, as Cloud SQL Proxy makes use of the Cloud SQL Admin API, we need to enable that by following these steps:

1. Enter Cloud SQL Admin API in the search bar at the top of the console and select it in the dropdown:

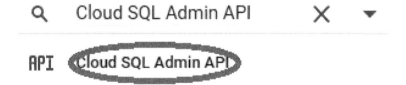

Figure 11.26 – Cloud SQL Admin API search

2. Click **Enable** (this may take a few minutes to complete):

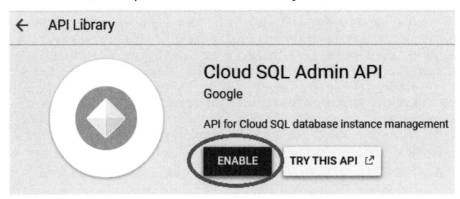

Figure 11.27 – Enable Cloud SQL Admin API

We also need to configure the service account Cloud SQL Proxy will use to access Cloud SQL:

1. From the navigation menu, select **IAM & Admin**:

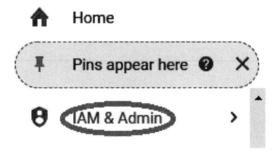

Figure 11.28 – IAM & Admin menu option

2. Click the pencil icon at the right-hand side of the member with the name **Compute Engine default service account** (this is the service account for our virtual machines):

Figure 11.29 – Edit service account

3. In the **Edit permissions** panel, click **ADD ANOTHER ROLE**:

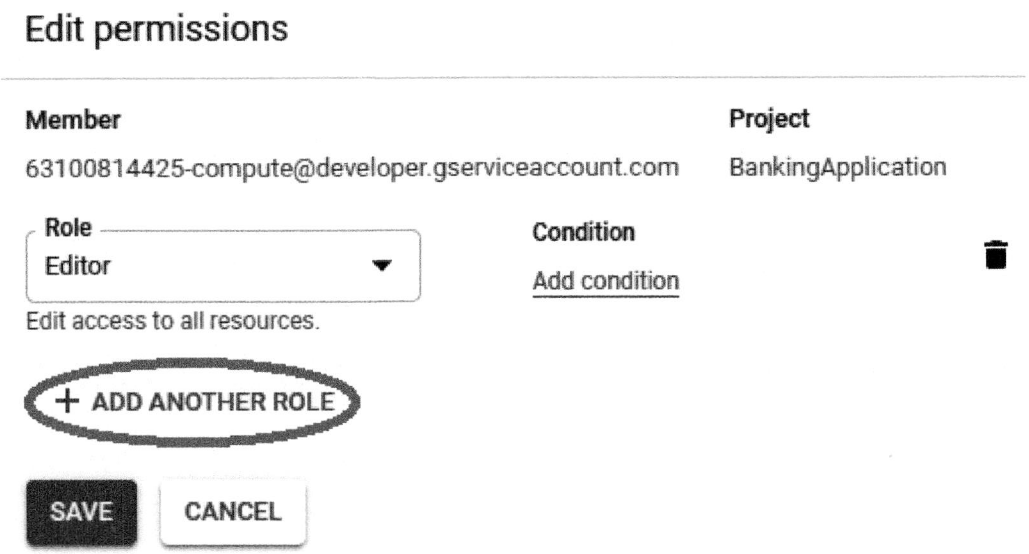

Edit permissions

Member   **Project**

63100814425-compute@developer.gserviceaccount.com   BankingApplication

Role

Editor ▼

Condition

Add condition

🗑

Edit access to all resources.

(+ ADD ANOTHER ROLE)

SAVE   CANCEL

Figure 11.30 – ADD ANOTHER ROLE

4.   Select **Cloud SQL Client** and click **SAVE**:

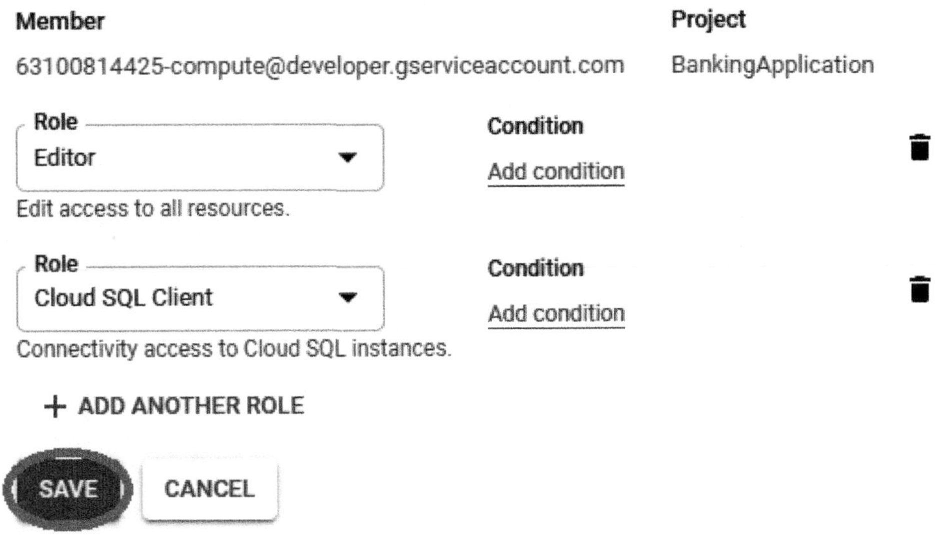

Member   **Project**

63100814425-compute@developer.gserviceaccount.com   BankingApplication

Role

Editor ▼

Condition

Add condition

🗑

Edit access to all resources.

Role

Cloud SQL Client ▼

Condition

Add condition

🗑

Connectivity access to Cloud SQL instances.

+ ADD ANOTHER ROLE

SAVE   CANCEL

Figure 11.31– Cloud SQL Client role

5. In the left-hand menu, select **Service Accounts**:

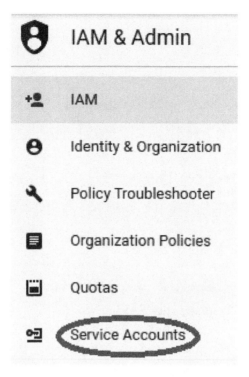

Figure 11.32 – Service Accounts menu option

6. Click on the service account to open the configuration:

Figure 11.33 – Open service account configuration

7. Click **EDIT** to enter edit mode:

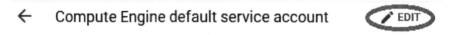

Figure 11.34 – Edit service account

8. Click **CREATE KEY**:

Service account status

Disabling your account allows you to preserve your policies without having to delete it.

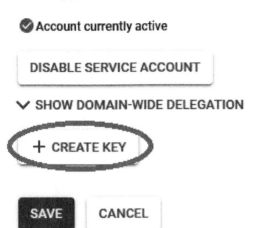

Account currently active

DISABLE SERVICE ACCOUNT

∨ SHOW DOMAIN-WIDE DELEGATION

+ CREATE KEY

SAVE   CANCEL

Figure 11.35 – CREATE KEY action

9.   Click **CREATE** (the key will automatically download to our local machine):

Create private key for "Compute Engine default service account"

Downloads a file that contains the private key. Store the file securely because this key can't be recovered if lost.

Key type

◉ JSON
   Recommended

○ P12
   For backward compatibility with code using the P12 format

CANCEL   CREATE

Figure 11.36 – Create the key

10. Click **CANCEL** as we don't need to update anything else on the service account:

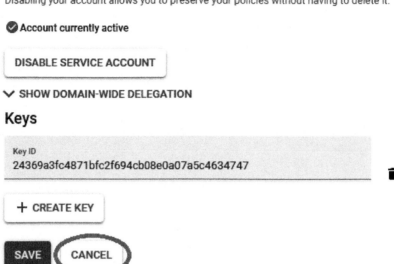

Figure 11.37 – Exit the update configuration

Now everything is in place, we can upload the credentials file to our Tomcat virtual machine and test the client works with the credentials by following these steps:

1. In our Tomcat virtual machine, click the cog icon and select **Upload file**:

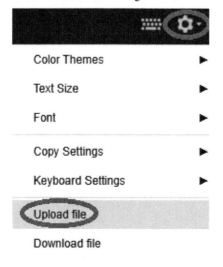

Figure 11.38 – Upload file menu option

2. Select your credentials file from the **Downloads** directory and click **Open**:

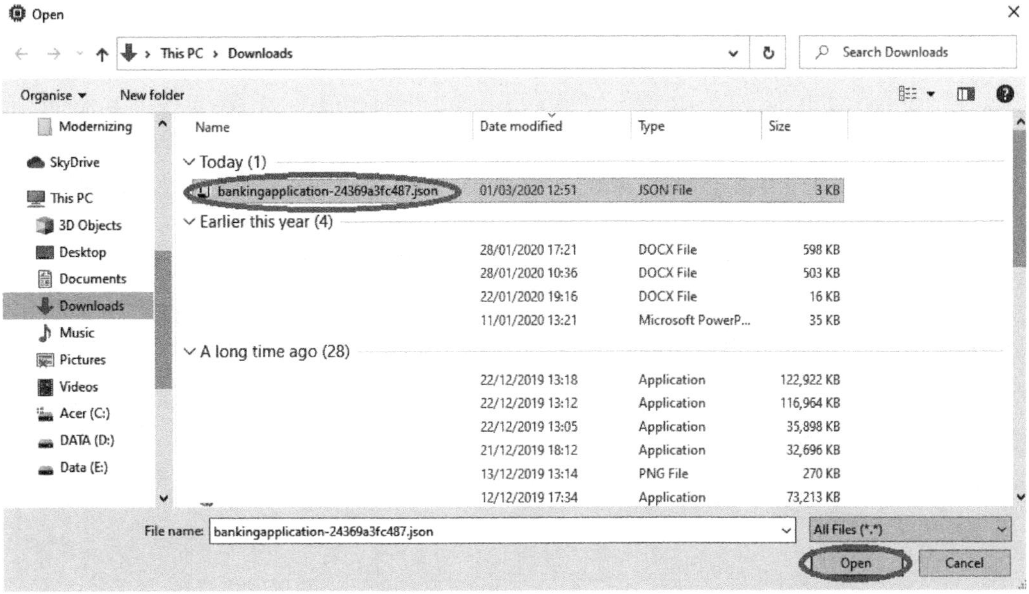

Figure 11.39 – Upload the credentials file

3. Rename the credentials file to `credentials.json` using the following command:

```
mv <generated_name>.json ./credentials.json
```

4. Start the proxy with the `credentials.json` file by entering the following command:

```
./cloud_sql_proxy -instances=bankingapplication:eur
ope-west2:mysql-service=tcp:3336 -credential_file=./
credentials.json
```

5. From another terminal window on the Tomcat virtual machine, enter the following command to log in to our Cloud SQL instance:

```
ql -h 127.0.0.1mys --port 3336 -u root -p
```

We will now make sure Cloud SQL Proxy starts at boot time as a service.

6. Enter the following commands to create two new directories:

```
sudo mkdir /var/run/cloud-sql-proxy
```
```
sudo mkdir /var/local/cloud-sql-proxy
```

7. Enter the following command to copy the credentials JSON file into the `/var/local/cloud-sql-proxy` directory:

```
sudo cp ~/credentials.json /var/local/cloud-sql-proxy
```

8. Create a file in `/lib/systemd/system` called `cloud-sql-proxy.service` with the following content:

```
cloud-sql-proxy.service
[Install]
WantedBy=multi-user.target

[Unit]
Description=Cloud SQL Proxy
Requires=networking.service
After=networking.service

[Service]
Type=simple
RuntimeDirectory=cloud-sql-proxy
WorkingDirectory=/usr/local/bin
ExecStart=/usr/local/bin/cloud_sql_proxy -dir=/var/
run/cloud-sql-proxy -instances=<instance_connection_
name>=tcp:3336 -credential_file=/var/local/cloud_sql_
proxy/credentials.json
Restart=always
StandardOutput=journal
User=root
```

9. Enter the following commands to load the new configuration, start the service, check the status, and make sure the service starts on reboot:

```
sudo systemctl daemon-reload
sudo systemctl start cloud-sql-proxy
sudo systemctl status cloud-sql-proxy
sudo systemctl enable cloud-sql-proxy
```

10. Test that we can connect to the Cloud SQL instance as we did previously:

```
mysql -h 127.0.0.1 --port 3336 -u root -p
```

Now all that remains is for us to update our environment variables in our configuration file as follows:

```
export BANKING_DATASOURCE_DIALECT="org.hibernate.dialect.
MySQL5InnoDBDialect"
```
```
export BANKING_DATASOURCE_URL="jdbc:mysql://127.0.0.1:3336/
banking?useSSL=false&allowPublicKeyRetrieval=true"
```

At this point, we have configured our application and are ready to proceed.

> **Important Note**
>
> The engine used by MySQL was updated from MyISAM to InnoDB in the latest release available in Cloud SQL. We needed to update the dialect to reflect this change, otherwise, the tables would not be created as the auto-create facilities in Hibernate would be using an engine that has been disabled.

We can now follow the standard procedure to update our application as follows:

1. Stop the Tomcat virtual machine.
2. Create an image from the Tomcat virtual machine.
3. Create an instance template from the image and virtual machine.
4. Apply the instance template to our Regional Managed Instance Group.

Once we have followed the preceding steps, our application will have been updated to use the following:

- Cloud Memorystore to manage our sessions
- Cloud SQL to host our relational database

We can now test the updated application by opening it in a web browser.

We have updated our solution to use Cloud SQL with Cloud SQL Proxy and so replaced the final virtual machine in our data layer with a Google Cloud service. In the next section, we will take a look at how Cloud Spanner can be used by an application.

Using Cloud Spanner

Although we will not be using Cloud Spanner for our application at this point, it is important to understand how to provision a Cloud Spanner instance and configure our application to use it. We will examine the following:

- Provisioning Cloud Spanner
- Updating our application build to use the open source Cloud Spanner JDBC library
- Updating our application settings to support this new configuration

The key thing is that, to our application, Cloud Spanner will look just like any JDBC-enabled relational database, and so we will not have to change any of the source code, just the configuration.

Provisioning Cloud Spanner

To provision Cloud Spanner, we need to perform the following steps:

1. From the navigation menu, select **Spanner**:

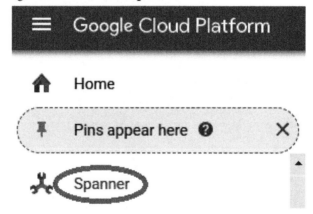

Figure 11.40 – Spanner menu item

2. Click **CREATE INSTANCE**:

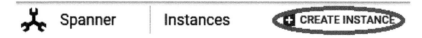

Figure 11.41 – CREATE INSTANCE action

3. Enter the **Instance name**:

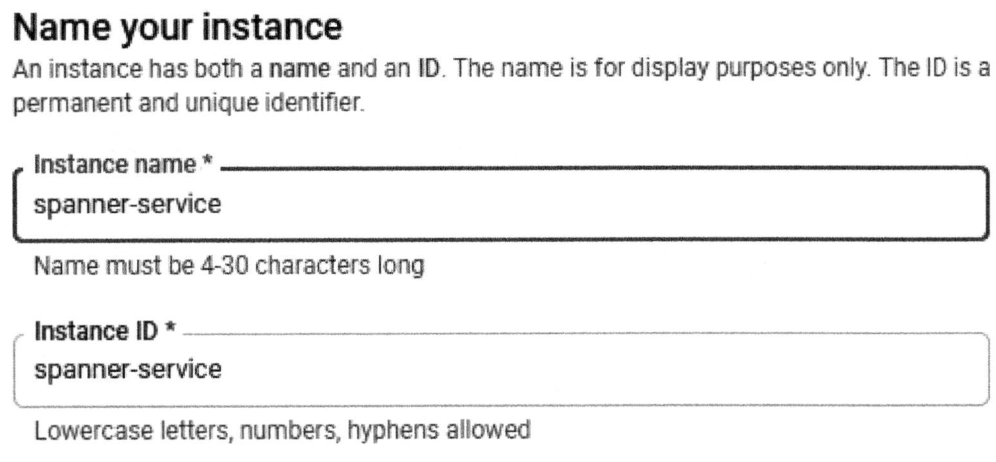

Name your instance

An instance has both a **name** and an **ID**. The name is for display purposes only. The ID is a permanent and unique identifier.

Instance name *

spanner-service

Name must be 4-30 characters long

Instance ID *

spanner-service

Lowercase letters, numbers, hyphens allowed

Figure 11.42 – Instance name and ID

4. Choose the region as the configuration:

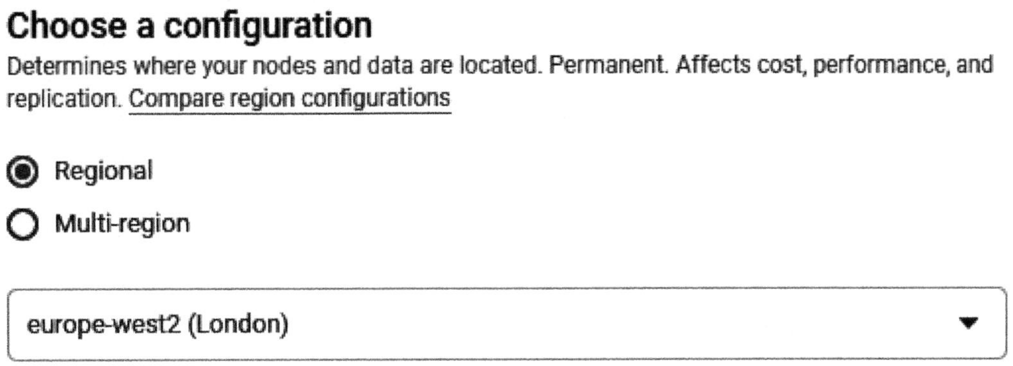

Choose a configuration

Determines where your nodes and data are located. Permanent. Affects cost, performance, and replication. Compare region configurations

● Regional

○ Multi-region

europe-west2 (London)   ▼

Figure 11.43 – Select a region

5. At the bottom of the page, click **CREATE**.

6. This could take a few minutes. Once complete, we create our banking database. Click **CREATE DATABASE**:

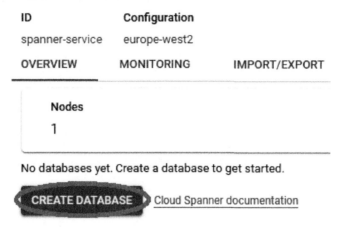

Figure 11.44 – Start creating the Spanner database

7. Enter banking and click **Continue**:

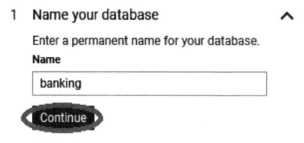

Figure 11.45 – Name the Spanner database

8. Click **Create**:

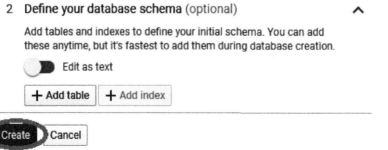

Figure 11.46 – Create the Spanner database

9. This is a long-running process and will shortly create the database. We will see a response like the following:

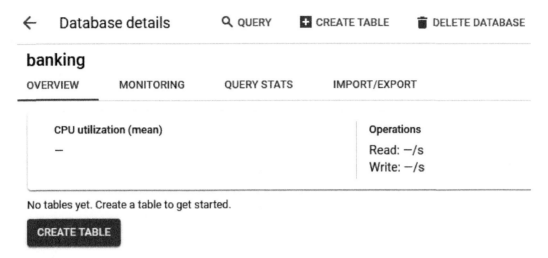

Figure 11.47 – Created Spanner database

We have now created our Cloud Spanner instance and are ready to make the changes needed to our application build to use it. The following section details how we update our build to use Cloud Spanner.

Updating the build

To switch over to using Cloud Spanner in our build, we would replace `runtimeOnly` `'mysql:mysql-connector-java'` in the dependencies section of our `build. gradle` file with the following:

```
implementation 'com.google.cloud:google-cloud-spanner-
hibernate-dialect:1.1.0'
```

```
implementation 'com.google.cloud:google-cloud-spanner-
jdbc:1.13.0'
```

The updates we made to our build were very minor and simply added the Hibernate support for the Cloud Spanner JDBC driver, and of course the Cloud Spanner JDBC driver itself. We now need to update our application settings to make use of these components.

Updating the application settings

To switch over to using Cloud Spanner at runtime, we would update our environment variables with the following:

```
export BANKING_DATASOURCE_DIALECT=com.google.cloud.spanner.
hibernate.SpannerDialect
```

```
export BANKING_DATASOURCE_DRIVER= com.google.cloud.spanner.
jdbc.JdbcDriver
```

```
export BANKING_DATASOURCE_URL= jdbc:cloudspanner:/projects/
{YOUR_PROJECT_ID}/instances/{YOUR_INSTANCE_ID}/databases/{YOUR_
DATABASE_ID}
```

```
export GOOGLE_APPLICATION_CREDENTIALS=<path_to_cloudspanner_
credentials_file>
```

We would then add the following to our `application.configuration` file:

```
spring.jpa.properties.hibernate.connection.driver_
class=${BANKING_DATASOURCE _DRIVER}
```

> **Important Note**
>
> Cloud Spanner is not identical to traditional relational databases. The Cloud Spanner JDBC driver allows us to map between SQL tables and Cloud Spanner tables, but we must understand that these are not the same thing. The key difference is that all tables *must* have primary keys.

We have now completed updating our application to use Cloud Spanner. This means we have completed examining how to update our solutions data layer and can move on to how to migrate the data from our MySQL virtual machine into our relational database services.

Importing data into Cloud SQL

Importing data into Cloud SQL is a key subject. If we are modernizing an existing application, then there will likely be a large amount of relational data already in existence and we need to be able to import this, so we don't lose any important information.

In order to import data into our Cloud SQL instance, we will first need to export that data from an existing MySQL database and place it in a location that Cloud SQL can import from. The following section examines these steps.

Exporting data from our MySQL virtual machine

To export the data from our MySQL virtual machine, perform the following steps:

1. In the command line, enter the following command:

```
mysqldump -u bankinguser -p --databases banking
--hex-blob --set-gtid-purged=OFF --single-transaction >
exported.sql
```

2. Enter the `bankinguser` password when prompted, as follows:

```
Enter password:
```

We now have a file called `exported.sql`, which we will upload to a Cloud Storage bucket. This means we need to create a Cloud Storage bucket by performing the following steps:

1. From the cloud console, in the navigation menu, select **Storage**:

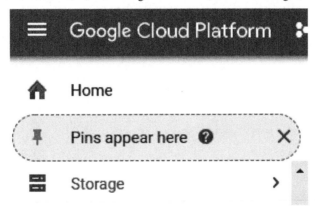

Figure 11.48 – Storage menu option

2. Click **CREATE BUCKET**:

Figure 11.49 – CREATE BUCKET

3. Enter a unique name for our bucket:

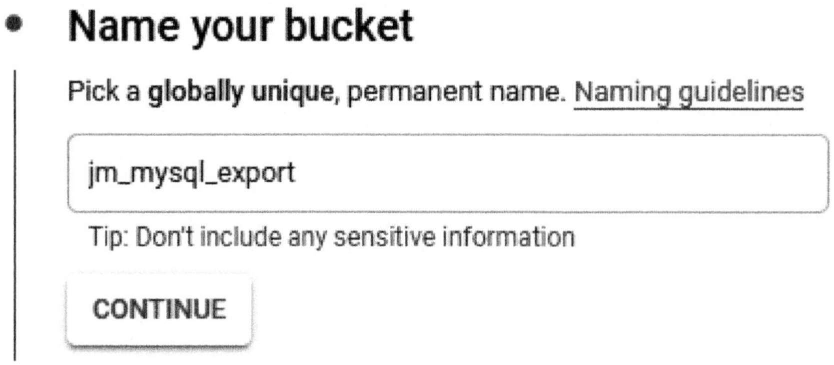

• Name your bucket

Pick a **globally unique**, permanent name. Naming guidelines

> jm_mysql_export

Tip: Don't include any sensitive information

CONTINUE

Figure 11.50 – Name our bucket

4. Choose where to store our data:

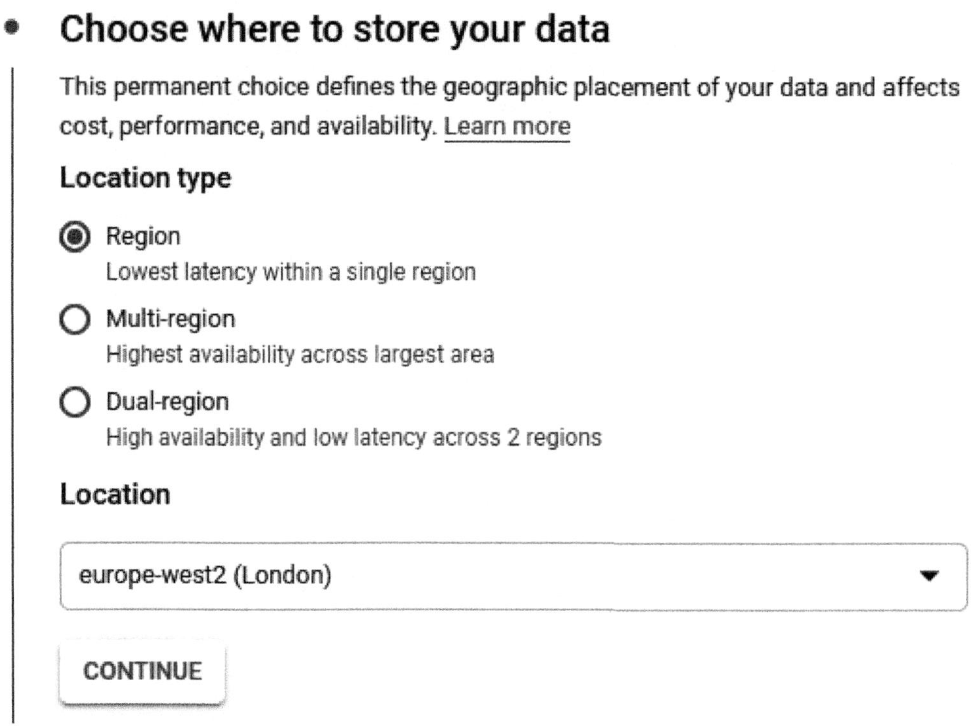

• Choose where to store your data

This permanent choice defines the geographic placement of your data and affects cost, performance, and availability. Learn more

Location type

◉ Region
Lowest latency within a single region

○ Multi-region
Highest availability across largest area

○ Dual-region
High availability and low latency across 2 regions

Location

> europe-west2 (London)   ▼

CONTINUE

Figure 11.51 – Bucket location

5. Click **CREATE**.

6. Our bucket will now be created, and we will see something like the following:

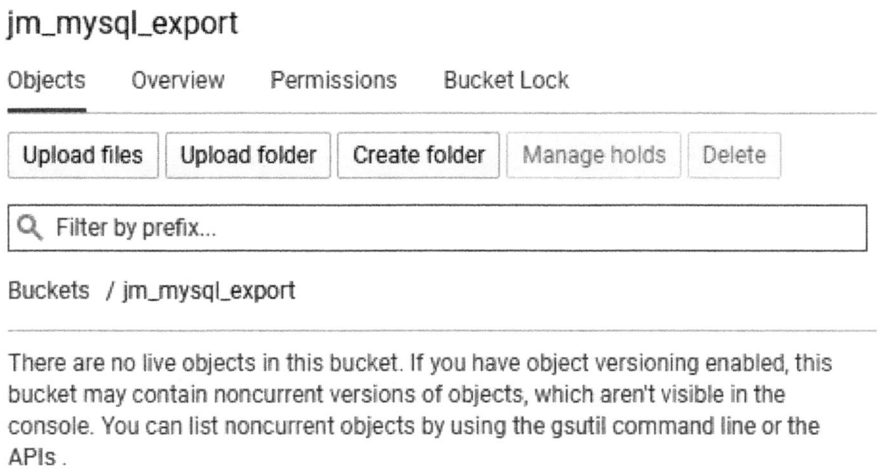

jm_mysql_export

Objects   Overview   Permissions   Bucket Lock

| Upload files | Upload folder | Create folder | Manage holds | Delete |

Q Filter by prefix...

Buckets / jm_mysql_export

There are no live objects in this bucket. If you have object versioning enabled, this bucket may contain noncurrent versions of objects, which aren't visible in the console. You can list noncurrent objects by using the gsutil command line or the APIs .

Figure 11.52 – Bucket details

To upload, we will need to use `gcloud` and `gsutil` in our MySQL virtual machine by performing the following steps:

1. Initialize `gcloud` using the `gcloud init` procedure we previously followed.

2. Log in to Google Cloud using the following command:

```
gcloud auth login
```

3. Open the link provided by using a web browser, and enter the authorization code generated from the web browser:

```
You are running on a Google Compute Engine virtual
machine.It is recommended that you use service accounts
for authentication.
You can run:
 $ gcloud config set account `ACCOUNT`
to switch accounts if necessary.
Your credentials may be visible to others with access
to this virtual machine. Are you sure you want to
authenticate with your personal account?
Do you want to continue (Y/n)? y
Go to the following link in your browser:
https://accounts.google.com/o/oauth2/auth?code_
challenge=2peIms-WI7b1BK1q-BgSNYooSuFUPIbnFezP
rYEfNdk&prompt=select_account&code_challenge_
method=S256&access_type=offline&redirect_
```

```
uri=urn%3Aietf%3Awg%3Aoauth%3A2.0%3Aoob&response_
type=code&client_id=32555940559.apps.googleusercontent.
com&scope=https%3A%2F%2Fwww.googleapis.
com%2Fauth%2Fuserinfo.email+https%3A%2F%2Fwww.googleapis.
com%2Fauth%2Fcloud-platform+https%3A%2F%2Fwww.googleapis.
com%2Fauth%2Fappengine.admin+https%3A%2F%2Fwww.
googleapis.com%2Fauth%2Fcompute+https%3A%2F%2Fwww.
googleapis.com%2Fauth%2Faccounts.reauth
```

```
Enter verification code:
```

4. Enter the following command, replacing <our_bucket_name> with the name chosen:

```
gsutil cp ./exported.sql gs://<our_bucket_name>/
```

5. A response like the following text will be generated, showing the file has been uploaded to our bucket:

```
Copying file://./exported.sql [Content-Type=application/
x-sql]...
```

```
/ [1 files][  6.2 KiB/  6.2 KiB]
```

```
Operation completed over 1 objects/6.2 KiB.
```

We are now ready to import the database into Cloud SQL.

Importing to Cloud SQL

Perform the following steps to import the database from our bucket into our Cloud SQL instance:

1. On the Cloud SQL **Overview** page, click **IMPORT**:

Figure 11.53 – IMPORT action

2. Browse to our file and click **Import**:

← Import data from Cloud Storage

Source

Choose the file you'd like to import data from
Browse for a file, or enter the path for one (bucket/folder/file). Make sure you have read access first. Learn more

| ☑ jm_mysql_export/exported.sql | Browse |

Indicate the format of the file you're importing

◉ SQL
A plain text file with a sequence of SQL commands, like the output of mysqldump

○ CSV
If your Cloud Storage file is a CSV file, select CSV. The CSV file should be a plain text file with one line per row and comma-separated fields.

Destination

Database ❓
Select a database only if your Cloud Storage import file does not specify any.

| banking ▼ |

When you import, a Cloud SQL service account will be granted read access to your Cloud Storage file and the bucket that contains it. This will be reflected in your permissions.

Figure 11.54 – Import the database

The import will now happen. After a few seconds or minutes, depending on the size of the import, we will get a notification that the import has been completed.

Cloud SQL versus Cloud Spanner

Importing data into Cloud Spanner is different from importing data into Cloud SQL. The reason for the difference is that Cloud Spanner is not a SQL database, it is a globally distributed and strongly consistent database service. This means it does not conform to any of the SQL standards.

The two simple approaches to importing data into Cloud Spanner from MySQL are the following:

- **CSV files**: We can export to CSV and import those CSV files into Cloud Spanner.

- **JDBC import tooling**: We can write a utility to read from MySQL and write to Cloud Spanner.

Because of the differences between Cloud Spanner and relational databases, there will often be differences between the schemas. This means that using Google Cloud Dataflow is the most common solution. Google Cloud Dataflow is the Google Cloud distributed **extract, transform, and load** (**ETL**) service. The focus of this book is modernizing applications rather than ETL, so we will leave that to a dedicated ETL book.

Summary

In this chapter, we have re-platformed our data layer. We migrated from using a virtual machine to manage our sessions to using Cloud Memorystore. We also migrated from using a virtual machine to host our relational database to using Cloud SQL. Making these changes provided us with the availability and scalability supplied by those services.

To fully make use of Cloud SQL, we switched from connecting directly to using Cloud SQL Proxy, which enhanced our security and availability stance by abstracting those concerns away from our application with regards to accessing our relational database.

Finally, we exported the database from our MySQL virtual machine and imported that into our Cloud SQL instance. In the real world, we would have data to migrate, so exploring how to do this was important.

In the next chapter, we will look at DevOps and how to automate building our application, provisioning the environment, and deploying the application in the Google Cloud.

12
Designing the Interim Architecture

We have now reached the point in this book where we will start to look at modernizing the software architecture of our application and refactoring it into microservices. There are a few more services we will be including in our infrastructure architecture to enable this modernization. The remaining chapters will examine implementing the changes we will discuss here. The focus of this chapter is to understand how our infrastructure and software architecture will be changed so that it's ready for the move to microservices. We will look at how utilizing Google Identity Platform and Google Cloud Pub/Sub impacts our infrastructure architecture, as well as how preparing for microservices impacts our software architecture.

In this chapter, we will cover the following topics:

- The infrastructure architecture
- The software architecture

The infrastructure architecture

In this section, we will review our infrastructure architecture as it currently stands, and then look at how we will need to adapt it to add support for Google Identity Platform and Google Cloud Pub/Sub.

Our starting point is the architecture we produced in *Chapter 11, Replatforming the Data Layer*:

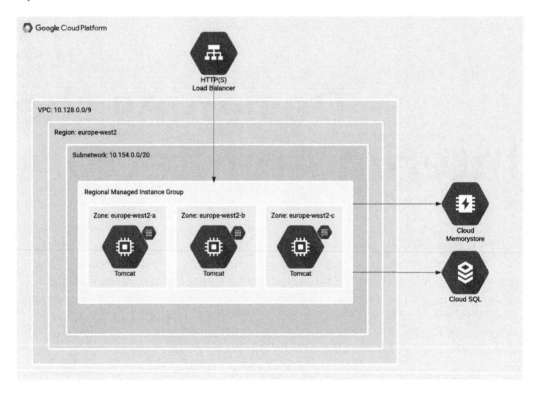

Figure 12.1 – Infrastructure architecture

In this architecture, we have made use of the following resources provided by Google Cloud:

- Relational Database Services using **Cloud SQL**
- Session-as-a-Service using **Cloud Memorystore**

- An auto-scaled cluster of Tomcat virtual machines using **Regional Managed Instance Groups**
- Load balancing using **HTTP(s) Load Balancer**
- Private networking using **Virtual Private Cloud (VPC)**
- Network security using **Firewall Rules**

This architecture has allowed us to reduce the operational overhead by replacing virtual machines with Google Cloud services. These services also addressed our concerns of availability, scalability, and network security.

With this, we have a robust basis for moving forward to start addressing more concerns. The specific concern we will be examining first is identity and authentication. Many traditional applications, such as our example application, handle those concerns themselves. We made use of the security modules provided by Spring Boot to handle identity and authentication. However, that means our application has that responsibility, so making changes to this can be difficult.

Let's examine a scenario. We have had a change request asking that users be given the ability to log in using their Google Identity or Facebook Identity. Normally, we would need to add all the code to handle this to our application.

This is where Identity Platform comes in.

Google Identity Platform

Google Identity Platform provides us with customer identity and authentication as a service. We only need to understand how to use Google Identity Platform rather than every protocol that's used by the various identity providers. This massively simplifies our code base and means that when we need to add a new identity provider, it is a matter of configuration and not development.

The identity providers that are currently supported are as follows:

- OpenID Connect
- SAML
- Google
- Twitter
- Facebook
- Microsoft

- LinkedIn
- Yahoo
- Play games
- GitHub
- Email/password
- Phone
- Anonymous

> **Important Note**
> Anonymous is a special identifier that's used for anonymous logins.

This is an impressive list of identity providers that we can use without having to code them. Adding Google Identity Platform to our infrastructure results in the following diagram:

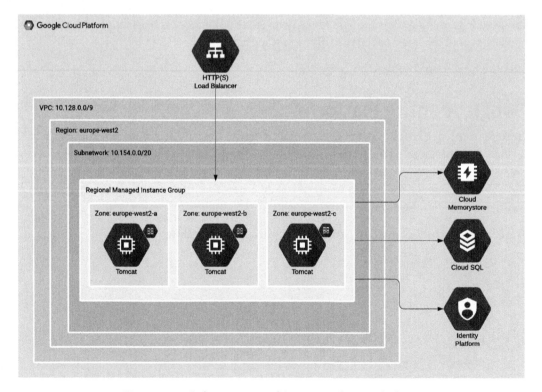

Figure 12.2 – Infrastructure architecture – Identity Platform

We will explore configuring Google Identify Platform and the changes that will be applied to our code base in more detail in *Chapter 14, Refactoring the Frontend and exposing REST Services*.

The next concern we will address is a consequence of moving to microservices, which we will address with Cloud Pub/Sub.

Cloud Pub/Sub

The microservices will need to communicate with each other, and we want to avoid direct dependencies that could easily result in a fragile architecture where the failure of one microservice could cause many others to fail. To prevent this situation and allow us to easily add behavior to another microservice, we will be applying domain events.

What are domain events? When a microservice has performed its task, it publishes an event to a topic. This event is a record that something has been done. Other microservices that are interested in the event subscribe to the topic and consume that event.

Let's look at an example. In our application, we want to transfer funds between two accounts. This can be accomplished by making a withdrawal from account A and a deposit to account B. However, we are talking about microservices here; is it good practice to have such a service deal with one account at a time? So, we invoke withdrawal on our service for account A and indicate that it is a transfer withdrawal. The details of the withdrawal are recorded in an event, which is then published. The microservice is listening for events and sees the transfer withdrawal. In response, it deposits the same amount to account B. This may seem complex at first glance, but it helps significantly with decoupling microservices, improving the reliability and extensibility of the solution.

Adding Cloud Pub/Sub to our architecture results in the following diagram:

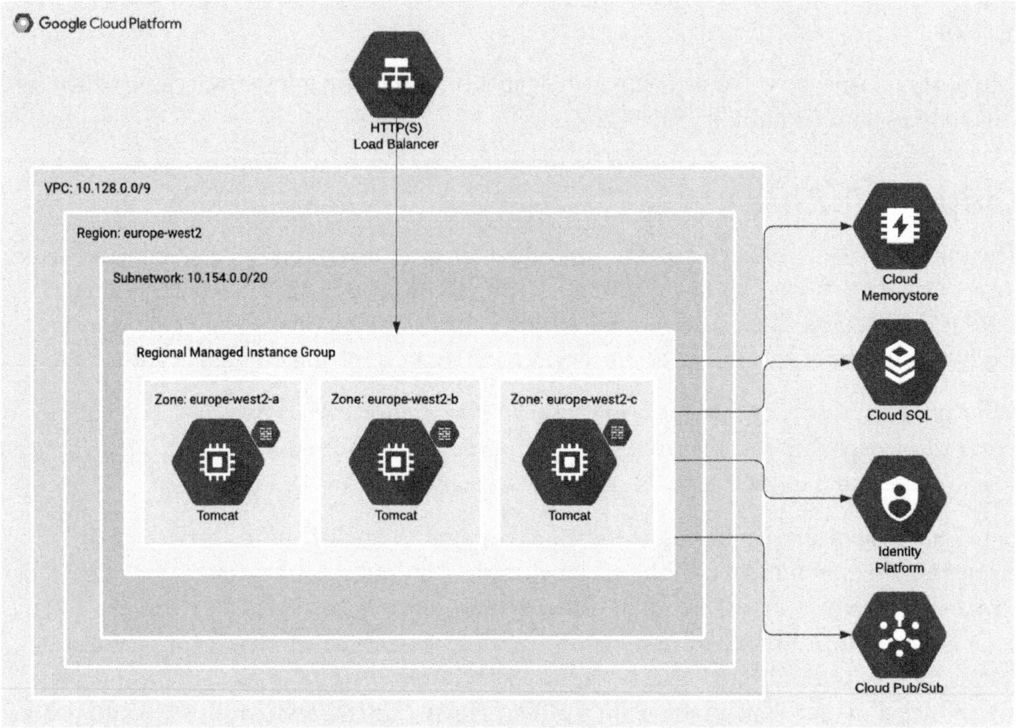

Figure 12.3 – Infrastructure architecture – Cloud Pub/Sub

We will explore using domain events and Cloud Pub/Sub in more detail in *Chapter 15, Handling Eventual Consistency with the Compensation Pattern*.

With that, we have finished looking at all the major changes we will make to our infrastructure architecture. Additional changes will be examined in *Chapter 16, Orchestrating your Application with Google Kubernetes Engine, Chapter 17, Going Serverless with Google App Engine*, and *Chapter 18, Future-Proofing Your App with Google Cloud Run*. Each of those chapters examines one of the options for hosting microservices in a Platform-as-a-Service or serverless environment.

We will now move on to examining the changes we need to make to our software architecture.

The software architecture

Before we start examining how our software architecture needs to change to become cloud native, we need to review the current software architecture.

The following diagram shows how the application is currently structured. This diagram has been simplified, so it does not show repositories or other supporting classes as these don't add much useful information to our refactoring efforts:

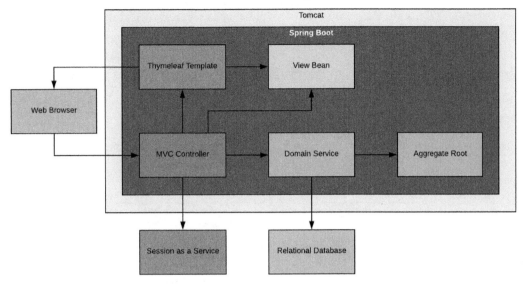

Figure 12.4 – Current software architecture (legacy)

To explain the architecture, we will run through how a request is processed. The user of a **Web Browser** navigates to the application. The URL used invokes an **MVC Controller**.

The **MVC Controller** checks if there is an existing session and if so, loads the state from **Session as a Service**. The **MVC Controller** then invokes a **Domain Service** with the information provided from the **Web Browser** and/or **Session**.

The **Domain Service** then retrieves an **Aggregate Root** from the **Relational Database** and invokes business logic on that **Aggregate Root**.

> **Important Note**
> Remember that an **Aggregate Root** is composed of *entities* and *value* objects.

If there are any state changes, the **Domain Service** then updates the **Relational Database** and returns a result to the **MVC Controller**.

Finally, the **MVC Controller** creates a **View Bean** (which can contain other beans) and hands over control to a **Thymeleaf Template**.

The **Thymeleaf Template** then renders an HTML page using the **View Bean** and returns that page to the **Web Browser**.

This is highly coupled (tightly bound) and deployed as a single unit in a WAR file. We will be refactoring over time to microservices that are independently buildable, testable, deployable, and scalable components.

However, we will not do this in one go. We will be taking an iterative and incremental approach to this refactoring.

Refactoring the frontend and exposing REST services

The first step in our refactoring process is to separate the user interface and expose the services of the application as REST services.

The following diagram shows that first step. This diagram has been simplified, so it does not show repositories or other supporting classes as these don't add much useful information to our refactoring efforts:

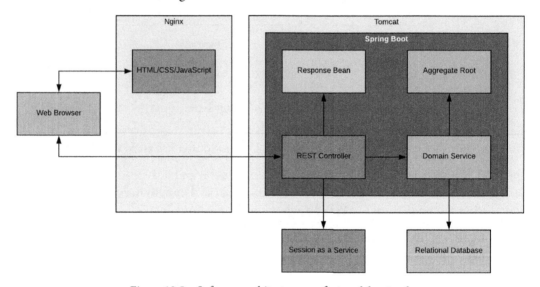

Figure 12.5 – Software architecture – refactored frontend

In this iteration of our software architecture, the user, at a **Web Browser**, navigates to the application. The URL that's used invokes a static HTML page hosted in Nginx.

The **Web Browser** renders this page, which contains all the view logic in it, using JavaScript and the AngularJS framework. The Web Browser executes the view logic and invokes the REST service exposed by the REST controller.

The REST controller acts almost exactly as it did in the previous iteration but instead of handing off control to **Thymeleaf**, it simply returns a **Response Bean**, which is converted by **Spring Boot** into a JSON representation of the bean and returned to the **Web Browser**.

The **Web Browser** then updates the document object model to populate it with the information returned from the REST service.

Important Note

Nginx acts as a reverse proxy when the URL is exposed by the REST controller. This is how we will initially implement the Strangler Pattern. Nginx will act as a facade for our deployment.

Separating the frontend and backend into two separately deployable units is what allows us to start refactoring the monolith into microservices. It is also the step that allows us to begin using Google Identity Platform.

Adding Google Identity Platform for identity and authentication

As we described earlier, instead of handling identity and authentication in our code base, we will use Google Identity Platform for those tasks.

The following diagram shows how Google Identity Platform fits into our architecture. This diagram has been simplified, so it does not show repositories or other supporting classes as these don't add much useful information to our refactoring efforts:

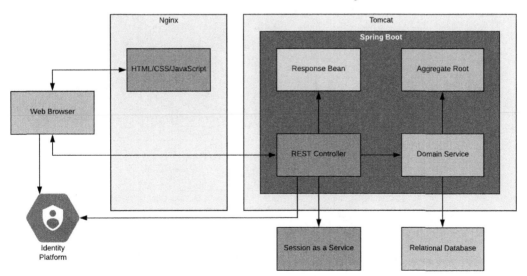

Figure 12.6 – Software architecture – Google Identity Platform

We will be using the Firebase SDK provided by Google, which simplifies identity and authentication for our user interface. Authentication will occur in the web browser rather than on the server, and we will pass a token from the browser to our REST services to prove we are authenticated and authorized to use the services. The REST controller will communicate with Google Identity Platform to verify that the user has authenticated.

Next, we will look at how our services can publish events and respond to events instead of just being invoked through a REST API.

Publishing events

The first change we will make is to enable publishing events from our application. The following diagram shows how this can be accomplished:

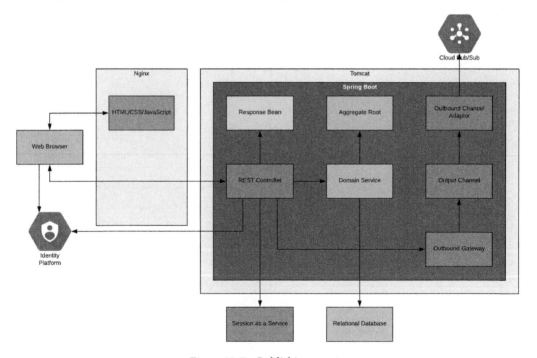

Figure 12.7 – Publishing events

The key elements we have added to our architecture are as follows:

- The **Outbound Channel Adaptor**: This is what converts between Spring Boot's internal Pub/Sub infrastructure and the Google Cloud Pub/Sub service. Using a different adaptor would allow us to connect to other Pub/Sub services without changing anything else.

- The **Outbound Channel**: This is the standard Spring Boot support for Pub/Sub.

- The **Outbound Gateway**: This is the component that places events onto the **Outbound Channel**.

We have placed the logic to allow outbound events to be published into the **REST Controller** rather than the **Domain Service**. This is because the **Domain Service** methods are transactional, and the **Relational Database** updates could be rolled back after all our code has been executed. Having this logic in the **REST Controller** allows us to make sure events are not falsely published, and that failure events can be published correctly.

The next section looks at how to respond to events.

Consuming events

As this section is all about responding to events, we have removed the elements that relate to the frontend from the diagram. Consuming events is not a frontend feature, so these elements would have complicated the following diagram:

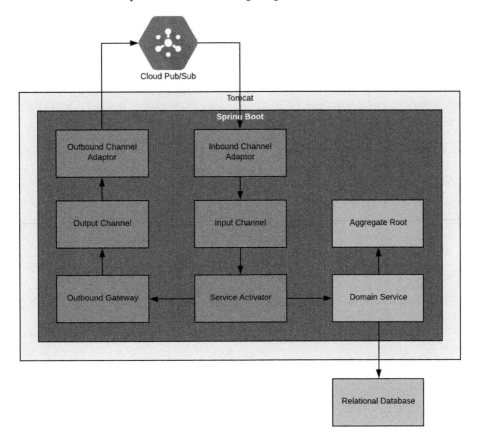

Figure 12.8 – Consuming events

In the preceding diagram, we have replaced the REST service with a **Service Activator**. This receives events from an input channel, which is populated by an inbound channel adaptor. This is the reverse sequence of the previous publishing scenario.

The key elements we have added to our architecture are as follows:

- The **Inbound Channel Adaptor**: This is what converts between Spring Boot's internal Pub/Sub infrastructure and the Google Pub/Sub service. Using a different adaptor would allow us to connect to other Pub/Sub services without changing anything else.

- The **Inbound Channel**: This is the standard Spring Boot support for Pub/Sub.

- The **Service Activator**: This is the component that receives events from the inbound channel and executes whatever logic we have decided on. Usually, we use this to invoke a **Domain Service** and then publish an event based on the response.

Our final step in refactoring our software architecture is to slice our application into microservices. This is not done in a single step but instead iteratively and incrementally.

Refactoring to microservices

As we mentioned previously, we will be using the Strangler pattern to refactor our application iteratively and incrementally to microservices. Our starting point was a single monolithic application.

The way we apply the Strangler pattern is to separate the frontend from the backend and place a facade between them. Doing so means that we can make changes to the backend without the frontend being aware of those changes. In our initial versions, we will make use of Nginx as a reverse proxy to act as this façade, as well as to host our static content (HTML/CSS/JavaScript). The following diagram illustrates the separation of the frontend and backend and the introduction of the façade:

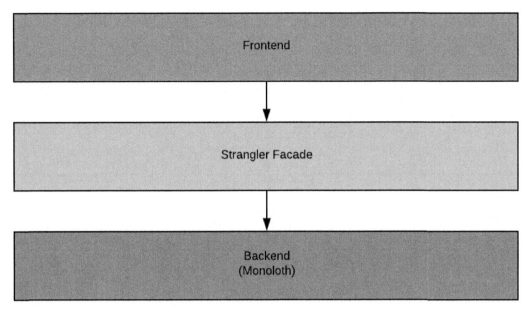

Figure 12.9 – Strangler facade

With the façade in place, we can start to separate the functionality we want to turn into microservices. As we do so, these microservices will be deployed and the **Backend (Monolith)** will begin to shrink, as illustrated in the following diagram:

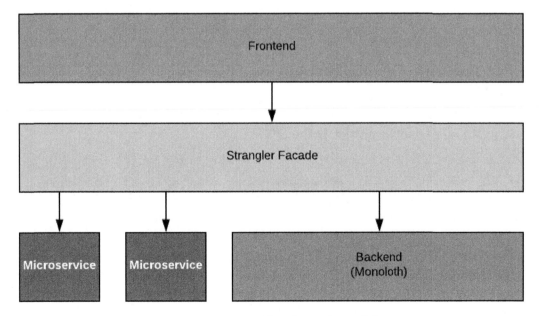

Figure 12.10 – Partially refactored monolith

Eventually, the monolith will have been completely removed, and only the microservices will remain:

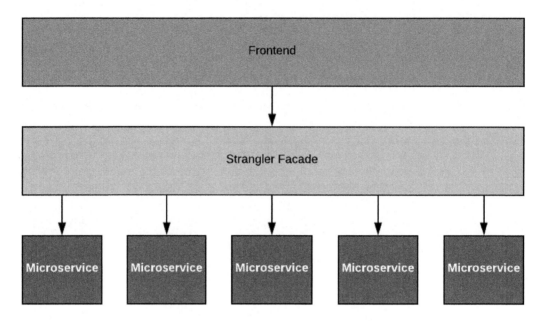

Figure 12.11 – Fully refactored to microservices

Now that we have looked at how we will be applying the Strangler pattern to refactor our application, we need to look at how to decide on the microservice boundaries.

Microservice boundaries

An important question to ask when working with microservices is, how big or small should they be? How can I define what should be a microservice? The approach we will be taking is based on **domain-driven design (DDD)**.

DDD is an approach to software engineering put forward by *Eric Evans* in his book of the same name. It is often explained as object-orientation done well. When using this approach, there are various building blocks we can use, all of which we have explained previously, and a key one is the **Aggregate Root**, which is made up of one or more *entities* (with one being the root) and zero or more *value* objects.

A key thing here is that the state of all the objects that comprise the Aggregate Root change together in a transaction. They help define the boundaries of a transaction. There are, of course, exceptions but over 95% of the time, a transaction will address a single Aggregate Root instance. We will explain how to handle the remaining 5% in *Chapter 15, Handling Eventual Consistency with the Compensation Pattern.*

Closely related to our Aggregate Root is another class called a Domain Service. A Domain Service acts on a specific Aggregate Root. As an example, if we have a class called Account as an Aggregate Root, then our Domain Service class would be called AccountService. This service orchestrates retrieving the Aggregate Root from a Repository (the abstraction of a persistent store), invoking the business logic methods of the Aggregate Root, and updating the Repository with the new state of the Aggregate Root.

We have identified what existing classes in our application a microservice would consist of using Aggregate Roots to define the boundary. All that remains is to put a Controller in place. We will follow the same naming conventions that we have for the Account service; this would be the AccountController. This basic structure and boundary of a microservice are illustrated in the following diagram:

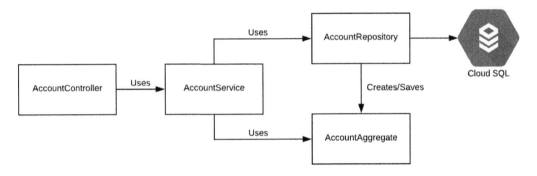

Figure 12.12 – Microservice structure

In the preceding diagram, we can see how the classes interact. To summarize, we have the following:

- **AccountController**: This is the entry point and boundary of our service. The purpose is to separate the different concerns. The controller handles the communication aspects of the service, including how it is invoked.

- **AccountService**: This is our orchestrator. It interacts with the **AccountRepository** to obtain and store instances of our **AccountAggregate**.

- **AccountRepository**: This is the layer of abstraction that handles communication with the persistent store to create, read, update, and delete information in the database. It is our object-relational mapping.

- **AccountAggregate**: This represents the thing that our service manages. In this case, this is a bank account.

In this section, we learned how to scope microservices and define boundaries based on DDD. This approach to defining boundaries helps us ensure that the services are not too big that they're monolithic, and not too small that they have excessive interactions.

Summary

In this chapter, we examined our infrastructure architecture and updated it to include Google Identity Platform. This allows us to offload identity and authentication from our code base and make use of an *as-a-service* offering from Google. We also updated it to include Google Cloud Pub/Sub to support the use of domain events, which we will examine more closely in *Chapter 15, Handling Eventual Consistency with the Compensation Pattern*.

We then examined our software architecture and looked at how we will refactor the application in the upcoming chapters.

In the next chapter, we will learn how to refactor the frontend and expose the backend with REST services.

13
Refactoring to Microservices

In this chapter, we will examine the packaging structure of our application and analyze how we can change that packaging structure to allow us to deploy our microservices as separate components. So far, the only deployment separation we have accomplished is separating the frontend from the backend. Using our analysis, we will restructure and repackage our code and move from WAR files to JAR files, finishing by wrapping our deployments in Docker containers, ready to be deployed in Google Kubernetes Engine, Google App Engine (Flexible), or Google Cloud Run.

In this chapter, we will cover the following topics:

- Analyzing the structure of the application backend
- Refactoring into microservices
- Refactoring the database
- The web frontend
- The Strangler Pattern revisited
- Containerizing the deployment units with Docker

Technical requirements

The code files for this chapter are available here: `https://github.com/PacktPublishing/Modernizing-Applications-with-Google-Cloud-Platform/tree/master/Chapter%2013`.

Analyzing the structure of the application backend

In this section, we will be analyzing the packaging structure and dependencies of our application backend to decide what code refactoring is needed to restructure and repackage so that a microservice only contains the interfaces and classes it needs. It would be a rare application that can simply be repackaged without some code changes being necessary.

The dependency structure between the components of our application is shown in the following diagram:

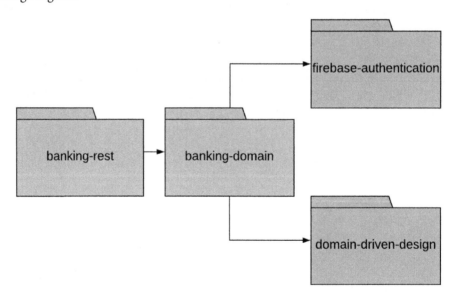

Figure 13.1 – Component dependencies (legacy)

The preceding diagram shows the WAR file **banking-rest**, which as well as providing its own classes contains the JAR files for **banking-domain**, **domain-driven-design**, and **firebase-authentication**. The last two of those are supporting JAR files and not specific to any service, so each microservice will have a copy of **domain-driven-design** and **firebase-authentication**. Our target is to separate **banking-rest** and **account-domain** into specific microservices, as shown in the following diagram:

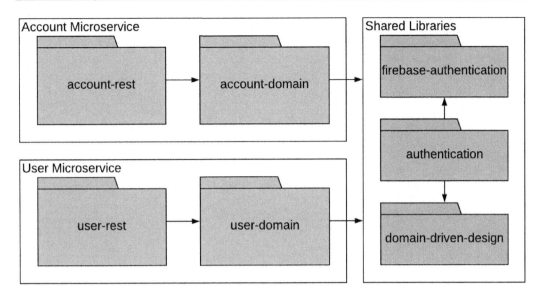

Figure 13.2 – Component dependencies (microservice)

The preceding separation looks straightforward, but the devil is in the details, so let's take a closer look at **banking-rest** and **banking-domain** in the following diagram:

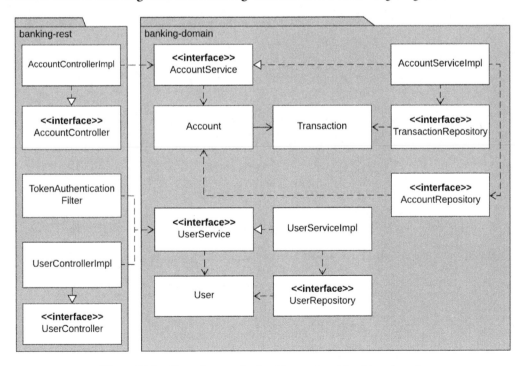

Figure 13.3 – Class diagram for banking-rest and banking-domain

In the preceding diagram, we can start to see a problem. All our microservices will need authentication but **UserService** is fulfilling two purposes, providing user profile functionality and authentication functionality. In the next section, we will learn how to refactor into two separate microservices and address the preceding problem.

Refactoring into microservices

The first thing we need to address is the multiple responsibilities of **UserService**. Each service should have one responsibility and **UserService** is providing both authentication functionality and user profile functionality. We can refactor like so:

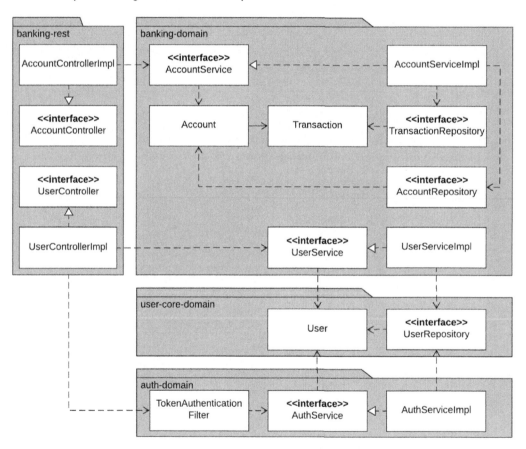

Figure 13.4 – Refactored to authentication and user services

What we have done in the preceding diagram is create two new JAR files called **user-core-domain** and **auth-domain**. We separated the common elements between **UserService** and **AuthService** into **user-core-domain**, placed the authentication capabilities that had previously been provided by **UserService** into **AuthService**, and moved **TokenAuthenticationFilter** into the **auth-domain** JAR file. This refactoring and repackaging provide much more flexibility than including all the code in each service – they just make use of a JAR file that provides the needed authentication.

The account microservice will now be structured as follows:

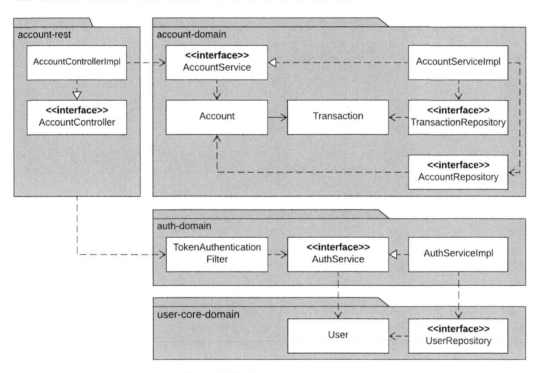

Figure 13.5 – Account microservice

In the preceding diagram, we can see that this account microservice is well organized and has a clear separation between the business functionality provided by **account-domain** and the authentication functionality provided by **auth-domain**.

The user microservice will be structured as follows:

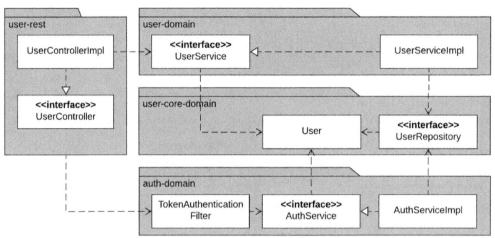

Figure 13.6 – User microservice

In the preceding diagram, we can once again see the clear separation of concerns between the business functionality provided by **user-domain** and the authentication functionality provided by **auth-domain**.

The refactored code can be found in this book's GitHub repository, in the Chapter 13 folder: https://github.com/PacktPublishing/Modernizing-Applications-with-Google-Cloud-Platform/tree/master/Chapter%20 13.

When refactoring from **banking-domain** into **account-domain**, **user-domain**, and **auth-domain**, we also took the opportunity to remove classes that are no longer required because we are using firebase authentication instead of handling all the authentication, registration, and other self-service tasks ourselves. Our refactoring of **banking-legacy-rest** into **account-rest** and **user-rest** was much simpler but required some additional changes to enable each microservice to have its own database, as well as to be able to use the user database for authentication. We will cover that in the next section.

Refactoring the database

A key concept of microservices is that they are independent of each other. This means that they should have separate databases. However, we would not want each microservice to have a copy of the tables used for authentication as this would lead to an unhealthy quantity of duplicated data. It would also lead to the risk of the authentication data getting out of sync. For this reason, we need a way of using two separate databases in a single microservice. These are the database for the **service** and the database for **authentication**.

Fortunately, there is a way to accomplish this using Spring Boot by making changes only to our configuration code and not our implementation code.

Our configuration for persistence was as follows:

```
@Configuration
@EnableJpaRepositories(
basePackages = {"uk.me.jasonmarston.domain.repository"})
@EnableTransactionManagement
public class PersistenceConfig {
}
```

The preceding configuration class simply enabled Spring Boot JPA support in Spring Boot, specified where the repository interface could be found, and enabled transactions. What we need to do is replace the preceding class with two new classes to configure the two databases.

Let's examine the `UserPersistenceConfig` class:

```
@Configuration
@EnableJpaRepositories(
basePackages = {"uk.me.jasonmarston.domain.user.repository"},
entityManagerFactoryRef = "userEntityManagerFactory",
transactionManagerRef = "userTransactionManager")
@EnableTransactionManagement
public class UserPersistenceConfig {
@Autowired
private Environment env;

...

}
```

In the preceding configuration class, we have again enabled JPA support in Spring Boot and enabled transactions. This time, when we specified where the repository interfaces could be found, we were more specific and provided the location for the `UserRepository` interface. We also provided references to two beans that will be defined in this class: `userEntityManagerFactory` and `userTransactionManager`. We will get to these shortly.

The next thing we need to do is declare our `userDataSource`, as follows:

```
@Primary
@Bean(name = "userDataSource")
@ConfigurationProperties(prefix = "spring.datasource")
public DataSource userDataSource() {
return DataSourceBuilder.create().build();
}
```

Note that when declaring the preceding bean, we provided the `@ConfigurationProperties` annotation and specified that the properties found in `application.properties` that apply to this bean are the ones that start with `spring.datasource`. We also applied the `@Primary` annotation to indicate that this is the primary `DataSource` for Spring Boot, as Spring Boot always requires a primary `DataSource`.

Next, we will declare our `userEntityManagerFactory` bean, as follows:

```
@Primary
@Bean(name = "userEntityManagerFactory")
public LocalContainerEntityManagerFactoryBean
userEntityManagerFactory(EntityManagerFactoryBuilder builder) {
Map<String, Object> properties = new HashMap<>();
properties.put("hibernate.hbm2ddl.auto", env.
getProperty("spring.jpa.hibernate.ddl-auto"));
properties.put("hibernate.dialect", env.getProperty("spring.
jpa.properties.hibernate.dialect"));
properties.put("hibernate.implicit_naming_strategy", env.
getProperty("spring.jpa.hibernate.naming_strategy"));

return builder
.dataSource(userDataSource())
.packages(User.class, Authority.class)
.properties(properties)
.build();
}
```

There are a few things to unpack in the preceding code. Firstly, it makes use of the userDataSource bean we declared previously since an EntityManagerFactory must be linked to a DataSource. Secondly, rather than explicitly specifying packages, we listed the classes that are annotated with @Entity (Spring Boot will deduce the package from the class). Thirdly, we provided properties for EntityManagerFactory by mapping properties from our application.properties file into the ones required for a manually configured EntityManagerFactory. Finally, we declared this as the primary EntityManagerFactory by applying the @Primary annotation for the same reason we did with our userDataSource bean.

> **Important Note**
>
> The hibernate.hbm2ddl.auto property is needed if we want Spring Boot to automatically create and update the tables in our new databases. In production, this would not be necessary or a wise thing to do.

Finally, we will declare our userTransactionManager bean, as follows:

```
@Primary
@Bean(name = "userTransactionManager")
public PlatformTransactionManager userTransactionManager(
final @Qualifier("userEntityManagerFactory")
LocalContainerEntityManagerFactoryBean
userEntityManagerFactory) {
return new JpaTransactionManager(userEntityManagerFactory.
getObject());
}
```

The method in the preceding code takes a LocalContainerEntityManagerFactoryBean as a parameter. We apply the @Qualifier annotation to the parameter to make sure our userEntityManagerFactory is injected by Spring Boot. Then, we create and return JpaTransactionManager, passing userEntityManagerFactory into the constructor. Once again, this bean is annotated with the @Primary annotation as Spring Boot needs a primary transaction manager.

Now, let's move on to the AccountPersistenceConfig class, as follows:

```
@Configuration
@EnableJpaRepositories(
basePackages = {"uk.me.jasonmarston.domain.account.
repository"},
```

```
entityManagerFactoryRef = "accountEntityManagerFactory",

transactionManagerRef = "accountTransactionManager")

@EnableTransactionManagement

public class AccountPersistenceConfig {

@Autowired

private Environment env;

...

}
```

The preceding code is almost identical to the `UserPersistenceConfig` class. The differences shown previously are simply the location of the repository and the names of the beans to be used for `EntityManagerFactory` and `TransactionManager`.

The declaration of the three beans in this class are also almost identical to the ones in the `UserPersistenceConfig` class, so we will simply examine the differences, starting with `accountDataSource`:

```
@Bean(name = "accountDataSource")

@ConfigurationProperties(prefix="spring.account-datasource")

public DataSource accountDataSource() {

return DataSourceBuilder.create().build();

}
```

The differences here are the bean's name and the prefix for the configuration properties. We must have a separate set of configuration properties for `DataSource` as it connects to a separate database, so it will have a different URL, user ID, and password.

The differences in `accountEntityManagerFactory` are as follows:

```
@Bean(name = "accountEntityManagerFactory")

public LocalContainerEntityManagerFactoryBean
accountEntityManagerFactory(EntityManagerFactoryBuilder
builder) {

...

return builder

.dataSource(accountDataSource())

.packages(Account.class, Transaction.class)

.properties(properties)

.build();

}
```

In this case, we have named the bean `accountEntityManagerFactory`, we are using `accountDataSource` rather than `userDataSource`, and we are identifying the packages to scan by passing in the `Account` and `Transaction` classes.

We will finish by looking at the `accountTransactionManager` bean:

```
@Bean(name = "accountTransactionManager")
public PlatformTransactionManager accountTransactionManager(
final @Qualifier("accountEntityManagerFactory")
LocalContainerEntityManagerFactoryBean
accountEntityManagerFactory) {
return new JpaTransactionManager(accountEntityManagerFactory.
getObject());
}
```

Again, the differences here are in the naming and references. Our bean is called `accountTransactionManager` and it uses the `accountEntityManagerFactory` bean.

The remaining difference is that none of the beans have the `@Primary` annotation as they are secondary rather than primary and we can only have one set of primary beans.

The last change we need to make is to `application.properties`, as follows:

```
# Primary datasource (User DataSource)
spring.datasource.jdbcUrl = ${USER_DATASOURCE_URL}
spring.datasource.username = ${USER_DATASOURCE_USERNAME}
spring.datasource.password = ${USER_DATASOURCE_PASSWORD}
spring.datasource.driverClassName=com.mysql.jdbc.Driver


# Account DataSource
spring.account-datasource.jdbcUrl = ${ACCOUNT_DATASOURCE_URL}
spring.account-datasource.username = ${ACCOUNT_DATASOURCE_
USERNAME}
spring.account-datasource.password = ${ACCOUNT_DATASOURCE_
PASSWORD}
spring.account-datasource.driverClassName=com.mysql.jdbc.Driver
```

The preceding changes provide the configuration needed for our separate databases.

We will need to create these databases and users and grant each user access to the appropriate database in **Google Cloud SQL** using the MySQL command-line tooling, as we covered in *Chapter 11, Re-platforming the Data Layer*.

Now that we have learned how the backend is refactored into microservices, we can move on and look at what changes are needed in the frontend.

The web frontend

The changes needed in the frontend are minimal and constrained to the two service modules we create to wrap around the REST endpoints. We simply remove banking/ from the start of all the relative URLs. While this is not strictly necessary, it does remove the suggestion that there is some sort of hierarchy in place with the REST services – they are simply endpoints.

Now, you may be wondering, if we are going to deploy the Spring Boot applications potentially on separate hosts, but definitely as separate deployment units, how do those URLs relative to the host of our frontend get mapped to those backend services?

As you will see in the next section, we will be hosting the frontend in NGINX, which is a high-performance web server and reverse proxy. We will be making use of the reverse proxy's functionality to map those URLs to the actual URLs and proxy the requests. Precisely how this will be implemented will depend on which platform we chose for deployment; that is, either **Google Kubernetes Engine**, **Google App Engine (Flexible)**, or **Google Cloud Run**.

Whichever platform we use, the result will be updating the /etc/NGINX/conf.d/ default.conf configuration file. The updated file will look something like this:

```
server {
    listen       80;
    server_name localhost;

    location / {
        root /usr/share/NGINX/html;
        index index.html;
    }

    location /account {
        proxy_pass http://<account_host_mapping>:8080
    }
```

```
location /user {
    proxy_pass http://<user_host_mapping>:8080
}
}
```

The preceding configuration tells NGINX that it should listen on port 80, serve web content from /user/share/NGINX/html by default, proxy to the account microservice on URLs starting with /account, and to the user microservice on URLs starting with /user.

The values for <account_host_mapping> and <user_host_mapping> will depend on the deployment option selected, as will the method for updating this file.

This mapping of local URLs and proxying to the actual microservices is how we implement the Strangler Facade from the Strangler Pattern. If we still had most of the service endpoints in a monolith, we would use the appropriate proxy statements to send all the requests, not split them into microservices and send them to the original monolith. Now, we will look a little more closely at the Strangler Pattern.

The Strangler Pattern revisited

We looked at the **Strangler Pattern** in *Chapter 12*, *Designing the Interim Architecture*. In that chapter, we looked at the different stages in the refactoring journey of using the Strangler Pattern. The following diagram shows the start of our journey:

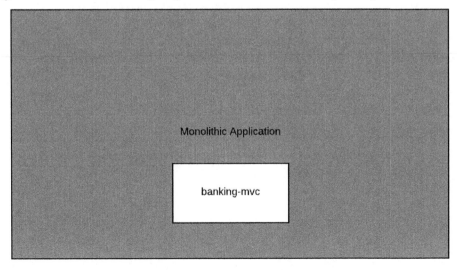

Figure 13.7 – Monolithic application

In the preceding diagram, we have the initial state with no Strangler Facade in play. The entire application is in our **banking-mvc** project, which is deployed as a JAR or WAR file.

The following diagram shows the first steps of refactoring toward microservices by breaking out the frontend from the backend:

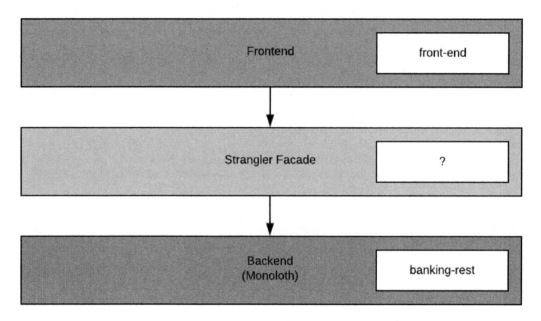

Figure 13.8 – Initial Strangler stage

In the preceding diagram, we have our frontend, which is our **front-end** project that holds all the static content for our web application. These are the stylesheets, JavaScript, HTML, and images needed for the user interface. We also have our backend, which is our **banking-rest** project, which contains all the rest services and domain classes for our banking application. Between the two, we have our Strangler Facade, which means that as we make changes and separate the microservices, the frontend will be completely unaware of these changes. We will examine the options for the Strangler Facade in the next few sections.

In the following diagram, we can see the final stage of our refactoring, which is using the Strangler Pattern and applying the Strangler Facade:

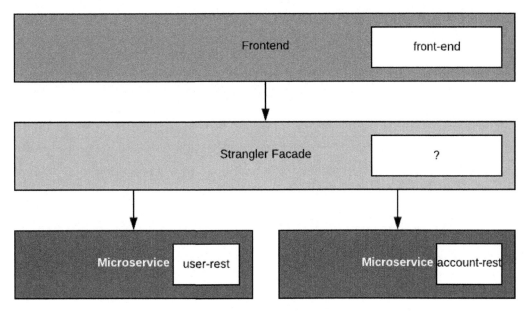

Figure 13.9 – Final Strangler stage

In the preceding diagram, our backend monolith of **banking-rest** has been replaced with two microservices, **user-rest** and **account-rest**. **front-end** is completely unaware of the change as the backend microservices and before that, the backend monolith is behind the Strangler Facade.

We will look at three options regarding how we will implement the Strangler Facade. The options we will examine are as follows:

- Google HTTP(s) Load Balancer Routing
- Google App Engine Dispatcher
- Apigee API Manager

In the next few sections, we will take a brief look at each of the options, starting with Google HTTP(s) Load Balancer Routing.

Google HTTP(S) Load Balancer Routing

With **Google HTTP(S) Load Balancer** in Google Cloud, we can make use of content-based load balancing, which routes requests to backend services based on the path of the HTTP(S) request. This is an extremely simple and flexible approach to implementing a Strangler Facade that works with both **Google Compute Engine** and **Google Kubernetes Engine**. We define a set of rules, and each rule says that if the URL matches this pattern, send the request to that service. We will be using this approach in *Chapter 16, Orchestrating Your Application with Google Kubernetes Engine*.

This approach does not work for **Google App Engine**, so we need to look at **Google App Engine Dispatcher**, which is covered in the next section.

Google App Engine Dispatcher

Unsurprisingly, **Google App Engine Dispatcher** works very much like the **HTTP(S) Load Balancer** approach. This solution is restricted to only being used with **Google App Engine** and maps our HTTP(S) URL paths to services deployed in **Google App Engine**. We define a set of rules, and each rule says that if the URL matches this pattern, send the request to that service. We will be using this approach in *Chapter 17, Going Serverless with Google App Engine*.

This just leaves us with the final common approach, **Apigee**, which is covered in the next section.

Apigee API Manager

The **Apigee** approach is where you use the API Gateway features of Apigee. This is usually done if you expect to have multiple applications exposing APIs rather than just a few APIs in a single application. API management solutions such as Apigee don't just offer an API Gateway, but also provide support for applying policies to transform, secure, and rate limit API usage. It also offers monitoring and development portal support. This is a much richer set of features than is needed for a simple application of the **Strangler Facade**, and it costs a significant amount more than using the other features. For these reasons, we will not use Apigee in this book. Instead, we will note that it is a valid solution and a great one when we are dealing with more than one application.

We will now learn how we can containerize our deployment units using Docker and add them to **Google Cloud Build**.

Containerizing the deployment units with Docker

The three deployment options we will be studying in the final three chapters of this book are **Google Kubernetes Engine**, **Google App Engine (Flexible)**, and **Google Cloud Run**. All these options are container-based, so we need to understand how to define a Docker image, how to build that image, and how to push it into a container registry.

We will begin by examining how we do this for our **front-end** project. The following source will be placed in a file called Dockerfile, at the root of our frontend project:

```
FROM NGINX:1.17.10-alpine
COPY WebContent /usr/share/NGINX/html
EXPOSE 80
```

The preceding code starts by declaring our image. This will build on top of the NGINX version 1.17.10-alpine image, which can be found in the Docker registry. We then copy our web content into the directory NGINX uses to serve web content, specifically /usr/share/NGINX/html. We finish by declaring that the container will expose a service on port 80.

It is important to understand that Docker images are made up of layers. Each layer adds on top of the previous layer and when taken together, they form an entire image. In the preceding file, the FROM, COPY, and EXPOSE commands define a layer in the Docker image. This layering improves deployment times as only changed layers need to be pushed to the container registry and transferred to the deployment environment.

So, how do we get from a Dockerfile to a Docker image and have that pushed to a container registry? We will be using **Google Cloud Build** for this, as shown in the following cloudBuild.yaml file:

```yaml
steps:
- name: 'gcr.io/cloud-builders/docker'
  args: ['build', '-t', 'gcr.io/$PROJECT_ID/front-end', '.']
  dir: 'front-end'
- name: 'gcr.io/cloud-builders/docker'
  args: ['push', 'gcr.io/$PROJECT_ID/front-end']
  dir: 'front-end'
```

In the preceding `cloudBuild.yaml` file, we are making use of the Docker cloud builder. The build is broken into two steps. The first step builds our image and tags it with `gcr.io/$PROJECT_ID/front-end`. The `$PROJECT_ID` part of the tag is a substitution variable and is provided by Google Cloud Build to identify which project the build is running in. It will be replaced by the actual project ID at build time. The second step pushes our newly built and tagged image to the **Google Container Registry** using that tag.

Now, let's look at the Dockerfile for our `user-rest` project. The `account-rest` project follows the same pattern, so we will not examine that project here:

```
FROM openjdk:8-jdk
ARG JAR_FILE=build/libs/user-rest-*.jar
COPY ${JAR_FILE} app.jar
RUN mkdir /credentials
EXPOSE 8080
ENTRYPOINT ["java","-jar","/app.jar"]
```

This time, we are using `openjdk` version 8-jdk as the base image we will build upon. We create an `ARG`, which is a variable to be used in our build of the Docker image. The `JAR_FILE` variable is set to the name of our JAR file from the `gradle` build. The name of this JAR includes the version number, which is why we used a wildcard in the name. The next statement copies the JAR file into our image and renames it `app.jar`. We then create a folder called `/credentials`, which will be used as a mount point later to expose the credential files for our service accounts. We declare that the service will be exposed on port `8080` and finally set the `ENTRYPOINT` property of our container to `java -jar /app.jar`. This tells the container that when it is started, this is the command that will be executed.

We will cover how the credential files and the environment variables get injected into our container in each of the final three chapters, as this depends on the deployment choices we make.

Now, let's turn our attention to the `cloudBuild.yaml` file for our `user-rest` project:

```
steps:
- name: 'gcr.io/cloud-builders/gradle'
  args: ['bootJar']
  env:
    - 'artifactory_contextUrl=${_ARTIFACTORY_URL}'
    - 'artifactory_password=${_ARTIFACTORY_PASSWORD}'
```

```
    - 'artifactory_user=${_ARTIFACTORY_USER}'
  dir: 'user-rest'
- name: 'gcr.io/cloud-builders/docker'
  args: ['build', '-t', 'gcr.io/$PROJECT_ID/user-rest', '.']
  dir: 'user-rest'
- name: 'gcr.io/cloud-builders/docker'
  args: ['push', 'gcr.io/$PROJECT_ID/user-rest']
  dir: 'user-rest'
```

The preceding cloudBuild.yaml file has three build steps. The first step uses the Gradle Cloud Builder and is set up mostly the same as what we had previously in our banking-legacy-rest project. The major difference in this step from our previous one is that we are using the bootJar task rather than the bootWar task. This is because we are building a standalone Spring Boot application as a JAR file with an embedded servlet container, rather than a WAR file to be deployed into a servlet container. The final two tasks build our image and push it to the **Google Container Registry**, as we did with the front-end project.

One of the great things about using **Google Cloud Build** is that we don't have to install and configure Docker or other tools needed to perform builds in our local environment, but instead use the secure environments provided by Google, which maintain those tools and install them.

To enable automation for all this, we will need to create new build triggers for our new projects – account-rest, account-domain, user-rest, user-domain, user-core-domain, and auth-domain – and delete the triggers for the old projects; that is, banking-legacy-rest and banking-domain. Then, we must replace our current local Git repository for our **Cloud Source Repository** with the projects from the Chapter 13 folder of this book's GitHub repository and then add, commit, and push all the changes (including deletions).

With that, we have learned how to define a Docker image, how to build that image, and how to push it to **Google Container Registry** using **Google Cloud Build**.

Summary

In this chapter, we examined the packaging structure of our application and analyzed the services and dependencies in our `banking-legacy-rest` and `banking-domain` projects. We realized that `UserService` was not following the single responsibility principle and had two distinct responsibilities: user profiles and authentication.

Based on this, we refactored the authentication responsibilities of `UserService` in `AuthService`, placing `AuthService` into its own project, along with `TokenAuthenticationFilter`. As both `UserService` and `AuthService` depend on `User` and `UserRepository`, we also placed `User` and `UserRepository` into their own project called `user-core-domain`. This allowed us to separate our concerns into two microservices, `user-rest` and `account-rest`. We then learned how to use two separate databases in our microservices to enable us to have a separate database for each microservice, as well as a shared database for authentication. Finally, we learned how to define container images using a Dockerfile, build the image using **Google Cloud Build**, and push the image to **Google Container Registry** using **Google Cloud Build**.

In the next chapter, we will learn how to refactor the frontend and expose the backend with REST services

Section 4: Refactoring the Application on Cloud-Native/PaaS and Serverless in Google Cloud

On completion of *Section 4*, you will have gained hands-on experience of using the options available to modernize your existing on-premises applications and migrating them to be cloud native inGoogle Cloud using the compute options in Google Cloud that supports containers including serverless - GKE, GAE and Cloud Run. You will refine the application to function as a microservice and serverless using relevant services from Google Cloud such as GAE, GKE and Google Cloud.

This part of the book comprises the following chapters:

14
Refactoring the Frontend and Exposing REST Services

We have been focusing on the infrastructure in the first part of this book. We examined how to rehost and re-platform our application, gaining some of the benefits of moving to the cloud without making major changes to the application itself.

We will now start to refactor our application toward microservices. To do this, we will need to separate out the frontend of the application so that it can be deployed separately when we move to microservices and expose the business logic to the frontend as **REpresentational State Transfer (REST)** services. We will also learn how to change the application to delegate identity and authentication to **Google Cloud** Identity Platform and use that to secure both the frontend and the REST services.

In this chapter, we will cover the following topics:

- Creating REST controllers
- Creating an AngularJS web frontend
- Authenticating in the web frontend
- Validating the authentication token in the REST controllers

Technical requirements

The code file for this chapter can be found here: `https://github.com/PacktPublishing/Modernizing-Applications-with-Google-Cloud-Platform/tree/master/Chapter%2014`.

Creating REST controllers

Before we create the frontend of our refactored application, we need to create controllers to expose our functionality as REST/**JavaScript Object Notation (JSON)** services. To accomplish this, we have created a new project called `banking-rest`. This lays the foundation for refactoring to microservices.

Let's examine our account controller. We have an interface called `AccountController`, as shown in the following code block:

AccountController.java

```java
public interface AccountController {
    ResponseEntity<?> depositFunds(final UUID id, final
DepositBean deposit, final User user);
    ResponseEntity<?> getAccount(final UUID id, final User
user);
    ResponseEntity<?> getAccounts(final User user);
    ResponseEntity<?> getBalance(final UUID id, final User
user);
    ResponseEntity<?> getDeposit(final UUID accountId, final
UUID id, final User user);
    ResponseEntity<?> getDeposits(final UUID id, final User
user);
    ResponseEntity<?> getTransaction(final UUID accountId,
final UUID id, final User user);
```

```
    ResponseEntity<?> getTransactions(final UUID id, final
User user);
    ResponseEntity<?> getWithdrawal(final UUID accountId,
final UUID id, final User user);
    ResponseEntity<?> getWithdrawals(final UUID id, final User
user);
    ResponseEntity<?> openAccount(final AccountNameBean
accountNameBean, final User user);
    ResponseEntity<?> withdrawFunds(final UUID id, final
WithdrawalBean withdrawal, final User user);
}
```

We have defined a contract for each of the operations we will be exposing as REST/JSON endpoints with this controller interface. When we examine an individual method declaration such as `withdrawFunds` in the preceding source code, we see that it returns a `ResponseEntity<?>` object. The question mark means we do not know at this point what the payload of the `ResponseEntity<?>` object will be. The reason we do not know is that we will always be returning some sort of response entity, but instead of, for instance, a `TransactionBean` object as the payload, there may be an error, so instead, we would have the payload be a `Message`. The `withdrawFunds` method takes as parameters a **universally unique identifier (UUID)** object called id, a `WithdrawalBean` object called `withdrawal`, and a `User` object called `user`.

These provide key information, as outlined here:

- `WithdrawalBean`: An object that represents the business data for the transaction—in this case, the amount to withdraw and a description of the withdrawal.

- `UUID`: A representation of the internal ID for the account we will be withdrawing cash from.

- `User`: The authenticated user. We will examine how authentication works in the *Validating the authentication token in the REST controllers* section.

We will now examine `AccountControllerImpl`, which is the `AccountController` implementation. Rather than list the whole file, we will examine it one part at a time. Here's the first part:

```
@RestController
public class AccountControllerImpl implements AccountController
{
    @Autowired
```

```
    private AccountService accountService;


    @Autowired
    private TransactionDetailsBuilderFactory
transactionDetailsBuilderFactory;


    @Autowired
    private TransactionIdentifierDetailsBuilderFactory
transactionIdentifierDetailsBuilderFactory;
...
}
```

In the preceding code snippet, we first declare that this class is a REST controller by applying the @RestController annotation at the class level. We then declare three services that Spring Boot will inject into our REST controller. We do this by using the @Autowired annotation.

The three services are listed here:

- AccountService: A domain service that orchestrates the domain objects and invokes the business logic methods of the domain object.

- TransactionDetailsBuilderFactory: A service that creates new instances of TransactionDetailsBuilder for us. TransactionDetailsBuilder will be used to construct a TransactionDetails object.

- TransactionIdentifierDetailsBuilderFactory: A service that creates new instances of TransactionIdentifierDetailsBuilder for us. TransactionIdentifierDetailsBuilder will be used to construct a TransactionIdentifierDetails object.

We will now look at the declaration for the depositFunds method, as follows:

```
@Override
@PreAuthorize("hasRole('USER')")
@RequestMapping(path = "/account/{id}/deposit",
    method=RequestMethod.POST,
    consumes = "application/json",
    produces = "application/json")
public ResponseEntity<?> depositFunds(
        @PathVariable("id") final UUID id,
```

```
                @NotNull @Valid @RequestBody final DepositBean
  deposit,
                @AuthenticationPrincipal final User user) {
  ...
  }
```

In the preceding code snippet, we first declare that this method is secured to only authenticated users that have been granted the USER role. This is done using the @ PreAuthorize("hasRole('USER')") annotation. We then declare that the method is mapped to a **Uniform Resource Locator** (**URL**) and that the URL has parameters (it is a dynamic URL).

In this case, we used the @RequestMapping annotation to specify the following:

- The path is "/account/{id}/deposit", where {id} is a path variable (more on this in a moment).

- The method only responds to **HyperText Transfer Protocol** (**HTTP**) POST actions.

- The method consumes JSON.

- The method produces JSON.

The parameters of the method are also marked up with annotations, as outlined here:

- The UUID id parameter is annotated with @PathVariable("id"). This indicates the variable is populated from the URL used to invoke this method.

- The DepositBean deposit parameter is annotated with @NotNull and @ Valid, which indicate to Spring Boot that it must apply those validations to the object before the method can be invoked. It is also annotated with @RequestBody, which enables the creation of a parameter from the JSON submitted via the request body of the HTTP POST action.

- The User user parameter is annotated with @AuthenticationPrincipal, which instructs Spring Boot to populate the object with the details of the currently authenticated user.

The code we have examined previously shows how we map between REST and our REST controller. We can now move on to the next part and learn what actually happens in our depositFunds method.

We will take the code a section at a time, based on the intent of that part of the method. We start by examining how we validate things that could not be validated with a simple declaration of an annotation, as follows:

```java
final Account account = accountService.getAccount(new
EntityId(id));

if(account == null || !account.getOwnerId().equals(user.
getUid())) {
    return ResponseEntity
                .badRequest()
                .body(new Message("Invalid Account"));
}

if(deposit.getAmount() == null || deposit.getDescription() ==
null) {
    return ResponseEntity
                .badRequest()
                .body(new Message("Invalid Transaction"));
}
```

In the preceding code snippet, we start by obtaining an account instance using the `id` parameter. We then check if the account exists and if it is owned by this user. If we fail that validation, we then return a response indicating the error. This is done by using the `ResponseEntity` object to indicate this is a bad request and putting into the body of the response a `Message` object indicating what the error was.

> **Important Note**
> We describe the error in general terms as we do not want to give away too much information and allow someone, for instance, to know an `id` exists for an account they do not own.

Now we have validated all the inputs, we can execute the business logic, as follows:

```java
final TransactionDetails.Builder builder =
            transactionDetailsBuilderFactory.create();

final TransactionDetails details = builder
        .forAccountId(new EntityId(id))
            .withAmount(new Amount(deposit.getAmount().
toString())))
```

```
        .withDescription(deposit.getDescription())
        .build();


final Transaction transaction = accountService
        .depositFunds(details);
```

In the preceding code snippet, we used our `TransactionDetailsBuilderFactory` service to create an instance of a `TransactionDetails.Builder` called `builder`. We then use that builder to build a `TransactionDetails` object called `details`, which we populate using the various objects passed into our method as parameters. Then we invoke the `depositfunds` method of `accountService` to perform the business logic and return to us a `Transaction` object called `transaction`.

Now we have successfully performed our business logic, we need to return information to the client that invoked the REST endpoint, as follows:

```
final URI location = ServletUriComponentsBuilder
        .fromCurrentRequest()
        .path("/{Id}")
        .buildAndExpand(transaction.getId().getId())
        .toUri();


return ResponseEntity.created(location).build();
```

We are doing two main things in the preceding code snippet. The first thing we do is to create a URL to return to the client. We do this by using `ServletUriComponentsBuilder` to incorporate the current path, append a path variable to that path, and populate that variable with the unwrapped `id` of the transaction. Finally, we use `ResponseEntity` to build a response for a created item. This indicates that the URL will be the body returned in an HTTP 201 response. The code 201 is a standard HTTP code that indicates the POST action was successful and the resource—in this case, a transaction—was created.

All the methods in our REST controllers follow this standard structure:

- Validate.

- Business operation.

- Encode response.

Now we have learned how to use the Spring Boot support for REST controllers, we can move on and learn about the web frontend.

Creating an AngularJS web frontend

Our web frontend will be a single-page web application using **HyperText Markup Language 5 (HTML5)**, **Cascading Style Sheets 3 (CSS3)**, AngularJS, and Bootstrap. There are a few other components, but these are the major ones. As our web frontend is to be deployed independently from the REST services, we have created a new project called frontend to hold our HTML, JavaScript, and other artifacts.

The first thing to be created is an index.html page that will be the only page accessed by the client. We will examine this page section by section, as we did with the REST controller in the previous section.

We first need to declare in our index.html file that we have a web page and it will be using AngularJS, as follows:

```html
<!DOCTYPE html>
<html ng-app="app">
    <head>
...
            <title>Internet Bank</title>
...
    </head>
    <body>
...
            <div class="container">
                <div ng-view></div>
            </div>
    </body>
</html>
```

This declares an HTML page and sets the ng-app attribute of the html tag to be app. This is a standard declaration you will find in any HTML5 web page. It also declares a div tag with the ng-view attribute. This indicates to AngularJS that the div tag content will be populated from a view component using the Angular router. We will learn about this in the *Routing* section.

So, how do we work our magic and get this to be a dynamic page? First, we need to include some script references in our head section to include all the AngularJS modules we will be using, as follows:

```
<script src="https://ajax.googleapis.com/ajax/libs/
angularjs/1.7.8/angular.min.js"></script>
<script src="https://ajax.googleapis.com/ajax/libs/
angularjs/1.7.8/angular-resource.min.js"></script>
<script src="https://ajax.googleapis.com/ajax/libs/
angularjs/1.7.8/angular-route.min.js"></script>
<script src="https://ajax.googleapis.com/ajax/libs/
angularjs/1.7.8/angular-animate.min.js"></script>
<script src="https://ajax.googleapis.com/ajax/libs/
angularjs/1.7.8/angular-touch.min.js"></script>
<script src="https://ajax.googleapis.com/ajax/libs/
angularjs/1.7.8/angular-cookies.min.js"></script>
<script src="https://code.jquery.com/jquery-3.4.1.js"></script>
```

The preceding code snippet includes the script files for the following:

- **AngularJS**: The core AngularJS code
- **AngularJS Resources**: Used to interact with our REST services
- **AngularJS Route**: Used to handle moving between views on a single page
- **AngularJS Animate**: Used to enable animation effects in the **user interface** (UI)
- **AngularJS Touch**: Used to enable gestures if we access through a device with a touchscreen
- **Angular Cookies**: Used to enable managing cookies within our application

We then include all the other supporting modules we will be using, as follows:

```
<script src="https://maxcdn.bootstrapcdn.com/bootstrap/3.3.7/
js/bootstrap.min.js"></script>
<script src="https://cdnjs.cloudflare.com/ajax/libs/1000hz-
bootstrap-validator/0.11.9/validator.min.js"></script>
```

```
<script src="https://cdnjs.cloudflare.com/ajax/libs/angular-ui-
bootstrap/2.5.0/ui-bootstrap-tpls.min.js"></script>
```

```
<script src="https://www.gstatic.com/firebasejs/7.2.3/firebase-
app.js"></script>
```

```
<script src="https://www.gstatic.com/firebasejs/7.2.3/firebase-
auth.js"></script>
```

```
<script src="https://cdn.firebase.com/libs/angularfire/2.3.0/
angularfire.min.js"></script>
```

The preceding code snippet includes the script files for the following:

- **Bootstrap**: Used to provide a clean, modern, and responsive (as in responsive design) UI.

- **Bootstrap Validator**: Used to implement HTML5 validation and extensions to that validation. Validation occurs interactively rather than waiting for a form to be submitted.

- **UI Bootstrap**: Used to integrate Bootstrap with AngularJS.

- **Firebase**: The core Firebase code.

- **Firebase Authentication**: Used to authenticate via the Google Identity Platform. We will examine this in detail in the next section.

- **AngularFire**: Used to integrate Firebase with AngularJS and simplify using Firebase.

We then add the Bootstrap style sheet and our custom style sheet for CSS specific to our application, as follows:

```
<link rel = "stylesheet" type = "text/css" href = "https://
cdnjs.cloudflare.com/ajax/libs/twitter-bootstrap/3.3.7/css/
bootstrap.min.css" />
```

```
<link rel = "stylesheet" type = "text/css" href = "app.css" />
```

That completes the setup needed for the frameworks we depend on for our single-page web application. The setup for Firebase Authentication is not complete, but we will cover that in the *Authenticating in the web frontend* section.

In the next section, we will learn about modules, which are the overall entry point for our application code.

Modules

Remember that `ng-app` attribute we added to the `html` tag for our web page? That is the runtime name of the module we will be using. The module is declared in the `head` section with the following `script` tag:

```
<script src="module.js"></script>
```

A module is the entry point of our application code and a container for the various artifacts of our application, such as controllers, components, services, and factories. Components need to be declared as dependencies in our module, but controllers register themselves against a module. Modules may also declare dependencies on other modules, so we can think of modules and the items they contain as a tree structure. The root can see down the tree, but the branches and leaves cannot see up the tree or at other branches and leaves at the same level unless a specific dependency is declared. A key idea of the module system is to remove the global scope and introduce isolation to prevent conflicts.

Our module script looks like this:

module.js

```
var app = angular.module('app', [
    'ngRoute', 'ui.bootstrap', 'firebase',
    'component.accountDeposit', 'component.accountDetail',
    'component.accountOpen', 'component.accountTable',
    'component.accountWithdraw', 'component.authenticate',
    'component.changePassword', 'component.signin',
    'component.signup', 'component.reset',
    'component.verifyEmail'
]);


app.factory("Auth", ["$firebaseAuth",
    function($firebaseAuth) {
        return $firebaseAuth();
    }
]);
```

The preceding script initializes our Angular module called `app` and saves it into a variable also called `app`. As part of the initialization, our module declares dependencies on the `ngRoute` (AngularJS Route), `ui.bootstrap` (UI Bootstrap), and **Firebase** modules. These are the foundational things that will be used either explicitly or implicitly by our application.

After the foundational dependencies come the dependencies on the modules containing our components, which we will examine in the next section. We will explain `Auth factory` in the *Authenticating in the web frontend* section.

Components

Components are the items in AngularJS we use to implement isolated views. Our components are placed in their own modules that the `app` module depends on. There are three files we use to define our components. The first file is the `module.js` module definition file and it contains the following declaration of the module:

```
angular.module('component.accountDeposit', [
    'service.account'
]);
```

In the preceding code snippet, our module has declared a dependency on the `service. account` module that will interact with our REST service for accounts.

Next, we have the implementation of our component in a file called `component.js`. This starts with the usual declaration of a function that is registered as a component in our module, as illustrated in the following code snippet:

```
angular.module('component.accountDeposit').
component('accountDeposit', {
    templateUrl: 'component/account-deposit/template.html',
    controller: ['Auth', '$location', '$timeout',
'$routeParams', '$rootScope', 'Account', function
AccountDetailController(Auth, $location, $timeout,
$routeParams, $rootScope, Account) {
    ...
    }]
});
```

The preceding code snippet uses `templateUrl` to define where our HTML code for the view is located, and `controller` to declare our function and the services it depends on.

We then declare a variable called `self` that allows functions defined within our controller to use instance variables in the `controller` function itself, and initialize any instance variables we need, as illustrated in the following code snippet:

```
var self = this;
self.accountId = $routeParams.accountId;
```

In the preceding code snippet, we have used the `$routeParams` service to get the `accountId` path variable out of the path to our view.

We then add the code to initialize the Bootstrap validator for our form, as follows:

```
$timeout(function() {
    jQuery('#deposit').validator();
    $rootScope.$apply();
}, 100);
```

The preceding code snippet creates a timer that will invoke our function in 100 **milliseconds (ms)**. We need to delay the execution of this code because, at this point, the view is still being built, so applying the change immediately would result in an error. This is a standard workaround for the problem of invoking `$apply()` on the `$rootScope` service when executing the setup for a component.

We then invoke our `Account` service to populate the account instance variable with the account information returned from our `Account` REST service, as follows:

```
Auth.$getAuth().getIdToken().then(function(token) {
    Account.setToken(token);
    self.account = Account.getUnique(self.accountId);
    $rootScope.$apply();
})
```

In the preceding code snippet, we are using the `getUnique` method of the `Account` service to retrieve the account details from our backend. We will learn about services in the *Services* section. Don't worry about the `Auth` method just yet. We will go into detail on that in the *Authenticating in the web frontend* section.

Finally, we declare a function that will be invoked on a button press in our view, as follows:

```
self.deposit = function() {
    Auth.$getAuth().getIdToken().then(function(token) {
        Account.setToken(token);
        self.account = Account.depositFunds(self.accountId,
{ amount: self.amount, description: self.description });
        $location.path('/accounts/' + self.accountId);
        $rootScope.$apply();
    })
}
```

In the preceding code snippet, we invoke the depositFunds method of the Account service to create a deposit against our bank account in our backend. We then invoke the path method of the $location service to inform the router of the view to open next.

> **Important Note**
>
> As part of the view path, we have included the accountId path variable so that the view will know to display the account we have been working with.

The final file we need to fully define our component is a view template called template. html. We will examine this file a section at a time, starting with this section:

```
<div class="row">
    <h1 ng-bind="$ctrl.account.name"></h1>
</div>
<div class="row">
    <h1 ng-bind="$ctrl.account.balance | number: 2"></h1>
</div>
<div class="row"> </div>
```

In the preceding markup, we have used the ng-bind attribute to bind those elements to instance variables in our component. The $ctrl reference is a reference to the function we registered as a component. Binding populates the element it is applied to with the data from the reference. In this case, we are binding to $ctrl.account.name and $ctrl. account.balance.

Next, we define the layout for our form, as follows:

```
<div class="row">
    <form id="deposit">
        <div class="col-md-4"></div>
        <div class="col-md-4">
...
        </div>
        <div class="col-md-4"></div>
    </form>
</div>
```

The preceding markup uses the Bootstrap grid system to lay out the form. The grid system divides the page into `row` and `column` elements. There are 12 columns in total, so in the preceding markup, we have assigned the `col-md-4` class to our three divisions. This means that each division will take up four of the columns in the grid. Notice also that the `form` element in the preceding snippet has been assigned an `id` value of `deposit`. This matches the ID used to register Bootstrap validation in our component function.

We will now examine the body of our form, as follows:

```
<div class="form-group">
    <label for="amount">Amount</label>
    <input min="0.01" max="999999.99" step="0.01" data-
required-error="An amount is required" id="amount"
placeholder="Enter amount" type="number" ng-model="$ctrl.
amount" class="form-control" required/>
    <div class="help-block with-errors"></div>
</div>
<div class="form-group">
    <label for="amount">Description</label>
    <input data-required-error="A description required"
id="amount" placeholder="Enter description" type="text" ng-
model="$ctrl.description" class="form-control" required/>
    <div class="help-block with-errors"></div>
</div>
<button type="submit" class="btn btn-primary btn-block" ng-
click="$ctrl.deposit()">Deposit Funds</button>
```

In the preceding markup, we have applied standard HTML5 validation such as `required` and the data `type` to our controls. We have also made use of the Bootstrap validator attributes to apply additional validation dynamically before the form is submitted. Validation errors are automatically bound to an element with the `help-block` and `with-errors` classes situated in the same element marked up with the `form-group` class. The value of the controls is bound to our controller using the `ng-model` attribute. Lastly, our **Submit** button is bound to the `$ctrl.deposit` function by adding the `ng-click` attribute to the button.

Now we have the three elements that compose a component, we need to update the `index.html` file to include our JavaScript files, as follows:

```
<script src="component/account-deposit/module.js"></script>
<script src="component/account-deposit/component.js"></script>
```

We will now look at how we navigate between views when we only have one HTML page.

Routing

Navigation between views is accomplished using the `$routingProvider` service of the ngRoute module. The following code from `config.js` is used to set up the rooting for our views:

```
angular.module('app').
    config(['$routeProvider', function config($routeProvider)
{
        $routeProvider.
        when('/', {
            template: '<signin></signin>'
        }).
        when('/signup', {
            template: '<signup></signup>'
        }).
...
        otherwise('/');
    }
]);
```

The preceding code snippet uses the `configure` method of our app module and so is invoked on startup. We use the `when` method to map a `path` to a `template`. A `template` is an HTML fragment that is rendered by the router when the `path` matches. So, how does this HTML fragment map to a component? The HTML tags shown in the preceding snippet are obviously not part of standard HTML. The router maps the tag name to our component name, so a tag such as `signin` would map to the `signin` component, and a tag such as `account-detail` would map to the `accountDetail` component. The reason for the dash separator is that HTML is not case-sensitive, so whenever a dash is seen in a tag it is removed and the next letter capitalized. Finally, we use the `otherwise` method to set the default path we will navigate to if an unmapped path is used.

We will now look at how services are defined.

Services

Services are also contained in their own modules. We have already discussed declaring a module, so we will move straight into defining our service, as follows:

```
angular.module('service.account').
        service('Account', ['$resource', function($resource) {
        var token = null;
        var account = null;
...
]);
```

In the preceding code snippet, we use the `service` method of our module to register our `Account` service and set up two instance variables. These variables are `token`, which holds the authentication token we will pass to our REST service, and `account`, which is our internal representation of the `$resource` instance we will initialize for our REST service.

We then define a `setToken` method for our service, as follows:

```
this.setToken = function(newToken) {
        if(token !== newToken) {
            token = newToken;
            account = $resource('bank/account/:accountId',
{accountId: '@accountId'}, {
...
                getUnique: {
```

```
                    method: 'GET',
                    params: {accountId: '@accountId'},
                    isArray: false,
                    headers: {
                        'Authorization': 'Bearer ' + token
                    }
                },
            });
    ...
        };
    };
```

If there is no pre-existing token that matches the value present in the `token` instance variable, this method creates an instance of the `$resource` instance configured with the path to our REST service and the parameters that can be inserted into that path. In the preceding code snippet, our path is `bank/account/:accountId`. This indicates that `accountId` is a path variable. The path variables are declared in the second parameter to `$resource` using a JSON structure such as `{accountId: '@accountId'}`. We define which operations our instance will support (in this case, `getUnique`) and define the `Authorization` header our operation will send. This instance is saved into the `account` instance variable. We will cover how the token is obtained in the *Authenticating in the web frontend* section.

Finally, we expose the methods of the `$resource` instance to the clients of our service by declaring a function that delegates to the `$resource` instance, as illustrated in the following code snippet:

```
this.getUnique = function(accountId, success, error) {
    return account.getUnique({accountId: accountId}, success,
error);
};
```

Now we have learned about the major elements of an AngularJS application, we will move on to how we handle authentication using Firebase.

Authenticating in the web frontend

There are two parts to authenticating in the web frontend. The first is the code and configuration of the web frontend itself to use the authentication framework, and the second is the service provided by Google to be the identity and authentication provider. In the following section, we will look at how to configure the Google Cloud Identity Platform for use with our web frontend.

Setting up Firebase and Google Identity Platform

Before we make use of Firebase and the Google Identity Platform, we will need to configure them both by performing the following steps:

1. From the navigation menu in Cloud Console, click **Identity Platform**, as illustrated in the following screenshot:

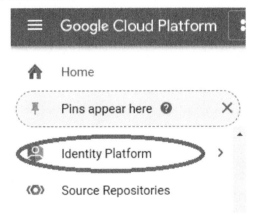

Figure 14.1 – Navigation menu: Identity Platform

2. If **Identity Platform** is not already enabled, click **ENABLE IDENTITY PLATFORM**, as illustrated in the following screenshot:

Figure 14.2 – Enabling Identity Platform

3. In the **Identity Providers** page, click **+ ADD A PROVIDER**, as illustrated in the following screenshot:

Identity Providers   + ADD A PROVIDER

Methods users can use to sign into your project. By default, all providers are disabled.

●	Name ↑	Enabled

No providers to display.

Figure 14.3 – Adding a provider

4. In the **New Identity Provider** page, select the **Email / Password** provider and click **SAVE**, as illustrated in the following screenshot:

Sign-in method

Select and configure an identity provider.

Select a provider
Email / Password   ▼

● Enabled

Configure email/password

Passwords

☑ Allow passwordless login
   Sign-in occurs via confirmation email link. Learn more

Templates

Templates for emails sent to users who sign up with email/password identity provider.

   CONFIGURE TEMPLATES

Import users

You can use the password hash parameters below to import users in bulk. Learn more

   VIEW PARAMETERS

   SAVE   CANCEL

Figure 14.4 – Creating a provider

5. Click **setup details**, as illustrated in the following screenshot:

Methods users can use to sign into your project. By default, all providers are disabled.

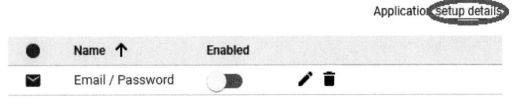

Figure 14.5 – Setup details

6. Copy and paste the snippet for **WEB** into a local text file and click **CLOSE**, as illustrated in the following screenshot:

Getting started

WEB   IOS   ANDROID

Copy and paste the snippet below at the bottom of your HTML, before other script tags. Learn more

```
<script src="https://www.gstatic.com/firebasejs/7.14.1/firebas
<script>
  var config = {
    apiKey: "AIzaSyALDS28rn2Gkqozr7q25a1mexgUozZVr-8",
    authDomain: "bankingapplication.firebaseapp.com",
  };
  firebase.initializeApp(config);
</script>
```

Figure 14.6 – Code snippet

Our **identity provider** (**IdP**) is now enabled, configured, and ready to use.

Next, we will configure the email verification and password change email settings so that the URL provided in those emails uses our application. We will do this by using the Firebase console at `https://console.firebase.google.com` and performing the following steps:

1. Click on the Firebase application created for our Google IdP, as illustrated in the following screenshot:

Figure 14.7 – Selecting Firebase project

2. From the navigation menu, click **Authentication**, as illustrated in the following screenshot:

Figure 14.8 – Navigation menu: Authentication

3. On the **Authentication** page, click **Templates**, as illustrated in the following screenshot:

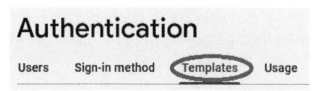

Figure 14.9 – Templates

4. Click the edit icon, as illustrated in the following screenshot:

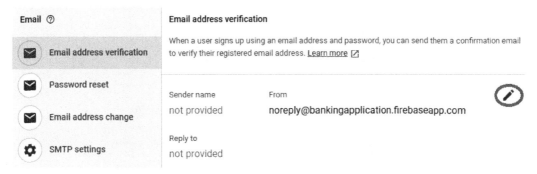

Figure 14.10 – Customizing the template

5. Set values for **Project public-facing name** and **Project support email**, as illustrated in the following screenshot:

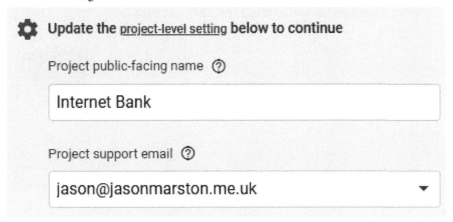

Figure 14.11 – Project public-facing name and support email

6. Click **customize action URL**, as illustrated in the following screenshot:

Figure 14.12 – Customize action URL

7. Enter the custom action URL for your application and click **Save**. The **Custom action URL** value will be the hostname of your application followed by /#!/__/ auth/action, as illustrated in the following screenshot:

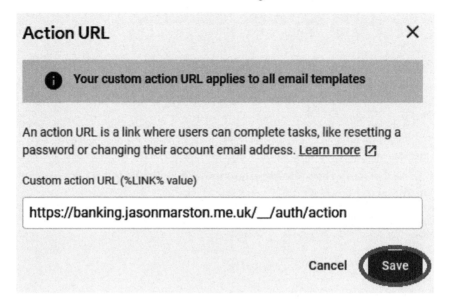

Figure 14.13 – Saving action URL

8. Click **Save**.

Firebase and the Google Identity Platform are now set up and ready to use. In the next section, we will learn how our AngularJS application uses Firebase Authentication.

Initializing Firebase Authentication

To configure AngularJS so that can use Firebase Authentication, we need to make use of the fragment we saved in *Step 6* when configuring the Google Identity Platform. We paste that fragment into our index.html file in the head section, as shown in the following code snippet:

```
<script>
    var config = {
        apiKey: "AIzaSyB-9eynwC5W856si5aJ4l1zw48SsICWbjQ",
        authDomain: "development-support.firebaseapp.com",
    };
    firebase.initializeApp(config);
</script>
```

The preceding fragment initializes the Firebase framework with the `apiKey` and `authDomain` values that were generated when we enabled the Google Identity Platform.

We now update our app module in `module.js` to make `$firebaseAuth` available to our application as a factory called `Auth`, as illustrated in the following code snippet:

```
app.factory("Auth", ["$firebaseAuth",
    function($firebaseAuth) {
        return $firebaseAuth();
    }
]);
```

Firebase Authentication is now ready to be used by our AngularJS application. We will now configure the Angular router to secure our views with Firebase Authentication.

Router updates

To secure our views using Firebase Authentication, we add the following code to our `config.js` file:

```
angular.module('app').
    run(["$rootScope", "$location", function($rootScope,
$location) {
        $rootScope.$on("$routeChangeError", function(event,
next, previous, error) {
            if (error === "AUTH_REQUIRED") {
                $location.path("/");
            }
        });
    }
]);
```

The preceding code snippet registers a listener on the `$routeChangeError` event and this is generated whenever there is an error with navigating to a view. It checks if the error is that the user is not authenticated and the view requires authentication. If this is the case, then the view is reset to the / path.

We can now apply guards to our routes, as follows:

```
when('/verify', {
    template: '<verify-email></verify-email>',
    resolve: {
        "currentAuth": ["Auth", function(Auth) {
            return Auth.$requireSignIn();
        }]
    }
}).
```

In the preceding example, we have registered that the user must be authenticated to access this view.

The following example stipulates that the user must be authenticated, and their email address must have been validated to access this view:

```
when('/change', {
    template: '<change-password></change-password>',
    resolve: {
        "currentAuth": ["Auth", function(Auth) {
            return Auth.$requireSignIn(true);
        }]
    }
}).
```

We will now look at how the authentication cycle works with Firebase Authentication.

The authentication cycle

In this section, we will sign in to the Angular frontend using the **Email / Password** identity option provided by Firebase and then route the request to the appropriate section in the application accordingly, based on whether the user is authenticated or not.

Signing in is accomplished with the following code fragment:

```
self.signIn = function() {
    Auth.$signInWithEmailAndPassword(self.email, self.
password).then(function() {
        // do nothing
    }).catch(function() {
```

```
            self.error = "Invalid credentials";
    });
}
```

We have used the `$signinWithEmailAndPassword` method of our `Auth` service and passed it the `self.email` and `self.password` variables. Signing in is an asynchronous operation, so the preceding method does not move us away from the sign-in view as, at this point, we do not know if authentication has succeeded or not, so cannot navigate to another view. If there is an error with authentication, then we update the `self.error` instance variable that is bound on our sign-in form to an error message display.

How do we trigger navigation on a successful sign-in? We use the following code:

```
Auth.$onAuthStateChanged(function(firebaseUser) {
    if(firebaseUser) {
        if(firebaseUser.emailVerified == true) {
            $location.path('/accounts');
        }
        else {
            $location.path('/verify');
        }
    }
});
```

The preceding code registers a listener on changes to the authentication state. If there is a `firebaseUser` object passed into our listener, then we have successfully authenticated. We next check if the email address has been verified. If the address has been verified, we can navigate to the account view using routing. If the address has not been verified, we navigate to the `verify` view, which allows the user to request verification emails.

Now we have signed in, we need to make use of the `firebaseUser` object to pass an authentication token to our `Account` service so that the service can provide that token to our REST service. We promised earlier to explain how this is done, as explained in the *Components* section in this chapter.

The preceding code uses the $getAuth method of our Auth service to obtain a Firebase user. We then invoke the getIdToken method of the Firebase user. This gives us the authentication token we will pass into our service. It is important to understand that repeated calls to this method do not give a different token each time. Tokens have an expiry date, and so a new token will only be issued when the current one is about to expire. Next, we invoke setToken on our Account service, which initializes our $resource instances and configures them to use the token as an Authorization header Bearer token.

We have learned how to sign in, how to detect the current authentication state, and how to enable our services to use a bearer token provided by our Firebase user. Next, we will look at how to sign out of our application.

The signout controller

Signing out is something that needs to be available to the user, no matter where they are in the application. For this reason, it is implemented as a controller rather than a component (view). The controller does not have a UI and is not in its own module. Instead, it is registered against the app module, as illustrated in the following code snippet:

```
app.controller('signout', ['$scope', 'Auth', '$location',
function SignoutController($scope, Auth, $location) {
    $scope.auth = Auth;


    Auth.$onAuthStateChanged(function(firebaseUser) {
        $scope.user = firebaseUser;
    });


    $scope.signOut = function() {
        $scope.auth.$signOut().then(function() {
            $location.path('/');
        });
    }
}]);
```

When a user signs in, it will register the preceding listener so that when they log out, this preceding listener is called and the $scope.auth value is set to null. The $scope object is associated with the page rather than a specific view, so it is always available to our controller. We sign out of the application by invoking the $signOut method of the Auth controller. If the signout is successful, we then navigate back to the default view.

In the next section, we will look at how we secure our REST controllers using the token we passed using the `Authorization` header.

Validating the authentication token in the REST controllers

In this section, we will learn about securing the backend of our banking application. Specifically, we now need to configure our application to secure the REST endpoints and validate the tokens that will be passed as `Authorization` headers to our endpoints. The validation will be delegated to a filter, which we will learn about in the next section.

The first step in securing our REST endpoints is to extend a `WebSecurityConfigurerAdapter` class and configure it as follows:

```
@Configuration
@EnableWebSecurity
@EnableGlobalMethodSecurity(
    securedEnabled = true,
    jsr250Enabled = true,
    prePostEnabled = true
)
public class SecurityConfig extends
WebSecurityConfigurerAdapter {
...
    @Bean
    public TokenAuthenticationFilter
tokenAuthenticationFilter() {
        return new TokenAuthenticationFilter();
    }
}
```

The preceding code uses annotations to enable web security and global method security. Global method security has three properties, as outlined here:

- The `securedEnabled` property enables the `@Secured` annotation.
- The `prePostEnabled` property enables `@PreAuthorize` annotations we will use to secure our REST endpoints.
- The `jsr250Enabled` property enables the `@RoleAllowed` annotation.

In the preceding code snippet, we have also registered a
`TokenAuthenticationFilter` class as a bean with Spring Boot. More on this class
later.

The following code snippet shows the `configure` method that is defined in our
`WebSecurityConfigurerAdapter` class:

```
@Override
protected void configure(final HttpSecurity http) throws
Exception {
    http.cors().and().sessionManagement()
    .sessionCreationPolicy(SessionCreationPolicy.STATELESS)
    .and().csrf().disable().formLogin().disable()
    .httpBasic().disable().authorizeRequests()
    .antMatchers("/", "/error", "/favicon.ico", "/**/*.png",
        "/**/*.gif", "/**/*.svg", "/**/*.jpg",
        "/**/*.html", "/**/*.css", "/**/*.js").permitAll()
    .anyRequest().authenticated();

    http.addFilterBefore(tokenAuthenticationFilter(),
    UsernamePasswordAuthenticationFilter.class);
}
```

The preceding code configures the Spring security framework to disable states (REST
services should be stateless), **cross-site request forgery** (**CSRF**), form logins, and basic
authentication. It enables authorization of requests and uses the `ant` matcher to list all the
URLs that do not need to be authenticated and require all other URLs to be authenticated
and authorized. Finally, it registers our `TokenAuthenticationFilter` class,
placing it before `UsernamePasswordAuthenticationFilter` in the filter chain. This
means it is encountered before the default authentication filter and so is used for
authentication instead.

Next, we will examine the `TokenAuthenticationFilter` class.

The authentication filter

`TokenAuthenticationFilter` is the class that handles validation of the bearer token passed in via the `Authorization` header. It initializes the Firebase Admin framework we will use to validate tokens. The code is illustrated in the following snippet:

```
public class TokenAuthenticationFilter extends
OncePerRequestFilter {
...

    private JwtValidation auth = null;

    public TokenAuthenticationFilter() {
        try {
            auth = JwtValidation.getInstance();
        } catch (final IOException e) {
            logError(e);
        }
    }
...
}
```

In the preceding code snippet, we have wrapped an instance of the Firebase Admin framework in a class called `JwtValidation`. This is also because we do not need access to the entire **application programming interface (API)**, just the token validation parts. Doing so also removes the direct dependency on Firebase and would allow us to change authentication frameworks easily if the need came up.

Important Note

To initialize the Firebase Admin API on our server (or on our local server), we will need to generate a key for our Firebase service account and download it to our server. We then need to create an environment variable called GOOGLE_APPLICATION_CREDENTIALS that holds the path to our credentials file.

Here is the standard code needed to implement the `doFilterInternal` function:

```
@Override
protected void doFilterInternal(
            final HttpServletRequest request,
            final HttpServletResponse response,
            final FilterChain filterChain)
                throws ServletException, IOException {
...
}
```

The preceding code gives us access to the request, response, and chain objects we will use to respond to requests.

The following code fragment shows how we obtain the token from the headers in the request and verify the token:

```
final String jwt = getJwtFromRequest(request);
if (StringUtils.hasText(jwt)) {
    final User user = userService.sync(auth.
verifyIdToken(jwt));
    user.setCredentials(jwt);

    final UsernamePasswordAuthenticationToken authentication
            = createAuthenticationToken(user);

    authentication.setDetails(
            new WebAuthenticationDetailsSource()
                .buildDetails(request));

    SecurityContextHolder.getContext()
            .setAuthentication(authentication);

    try {
        filterChain.doFilter(request, response);
    }
...
}
```

In the preceding code snippet, we use the `getJwtFromRequest` private method to simplify our code when obtaining a token from the request. If there is a token, we verify the token and then use it to synchronize with the user service. Synchronizing obtains a `user` object and updates it with any changes we want to propagate from Google Identity Platform, such as a new photograph. Once we have our user, we add the token to it using the `credentials` method. Next, we create a Spring Boot `UsernamePasswordAuthenticationToken` instance for the user, associate the Spring Boot token with the current request, and set the token to be the authentication token of the Spring Boot context. Finally, we continue along the filter chain.

We have not shown the exception-handling code in the preceding code fragment or the private methods that simplify the code. These are simple methods, and they can be found in the GitHub repository: `https://github.com/PacktPublishing/Modernizing-Applications-with-Google-Cloud-Platform/tree/master/Chapter%2014/banking-rest/src/main/java/uk/me/jasonmarston/auth/filter/impl/TokenAuthenticationFilter.java`.

Summary

In this chapter, we learned how to create REST controllers to expose our business services as REST/JSON APIs and how to create a web frontend using AngularJS. We also learned how to secure our web frontend using Firebase Authentication, and how to secure our REST controllers using tokens passed from our web frontend. This sets the foundation for refactoring to microservices.

In the next chapter, we will look at DevOps and how to automate building our application, provisioning the environment, and deploying the application in the Google Cloud.

15

Handling Eventual Consistency with the Compensation Pattern

We will now turn our attention to how microservices communicate with each other and how we handle transactions when each microservice is invoked in the context of its own transaction. We will learn how to handle that issue using eventual consistency, and as a byproduct, we will also see how we can reduce the coupling between our services. We will then learn how to handle errors and do what under commitment control would have been a rollback, by using the compensation pattern. Then, we will learn how to implement what we have learned and how to set up Google Cloud Pub/Sub to support that implementation. Finally, we will deploy and test our updated application.

In this chapter, we will cover the following topics:

- The distributed transaction problem
- The compensation pattern
- Creating topics and subscriptions with Google Cloud Pub/Sub
- Implementing eventual consistency and the compensation pattern
- Deploying and testing the application

Technical requirements

The code file for this chapter can be found here: `https://github.com/PacktPublishing/Modernizing-Applications-with-Google-Cloud-Platform/tree/master/Chapter%2015`

The distributed transaction problem

With microservices, each service is a transaction boundary and acts on an **aggregate root**. Thus, if we place an order using an **Order** microservice and allocate stock using a **Stock** microservice, those operations happen in separate transactions. We could of course have the Order microservice call the Stock microservice, but this would mean the two microservices are tightly bound. The Order microservice would depend on the Stock microservice and fail if the Stock microservice were unavailable for some reason. It could also lead to a complex web of interdependent microservices that would not be able to be built, tested, deployed, or scaled independently.

A better solution is for us to use **domain events** and an **event bus**. Domain events are a record of something that happened in the business logic of our microservice and contain details of the change (or details of a failed change). In the preceding example, for instance, when we successfully place an order, we would create and publish an instance of an `OrderConfirmedEvent`. The Stock microservice would subscribe to this **event** and allocate the stock for the Order the `OrderConfirmedEvent` relates to.

> **Important Note**
> The **publish/subscribe (pub/sub)** model is not point-to-point. We can have many subscriptions and have an event delivered to multiple clients that are interested in the event.

We have applied this pattern to our application, as shown in the following diagram:

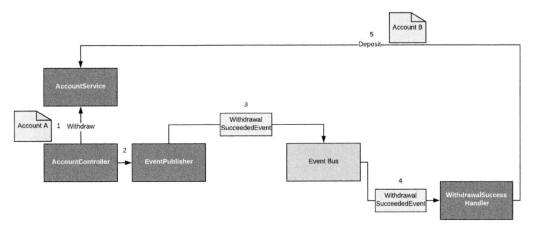

Figure 15.1 – Eventual consistency: transfer funds

The preceding diagram shows the flow for transferring funds between accounts, as follows:

1. The `AccountController` invokes the `withdraw` method on the `AccountService` using **Account A**.

2. On a successful withdrawal, the `AccountController` uses the `EventPublisher` to publish the `WithdrawalSucceededEvent`.

3. The `EventPublisher` puts the `WithdrawalSucceededEvent` onto the event bus (in this case, Google Pub/Sub) on a topic named `accountTopic`.

4. The `WithdrawalSuccessHandler` has subscribed to the `accountTopic` and thus receives the `WithdrawalSucceededEvent`.

5. The `WithdrawalSuccessHandler` invokes the `deposit` method on the `AccountService` using **Account B**.

This may at first glance look overly complicated, but it achieves loose coupling by removing direct dependencies between microservices. It also enables extensibility as we could, for instance, have other microservices (such as know-your-client, fraud detection, or auditing) subscribe to our `WithdrawalSucceededEvent` without having to change the **Account** microservice in any way.

> **Important Note**
>
> The aforementioned `AccountController` and `WithdrawalSuccessHandler` are both within our Account microservice; they are simply different entry points to the service.

So, what happens when something goes wrong and our two microservice instances are supposed to be in sync? We cover that in the next section with the compensation pattern.

Operations can fail anywhere, even in an eventual consistent workflow. But we still need to ensure that our application can survive and continue working after a failure, and this is where a compensating transaction pattern comes in. A compensating transaction pattern is, in essence, a mechanism to undo changes that may have caused an operation to fail. With the help of this pattern, we can bring the application back to a stage where it was working. Of course, this is an oversimplification and there are many nuances involved. Let's take a look at an example to better understand how this pattern works.

The compensation pattern

Using our example of an Order and a Stock microservice from the previous section, we will now look at what happens if we have no stock to allocate for the order. These two microservices are decoupled, so do not share a traditional transaction boundary. We need a mechanism for the Stock microservice to inform the Order microservice that it could not allocate the required stock, and so it should reverse the confirmation. We will do this by again using **events**. The Stock microservice would publish an `AllocationFailedEvent` and the Order microservice would subscribe to that event and revert the state of the order to **pending**.

We have applied this pattern to our application, as shown in the following diagram:

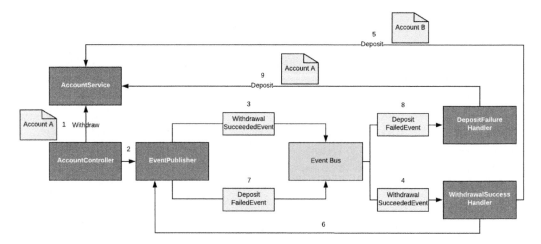

Figure 15.2 – Compensation pattern: transfer funds

The preceding diagram shows the flow for a failure in transferring funds between accounts, as follows:

1. The `AccountController` invokes the `withdraw` method on the `AccountService` using **Account A**.

2. On a successful withdrawal, the `AccountController` uses the `EventPublisher` to publish the `WithdrawalSucceededEvent`.

3. The `EventPublisher` puts the `WithdrawalSucceededEvent` onto the event bus (in this case, Google Pub/Sub) on a topic named `accountTopic`.

4. The `WithdrawalSuccessHandler` has subscribed to the `accountTopic` and thus receives the `WithdrawalSucceededEvent`.

5. The `WithdrawalSuccessHandler` invokes the `deposit` method on the `AccountService` using **Account B**.

6. On a failed deposit, the `WithdrawalSuccessHandler` uses the `EventPublisher` to publish the `DepositFailedEvent`.

7. The `EventPublisher` puts the `DepositFailedEvent` onto the event bus (in this case, Google Pub/Sub) on a topic named `accountTopic`.

8. The `DepositFailureHandler` has subscribed to the `accountTopic` and thus receives the `DepositFailedEvent`.

9. The `DepositFailureHandler` invokes the `deposit` method on the `AccountService` using **Account A** to deposit the funds back to the original account.

Using an event rather than having everything in a single transaction under commitment control means that the account books may not balance for a second or so, but they will eventually be consistent. That is the drawback of using events. However, the real world is not under commitment control, and if everything balances within a reasonable time, this is not a real issue.

An interesting side effect of using compensations in our application is that the deposit transaction made to reverse the withdrawal from a failed transfer will show up in the account history. We get more detail than we would have for a normal failed transaction. In the **user interface** (**UI**) for our application transfer, withdrawals and deposits in the transaction history for an account will show up with a pale blue background, and compensation deposits will show up with a pale yellow background.

We will now move on to provisioning the topics and subscriptions our implementation of domain events and the compensation pattern will need.

Creating topics and subscriptions with Google Cloud Pub/Sub

We will now provision two **topic** and **subscription** pairs. The reason we have two pairs is that we will need to use the dead-letter functionality of Google Cloud Pub/Sub. The dead-letter functionality is to place a message (event) that was not acknowledged as delivered into another topic after a certain number of failed delivery attempts. This means that we are storing each event that could not be processed into that topic, which allows us to correct the problem later. The first pair is for dead letters, and the second pair is for our application to publish and subscribe to.

To create the necessary topic and subscription pairs, we will take the following steps in the cloud console:

1. From the navigation menu, click **Pub/Sub**, as illustrated in the following screenshot:

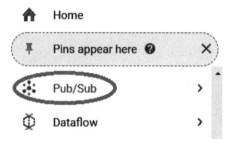

Figure 15.3 – Navigation menu: Pub/Sub

2. On the **Topics** page, click **CREATE TOPIC**, as illustrated in the following screenshot:

Figure 15.4 – Creating a topic

3. Provide a value for **Topic ID** (in our case, `accountFailureTopic`), and click **CREATE TOPIC**, as illustrated in the following screenshot:

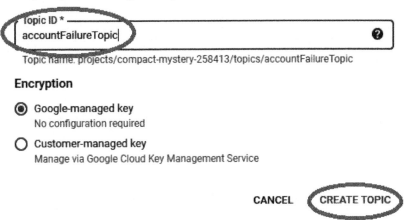

Create a topic

A topic forwards messages from publishers to subscribers.

Topic ID *
accountFailureTopic   ?

Topic name: projects/compact-mystery-258413/topics/accountFailureTopic

Encryption

◉ Google-managed key
No configuration required

○ Customer-managed key
Manage via Google Cloud Key Management Service

CANCEL   CREATE TOPIC

Figure 15.5 – Creating a topic with the topic identifier (ID)

4. From the **Pub/Sub** menu, click **Subscriptions**, as illustrated in the following screenshot:

Figure 15.6 – Pub/Sub menu: Subscriptions

5. On the **Subscriptions** page, click **CREATE SUBSCRIPTION**, as illustrated in the following screenshot:

Figure 15.7 – Creating a subscription

6. Provide a value for **Subscription ID** (in our case,
    `accountFailureSubscription`), select `accountFailureTopic` for the
    Pub/Sub Topic, and click **CREATE**, as illustrated in the following screenshot:

Figure 15.8 – Creating a subscription with ID and topic

7. From the **Pub/Sub** menu, click **Topics**, as illustrated in the following screenshot:

Figure 15.9 – Pub/Sub menu: Topics

8. On the **Topics** page, click **CREATE TOPIC**, as illustrated in the following screenshot:

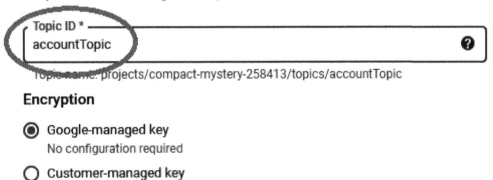

Figure 15.10 – Creating a topic

9. Provide a value for **Topic ID** (in our case, `accountTopic`), and click **CREATE TOPIC**, as illustrated in the following screenshot:

Create a topic

A topic forwards messages from publishers to subscribers.

Topic ID *
accountTopic

projects/compact-mystery-258413/topics/accountTopic

Encryption

⦿ Google-managed key
No configuration required

○ Customer-managed key
Manage via Google Cloud Key Management Service

CANCEL

Figure 15.11 – Creating a topic with the Topic ID

10. From the **Pub/Sub** menu, click **Subscriptions**, as illustrated in the following screenshot:

Figure 15.12 – Pub/Sub menu: Subscriptions

11. On the **Subscriptions** page, click **CREATE SUBSCRIPTION**, as illustrated in the following screenshot:

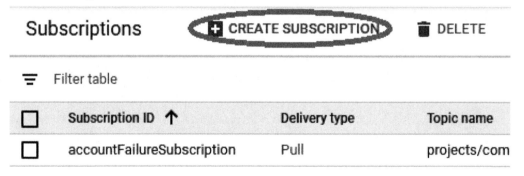

Figure 15.13 – Creating a subscription

12. Provide a value for **Subscription ID** (in our case, `accountSubscription`), and select our `accountTopic` topic:

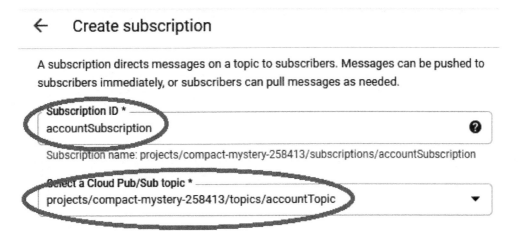

Figure 15.14 – Creating a subscription with ID and topic

13. Check **Enable dead lettering**, select `accountFailureTopic` for the dead-letter topic, and click **CREATE**, as illustrated in the following screenshot:

Dead lettering

☑ Enable dead lettering

Subscriptions may configure a maximum number of delivery attempts. When a message cannot be delivered, it is republished to the specified dead-letter topic.

Select a dead-letter topic *
projects/compact-mystery-258413/topics/accountFailureTopic   ▼

Maximum delivery attempts *
5

Maximum delivery attempts is from 5 to 100.

CREATE

Figure 15.15 – Dead lettering

We have now created the two topic and subscription pairs we need for our application. We have enabled dead lettering on our `accountSubscription` topic and configured it to send messages that have failed to be delivered five times to our `accountFailureTopic` topic.

We are now ready to move on and learn about how to implement what we have learned about eventual consistency and the compensation pattern.

Implementing eventual consistency and the compensation pattern

In this section, we examine the code required to implement eventual consistency and compensations. Before jumping into our code, we will briefly discuss Spring Integration, which gives us a standardized way of handling enterprise integration patterns in our code, much as Spring Data gives us a standardized way of handling object-relational mapping and transactional databases. We do not need to get down to the low-level detail of the Google Pub/Sub **application programming interface (API)** as that is abstracted for us by Spring Integration. The major components of Spring Integration we will need to understand are listed here:

- `ChannelAdapter`: A channel adapter is an interface provided by Spring that handles the low-level details of communicating with a provider. In our case, Spring Integration provides a `PubSubInboundChannelAdapter` component, which implements this interface to handle Google Cloud Pub/Sub and receives messages from it. We just need to provide the basic configuration for the endpoint it will be dealing with and the channel the messages received should be placed on.

- `Channel`: This is the core of Spring Integration. Messages are placed on and received from channels. This is how communication happens between Spring Integration components.

- `Router`: This receives a message from one channel, and then decides which channel to place that message on.

- `Transformer`: This receives a message from a channel, performs some sort of transformation on it, and places it on another channel.

- `MessageHandler`: This is an interface provided by Spring Integration that we need to implement. We place the business logic for handling the message received in that implementation class. An exception to this is the `PubSubMessageHandler` interface, which is provided by Spring Integration and handles the low-level details of communicating with Google Cloud Pub/Sub and publishing messages to it.

Now we have a basic understanding of Spring Integration, we can start to look at our implementation of eventual consistency and compensations, starting with our events. The following code segment is for our `WithdrawalSucceededEvent` class:

```
public class WithdrawalSucceededEvent {
    private UUID accountId;
    private UUID referenceAccountId;
    private String description;
```

```
    private UUID journalCode;
    private BigDecimal amount;
    private boolean isCorrection;

    public WithdrawalSucceededEvent() {
    }

    public WithdrawalSucceededEvent(TransactionDetails
details) {
...
    }
    // getters and setters here
}
```

The preceding code defines a simple **Plain Old Java Object** (**POJO**) that has private instance variables for each of the attributes of the event. It has a no arguments constructor that will be used to create it from a **JavaScript Object Notation** (**JSON**) representation and a constructor that takes a `TransactionDetails` object and is used to set all the fields from the values in that object.

The next thing we will need to do is define an interface to be used for publishing events, as follows:

```
@MessagingGateway(defaultRequestChannel =
"objectOutputChannel")
public interface AccountEventPublisher {
    <T> void publish(T event);
}
```

We have annotated this interface with the `@MessagingGateway` annotation. This informs Spring Integration that this interface will be used to publish messages to `objectOutputChannel`. The method declared uses Java generics, so we do not have to declare methods explicitly for each type of event we want to publish.

Next, we declare a configuration class, as follows:

```
@Configuration
@EnableIntegration
public class IntegrationConfig {
    @Bean
```

```
@Transformer(
        inputChannel="objectOutputChannel",
        outputChannel="textOutputChannel")
ObjectToJsonTransformer objectToJsonToTransformer() {
    return new ObjectToJsonTransformer();
}


@Bean
@ServiceActivator(inputChannel = "textOutputChannel")
public MessageHandler messageSender(final PubSubTemplate
pubsubTemplate) {
    return new PubSubMessageHandler(pubsubTemplate,
"accountTopic");
}
...
}
```

We have annotated our `IntegrationConfig` configuration class with the `@Configuration` annotation to inform Spring Boot that this class contains configuration, and with the `@EnableIntegration` annotation to enable Spring Integration. We then declared two beans. The first is a `Transformer` bean that takes an object from the `objectOutputChannel` channel and uses the `ObjectToJsonTransformer` class to convert the object to a JSON string representation of the object and place it on the `textOutputChannel` channel. When the `Transformer` component transforms from an object to a JSON string representation, it sets a `json__TypeId__` header in the message to the fully-qualified class name of the class it transformed from. We will need this later to convert the string back to a Java object. The second bean is a `MessageHandler` bean that handles placing the string representation of our object onto our Google Cloud Pub/Sub `accountTopic`. This is all the code we need to take any Java object that can be converted into a JSON string representation and publish it to a topic in Google Cloud Pub/Sub.

Now that we have learned how to publish messages into our topic, we will look at the beans needed to receive an event from our subscription, as follows:

```
@Bean
public PubSubInboundChannelAdapter
accountMessageChannelAdapter(
        @Qualifier("textInputChannel") final MessageChannel
inputChannel,
```

```
            final PubSubTemplate pubSubTemplate) {
    PubSubInboundChannelAdapter adapter =
            new PubSubInboundChannelAdapter(
                    pubSubTemplate,
                    "accountSubscription");
    adapter.setOutputChannel(inputChannel);
    adapter.setAckMode(AckMode.MANUAL);
    return adapter;
}
```

The bean shown in the preceding code snippet is a `PubSubInboundChannelAdapter` bean and it uses the `@Qualifier` annotation to bind the `inputChannel` instance variable to `textInputChannel` so that messages received from the `accountSubscription` subscription will be placed on the `textInputChannel` instance variable. Finally, it sets the acknowledgment mode to `MANUAL` so that we can decide how to handle errors in our code rather than automatically acknowledging every message and having them automatically removed from the subscription.

We now turn our attention toward what to do with text messages that have been placed on our `textInputChannel` instance variable, as follows:

```
@Bean
@Router(inputChannel="textInputChannel")
public HeaderValueRouter headerValueRouter() {
    final HeaderValueRouter router =
            new HeaderValueRouter("json__TypeId__");
    router.setChannelMapping(
            "class " + WithdrawalSucceededEvent.class.
getCanonicalName(),
            "textWithdrawalSucceededInputChannel");
    router.setChannelMapping(
            "class " + DepositFailedEvent.class.
getCanonicalName(),
            "textDepositFailedInputChannel");
    return router;
}
```

In the preceding code snippet, we have created a `HeaderValueRouter` bean. This bean receives a text message on the `textInputChannel` instance variable and routes it to either `textWithdrawalSucceededChannel` or `textDepositFailedInputChannel`, depending on the value of the `json__TypeId__` header.

These two beans are not managed by Spring Integration, so we must create them, like this:

```java
@Bean
public MessageChannel objectWithdrawalSucceededInputChannel() {
    return new DirectChannel();
}


@Bean
public MessageChannel objectDepositFailedInputChannel() {
    return new DirectChannel();
}
```

The preceding code needs little explanation as it is simply creating new instances of `DirectChannel` and registering them as beans with Spring Boot. The name of each bean is automatically set by Spring Boot to be the name of the method.

We now register beans to transform from JSON strings to Java objects. We have two of these, one for each channel created in the preceding code snippet:

```java
@Bean
@Transformer(


    inputChannel="textWithdrawalSucceededInputChannel",


    outputChannel="objectWithdrawalSucceededInputChannel")
JsonToObjectTransformer withdrawalSucceededTransformer() {
    return new
JsonToObjectTransformer(WithdrawalSucceededEvent.class);
}


@Bean
@Transformer(
        inputChannel="textDepositFailedInputChannel",
        outputChannel="objectDepositFailedInputChannel")
```

```
JsonToObjectTransformer depositFailedTransformer() {
      return new JsonToObjectTransformer(DepositFailedEvent.
class);
}
```

The beans shown in the preceding code snippet are again straightforward and simply bind to an input channel and an output channel. They create an instance of the `JsonToObjectTransformer` class and pass into the constructor the Java class that instance should transform the JSON string representation into. The `DepositFailedEvent` will be placed onto the `objectDepositFailedInputChannel` and the `WithdrawalSucceededEvent` will be placed onto the `objectWithdrawalSucceededInputChannel`.

The final beans we will register are the handlers for the two object channels, as illustrated in the following code snippet:

```
@Bean
@ServiceActivator(inputChannel =
"objectWithdrawalSucceededInputChannel")
public MessageHandler withdrawalSuccededReceiver() {
      return new WithdrawalSuccessHandler();
}


@Bean
@ServiceActivator(inputChannel =
"objectDepositFailedInputChannel")
public MessageHandler depositFailedReceiver() {
      return new DepositFailureHandler();
}
```

The preceding code creates an instance of our `WithdrawalSuccessHandler`, binding it to the `objectWithdrawalSucceededInputChannel`, and an instance of our `DepositFailureHandler`, binding it to the `objectDepositFailedInputChannel`.

That completes the foundational code we need to receive, route, and transform our messages so that they become Java objects and can be handled by the correct handler.

There is behavior that is common to all handlers, so we have created an abstract class to hold that common behavior that our concrete implementations will inherit from, as illustrated in the following code snippet:

```
public abstract class AbstractMessageHandler implements
MessageHandler {
        protected final void ack(final Message<?> message) {
            getOriginalMessage(message).ack();
        }

        protected final void nack(final Message<?> message) {
            getOriginalMessage(message).nack();
        }

        private BasicAcknowledgeablePubsubMessage
getOriginalMessage(
                final Message<?> message) {
            return message.getHeaders().get(
                    GcpPubSubHeaders.ORIGINAL_MESSAGE,

        BasicAcknowledgeablePubsubMessage.class);
        }
}
```

The abstract class shown in the preceding code snippet provides two protected methods to handle acknowledging and nacking the message. Nacking is explicitly putting a message back onto a queue rather than waiting for it to time out and automatically return to the queue.

Now, we arrive at our business logic for handling receipt of a WithdrawalSucceededEvent, as illustrated in the following code snippet:

```
public class WithdrawalSuccessHandler extends
AbstractMessageHandler {
        @Autowired
        private AccountService accountService;

        @Autowired
        private TransactionDetailsBuilderFactory
transactionDetailsBuilderFactory;
```

```
    @Autowired
    private TransferIdentifierDetailsBuilderFactory
transferIdentifierDetailsBuilderFactory;

    @Autowired
    private AccountEventPublisher accountEventPublisher;
...
}
```

In the preceding code snippet, we autowired the beans our business logic will use. Notice that we included the `AccountEventPublisher`; this is because we want to be able to publish a `DepositFailedEvent` if we are unable to deposit funds into the destination account.

Now, we implement the `handleMessage` method, which we will use to respond to receipt of a `WithdrawalSucceededEvent`. The code is illustrated in the following snippet:

```
@Override
public void handleMessage(final Message<?> message)
            throws MessagingException {
    final WithdrawalSucceededEvent event =
                (WithdrawalSucceededEvent) message.
getPayload();
        // only process transfers
    if(event.getAccountId().equals(event.getReferenceAccountId()))
{
            this.ack(message);
            return;
        }
...
}
```

The preceding code obtains the payload of the message, which is our `WithdrawalSucceededEvent` object, and checks to make sure it is ready for a transfer. If it is not for a transfer, it acknowledges the method and returns without doing any more processing.

So, now we know we are dealing with a transfer, we need to create objects we will pass to the account service to enact, as follows:

```
final TransactionDetails.Builder transactionDetailsBuilder =
        transactionDetailsBuilderFactory.create();

final TransactionDetails transactionDetails =
transactionDetailsBuilder
        .forAccountId(new EntityId(event.
getReferenceAccountId()))
        .withReferenceAccountId(new EntityId(event.
getAccountId()))
...
        .build();
```

Notice in the preceding code snippet that we have set the `AccountId` value to the `ReferenceAccountId` value of the event, and the `ReferenceAccountId` value to the `AccountId` value of the event. This is because we are now dealing with the other side of the transfer.

Next, we will create objects we will pass to the account service to determine if this event has already been processed. With pub/sub systems, messages are delivered at least once, so they may have been delivered more than once. Because of that, we need to ensure that messages are idempotent and do nothing when being repeated. This is achieved in the following way:

```
final TransferIdentifierDetails.Builder
transactionIdentifierBuilder =
        transferIdentifierDetailsBuilderFactory.create();

final TransferIdentifierDetails identifierDetails =
        transactionIdentifierBuilder

    .forAccountId(transactionDetails.getAccountId())

    .forJournalCode(transactionDetails.getJournalCode())

    .asCorrection(transactionDetails.isCorrection())
                .build();
```

Now, we get to the code that processes our `WithdrawalSucceededEvent`, as illustrated here:

```
try {
    if(accountService.getTransfer(identifierDetails) == null)
{
        accountService.depositFunds(transactionDetails);
    }
    this.ack(message);
}
```

The preceding code first tests if the deposit for our transfer has already happened by calling the `getTransfer` method of `accountService`. If `null` is returned, then we have not yet deposited funds, so we can call `depositFunds` on our `accountService` and acknowledge the message, which removes it from the subscription.

All that remains now is to handle any exceptions thrown by our `accountService` service, as follows:

```
catch(final RuntimeException e) {
    if(accountService.getTransfer(identifierDetails) != null)
{
        this.ack(message); // another handler instance
worked
        return;
    }
    final TransactionDetails failureDetails =
            transactionDetailsBuilder
                    .asCorrection(true)
                    .build();
    final DepositFailedEvent depositFailedEvent =
            new DepositFailedEvent(failureDetails);
    accountEventPublisher.publish(depositFailedEvent);
    this.ack(message);
}
```

In the preceding `catch` block, we first check if another instance has successfully processed the transfer deposit. If it has, then we acknowledge the message and return it.

If another instance has not successfully made the transfer deposit, then we publish a
DepositFailedEvent so that we can compensate and reverse the withdrawal. Notice
that we specify that DepositFailedEvent should be handled as a compensation by
passing true to the asCorrection method of transactionDetailsBuilder.

We will now examine the DepositFailureHandler. This follows the same patterns
as WithdrawalSuccessHandler, including the switching of the AccountId and
ReferenceAccountId values, so we will skip straight to the business logic, as follows:

```
try {
        if(accountService
                    .getTransfer(transactionIdentifierDetails) ==
null) {
                accountService.depositFunds(transactionDetails);
        }
        this.ack(message);
}
```

The preceding business logic is identical to our WithdrawalSuccessHandler, but
remember that it is acting on the original account to deposit the funds back into that
account as a correction (compensation).

Again, we have a catch block to handle exceptions thrown by our accountService
service, as illustrated in the following code snippet:

```
catch(final RuntimeException e) {
        if(accountService
                    .getTransfer(transactionIdentifierDetails) !=
null) {
                this.ack(message); // another handler instance
worked
        }
}
```

The preceding exception-handling code is much simpler than the code for
WithdrawalSuccessHandler. This is because if we cannot enact the compensation
by depositing the funds back into the original account, something serious has happened
and after five retries, the message will end up on our dead-letter topic. Messages on a
dead-letter topic are to be handled outside of the application and are extremely rare. An
example of a reason why this could happen is a database outage.

The last piece of the puzzle is in our `AccountControllerImpl` class, as illustrated in the following code snippet:

```
@RestController
public class AccountControllerImpl implements AccountController
{
        @Autowired
        private AccountEventPublisher accountEventPublisher;
...

        public ResponseEntity<?> withdrawFunds(@
PathVariable("id") final UUID id,
                @RequestBody final WithdrawalBean withdrawal,
                @AuthenticationPrincipal final User user) {
...
            final WithdrawalSucceededEvent event =
                    new
WithdrawalSucceededEvent(successDetails);

            accountEventPublisher.publish(event);
...
        }
}
```

Our controller shown in the preceding code snippet invokes the `publish` method of our `accountEventPublisher` after the withdrawal has been successful.

We have now covered all the classes and code we need to handle eventual consistency and compensations. The implementation in this section publishes a `WithdrawalSucceededEvent` after every successful withdrawal. The event is routed to our `accountTopic` and received from our `accountSubscription`, where it is delivered to our `WithdrawalSuccessHandler`. If the withdrawal is a transfer withdrawal (has a `ReferenceAccountId` value), then we try to deposit funds into the destination account. If that deposit fails, then we publish a `DepositFailedEvent` event, which goes through the same routing already outlined and is delivered to our `DepositFailureHandler`, which deposits the funds back into the originating account.

So, what next? We need to deploy and test our updated application to make sure everything is wired together correctly and works **end to end (E2E)**.

Deploying and testing the application

In order to build, deploy, and test our application, we need to copy the content of *Chapter 14, Refactoring the Frontend and Exposing REST Services*, in the GitHub repository for this book (`https://github.com/PacktPublishing/Modernizing-Applications-with-Google-Cloud-Platform/tree/master/Chapter%2014`) into the local repository we set up for pushing to our **Google Cloud** source repository in *Chapter 5, Implementing DevOps with Google Cloud Platform*.

Now we have all the code in our repository, we are ready to set up for deployment, as follows:

1. Push the code into the Google Cloud source repository by entering the following commands at a command line in our repository directory:

   ```
   git add -A .
   git commit -m "code drop"
   git push
   ```

2. Set up two new build triggers for our `banking-legacy-rest` and `front-end` projects by following the procedure for creating triggers we learned about in *Chapter 5, Implementing DevOps with Google Cloud Platform*.

3. Create a key for our Firebase service account and download it to our local machine using the procedure we learned about in *Chapter 5, Implementing DevOps with Google Cloud Platform*.

4. Rename the JSON file containing our credentials to `firebase.json` and upload it to our Tomcat **virtual machine (VM)**.

5. In the Tomcat VM, create a folder called `/credentials` and copy the `credentials.json` file from `/var/local/cloud-sql-proxy` and the newly uploaded `firebase.json` file into the `/credentials` folder.

6. Set up the environment variables for our credentials by adding the following lines to the end of the `setupenv.sh` file:

   ```
   export PUB_SUB_CREDENTIALS="file:/credentials/
   credentials.json"
   export GOOGLE_APPLICATION_CREDENTIALS="/credentials/
   firebase.json"
   ```

7. In the `/opt/bitnami/apache/conf/vhosts` folder, update the `tomcat-https-vhost.conf` file to change the reverse proxy section to match the following:

```
# Reverse proxy to Tomcat for non-WebSockets requests
ProxyPass /bank ajp://localhost:8009/bank
ProxyPassReverse /bank ajp://localhost:8009/bank
# BEGIN: Support domain renewal when using mod_proxy
within Location
```

The preceding code enables the reverse proxy functionality in Apache so that requests to `hostname/bank` or `hostname/bank/*` are sent to Tomcat rather than being served by Apache.

8. Update the `startup.sh` file we placed into a storage bucket in *Chapter 5, Implementing DevOps with Google Cloud Platform*, and replace the last line with the following code:

```
#sudo gsutil cp gs://jm-application/ROOT.war /opt/
bitnami/tomcat/webapps/ROOT.war

sudo gsutil cp gs://jm-application/bank.war /opt/bitnami/
tomcat/webapps/bank.war

sudo gsutil cp gs://jm-application/front-end.tar.gz /opt/
bitnami/apache/htdocs/front-end.tar.gz

sudo tar -xvf /opt/bitnami/apache/htdocs/front-end.tar.gz
--directory /opt/bitnami/apache/htdocs
```

9. Replace the version of `startup.sh` in our storage bucket with this updated version.

10. Trigger our builds one at a time, waiting for each to complete before moving on to the next in the following sequence:

    A. `firebase-authentication`

    B. `domain-driven-design`

    C. `banking-domain`

    D. `banking-legacy-rest`

    E. `front-end`

> **Important Note**
>
> You will need to ensure the Artifactory VM is running for the builds to work and that the Cloud SQL database is started for the testing to work.

11. Restart the Tomcat VM.

We have built and deployed our updated application, so we are now ready to test the application using a web browser. Open a web browser and navigate to the **Uniform Resource Locator** (**URL**) for our application. In our examples, we have used `https://banking.jasonmarston.me.uk`.

Summary

In this chapter, we learned about the distributed transaction problem with microservices and how to solve this using eventual consistency. We learned how to use the compensation pattern to correct failures in eventual consistency scenarios and reverse actions to simulate rollback behavior. We then created topic and subscription pairs that we need for our application to run and examined how eventual consistency and the compensation pattern are implemented in our application. Finally, we built, deployed, and tested our application.

In the next chapter, we will learn how to take our container images and orchestrate them in **Google Kubernetes Engine**.

16

Orchestrating Your Application with Google Kubernetes Engine

The remaining three chapters of this book cover the three major options for deploying our application as cloud-native microservices, which are **Google Kubernetes Engine (GKE)**, Google App Engine, and Cloud Run. This chapter focuses on GKE, which serves as a platform for deploying microservices, though not serverless ones. We will cover provisioning a cluster, configuring the environment and microservices, deploying our application, and configuring public access to the application.

In this chapter, we will cover the following topics:

- Introducing **GKE**
- Configuring the environment
- Deploying and configuring the microservices

- Configuring public access to the application

- When to use GKE

Now, let's look at what exactly GKE is and how to provision and use it.

Technical requirements

The code files for this chapter are available here: `https://github.com/` `PacktPublishing/Modernizing-Applications-with-Google-Cloud-` `Platform/tree/master/Chapter%2016`.

Introducing GKE

GKE is a container management and orchestration service based on **Kubernetes**, which is an open source container management and orchestration system.

So, what do we mean by management and orchestration? Kubernetes handles deploying, configuring, and scaling our container-based microservices.

There are two major parts to Kubernetes.

The first part is **masters**, also known as the control plane. This hosts the following services:

- **The API server**: Handles all communications between all components.

- **The cluster store (etcd)**: Holds the configuration and state of the cluster.

- **The controller manager**: Monitors all components and ensures they match the desired state.

- **The scheduler**: Watches the cluster store for new tasks and assigns them to a cluster node.

- **The cloud controller manager**: Handles the specific integrations needed for a cloud service provider. An example in our case is to provision an HTTP(s) load balancer for our application.

The second major part is Nodes (part of Node pools). This is where our application runs. Nodes do three basic things:

- Watch the API server for new work

- Execute the new work

- Report the status of the work to the control plane

As we are using GKE rather than hosting Kubernetes on our virtual machines, we do not need to concern ourselves with the masters. These are hosted and managed by **Google Cloud**. This means tasks such as upgrading the version of Kubernetes are managed for us by Google Cloud rather than us having to manually handle them. GKE also provides a facility called cluster autoscaling, which means that if the **Nodes** in our cluster become fully utilized and we need to deploy more workloads, the cluster will be horizontally scaled out to add the needed capacity, and once the capacity is no longer needed, the cluster will be horizontally scaled in to control costs.

The following diagram shows the architecture of GKE:

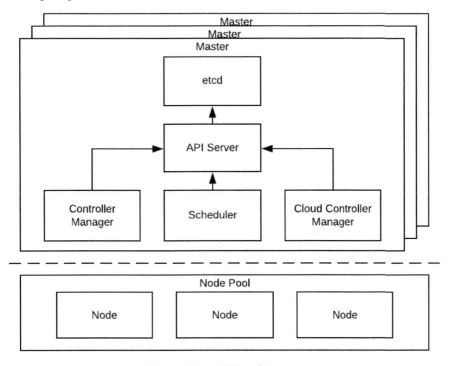

Figure 16.1 – GKE architecture

Now that we have gained an understanding of what GKE is, we will move on and learn how to create a GKE cluster.

Modes of operation

GKE offers two different modes of operation, each providing two different levels of control and customizability over your GKE clusters:

- **Autopilot**: As the name suggests, Autopilot mode takes control of the entire cluster and Node infrastructure, managing it for you. Clusters running in this mode are preconfigured and optimized for production workloads. The developer only needs to pay for the resources that are used by your workloads.

- **Standard**: On the other side of the spectrum, Standard mode gives developers complete control and customizability over the clusters and node infrastructure, allowing them to configure standard clusters whichever way suits their production workloads.

We will use Standard mode to create GKE clusters for our deployment.

Creating a GKE cluster

Now, let's create a GKE cluster by performing the following steps:

1. From the cloud shell, enter the following command to set up the project:

   ```
   gcloud config set project bankingapplication
   ```

2. Enter the following command to create the cluster:

   ```
   gcloud container clusters create banking-cluster --zone
   europe-west2-c --enable-ip-alias --machine-type=n1-
   standard-2 --num-nodes 1 --enable-autoscaling --min-nodes
   1 --max-nodes 4
   ```

   The preceding command will create a new GKE cluster called `banking-cluster` hosted in the `europe-west2-c` zone. We used the `--enable-ip-alias` switch to join the cluster to our VPC so that we can use the private IP address of our **Cloud SQL** database. We have specified that we will use the `n1-standard-2` machine type for the Nodes and that our pool will initially have one Node. Finally, we enabled cluster autoscaling and set the limits to be a minimum of one Node and a maximum of four Nodes. This is a long-running task, so it will take a few minutes to complete.

3. In the cloud console, from the **Navigation** menu, select **Kubernetes Engine**:

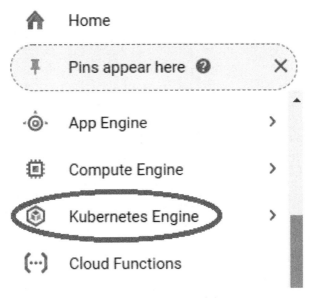

Figure 16.2 – Navigation menu – Kubernetes Engine

After a few minutes, you will see the status change to a green tick, as follows:

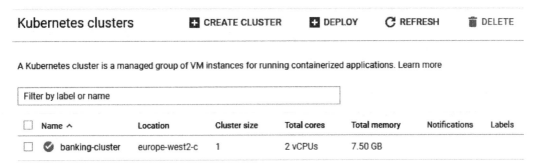

Figure 16.3 – Kubernetes cluster (status)

With that, we have learned about GKE and created our cluster for use in the rest of this chapter. Now, let's turn our attention to providing configuration to our application.

Configuring the environment

A well-designed microservice will have its configuration externalized so that it can take the configuration from the environment it is deployed to. This means we can deploy the same container to a development environment, test environment, and deployment environment and not have specific versions for each. Another particularly good reason to externalize configuration such as usernames, passwords, and other credentials is to keep them out of the source code repository, so we must keep them secret. We will be making use of manifests extensively in this chapter. Manifests declare what the state should be, and Kubernetes does what it needs to do to bring the cluster into that state. Manifests are idempotent, so if a manifest is applied multiple times, no changes are made except for the first time it is applied. If the contents of a manifest are changed and it is applied, then Kubernetes will update its state to address the difference between the two instances of the manifest.

Kubernetes ConfigMaps and Secrets

In **Kubernetes**, this externalized configuration is provided by **ConfigMaps** and **Secrets**.

A ConfigMap is an API object that provides name-value pairs. These pairs can either be simple, such as HOSTNAME: localhost, or the value can be the contents of a file and later used as a file by our container.

Secrets differ from ConfigMaps in that they have the values encoded using Base64. It is important to remember that this is encoding and not encryption; the encoding is pure so that the values are not easily read from the configuration. Due to Secrets only being encoded rather than encrypted, we will use **Google Secret Manager** to handle our truly secret configuration.

Google Secret Manager

Google Secret Manager is a secure central service for storing and managing sensitive information such as passwords for use by applications in **Google Cloud**. These secrets can be accessed by service accounts that have been granted the **Secret Manager Secret Accessor** and **Secret Manager Viewer** roles. Add these roles to the **Compute Engine default service account** before moving on to create our secrets.

We will add the secret keys used by our application by following these steps:

1. From the cloud console, from the **Navigation** menu, select **Security | Secret Manager**:

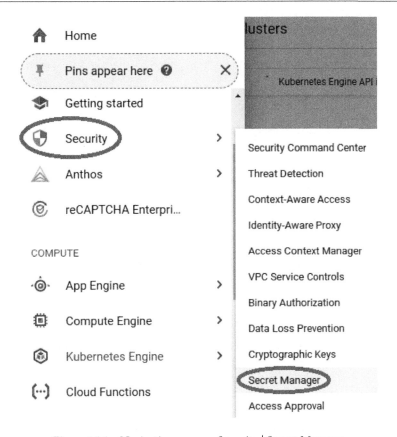

Figure 16.4 – Navigation menu – Security | Secret Manager

2. Click **CREATE SECRET**:

Security

Secret Manager

Secret Manager lets you store, manage, and secure access to your application secrets. Learn more

Figure 16.5 – Secret Manager – CREATE SECRET

3. Enter the name and value of the secret, select the region (we used `europe-west4`), and click **CREATE SECRET**:

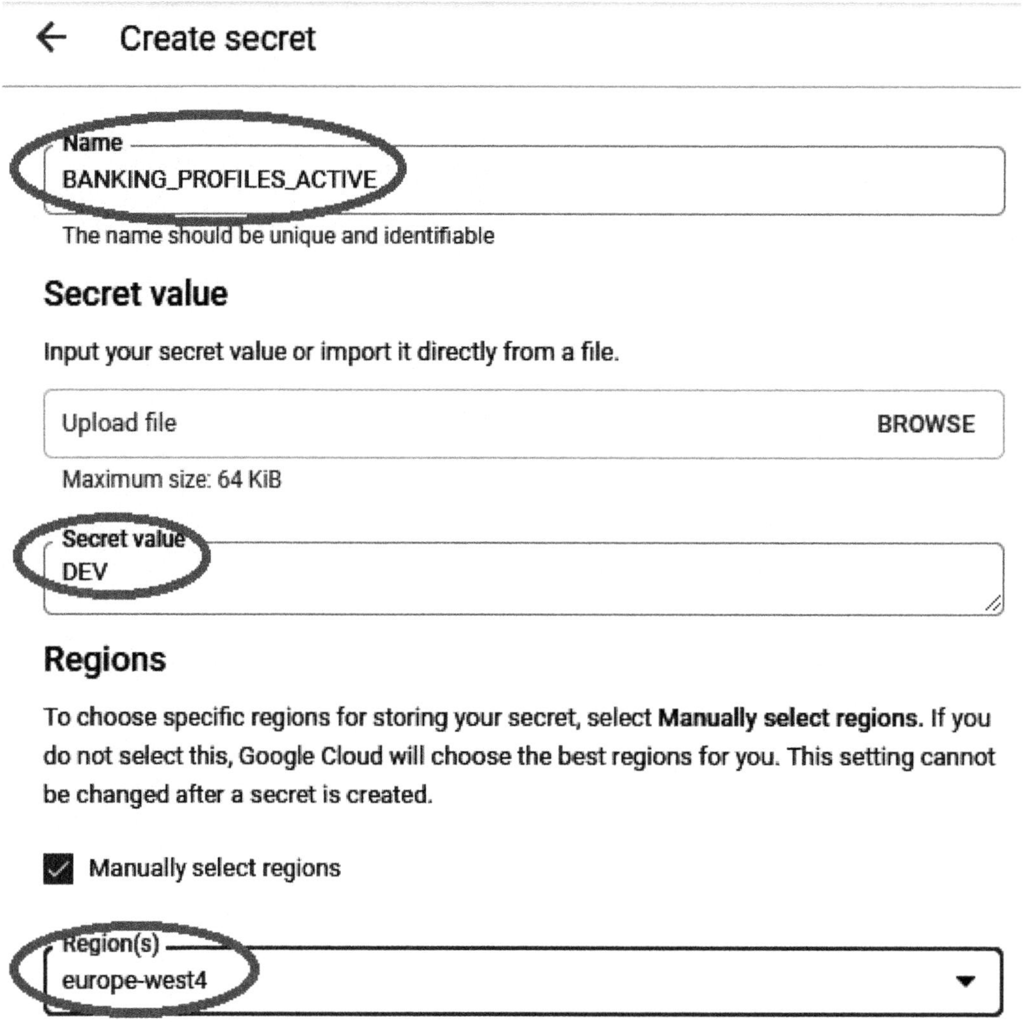

 **Create secret**

Name
BANKING_PROFILES_ACTIVE

The name should be unique and identifiable

Secret value

Input your secret value or import it directly from a file.

Upload file   **BROWSE**

Maximum size: 64 KiB

Secret value
DEV

Regions

To choose specific regions for storing your secret, select **Manually select regions**. If you do not select this, Google Cloud will choose the best regions for you. This setting cannot be changed after a secret is created.

☑ Manually select regions

Region(s)
europe-west4   ▼

Figure 16.6 – The Create secret screen

4. You will see the success page, as follows. Click the left arrow at the top:

← Secret details   🗑 DELETE

Details for "BANKING_PROFILES_ACTIVE"

projects/292730690469/secrets/BANKING_PROFILES_ACTIVE

Regions

europe-west4

Versions   + NEW VERSION   ENABLE SELECTED   DISABLE SELECTED

	Version	Status	Created on ↓	Actions
☐	1	✔ Enabled	5/21/20, 11:31 AM	⋮

Figure 16.7 – Successfully created secret

5. At this point, we will see a list of all the secrets we have configured and can click **+ CREATE SECRET** to create another secret:

Secret Manager   (+ CREATE SECRET)

Secret Manager lets you store, manage, and secure access to your application secrets.
Learn more

≂ Filter table

	Name ↑	Labels	Created	Actions
☐	BANKING_PROFILES_ACTIVE		5/21/20, 11:31 AM	⋮

Figure 16.8 – Secret Manager

6. Create a secret for each item in the following list:

```
--ACCOUNT_DATASOURCE_CLOUD_SQL_INSTANCE:
bankingapplication:europe-west2:mysql-instance
```
```
--ACCOUNT_DATASOURCE_PASSWORD: <your_db_password>
```
```
--ACCOUNT_DATASOURCE_URL: jdbc:mysql:///account
```
```
--ACCOUNT_DATASOURCE_USERNAME: <your_db_user>
```

```
--BANKING_DATASOURCE_DDL_AUTO: update
```

```
--BANKING_DATASOURCE_DIALECT: org.hibernate.dialect.
MySQL5InnoDBDialect
```

```
--BANKING_INITIAL_ADMIN_EMAIL: <your_admin_email>
```

```
--BANKING_PROFILES_ACTIVE: DEV
```

```
--GKE_ACCOUNT_DATASOURCE_URL: jdbc:mysql://localhost:3306/
account?useSSL=false&allowPublicKeyRetrieval=
true&useUnicode=yes&characterEncoding=UTF-8
```

```
--GKE_USER_DATASOURCE_URL: jdbc:mysql://localhost:3306/
user?useSSL=false&allowPublicKeyRetrieval=
true&useUnicode=yes&characterEncoding=UTF-8
```

```
--USER_DATASOURCE_CLOUD_SQL_INSTANCE:
bankingapplication:europe-west2:mysql-instance
```

```
--USER_DATASOURCE_PASSWORD: <your_db_password>
```

```
--USER_DATASOURCE_URL: jdbc:mysql:///user
```

```
--USER_DATASOURCE_USERNAME:   <your_db_username>
```

On inspecting the preceding list of secrets, we will notice that ACCOUNT_DATASOURCE_
URL and USER_DATASOURCE_URL are different from what we have used previously, as
well as that GKE_ACCOUNT_DATASOURCE_URL and GKE_USER_DATASOURCE_URL
match the old values for them. This is in preparation for the following chapters. We will
use the GKE_ versions in this chapter.

We now have secrets for every environment variable that could be moved to be a secret.
But how do we use these secrets in our application? Following our strategy of minimizing
code changes, we utilized the support for Google Secret Manager that's provided by Spring
Boot by updating our build.gradle dependencies to add the following:

```
implementation 'org.springframework.cloud:spring-cloud-gcp-
starter-secretmanager:1.2.2.RELEASE'
```

Next, we created a new configuration file in our resources folder called bootstrap.
properties with the following content:

```
spring.cloud.gcp.secretmanager.enabled = true
spring.cloud.gcp.secretmanager.bootstrap.enabled = true
spring.cloud.gcp.secretmanager.secret-name-prefix = GCP_
```

The preceding configuration enables Google Secret Manager's support and enables it to work at bootstrap time, which is before our `application.properties` file is processed. This allows us to inject the secrets into `application.properties` in the same way we previously injected the environment variables. Finally, the configuration declares that variables prefixed with `GCP_` are the ones that will be loaded from Google Secret Manager.

Finally, we must update our `application.properties` file:

```
spring.profiles.active = ${GCP_BANKING_PROFILES_ACTIVE}
spring.jpa.hibernate.ddl-auto = ${GCP_BANKING_DATASOURCE_DDL_
AUTO}
spring.jpa.properties.hibernate.dialect = ${GCP_BANKING_
DATASOURCE_DIALECT}
spring.datasource.jdbcUrl = ${GCP_GKE_USER_DATASOURCE_URL}
spring.datasource.username = ${GCP_USER_DATASOURCE_USERNAME}
spring.datasource.password = ${GCP_USER_DATASOURCE_PASSWORD}
spring.account-datasource.jdbcUrl = ${GCP_GKE_ACCOUNT_
DATASOURCE_URL}
spring.account-datasource.username = ${GCP_ACCOUNT_DATASOURCE_
USERNAME}
spring.account-datasource.password = ${GCP_ACCOUNT_DATASOURCE_
PASSWORD}
logging.level.org.springframework: ${BANKING_LOGGING_LEVEL}
logging.level.org.hibernate: ${BANKING_LOGGING_LEVEL}
logging.level.com.zaxxer: ${BANKING_LOGGING_LEVEL}
logging.level.io.lettuce: ${BANKING_LOGGING_LEVEL}
logging.level.uk.me.jasonmarston: ${BANKING_LOGGING_LEVEL}
banking.initial.admin.email = ${GCP_BANKING_INITIAL_ADMIN_
EMAIL}
```

In the preceding source code, we have not included the entire `application.properties` file, just the items that obtain their values from Google Secret Manager or environment variables.

These configuration changes of adding the dependencies, adding the `bootstrap.properties` file, and updating the `application.properties` file means that we do not have to make any source code changes to make use of Google Secret Manager.

Now that we can access our application secrets from Google Secret Manager, we will learn how Kubernetes provides environment variables and other configurations to our application.

Kubernetes ConfigMaps

Our application has externalized configuration it obtains from environment variables. As this is not sensitive information, we can make use of a ConfigMap. The following `account-env.yaml` manifest file shows how we can accomplish this:

```
apiVersion: v1
kind: ConfigMap
metadata:
  name: account-env-configmap
data:
  BANKING_LOGGING_LEVEL: WARN
  GOOGLE_APPLICATION_CREDENTIALS: /secrets/credentials.json
  GOOGLE_CLOUD_PROJECT: bankingapplication
```

In the preceding ConfigMap manifest, we provided the details for our logging level, the location of our credentials, and the Google Cloud project the credentials are for. Once we have updated those details, we can apply the ConfigMap to our cluster. To do this, upload the file to our cloud shell and execute the following command:

```
kubectl apply -f account-env.yaml
```

We can delete the ConfigMap by executing the following command:

```
kubectl delete -f account-env.yaml
```

The preceding `apply` command creates the **ConfigMap** needed for the account's microservice environment variables. We must repeat the same procedure for `user-env.yaml` to provide the environment variables needed for the user microservice.

Next, we will create a ConfigMap that holds the configuration for our Nginx service. This will be our initial approach to creating a Strangler Facade. The following `nginx-config.yaml` manifest file shows how we can accomplish this:

```
apiVersion: v1
kind: ConfigMap
metadata:
  name: nginx-configmap
```

```
data:
  default.conf: "server {\r\n
\    listen 80;\r\n
\    server_name www.banking.jasonmarston.me.uk;\r\n
\r\n
\    location / {\r\n
\        root /usr/share/nginx/html;\r\n
\        index index.html;\r\n
\r\n
\        location /account {\r\n
\            proxy_pass http://account-svc:8080;\r\n
\        }\r\n
\r\n
\        location /user {\r\n
\            proxy_pass http://user-svc:8080;\r\n
\        }\r\n
\    }\r\n
}\r\n"
```

We will upload this file to our cloud shell and execute the following command to create the ConfigMap:

```
kubectl apply -f nginx-config.yaml
```

We can delete the ConfigMap by executing the following command:

```
kubectl delete -f nginx-config.yaml
```

The preceding `apply` command creates the ConfigMap needed for the Nginx reverse proxy configuration to route requests to our account and user microservices. This will look like a file to our microservices rather than the simple name and value pairs we used previously.

We will now move on and examine **Kubernetes Secrets** in the next section.

Kubernetes Secrets

We are not finished with the externalized configuration yet. When interacting with **Google Cloud Pub/Sub**, **Google Cloud Identity Platform**, and **Google Cloud SQL**, our application makes use of a credentials file for our service account. Specifically, we used the Compute Engine default service account. We need to upload a copy of that credentials file to our cloud shell and name it `credentials.json`. Once that is done, we can create the Secret by executing the following command:

```
kubectl create secret generic credentials-secret --from-
file=credentails.json=./credentials.json
```

We can delete the Secret by executing the following command:

```
kubectl delete secret credentials-secret
```

The preceding `create` command creates the Secret needed for each of the Google Cloud services we will be using. This will look like a file to our microservices rather than the simple name and value pairs we used previously. The name of the Secret is set to look like a filename and the value populated from the content of the file is passed to the command.

The externalized configuration of our microservices is now in place and ready to be used when we deploy our application. We will now move on and examine how containers are deployed and managed in Kubernetes.

> **Important Note**
>
> We will need `credentials-secret` later in this chapter, so if you have deleted it, please recreate it.

Deploying and configuring the microservices

Kubernetes has several abstractions that represent the state of our system. The key abstractions when deploying our microservices are as follows:

- Pod
- ReplicaSet
- Deployment
- Horizontal Pod Autoscaler
- Service

We will examine each of these abstractions and how we can use them in the following sections.

Kubernetes Pods

A **Pod** is the smallest unit of deployment in Kubernetes. A Pod is a wrapper around one or more containers that share a network address space and share resources such as volumes. Most of the time, a Pod consists of a single container, but sometimes, it is useful to have multiple containers working together when tight coupling between the containers exists. In our application for our microservices, we will have the container of our microservice and a container for the **Cloud SQL proxy**. This is called a sidecar pattern and allows us to keep our microservice containers simple and still make use of capabilities such as the Cloud SQL proxy.

We will examine the layout of a Pod manifest by taking it a section at a time:

```
apiVersion: v1
kind: Pod
metadata:
  name: account-pod
spec:
  containers:
```

The start of our preceding manifest declares the version of the API we are using, specifies we are declaring a Pod, provides a name of `account-pod` for our Pod, and starts the specification for the containers we will be using.

The next section deals with the declarations for our `account` container:

```
- name: account
  image: gcr.io/bankingapplication/account-rest:latest
  ports:
  - containerPort: 8080
  volumeMounts:
  - name: secrets-volume
    mountPath: /secrets
    readOnly: true
  envFrom:
  - configMapRef:
      name: account-env-configmap
```

This part of the manifest declares that the container we are using will be called `account` and that the image will be pulled from `gcr.io/bankingapplication/account-rest:latest`. Our container's service will be exposed on port `8080` and mount two volumes, `/firebase` and `/pubsub`, in `read only` mode. Finally, our container will populate the environment variables from our `account-env-secret`.

Next, we have the declaration of the container for the Cloud SQL proxy:

```
  - name: cloudsql-proxy
    image: gcr.io/cloudsql-docker/gce-proxy:1.21
    command: ["/cloud_sql_proxy",
              "-instances=bankingapplication:europe-
west2:mysql-instance=tcp:3306",
              "-ip_address_types=PRIVATE",
              "-credential_file=/secrets/credentials.json"]
    securityContext:
      runAsUser: 2 # non-root user
      allowPrivilegeEscalation: false
    volumeMounts:
    - name: secrets-volume
      mountPath: /secrets
      readOnly: true
```

This part of the manifest declares that the container we are using will be called `cloud-sql-proxy` and that the image will be pulled from the Cloud SQL Auth proxy GitHub releases page. The latest release of the Cloud SQL Auth proxy Docker image, at the time of writing, is 1.23. and referenced as `gcr.io//cloudsql-docker/gce-proxy:1.21`. When starting the Cloud SQL proxy, the `/cloud_sql_proxy` command will be invoked, passing in the parameters needed to connect to our **Cloud SQL** database on the private IP address using the credentials from our service account. We have also secured the container to ensure it does not run as root, and privileges cannot be promoted to root. Finally, our container will mount a volume called `/secrets` in `read only` mode.

That last part of our configuration is the volume we used previously:

```
  volumes:
  - name: secrets-volume
    secret:
      secretName: credentials-secret
```

In the preceding code, we exposed our Secret as a volume that can be mounted by containers in our Pod. Specifically, we have exposed the credentials file, which is used to externalize the security configuration that's used to connect to Google Cloud services.

Assuming we have created the preceding file in our cloud shell, we can deploy the Pod by executing the following command:

```
kubectl apply -f account-pod.yaml
```

We can delete the Pod by executing the following command:

```
kubectl delete -f account-pod.yaml
```

The problem with Pods is that, on their own, they are limited. We have declared our account-pod, but that just gives us a single instance of our Pod. What do we do if we need to scale and have multiple Pod instances? That is where **ReplicaSets** come in.

Kubernetes ReplicaSets

The purpose of a **ReplicaSet** is to maintain a set of stateless Pods that are replicas. The ReplicaSet keeps the desired number of Pods active. It acts as a wrapper around our Pod definition. The following manifest shows the declaration of a ReplicaSet:

```
apiVersion: apps/v1
kind: ReplicaSet
metadata:
  name: account-rs
spec:
  replicas: 2
  selector:
    matchLabels:
      name: account-pod
  template:
...
```

The preceding code declares a ReplicaSet called account-rs that has two Pod replicas in it. We match that to our Pod by using a selector. Our selection has a label match declared using the name tag and stating it needs to be account-pod. The omitted part of the file after template is the content from our Pod manifest file, omitting the first two lines of that declaration.

Assuming we have created the preceding file in our cloud shell, we can deploy the ReplicaSet by executing the following command:

```
kubectl apply -f account-rs.yaml
```

We can delete the ReplicaSet by executing the following command:

```
kubectl delete -f account-rs.yaml
```

So, now, we can have a stable set of stateless Pods active, but how do we manage different deployment strategies? How do we keep some Pods running while we roll out updates to the ReplicaSet? This is handled by Deployments, and just like how ReplicaSets wrap around Pods, **Deployments** wrap around ReplicaSets, as we will see in the next section.

Kubernetes Deployments

The purpose of a **Deployment** is to change Pods and ReplicaSets at a controlled rate. In practice, we do not declare ReplicaSets directly but wrap them with Deployments. Deployments allow us to apply strategies to updates such as rolling updates and provide us with the ability to roll back updates. The following manifest shows the declaration of a Deployment:

```
apiVersion: apps/v1
kind: Deployment
metadata:
  name: account-deployment
spec:
  replicas: 2
  strategy:
    type: RollingUpdate
    rollingUpdate:
      maxUnavailable: 1
      maxSurge: 1
  selector:
    matchLabels:
      name: account-pod
  template:
...
```

The preceding manifest code declares a **RollingUpdate** strategy, states that only one Pod in the ReplicaSet may be unavailable at a time, and that the number of Pods may be one bigger than the ReplicatSet size while an update is underway. As with the ReplicatSet manifest, it uses a selector to link to the Pod definition.

Assuming we have created the preceding file in our cloud shell, we can deploy the Deployment by executing the following command:

```
kubectl apply -f account-deployment.yaml --record
```

The purpose of the `--record` switch in the preceding command is to create a rollback point that we can use if there is a problem with the update. We can see the available revisions by executing the following command:

```
kubectl rollout history deployment account-deployment
```

We can roll back to a revision by executing the following command:

```
kubectl rollout undo deployment account-deployment
--to-revision=1
```

We can delete the Deployment by executing the following command:

```
kubectl delete -f account-deployment.yaml
```

With that, we have organized how we can deploy our containers in a way that protects the availability of existing services and allows us to roll back updates to previous update points. Now, let's look at how we can automatically horizontally scale our Pods in and out. This is covered in the next section.

Kubernetes Horizontal Pod Autoscalers

The purpose of a **Horizontal Pod Autoscaler** (**HPA**) is to add and remove Pods in a ReplicaSet based on the resource metrics we define to best match the resource consumption to our workload needs.

The following manifest declares an HPA for our Deployment:

```
apiVersion: autoscaling/v1
kind: HorizontalPodAutoscaler
metadata:
  name: account-hpa
spec:
```

```
scaleTargetRef:
  apiVersion: apps/v1
  kind: Deployment
  name: account-deployment
minReplicas: 1
maxReplicas: 10
targetCPUUtilizationPercentage: 75
```

The preceding manifest declares an HPA called account-hpa. It specifies that the HPA is for the Deployment called account-deployment. It then specifies that the minimum number of replicas is 1 and that the maximum number is 10. Finally, it declares that we scale up if the CPU utilization goes over 75%.

Assuming we have created the preceding file in our cloud shell, we can deploy the HPA by executing the following command:

```
kubectl apply -f account-hpa.yaml
```

We can delete the HPA by executing the following command:

```
kubectl delete -f account-hpa.yaml
```

This concludes what we need to do for our microservices to run, scale, and be effectively managed to remove downtime while updating the application. We will now move on to how we can access these Pods in a ReplicaSet as a unit without having to address a specific Pod. We will do this using Services.

Kubernetes Services

The purpose of **Services** is to present a frontend for our ReplicaSets or Pods and provide a single point of entry that will load balance across the Pods that have been identified.

The following manifest declares a Service for our Pods, identified by the name account-pod:

```
apiVersion: v1
kind: Service
metadata:
  name: account-svc
spec:
  type: NodePort
  selector:
```

```
    name: account-pod
 ports:
 - protocol: TCP
   port: 8080
   targetPort: 8080
```

The preceding manifest declares a Service called `account-svc` that routes requests to the `account-pod` instances in our ReplicaSet. It maps the port our service exposes, which is `8080`, to the port our Pods expose, which is also `8080`.

Of note here is the type of Service. The type is important because of the behavior it describes. The following are the most important types:

- **ClusterIP**: Exposes the service on a cluster internal IP address. The service can be accessed by other Pods from within the cluster

- **NodePort**: Builds on top of the ClusterIP and allows external access to the Pods on the node ports that have been generated by the service for each **Node**. This external access balances within a Node but not across Nodes and is often used in conjunction with **Ingress**, as we will see in the next section.

- **LoadBalancer**: Builds on top of **ClusterIP** or **NodePort** and creates a **Google Cloud HTTP(s) load balancer** to route traffic from outside our cluster to the service in our cluster. This external access balances across Nodes and is often used in conjunction with Ingress, as we will see in the next section.

Assuming we have created the preceding file in our cloud shell, we can deploy the Service by executing the following command:

```
kubectl apply -f account-service.yaml
```

We can delete the Service by executing the following command:

```
kubectl delete -f account-service.yaml
```

We now have the manifests needed to create a Deployment that manages a ReplicaSet that manages instances of our Pod. We also have the manifests for an HPA and a Service. We will now look at how we can automate applying these manifests and the manifests for our ConfigMap instances using **Google Cloud Build**.

Automating the deployment of our components

In this section, we will learn how to automate the deployment of our application components. The source code for this deployment can be found in the Chapter 16 folder of this book's GitHub repository: https://github.com/PacktPublishing/ Modernizing-Applications-with-Google-Cloud-Platform/tree/ master/Chapter%2016. In this folder, there is a project called gke-deploy. Copy that into the local repository that is linked to **our Google Cloud source repository**.

The structure of our project is as follows:

```
gke-deploy
    certificate
        certificate.yaml
        cloudBuild.yaml
    ingress
        cloudBuild.yaml
        cloudBuild2.yaml
        ingress.yaml
        ingress2.yaml
    microservices
        account
            account-deployment.yaml
            account-env.yaml
            account-hpa.yaml
            account-service.yaml
        front-end
            front-end-deployment.yaml
            front-end-hpa.yaml
            front-end-service.yaml
            nginx-config.yaml
        user
            user-deployment.yaml
            user-env.yaml
            user-hpa.yaml
            user-service.yaml
        cloudBuild.yaml
```

For now, ignore the certificate and ingress folders – we will cover those in the next section. In this section, we are focusing on deploying the three microservices and all the components and configurations they need to run. In Google Cloud Build, create a new build trigger using the `gke-deploy/microservice/cloudBuild.yaml` file. The content of this file is shown in the following fragments.

The first fragment deploys all the component parts needed for our `account` microservice:

```
steps:
- name: 'gcr.io/cloud-builders/kubectl'
  args: ['apply', '-f', 'account-env.yaml', '-f', 'account-deployment.yaml', '-f', 'account-hpa.yaml', '-f', 'account-service.yaml']
  dir: 'gke-deploy/microservices/account'
  env:
  - 'CLOUDSDK_COMPUTE_ZONE=europe-west2-c'
  - 'CLOUDSDK_CONTAINER_CLUSTER=banking-cluster'
```

The following fragment deploys all the components needed for our `user` microservice:

```
- name: 'gcr.io/cloud-builders/kubectl'
  args: ['apply', '-f', 'user-env.yaml', '-f', 'user-deployment.yaml', '-f', 'user-hpa.yaml', '-f', 'user-service.yaml']
  dir: 'gke-deploy/microservices/user'
  env:
  - 'CLOUDSDK_COMPUTE_ZONE=europe-west2-c'
  - 'CLOUDSDK_CONTAINER_CLUSTER=banking-cluster'
```

The final fragment deploys all the components needed for our `front-end` microservice:

```
- name: 'gcr.io/cloud-builders/kubectl'
  args: ['apply', '-f', 'nginx-config.yaml', '-f', 'front-end-deployment.yaml', '-f', 'front-end-hpa.yaml', '-f', 'front-end-service.yaml']
  dir: 'gke-deploy/microservices/front-end'
  env:
  - 'CLOUDSDK_COMPUTE_ZONE=europe-west2-c'
  - 'CLOUDSDK_CONTAINER_CLUSTER=banking-cluster'
```

The preceding build will provision all the items we discussed previously, except for the credential's secret. That is deployed manually before the other items are automatically deployed using Google Cloud Build. Once the build trigger is in place, we can add, commit, and push to our Google Cloud source repository and watch the deployment happen.

Once the build has been completed successfully, our microservices will be provisioned in GKE and ready to use. But how do we test and use our application? The services are ready but have not been exposed on public endpoints with hostnames provided by DNS. We will cover how to do that in the following section.

Configuring public access to the application

We will now look at how we can expose our services to the outside world and make them available on public endpoints. The services we have created thus far are of the `NodePort` type, which means they are exposed on the IP address of the Node they are running on, using a port generated by the Service. The IP address of each Node is a private IP address on our VPC. To expose our services securely to the outside world, we need to have three things in place. First, we need a public static IP address so that we can map our hostname in our DNS to that address. Next, we need an SSL certificate so that we can use HTTPS. Finally, we need a method that will let us route traffic from the public IP address/ hostname to our services. This method is called **Ingress**.

We create the public static IP address called `banking-ip` as we did when setting up the **Google HTTP(s) load balancer** for our virtual machine infrastructure. Please ensure that the A (address) record that's set up in your DNS provider matches the hostname we will use to resolve to our public static IP address.

Now, we will learn how to use a **Google-managed certificate** to enable HTTPS for our application.

Kubernetes-managed certificates

Kubernetes-managed certificates are wrappers around Google-managed certificates, which are SSL certificates that Google creates and manages for us. These certificates are limited compared to self-managed certificates in that they do not demonstrate the identity of the organization and do not support wildcards.

Support for Kubernetes-managed certificates is in beta, so we may run into problems when asking Google Cloud to provision a certificate for us. The problem is that if there is already a managed certificate existing in our Google Cloud project for the hostname we want to use, the provisioning will fail. To check the existing certificates, enter the following commands in the cloud shell:

```
gcloud config set project bankingapplication
gcloud beta compute ssl-certificates list
```

If you see a conflicting certificate, you can delete it with the following command:

```
gcloud beta compute ssl-certificates delete <certificate_name>
```

We are now ready to learn how Kubernetes-managed certificates are provisioned. In the certificate folder of our gke-deploy project, there are two files: certificate.yaml and cloudBuild.yaml. The certificate.yaml file is the manifest for our managed certificate and looks like this:

```
apiVersion: networking.gke.io/v1beta1
kind: ManagedCertificate
metadata:
  name: banking-certificate
spec:
  domains:
    - www.banking.jasonmarston.me.uk
```

In the preceding manifest, we have declared that our certificate is named banking-certificate and that it is for the www.banking.jasonmarston.me.uk document.

The cloudBuild.yaml file defines the build for our certificate:

```
steps:
- name: 'gcr.io/cloud-builders/kubectl'
  args: ['apply', '-f', 'certificate.yaml']
  dir: 'gke-deploy/certificate'
  env:
    - 'CLOUDSDK_COMPUTE_ZONE=europe-west2-c'
    - 'CLOUDSDK_CONTAINER_CLUSTER=banking-cluster'
```

The preceding listing uses the `kubectl` cloud builder to apply our `certificate.yaml` file.

We will not execute the cloud build for our certificate yet as it goes hand in hand with our Ingress. Instead, we will apply both the certificate and Ingress in the next section.

Kubernetes Ingress

Ingress is a Kubernetes object that exposes one or more Services to clients outside of our cluster. It defines a set of rules for routing traffic from specific URLs to specific services. The initial version of the Ingress manifest file (`ingress.yaml`) we will examine looks as follows:

```yaml
apiVersion: networking.k8s.io/v1beta1
kind: Ingress
metadata:
  name: banking-ingress
  annotations:
    kubernetes.io/ingress.allow-http: "false"
    kubernetes.io/ingress.global-static-ip-name: banking-ip
    networking.gke.io/managed-certificates: banking-certificate
spec:
  rules:
    - host: www.banking.jasonmarston.me.uk
      http:
        paths:
          - path:
            backend:
              serviceName: front-end-svc
              servicePort: 80
```

The annotations in our preceding metadata section define that we will only accept HTTPS traffic, we will use the public static IP address called `banking-ip`, and we will use the certificate called `banking-certificate` to enable SSL. The content in the `spec` section defines a rule that all incoming traffic that will host `www.banking.jasonmarston.me.uk` on any path will be routed to our `front-end-svc` service on port `80`. While this works, it does mean that all traffic to `user-svc` and `account-svc` goes through `front-end-svc`, which can create a bottleneck. Instead, in `ingress2.yaml`, we have specified additional rules, as shown in the following fragment:

```
spec:
  rules:
    - host: www.banking.jasonmarston.me.uk
      http:
        paths:
          - path: /account
            backend:
              serviceName: account-svc
              servicePort: 8080
          - path: /account/*
            backend:
              serviceName: account-svc
              servicePort: 8080
          - path: /user/*
            backend:
              serviceName: user-svc
              servicePort: 8080
          - path:
            backend:
              serviceName: front-end-svc
              servicePort: 80
```

In the preceding fragment, we have specified that traffic to `/account` or `/account/*` will be routed to our `account-svc` on port `8080`, traffic to `/user/*` will be routed to our `user-svc` on port `8080`, and all other traffic will be routed to `front-end-svc` on port `80`. This means that `front-end-svc` is no longer a bottleneck and traffic is routed directly to the service intended.

Now, we can set up Cloud Build triggers for our managed certificate and Ingress manifests. Use `cloudBuild2.yaml` for the Ingress build. Once these have been set up, run them manually from Cloud Console.

Provisioning certificates and setting up Ingress can be a lengthy process. Kubernetes needs to create a Google HTTP(s) load balancer and provision the certificate. We have found that it typically takes approximately 30 minutes from completion of the cloud builds to the application being available.

You would see the following sorts of errors in the browser if the Ingress is not ready yet:

- *This site can't be reached*: Generally, the Google HTTP(s) load balancer has not been provisioned yet.
- *Certificate or Cypher error messages*: The certificate has either not been provisioned yet or the provisioned certificate has not been applied and propagated to where it is needed yet.

We now have a fully working GKE-based environment for our banking application.

When to use GKE

GKE should be used as the deployment environment when containers are under discussion and we need complex orchestration.

The following list explains some reasons why we would want to use GKE to host our containers:

- We need **Stateful** containers.
- We need to use ConfigMaps or Secrets.
- We need to have complex **Ingress** routing.
- We need the services to be hosted on a **VPC.**
- We need to always have at least one instance of our container active.
- We have special host needs such as GPUs or Windows operating systems on our Nodes.

Now that we have learned about when to use GKE, we can move on to the next section and review what we have learned in this chapter.

Summary

In this chapter, we learned about GKE and how it orchestrates and manages the deployment, configuration, and scaling of our container-based microservices. We learned how to provide configuration for our microservices using **Kubernetes ConfigMaps** and **Secrets**, and how to manage true secrets using **Google Secret Manager**. We then learned how to configure and deploy our microservices and how to expose them securely to a public endpoint so that they can be accessed from outside the cluster. Finally, we learned when to use GKE.

With the information provided in this chapter, we can decide whether GKE is appropriate for hosting our application microservices and if it is, how to provision a GKE cluster, deploy and configure our microservices, and provide a public endpoint for users of the application to access via a web browser.

In the next chapter, we will learn how to deploy and run our microservices in the most mature serverless platform on Google Cloud, **Google App Engine (Flexible)**.

17

Going Serverless with Google App Engine

Container-based microservices is a very useful and modern approach that offers portability and flexibility by allowing you to migrate your applications seamlessly from one compute service to another with very little or no operational overhead and is available on **Google Compute Engine (GCE)**, **Google App Engine (GAE)**, **Google Cloud Run**, and **Google Kubernetes Engine (GKE)**.

In this chapter, we turn our attention to **Google App Engine** (flexible), which is Google's longest serving and most mature *serverless* offering. The **Google App Engine flexible environment** does *not* offer the complex orchestration that Google Kubernetes Engine does, but if such orchestration is not required, then the Google App Engine flexible environment is the simplest, most mature, and cost-effective option available for running container-based microservices.

In the next chapter, we will look at a table that compares App Engine, Cloud Run, and Google Kubernetes deployments.

In this chapter, we will cover the following topics:

- Google App Engine
- Deploying containers to the App Engine flexible environment
- When to use Google App Engine

Technical requirements

The code files for this chapter are available here: `https://github.com/PacktPublishing/Modernizing-Applications-with-Google-Cloud-Platform/tree/master/Chapter%2017`.

Introducing Google App Engine

We have described Google App Engine as a serverless offering, but what do we mean by that? Serverless is a method of providing the runtime environment needed by an application without binding the application to a specific server infrastructure. The application only has access to the features provided by the environment, and we do not have to worry about patching or maintaining the underlying infrastructure. The application is automatically scaled out when demand increases and scaled back in when demand decreases.

Google App Engine is designed to host services that communicate on ports 80 or 443 using the HTTP(S) protocol, specifically, web applications. It also manages connectivity to Google Cloud SQL as it is quite a common pattern for web applications to connect to relational databases. There are two flavors of Google App Engine – *Standard* and *Flexible*. We will examine Standard first.

Google App Engine standard environment

The Google App Engine standard environment is based on out-of-the-box containers that have been pre-configured with popular runtime stacks for web applications. At the time of writing, the runtime stacks available are as follows:

- Python
- Java
- Node.js

- PHP
- Ruby
- Go

If the runtime stack for our application is a supported one, then the Google App Engine Standard Environment is a fantastic choice for running an application. However, if the runtime stack is not supported, then we need to use the Google App Engine flexible environment.

Google App Engine flexible environment

The Google App Engine flexible environment allows us to customize a container based on one of the runtime images for the various programming languages mentioned previously or provide our own custom container for a runtime stack not in the preceding list. The flexibility for the runtime provided by the Google App Engine flexible environment comes at a price. The price is mostly in terms of complexity, as we must create and maintain a custom container image. The other impacts are as follows:

- Deployment times are measured in minutes rather than seconds.
- Startup times are measured in minutes rather than seconds.
- The service cannot scale down to zero instances.
- Pricing is based on the usage of vCPU, memory, and persistent disks rather than instance hours.

Now that we have learned about Google App Engine, including the two flavors available, Standard and Flexible, we will learn how to make use of the Google App Engine flexible environment and deploy our application microservices.

Components of App Engine and the hierarchy of an application deployed on App Engine

An **App Engine** app is made up of a single application resource that consists of one or more microservices.

Each service can be configured to use different runtimes and to operate with different performance settings, meaning you can have a service with the runtime *Go*, a second service with the runtime *Node.js*, and a third service with runtime Python all part of the same single application.

Within each service, you deploy versions of that service. Each version then runs within one or more instances, depending on how much traffic you configured it to handle:

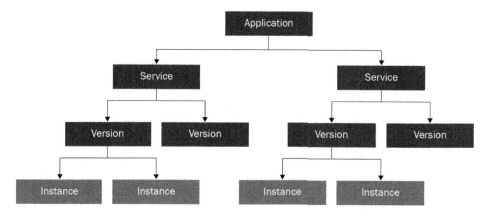

Figure 17.1 – App Engine hierarchy of an application

Deploying containers to the App Engine flexible environment

In this section, we will learn about what is needed to deploy an updated version of our banking application using the Google App Engine flexible environment.

Before deploying our microservices with the Google App Engine flexible environment, we need to make a few changes in our projects to account for the environment differences between Google App Engine and Google Kubernetes Engine.

Application configuration updates

To update our application configuration to be ready to deploy to the Google App Engine flexible environment, we need to make a few small changes to make sure we pick up the externalized configuration of our application.

The changes made to our application configuration are as follows:

1. Firstly, in our user-rest and account-rest projects, we need to update the application.properties file to replace instances of GCP_GKE_*, such as the following:

    ```
    spring.datasource.jdbcUrl = ${GCP_GKE_USER_DATASOURCE_
    URL}
    ```

```
spring.account-datasource.jdbcUrl = ${GCP_GKE_ACCOUNT_
DATASOURCE_URL}
```

2. The instances of GCP_GKE_* are replaced with GCP_*, as shown next:

```
spring.datasource.jdbcUrl = ${GCP_USER_DATASOURCE_URL}
spring.account-datasource.jdbcUrl = ${GCP_ACCOUNT_
DATASOURCE_URL}
```

3. Next, we need to add configuration to make use of the connectivity to Google Cloud SQL provided by Google App Engine rather than *Google Cloud SQL Proxy*:

```
spring.datasource.socketFactory = com.google.cloud.sql.
mysql.SocketFactory
spring.datasource.cloudSqlInstance = ${GCP_USER_
DATASOURCE_CLOUD_SQL_INSTANCE}
spring.account-datasource.socketFactory = com.google.
cloud.sql.mysql.SocketFactory
spring.account-datasource.cloudSqlInstance = ${GCP_
ACCOUNT_DATASOURCE_CLOUD_SQL_INSTANCE}
```

The previous code fragment declares that *Spring Boot* will use the SocketFactory method provided by Google to connect to our Google Cloud SQL instance. This is done twice, once for the default (user) data source, and once for the account data source. The names of the Cloud SQL instances are retrieved from *Google Secret Manager*, as indicated by the GCP_ prefix variable.

4. Now we have updated the application.properties file in our user-rest and application-rest microservices to reflect the fact that Google App Engine manages connections to databases for us. Rather than using the Google Cloud SQL proxy, we can move on to the frontend microservice.

5. A requirement for custom containers in Google App Engine (flexible) is for them to listen on port 8080 for HTTP traffic. The user-rest and account-rest microservices already expose port 8080, but until now the front-end microservice has been listening on port 80.

6. To change front-end to listen on and expose port 8080, we need to create a file called default.conf as follows:

```
server {
    listen        8080;
    server_name app.banking.jasonmarston.me.uk;
```

```
location / {
        root /usr/share/nginx/html;
        index index.html;
    }
}
```

7. The preceding configuration instructs `Nginx` to listen on port `8080` for the hostname `app.banking.jasonmarston.me.uk` and serve up static content from the `/usr/share/nginx/html` folder.

8. Next, we need to apply the preceding configuration file to our container and change the port exposed to be port `8080`:

```
FROM nginx:1.17.10-alpine
COPY WebContent /usr/share/nginx/html
COPY default.conf /etc/nginx/conf.d/default.conf

EXPOSE 8080
```

9. The previous `Dockerfile` copies our `default.conf` file into the container image at the location where `Nginx` expects to find a default configuration and exposes port `8080` for the container.

   The changes to our `front-end`, `user-rest`, and `account-rest` projects can be found in the `Chapter 11` folder of the GitHub repository for the book: `https://github.com/PacktPublishing/Modernizing-Applications-with-Google-Cloud-Platform/tree/master/Chapter%2017`.

10. To action these changes, copy the `Chapter 11` folder into our local Git repository folder, and then add, commit, and push the updates to our Google Cloud source repository.

Now that we have completed the configuration changes to our application, the next step is to deploy the `appengine` service by updating the `app.yaml` file, which acts as a deployment descriptor for a specific `appengine` service version. App Engine also provides an option to serve the application on a custom domain in addition to the preconfigured `appspot` domain. This is done using a routing file called a `dispatch.yaml` file, which configures routing to specific services based on a domain, which we will also cover in the following section.

Deployment configuration

There are various configuration files associated with Google App Engine apps and services deployed within those apps. The two configuration files used in this chapter are app.yaml, which is used to configure a specific microservice, and dispatch.yaml, which is used to configure the routing of HTTP(S) requests to microservices. This means that we will have one app.yaml file per microservice and one dispatch.yaml file for the application. The configuration files we will be dealing with for deployment can be found in the gae-deploy project in the Chapter 11 folder of the GitHub repository for the book: https://github.com/PacktPublishing/Modernizing-Applications-with-Google-Cloud-Platform/tree/master/Chapter%2017.

We will now examine the app.yaml file for our account microservice one fragment at a time:

```
runtime: custom
env: flex
service: account
```

In the preceding fragment, we have specified that we are using the Google App Engine flexible environment rather than Standard by providing flex as the value for env:. We are providing a custom runtime stack by specifying custom for runtime:, and we are calling the instance we will be deploying to account by providing account as the name for the service attribute:.

Next, we move on to the environment fragment:

```
env_variables:
    BANKING_LOGGING_LEVEL: WARN
    GOOGLE_CLOUD_PROJECT: bankingapplication
```

The previous environment fragment declares the environment variables that we could not transfer into being *secrets* handled by *Google Secret Manager*.

Next, we specify the resources for our instance:

```
resources:
    cpu: 1
    memory_gb: 1
```

The previous `resources` fragment declares that our instance requires 1 CPU and 1 GB of RAM.

Now we declare our autoscaling rules:

```
automatic_scaling:
  min_num_instances: 1
  max_num_instances: 10
  cool_down_period_sec: 180
  cpu_utilization:
    target_utilization: 0.75
  target_concurrent_requests: 100
```

The previous automatic scaling section specifies that we will have between 1 and 10 instances active at any time (inclusive), while there will be a 3-minute delay between scaling actions to prevent excessive scaling activity, and our target CPU utilization is 75%.

Next, we move on to health checks:

```
liveness_check:
  path: "/healthcheck"
  check_interval_sec: 30
  timeout_sec: 4
  failure_threshold: 2
  success_threshold: 2
  initial_delay_sec: 30
readiness_check:
  path: "/healthcheck"
  check_interval_sec: 5
  timeout_sec: 5
  failure_threshold: 5
  success_threshold: 2
  app_start_timeout_sec: 100
```

The previous fragment declares two health checks. First is a readiness check, which is used to register the instance with the load balancer when startup has completed and a successful HTTP status code is returned from the service. Second is the liveness check, which is used to move an instance in or out of the load balancer depending on the status.

The final fragment is for our connection to the database:

```
beta_settings:
   cloud_sql_instances: bankingapplication:europe-west2:mysql-
instance
```

The previous fragment declares the Cloud SQL instance our application will connect to. Note that this must be on a public endpoint rather than a private one. We have a similar `app.yaml` file for each of the microservices that make up our application.

Next, we will look at the `dispatch.yaml` file, which we use to configure routing to our microservices:

```
dispatch:
   - url: "app.banking.jasonmarston.me.uk/"
     service: default

   - url: "app.banking.jasonmarston.me.uk/user/*"
     service: user

   - url: "app.banking.jasonmarston.me.uk/account"
     service: account

   - url: "app.banking.jasonmarston.me.uk/account/*"
     service: account
```

In the previous file, we map the URLs to our microservices. Each of the rules maps a location under `hostname app.banking.jasonmarston.me.uk` to a specific microservice. This completes the configuration of our components and deployments for Google App Engine (flexible), so we will now move on to how to deploy these components and configurations.

Deployment prerequisites

To deploy our microservices in the Google App Engine flexible environment, there are a few things we need to set up. The first of these is setting the service account permissions for Google Cloud Build, as shown next:

GCP Service	Role ❓	Status
Cloud Functions	Cloud Functions Developer	DISABLED ▾
Cloud Run	Cloud Run Admin	ENABLED ▾
App Engine	App Engine Admin	ENABLED ▾
Kubernetes Engine	Kubernetes Engine Developer	ENABLED ▾
Compute Engine	Compute Instance Admin (v1)	DISABLED ▾
Firebase	Firebase Admin	DISABLED ▾
Cloud KMS	Cloud KMS CryptoKey Decrypter	DISABLED ▾
Service Accounts	Service Account User	ENABLED ▾

Figure 17.2 – Cloud Build service account permissions

The next step is to grant permissions to our `appengine` service account to allow it to use Google Secret Manager. We do this by adding the following roles to our `bankingapplication@appspot.gserviceaccount.com` account:

- Secret Manager Secret Accessor
- Secret Manager Viewer

These roles are shown next:

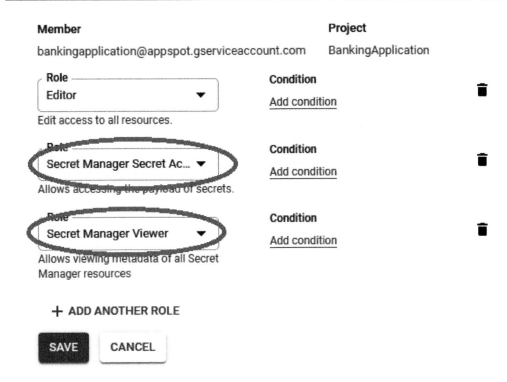

Figure 17.3 – App Engine service account roles

Lastly, we will create an application to host the microservices we are deploying:

1. From the **Navigation** menu, click **App Engine**:

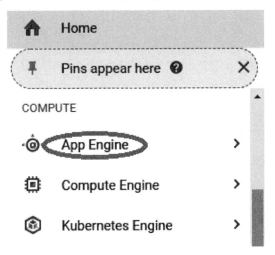

Figure 17.4 – Nav menu: App Engine

2. On the **App Engine** page, click **Create Application**:

Figure 17.5 – Create Application

3. Select a region (we chose `europe-west2`) and then click **Create app**:

Figure 17.6 – Selecting a region and creating an app

4.   Click **Cancel**:

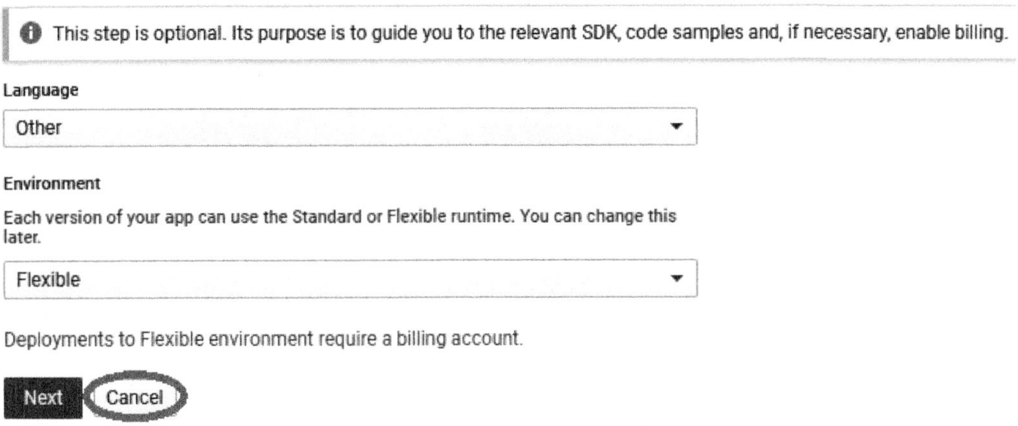

> ℹ This step is optional. Its purpose is to guide you to the relevant SDK, code samples and, if necessary, enable billing.

Language

| Other | ▾ |

Environment

Each version of your app can use the Standard or Flexible runtime. You can change this later.

| Flexible | ▾ |

Deployments to Flexible environment require a billing account.

[Next] (Cancel)

Figure 17.7 – Canceling the optional step

5.   Review the success message:

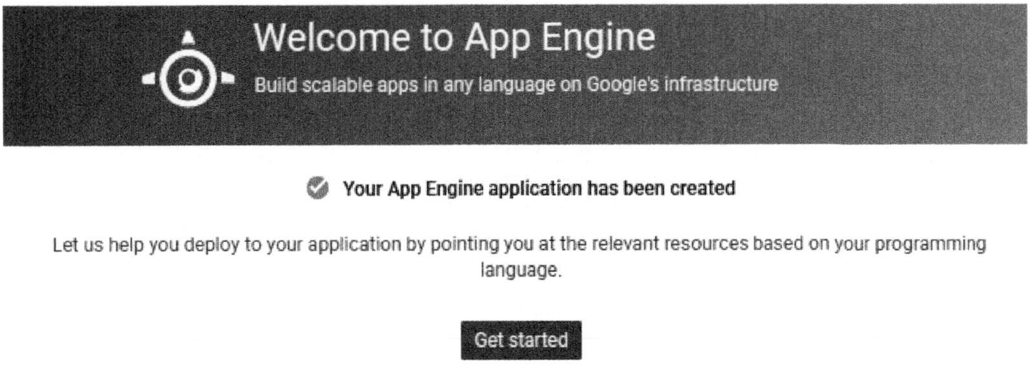

Welcome to App Engine
Build scalable apps in any language on Google's infrastructure

✅ **Your App Engine application has been created**

Let us help you deploy to your application by pointing you at the relevant resources based on your programming language.

[Get started]

Figure 17.8 – App Engine created

6. From the **Navigation** menu, select **App Engine** > **Settings**:

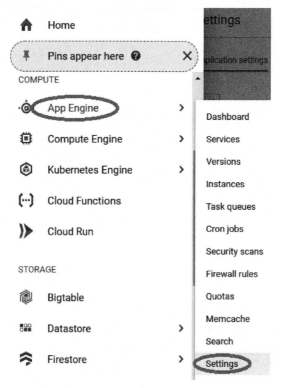

Figure 17.9 – Nav menu: App Engine > Settings

7. On the **Settings** page, select **Custom domains** and then click on the **Add a custom domain** button:

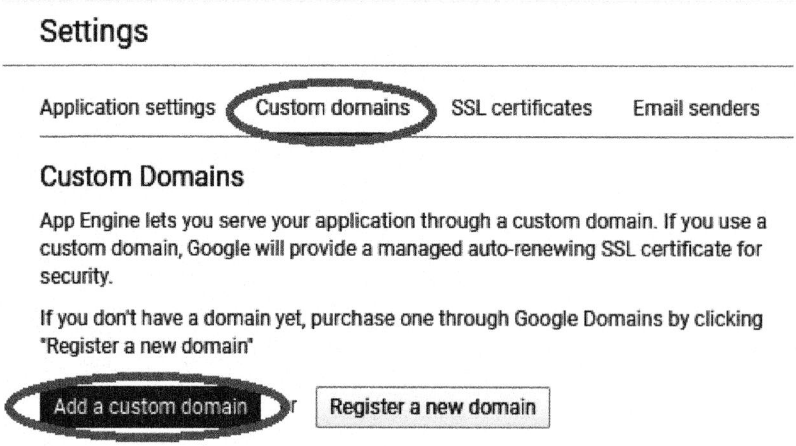

Figure 17.10 – Custom domains: Adding a custom domain

8. Select a validated domain and then click **Continue**:

Application settings
Custom domains
SSL certificates
Email senders
To point your own domain names to your App Engine app, follow these steps.
1 Select the domain you want to use
jasonmarston.me.uk
Continue
2 Point your domain to banking-279608
3 Update your DNS records to enable security
Cancel

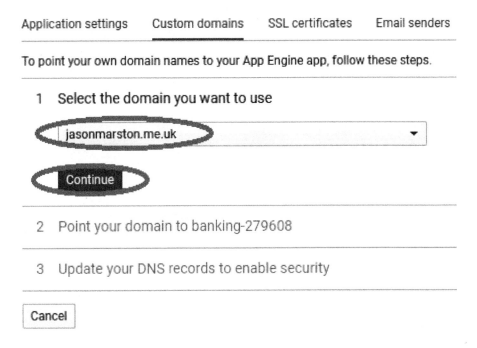

Figure 17.11 – Custom domains: Continue

9. Provide a hostname (deleting any existing hostnames) and then click **Save mappings**:

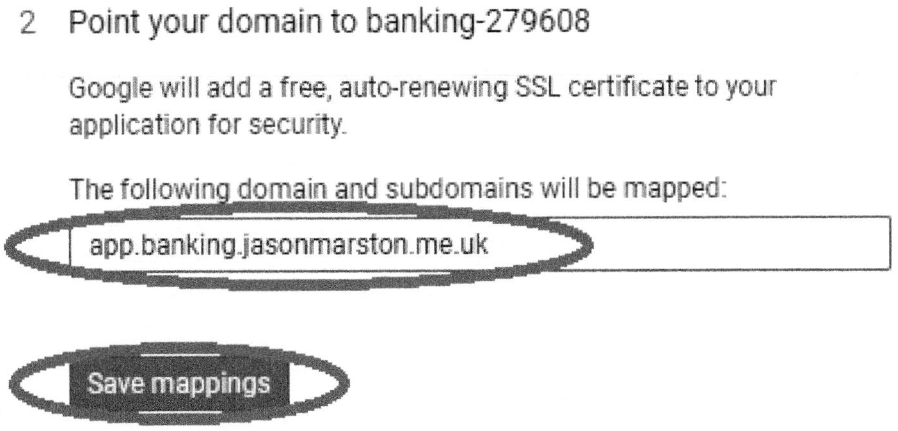

2 Point your domain to banking-279608
Google will add a free, auto-renewing SSL certificate to your application for security.
The following domain and subdomains will be mapped:
app.banking.jasonmarston.me.uk
Save mappings

Figure 17.12 – Save mappings

10. Click **Continue**:

2   Point your domain to bankingapplication

Google will add a free, auto-renewing SSL certificate to your application for security.

The following domain and subdomains will be mapped:

Status	Domain
✔	app.banking.jasonmarston.me.uk

Figure 17.13 – Continue

11. Update your DNS with your DNS provider and then click **Done**:

3   Update your DNS records to enable security

Add the following DNS records with your domain registrar for jasonmarston.me.uk:

Type	Data	Alias
A	216.239.32.21	
A	216.239.34.21	
A	216.239.36.21	
A	216.239.38.21	
AAAA	2001:4860:4802:32::15	
AAAA	2001:4860:4802:34::15	
AAAA	2001:4860:4802:36::15	
AAAA	2001:4860:4802:38::15	
CNAME	ghs.googlehosted.com	app.banking

DNS changes can take up to 24 hours to take effect. Your SSL certificate will take several minutes to activate.

Figure 17.14 – Updating the DNS

We have updated the permissions for our Google Cloud Build service account and our Google App Engine service account. We have also created the application we will deploy our microservices to, and mapped the DNS hostname we will use for the application. We can now move on to setting up the automation of our deployment.

Automating deployment

Once again, we are declaring a build using a `cloudBuild.yaml` file. In this instance, we are using a cloud builder we have not used before. This is the `cloud-sdk` cloud builder. The `cloud-sdk` cloud builder provides up-to-date versions of the command-line tools for use with Google Cloud. These tools include `gcloud`, `gsutil`, and `bq`. We use this instead of the `gcloud` cloud builder as the version of the `gcloud` command-line tool is more up to date in the `cloud-sdk` cloud builder than in the `gcloud` cloud builder.

We will examine the `cloudBuild.yaml` file for deploying our application one step at a time, starting with the following fragment for `front-end`:

```
steps:
- name: 'gcr.io/google.com/cloudsdktool/cloud-sdk'
  args:
  - 'gcloud'
  - 'app'
  - 'deploy'
  - '--image-url'
  - 'gcr.io/bankingapplication/front-end:latest'
  - 'front-end/app.yaml'
  dir: 'gae-deploy'
```

The preceding fragment instructs Google Cloud Build to use the `gcloud app deploy` command to deploy our `front-end` microservice from the `front-end` image in Google Container Registry. It also applies the `app.yaml` configuration to the microservice as part of the deployment.

The next fragment deals with the `user` microservice:

```
- name: 'gcr.io/google.com/cloudsdktool/cloud-sdk'
  args:
  - 'gcloud'
  - 'app'
  - 'deploy'
  - '--image-url'
```

```
- 'gcr.io/bankingapplication/user-rest:latest'
- 'user/app.yaml'
dir: 'gae-deploy'
```

The preceding fragment instructs Google Cloud Build to use the `gcloud app deploy` command to deploy our `user` microservice from the `user-rest` image in Google Container Registry. It also applies the `app.yaml` configuration to the microservice as part of the deployment.

The next fragment deals with the `account` microservice:

```
- name: 'gcr.io/google.com/cloudsdktool/cloud-sdk'
  args:
  - 'gcloud'
  - 'app'
  - 'deploy'
  - '--image-url'
  - 'gcr.io/bankingapplication/account-rest:latest'
  - 'account/app.yaml'
  dir: 'gae-deploy'
```

The preceding fragment instructs Google Cloud Build to use the `gcloud app deploy` command to deploy our `account` microservice from the `account-rest` image in Google Container Registry. It also applies the `app.yaml` configuration to the microservice as part of the deployment.

Now that we have declared steps for each of our microservices, our build configuration needs a step for the routing in our application, as shown next:

```
- name: 'gcr.io/google.com/cloudsdktool/cloud-sdk'
  args:
  - 'gcloud'
  - 'app'
  - 'deploy'
  - 'dispatch.yaml'
  dir: 'gae-deploy'
timeout: 1800s
```

The preceding fragment instructs Google Cloud Build to use the `gcloud app deploy` command to apply the `dispatch.yaml` configuration to the application in order to route HTTP requests to the correct microservice. The final line updates the timeout to be 30 minutes, since deployment to Google App Engine (flexible) is a time-consuming process.

Our next step is to copy the `Chapter 11` folder into our local Git repository folder, and then add, commit, and push the updates to our Google Cloud source repository.

Now that all the configuration for our application is in our Google Cloud source repository, we can create a Cloud Build trigger to execute the build defined by the preceding `cloudBuild.yaml` file. Once this trigger has been created, we can trigger it and then wait a while (approximately 20 to 25 minutes) for the deployment to complete.

Once the build has been completed successfully, we can test the application by using a web browser to access `https://app.banking.jasonmarston.me.uk`.

We will now look at when to choose Google App Engine for our microservices.

When to use Google App Engine

The choice between **Google App Engine**, **Google Kubernetes Engine**, and **Google Cloud Run** can be a tricky one and, in a professional environment, is often determined by company policies. If we have total freedom, it can still be a subjective choice. However, the following is some guidance to help with the decision-making process.

Consider using Google App Engine when the following criteria apply:

- The services are HTTP(S) based.
- The services are stateless.
- There is a small number of services.
- The services do not require complex orchestration.
- Google Cloud Run is not available in the region you wish to deploy to.

The previous guidance comes down to two major concerns. Are the microservices stateless web apps, and do we need to coordinate between them? If, based on the previous list of considerations, Google App Engine is not a good fit, then we need to consider Google Kubernetes Engine or Google Cloud Run.

That concludes our chapter on going serverless with the Google App Engine flexible environment. We will finish up with a brief review of the chapter.

Summary

In this chapter, we learned about Google App Engine in both of its flavors – Standard and Flexible. We looked at the changes needed to our microservices to allow them to run effectively in the Google App Engine flexible environment, and the configuration we would need to add for Google App Engine. We then learned how to automate the deployment and configuration of our microservices in a Google App Engine application. Finally, we learned some guidelines on how to decide whether the Google App Engine flexible environment is a good match for the application we wish to deploy.

In the next chapter, we will learn about Google Cloud Run and how to deploy and configure our application in the very latest serverless environment available in Google Cloud, thereby futureproofing our application deployment.

18
Future Proofing Your App with Google Cloud Run

In this chapter, we look at the final option for deploying microservices that we will be considering in this book – **Google Cloud Run**. This is the latest serverless offering from Google and is built from the ground up with containers in mind. Google Cloud Run does not offer the complex orchestration that Google Kubernetes Engine does, but if such orchestration is not required, then Google Cloud Run is the latest and most container-centric option available for our container-based microservices.

In this chapter, we will cover the following topics:

- Cloud Run
- Deploying containers to Google Cloud Run
- When to use Cloud Run

Technical requirements

The code files for this chapter are available here: `https://github.com/PacktPublishing/Modernizing-Applications-with-Google-Cloud-Platform/tree/master/Chapter%2018`.

Cloud Run

Google Cloud Run is Google's serverless platform for containers. Being serverless, Google Cloud Run abstracts away all the infrastructure management concerns, allowing us to focus on what is important, which is running the containers that host the microservices for our application. It was built using the Knative open source project, created by Google, and is designed to provide the environment in which to run serverless applications using Kubernetes. The next section examines Knative in more detail.

The Knative stack

The idea of Knative is to simplify the configuration and deployment of containers to Kubernetes by being idiomatic. This means that instead of having to declare manifests for Pods, Stateless Sets, Deployments, Horizontal Pod Autoscalers, Services, Ingress, and so on, these things are set up by default.

The following diagram illustrates the Knative stack:

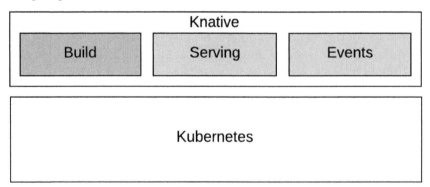

Figure 18.1 – Knative primitives

In the preceding diagram, we see that Knative is underpinned by Kubernetes. Kubernetes is the platform Knative runs on. So, on top of that platform, Knative is an open source community project that adds components for deploying, running, and managing serverless, cloud-native applications in Kubernetes, which are discussed in the following subsections.

Build

Build covers the primitives for building containers to wrap our microservices. The concept is that developers are good at writing code for applications and containers are not applications. For this reason, Knative includes support for simplifying the build of containers for developers. As we are using Knative via Google Cloud Run in Google Cloud this concern is handled by Google Cloud Build, so we will not need to use this aspect of Knative.

Serving

Serving covers the capabilities provided by Knative as Kubernetes **Custom Resource Definitions (CRDs)**. Knative builds on Kubernetes and Istio to deploy and serve containers.

The CRDs provided by Knative for serving are as follows:

- **Service**: Manages the life cycle of our workload, coordinating a route and configuration.

- **Route**: Maps a network endpoint to one or more revisions depending on the deployment strategy.

- **Configuration**: Describes the desired state of our workload and creates a revision to match the desired state.

- **Revision**: A point-in-time snapshot of the code and configuration, allowing for rollbacks, blue/green deployments, and canary deployments. These are created by updates to a configuration.

The following diagram illustrates the relationship between these CRDs:

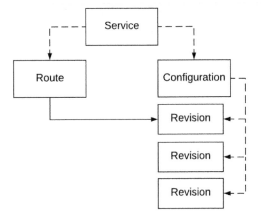

Figure 18.2 – Knative resource types

The only resource listed previously that we create or update using a manifest is the service. We will cover this manifest in the *Deploying containers to Cloud Run* section. All other resource types are managed by the **Service** (manages the **Route** and **Configuration**), or by the **Configuration** (manages the **Revision**).

We now move on to the final group of primitives for triggering our microservices, which are known in **Knative** as events.

Events

Events is an especially important part of Knative and provides an abstraction around various types of trigger. The following trigger types are supported with Google Cloud Run:

- **HTTPS**: All services have an HTTPS URL. This is the standard programming model developers will be familiar with and is often implemented using REST/JSON.

- **gRPC**: Generally used for service-to-service communications (this is Google's open source Remote Procedure Call protocol).

- **Pub/Sub**: Converts the receipt of a pub/sub event into an HTTPS request/response.

- **Schedule**: Like a cron job, these are tasks to be run at a specific time/date.

- **Asynchronous Cloud Tasks**: Adding tasks to a queue to be processed later (fire and forget).

- **Webhook Targets**: Also called a web callback or HTTP push API.

This abstraction provides a standard programming model for each of the trigger types and removes much of the boilerplate code usually needed to handle events for these types of triggers. In this book, we have only made use of the HTTPS trigger type. By way of independent study after completing this chapter, we would recommend studying and experimenting with the pub/sub trigger type as this has the potential to simplify our code base again and remove much of the code for handling the receiving of events from Google Cloud Pub/Sub.

We will now move on and examine the two varieties of Google Cloud Run available to us.

Cloud Run environments

As we mentioned earlier, there are two flavors of Google Cloud Run available to us. These flavors are as follows:

- Fully managed
- Cloud Run for Anthos

We will take a closer look at each flavor in the following sections.

Fully managed

Fully managed Google Cloud Run is the default environment we will be dealing with and the version we will use in this book. The fully managed version hides all of the infrastructure away from us and only presents a control plane where we can deploy and manage our workloads. In this version, we have no visibility of Masters or Nodes, and have no access to `kubectl`. This is the simplest version available to us and is fully serverless.

Cloud Run for Anthos

With Cloud Run for Anthos, we install Google Cloud Run on a Google Kubernetes Engine cluster of our choice. The cluster can be in Google Cloud or on-premises for a hybrid cloud environment. The following diagram helps to visualize this stack:

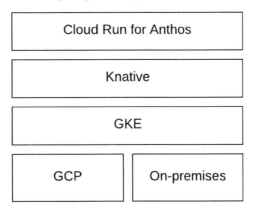

Figure 18.3 – Cloud Run for Anthos

Some of the key differences between the preceding stack and the fully managed version of Google Cloud Run are as follows:

- **Pricing**: Cloud Run for Anthos is billed as part of Anthos, whereas the fully managed version is pay-per-use.

- **Machine types**: Can be chosen with Cloud Run for Anthos (including custom machine types).

- **Autoscaling**: Limited by the capacity of the GKE cluster with Cloud Run for Anthos.

Now that we have learned about Google Cloud Run and Knative, we will look at how to deploy our containers to Google Cloud Run.

Deploying containers to Google Cloud Run

To deploy our application to Google Cloud Run, there are a few changes we need to make to the packaging of our frontend.

Frontend configuration

As Google Cloud Run has no configuration available for ingress or path-based routing of HTTP(S) requests, we will need to implement the reverse proxy approach to the Strangler Façade pattern. The following `default.conf` configuration file declares how the various URL paths will be handled:

```
server {
    listen       80;
    server_name app.banking.jasonmarston.me.uk;
    location / {
        root /usr/share/nginx/html;
        index index.html;
    }
    location /account {
        proxy_ssl_server_name on;
        proxy_pass https://account.banking.jasonmarston.me.uk;
    }
    location /user {
        proxy_ssl_server_name on;
        proxy_pass https://user.banking.jasonmarston.me.uk;
    }
}
```

In the preceding `default.conf` file, any path starting with `/account` after the hostname is routed to the `https://account.banking.jasonmarston.me.uk` endpoint, which we will later configure to be the endpoint for our account service. Any path starting with `/user` after the hostname is routed to the `https://user.banking.jasonmarston.me.uk` endpoint, which we will configure to be the endpoint for our account service. All other paths will be handled by this service, which will have an endpoint of `https://app.banking.jasonmarston.me.uk`.

Next, we make sure that our `Dockerfile` exposes Nginx on port `80`:

```
FROM nginx:1.17.10-alpine
COPY WebContent /usr/share/nginx/html
COPY default.conf /etc/nginx/conf.d/default.conf


EXPOSE 80
```

The changes to the `default.conf` and `Dockerfile` files discussed previously are the only changes we needed to make to our frontend microservice. We can now look at how we describe our microservices to Google Cloud Run using manifest files written in YAML.

Service manifest

Each of the microservices that we will be deploying to Google Cloud Run will have a manifest that declares the information needed by Google Cloud Run to deploy and run the microservices. We will examine a manifest a fragment at a time, starting with the following fragment:

```
apiVersion: serving.knative.dev/v1
kind: Service
metadata:
  name: account
```

The preceding fragment declares that we are using version 1 of the `service.knative.dev` API and the kind of resource we are describing is a Service called `account`.

Next, we will specify the services that Google Cloud Run will provide to our microservice:

```
spec:
  template:
    metadata:
      annotations:
        run.googleapis.com/cloudsql-instances:
bankingapplication:europe-west2:mysql-instance
```

The preceding fragment used the `run.googleapis.com/cloudsql-instances` annotation to declare that Google Cloud Run will manage connectivity to the Google Cloud SQL instance declared.

Next, we specify the containers for our microservice:

```
spec:
  containers:
  - image: gcr.io/bankingapplication/account-rest:latest
    ports:
    - containerPort: 8080
    resources:
      limits:
        cpu: 1000m
        memory: 512Mi
    env:
    - name: BANKING_LOGGING_LEVEL
      value: WARN
    - name: GOOGLE_CLOUD_PROJECT
      value: bankingapplication
```

The preceding fragment declares that the container is based on the gcr.io/
bankingapplication/account-rest:latest image and is exposed on port
8080. It specifies the resource requirements for our container in terms of CPU and RAM,
and finally, it declares the two environment variables our microservice needs and could
not externalize in Google Secret Manager.

The preceding manifest is straightforward. We did not have to declare a Deployment,
a Horizontal Pod Autoscaler, or a Service. All these things were handled for us
automatically by Google Cloud Run. The Knative design goal of removing the *boring but
difficult* parts of deploying microservices has been accomplished.

We will have a manifest like the one above for each of our three microservices –
account, user, and front-end. These manifests will be used by Google Cloud Build
to automate the deployment of our microservices, as we will see in the next section.

Google Cloud Build

To use Google Cloud Build with Google Cloud Run, we need to make sure that the service
account used by Google Cloud Build has permission to deploy our microservices to
Google Cloud Run.

To accomplish this, we perform the following steps:

1. In the Cloud Console from the navigation menu, select **Cloud Build | Settings**.

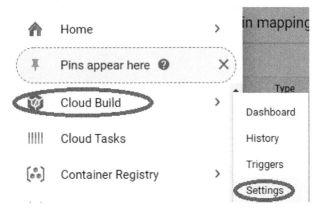

Figure 18.4 – Nav Menu: Cloud Build | Settings

2. Enable the **Cloud Run Admin** role by selecting **ENABLED** in the **Status** column.

Settings

Service account permissions

Cloud Build executes builds with the permissions granted to the Cloud Build service account tied to the project. You can grant additional roles to the service account to allow Cloud Build to interact with other GCP services.

Service account email: 63100814425@cloudbuild.gserviceaccount.com

GCP Service	Role ❓	Status
Cloud Functions	Cloud Functions Developer	DISABLED ▾
Cloud Run	Cloud Run Admin	ENABLED ▾
App Engine	App Engine Admin	ENABLED ▾
Kubernetes Engine	Kubernetes Engine Developer	ENABLED ▾
Compute Engine	Compute Instance Admin (v1)	DISABLED ▾
Firebase	Firebase Admin	DISABLED ▾
Cloud KMS	Cloud KMS CryptoKey Decrypter	DISABLED ▾
Service Accounts	Service Account User	ENABLED ▾

Roles not listed here can be managed in the IAM section

Figure 18.5 – Service account permissions

Google Cloud Build now has the Cloud Run Admin role applied to its service account, and so will be able to deploy containers to Google Cloud Run.

We will now examine the `cloudBuild.yaml` file that we will configure a Google Cloud Build trigger to use. We will do this by breaking the file down into fragments, each containing a build step. The first step is as follows:

```yaml
steps:
- name: 'gcr.io/cloud-builders/gcloud'
  args:
  - 'beta'
  - 'run'
  - 'services'
  - 'replace'
  - 'gcr-deploy/user.yaml'
  - '--platform'
  - 'managed'
  - '--region'
  - 'europe-west4'
```

The preceding step uses the `gcloud` cloud builder to invoke a `gcloud` command that, if entered at a command line, would look like the following:

```
gcloud beta run services replace gcr-deploy/user.yaml
--platform managed --region europe-west4
```

This instructs `gcloud` to deploy a revision of our user service described by the `user.yaml` file to the fully managed version of Google Cloud Run in the `europe-west4` region.

In the next step, we make our user service publicly available:

```yaml
- name: 'gcr.io/cloud-builders/gcloud'
  args:
  - 'run'
  - 'services'
  - 'add-iam-policy-binding'
  - 'user'
  - '--member=allUsers'
  - '--role=roles/run.invoker'
```

```
  - '--platform'
  - 'managed'
  - '--region'
  - 'europe-west4'
```

The preceding step uses the `gcloud` cloud builder to invoke a `gcloud` command that, if entered at a command line, would look like the following:

```
gcloud beta run services add-iam-policy-binding user
--member=allUsers --role=roles/run.invoker --platform managed
--region europe-west4
```

This instructs `gcloud` to apply an IAM policy binding that grants `role roles/run.invoker` to all users.

The preceding pair of steps is repeated twice more, once for each of our remaining microservices, `account`, and `front-end`.

To apply all the preceding code from this chapter and deploy our application microservices into Google Cloud Run, we will first need to copy the projects from the `Chapter 12` folder of the GitHub repository over to our local Git repository for our Google Source Repository. We can then add, commit, and push the changes to make the changes available in Google Cloud.

We then create a Google Cloud Build trigger for the `gcr-deploy` project containing our manifests and `cloudBuild.yaml` file.

To create the required build trigger, perform the following steps:

1. In the Cloud Console, from the navigation menu, select **Cloud Build | Triggers**.

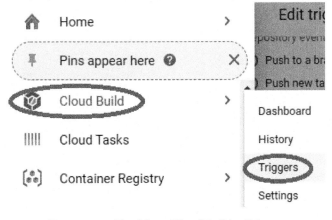

Figure 18.6 – Nav Menu: Cloud Build > Triggers

2. On the **Triggers** page, click **+ CREATE TRIGGER**.

Triggers   →ʘ CONNECT REPOSITORY   (+ CREATE TRIGGER)

Figure 18.7 – CREATE TRIGGER

3. Enter the name of the trigger. We used `gcr-deploy`.

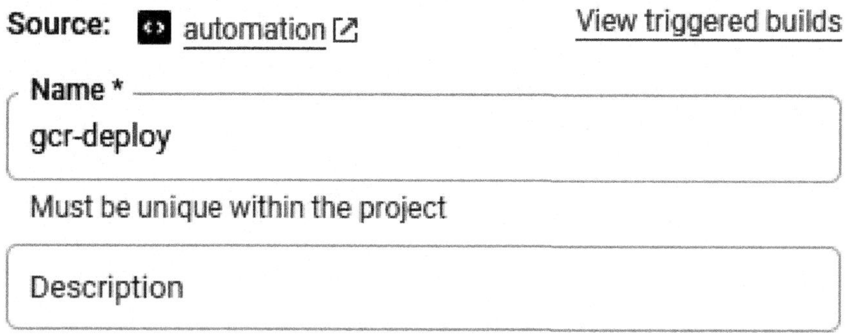

Source: `<>` automation ↗   View triggered builds

┌ **Name *** ──
│ gcr-deploy
└───

Must be unique within the project

┌───
│ Description
└───

Figure 18.8 – Trigger name

4. Provide an **Included files filter (glob)** to ensure that the trigger only executes on updates found in our project. We used `gcr-deploy/**` as our filter.

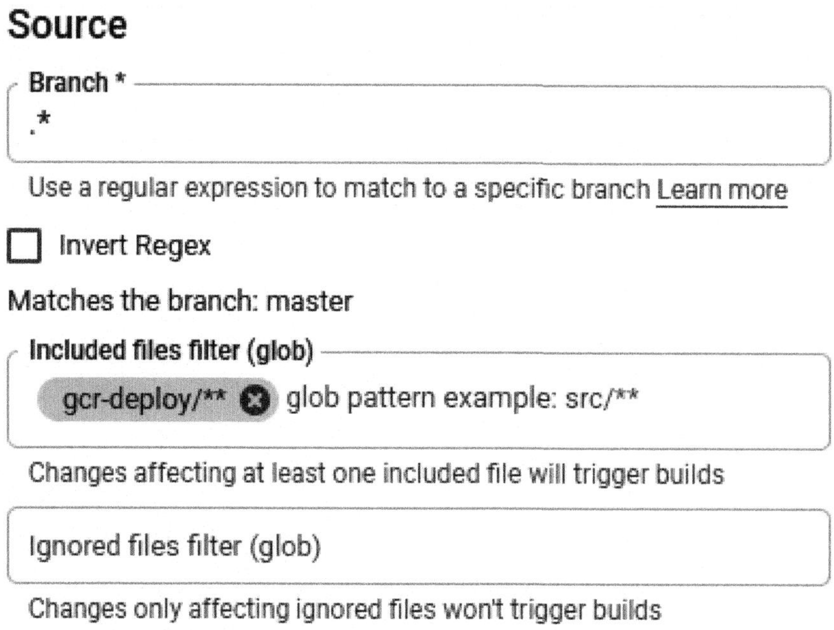

Source

┌ **Branch *** ──
│ .*
└───

Use a regular expression to match to a specific branch Learn more

☐ Invert Regex

Matches the branch: master

┌ **Included files filter (glob)** ─────────────────────
│ (gcr-deploy/** ⊗) glob pattern example: src/**
└───

Changes affecting at least one included file will trigger builds

┌───
│ Ignored files filter (glob)
└───

Changes only affecting ignored files won't trigger builds

Figure 18.9 – Included files filter (glob)

5. Provide the **Cloud Build configuration file location**. We used `/gcr-deploy/cloudBuild.yaml`. Click **SAVE**.

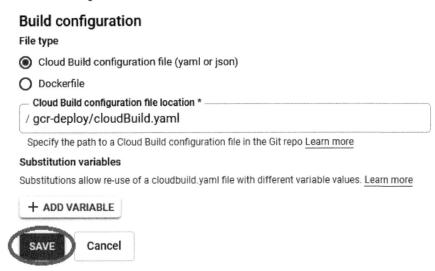

Build configuration

File type

◉ Cloud Build configuration file (yaml or json)

○ Dockerfile

┌─ **Cloud Build configuration file location *** ─────────────────────
│ / gcr-deploy/cloudBuild.yaml
└───

Specify the path to a Cloud Build configuration file in the Git repo Learn more

Substitution variables

Substitutions allow re-use of a cloudbuild.yaml file with different variable values. Learn more

   + ADD VARIABLE

   SAVE   **Cancel**

Figure 18.10 – Build configuration

6. Execute the `gcr-deploy` trigger by clicking **Run trigger**.

Name	Description	Event	Filter	Build configuration	Status		
account-domain	–	Push to branch	.*	account-domain/cloudBuild.yaml	Enabled ▾	Run trigger	⋮
account-rest	–	Push to branch	.*	account-rest/cloudBuild.yaml	Enabled ▾	Run trigger	⋮
auth-domain	–	Push to branch	.*	auth-domain/cloudBuild.yaml	Enabled ▾	Run trigger	⋮
domain-driven-design	–	Push to branch	.*	domain-driven-design/cloudBuild.yaml	Enabled ▾	Run trigger	⋮
firebase-authentication	–	Push to branch	.*	firebase-authentication/cloudBuild.yaml	Enabled ▾	Run trigger	⋮
front-end	–	Push to branch	.*	front-end/cloudBuild.yaml	Enabled ▾	Run trigger	⋮
gae-deploy	–	Push to branch	.*	gae-deploy/cloudBuild.yaml	Enabled ▾	Run trigger	⋮
gcr-deploy	–	Push to branch	.*	gcr-deploy/cloudBuild.yaml	Enabled ▾	Run trigger	⋮
user-core-domain	–	Push to branch	.*	user-core-domain/cloudBuild.yaml	Enabled ▾	Run trigger	⋮
user-domain	–	Push to branch	.*	user-domain/cloudBuild.yaml	Enabled ▾	Run trigger	⋮
user-rest	–	Push to branch	.*	user-rest/cloudBuild.yaml	Enabled ▾	Run trigger	⋮

automation   Cloud Source Repository ⋮ ⌃

Figure 18.11 – Run trigger

7. Deploying to Google Cloud Run is a long-running process, so it will take a few minutes for the build invoked by the trigger to complete. Once it has been completed successfully, we will see something like the following on the **Build history** page:

Build history   **❚❚ STOP STREAMING BUILDS**

	Build	Source	Ref	Commit	Trigger Name	Created	Duration
✓	45a1467a	automation ⬀	master	0ce37c2 ⬀	gcr-deploy	6/17/20, 11:56 AM	2 min 39 sec

Figure 18.12 – Build history

We have, at this point, deployed our microservices to Google Cloud Run. The remaining step is to configure our domain name mappings, which we will cover in the next section.

Domain name mapping

The final step in configuring our application microservice deployment is to provide custom domain name mappings for our three microservices.

We will do this by performing the following steps:

1. In the Cloud Console from the navigation menu, select **Cloud Run**.

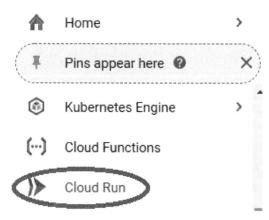

Figure 18.13 – Nav Menu: Cloud Run

2. On the **Cloud Run | Services** page, click **MANAGE CUSTOM DOMAINS**.

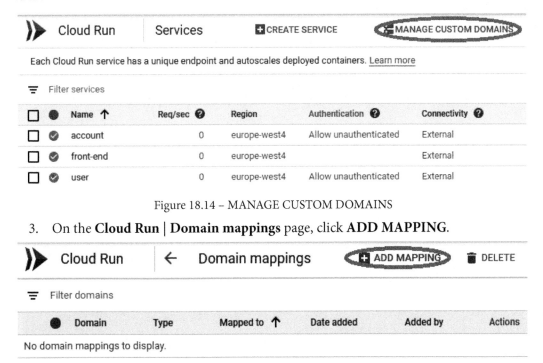

Figure 18.14 – MANAGE CUSTOM DOMAINS

3. On the **Cloud Run | Domain mappings** page, click **ADD MAPPING**.

Figure 18.15 – ADD MAPPING (account)

4. Select **account** for the service, a verified domain for the domain, and enter a hostname. We used `account.banking`, so our fully qualified endpoint would be `https://account.banking.jasonmarston.me.uk`. Click **CONTINUE**.

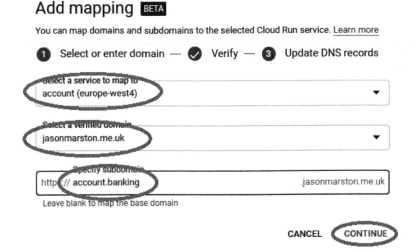

Figure 18.16 – Account mapping

5. Verify that you have a matching CNAME record in your DNS configuration and then click **DONE**.

Add mapping

You can map domains and subdomains to the selected Cloud Run service. Learn more

✓ Select or enter domain — ✓ Verify — ③ Update DNS records

Update the DNS records on your domain host with the records below. You can view these again using the "DNS records" button in the domain mappings table. Learn more

DNS records for **account.banking.jasonmarston.me.uk**

Name	Type	Data
account.banking	CNAME	ghs.googlehosted.com. 🗐

(DONE)

Figure 18.17 – Confirming Add mapping (account)

6. On the **Cloud Run | Domain mappings** page, click **ADD MAPPING**.

Figure 18.18 – ADD MAPPING (user)

7. Select **user** for the service, a verified domain for the domain, and enter a hostname. We used user.banking, so our fully qualified endpoint would be https://user.banking.jasonmarston.me.uk. Click **CONTINUE**.

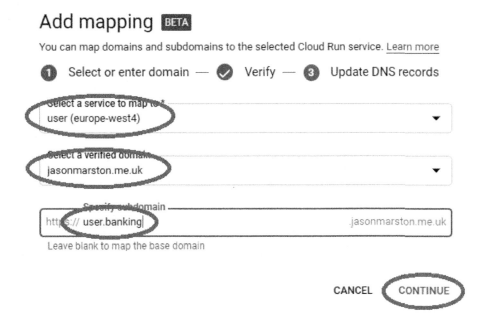

Figure 18.19 – User mapping

8. Verify that you have a matching CNAME record in your DNS configuration and click **DONE**.

Add mapping BETA

You can map domains and subdomains to the selected Cloud Run service. Learn more

✓ **Select or enter domain** — ✓ **Verify** — ③ **Update DNS records**

Update the DNS records on your domain host with the records below. You can view these again using the "DNS records" button in the domain mappings table. Learn more

DNS records for user.banking.jasonmarston.me.uk

Name	Type	Data
user.banking	CNAME	ghs.googlehosted.com.

Figure 18.20 – Confirming Add mapping (user)

9. On the **Cloud Run | Domain mappings** page, click **ADD MAPPING**.

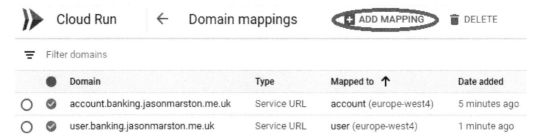

Figure 18.21 – ADD MAPPING (frontend)

10. Select **front-end** for the service, a verified domain for the domain, and enter a hostname. We used app.banking, so our fully qualified endpoint would be https://app.banking.jasonmarston.me.uk. Click **CONTINUE**.

Figure 18.22 – Frontend mapping

11. Verify that you have a matching CNAME record in your DNS configuration and then click **DONE**.

Add mapping

You can map domains and subdomains to the selected Cloud Run service. Learn more

✓ Select or enter domain — ✓ Verify — ❸ Update DNS records

Update the DNS records on your domain host with the records below. You can view these again using the "DNS records" button in the domain mappings table. Learn more

DNS records for **app.banking.jasonmarston.me.uk**

Name	Type	Data
app.banking	CNAME	ghs.googlehosted.com.

DONE

Figure 18.23 – Confirming Add mapping (frontend)

12. Within a few minutes, we will see the three verified mappings, as shown in the following screenshot:

Figure 18.24 – Completed mapping set

Our application is now fully deployed and configured. We can test whether the application is working as expected by using a web browser and opening the https://app.banking.jasonmarston.me.uk URL.

We will now learn about when to use Cloud Run.

When to use Cloud Run

It is the view of the author that Google Cloud Run should be the default deployment environment when containers are under discussion. The question then becomes, when should we not use Google Cloud Run to host our containers?

The following list includes some of the reasons when we would not use Google Cloud Run to host our containers:

- We need stateful containers.

- We need to use ConfigMaps or Secrets.

- We need to have complex ingress routing.

- We need the services to be hosted on a VPC (it is possible to use a VPC connector to access private IP addresses, but Google Cloud Run is not hosted in our VPC).

- We always need to have at least one instance of our container active (it is not currently possible to set the minimum number of instances to anything other than zero).

There are exceptions to the preceding list, specifically around ConfigMaps and Secrets, and the VPC. If we are using Google Cloud Run for Anthos instead of fully managed Google Cloud Run, we can make use of ConfigMaps and Secrets. As regards the VPC, if, when we create our Google Kubernetes Engine, we specify that it will join our VPC, then we, of course, gain full access to the VPC.

Now that we have learned about when to use Google Cloud Run, and when not to, we can move on to the next section and review what we have learned in this chapter.

Summary

In this chapter, we learned about Google Cloud Run and Knative, the open source project it is built upon. We learned that Google Cloud Run is a serverless platform for hosting our container-based microservices, and a key design goal is to remove the *boring but difficult* parts of deploying microservices, such as configuring Horizontal Pod Autoscalers, Services, and Ingress. We learned how to automatically deploy our microservices to Google Cloud Run using a custom domain name.

Deploying apps with Cloud Run is one of the easiest ways to future-proof your application. It also helps ensure that the apps you develop can stand the test of time and continue to live on within the fast-changing world of cloud-native. That said, Cloud Run still has its limitations, especially when it comes to complex orchestration. Thankfully, as with almost everything else that the cloud and Google Cloud offer, there are alternatives to future-proofing your app, too.

And finally, we would like to thank you for sharing this 400-page long experience with us. We, perhaps like yourself, started our cloud computing journey at the end of a similar book and are very grateful that we get to continue contributing to our passion and career, now in the form of a new book.

But we're sure you need to start working on your cloud-native applications, so we'll say goodbye for now and let you get cracking. Happy coding!

Appendix A
Choosing the Right Migration Strategy

In this book, we've explored numerous services and methodologies that achieve the same end goal: to bring a system onto Google Cloud Platform. To someone new, this complex web of interrelated technologies and practices might seem overkill. But there's a simple reason why we have a myriad of options instead of a single plug and play option – not every project is the same, but they are usually similar. For instance, as a developer, some of your projects might require you to migrate an application as quickly as possible or they might not have any deadlines at all; getting every function and feature onto the cloud is all that matters. So, in a way, we can group almost all cloud projects into broad categories that are defined by certain requirements. And to give more structure to development efforts, each cloud project category has an appropriate strategy that is usually the best way of getting started on the cloud. These strategies contain best practices, principles, services, and more that developers can apply in a well-tested sequence of events.

In essence, as soon as you define the requirements for a cloud project, you can usually find a corresponding migration strategy and path that you can adopt as a guide. Then, you can build the rest of your migration roadmap on top of that.

In the brief example we just mentioned, we talked about the two extreme ends on a spectrum of cloud migration options. However, as will be discussed in *Appendix B*, there are a total of six main migration strategies, each with its own nuances.

This appendix explains Google's intuitive and powerful four-step (**Assess**, **Plan**, **Migrate**, and **Optimize**) migration process to simplify the process of understanding its advantages, disadvantages, unique characteristics, and considerations before finally choosing a migration strategy.

Step 1 – assess

The assessment phase is critical for defining your starting point, which, in turn, dictates everything from your first-mover application to the migration path.

To better organize our efforts, the assessment phase can be divided into the following steps:

1. Creating an inventory/portfolio of your applications and grouping them based on similar properties

2. Bringing your development teams up to speed

3. Choosing your first-mover application

Cataloging existing applications

Creating an inventory of your existing applications/workloads and then cataloging them into similar groups is an important step, even if you already have a rough idea of which application you'll be migrating first. This is because your IT infrastructure is likely interconnected and dependent on different applications and workloads to fully function – choosing an application without fully understanding its impact on the rest of the infrastructure is not a smart move.

Additionally, we say *applications/workloads* because your catalog shouldn't just include the list of your applications, but also other elements associated with your application. These can be (but are not limited to) the following:

*   Dependencies that are used within each app

*   Shared databases, storage and messaging systems, and so on

*   Servers that these apps are hosted on

*   Third-party licenses and compliance requirements and restrictions

*   Hardware requirements

All of this information gives you additional insights into the inner workings of all your applications in a single place, which is something you'll need time and time again throughout the migration process.

Finally, the most common method of building this catalog would be to enter the details of each application manually. But if you have a really large ecosystem or one that changes very often, then there are ways to automate this process (but that's outside the scope of this appendix).

Educating teams

As a migration officer, you'll likely be working with different development teams (each in charge of a different application/workload), and ensuring that the development team(s) you're working with understands and is fully on board with this change is crucial for productivity. The biggest difference between the top cloud performers and everyone else is their corporate culture. Every organizational change involves moving employees from a familiar environment to one that's not. And the best way to ensure a smooth transition is to bring your team up to speed in terms of your migration strategy, development roadmap, and goals.

In addition to this, you'll need to consult business owners on the process of certifying team members to ensure they have the necessary expertise to operate. You may also need to create the right training environments and introduce team members to the right resources and learning paths.

And finally, working with internal in-house teams will provide qualitative information about applications that may have been missed in the earlier quantitative assessment.

Choosing what to migrate first

With details of your application ecosystem well established, it's time to choose which application will be migrated first, or in which order your applications will be migrated.

There is a systematic way to do this and that is to evaluate each application/workload against a series of important criteria. By doing this, you can ensure the least disruption to business operations and also a smooth overall transition. However, not every criterion mentioned here can be applied to every project/every business. That said, here is what you're looking for in your first-mover application:

- **Moderately business-critical**: Ideally, we're looking for applications that sit between the most business-critical and least business-critical applications. The reason we're avoiding core business applications such as security or payments as the first-mover advantage is that you might face bugs and other issues during deployment, and we don't want to disrupt central business operations.

At the same time, we're also avoiding the least business-critical applications or applications that are rarely used because, first, you're looking at a smaller user base, which is important for testing, and second, you'll have to divert additional resources to an app that doesn't already have them (such as extra developers), which may be a wasted effort in the long run.

- **Similar to the majority of your applications**: We also want to rule out any edge cases or applications that run in significantly different environments or under unique circumstances. We want an application that can somewhat mimic the behavior of other applications and be a good representation of what to expect through the rest of the migration. Additionally, the solutions that worked on the first-mover application can be applied to others in the future right away.

Capable and innovative teams

We're also looking for applications that are run/maintained not only by teams that have the necessary knowledge to work in a cloud environment but also by innovative teams. High-performing teams with a proven track record of creative problem solving are more likely to be able to meet the challenges that may arise during migration.

The effort required for migration

It's also important to consider the number of dependencies (and other components such as databases, messaging systems, storage systems, and so on) an application has. More dependencies will complicate the process, so lower is generally better. That said, we still want to meet our previous criterion and avoid edge cases. So, if you have no choice but to choose from applications with dependencies, try to choose the ones that are loosely coupled to their dependencies for easier migration.

Additionally, you also want to consider the amount of refactoring involved. The goal with the first-mover app is to not just deploy it but also optimize it before other applications/workloads can be migrated. So, prioritize apps that do not need a lot of refactoring because those can be migrated alongside others simultaneously.

License restrictions and compliance

If you're using any third-party services, tools, or other components, make sure to check if their User License (or Terms of Service) allows you to use them on a cloud environment (public or private) such as Google Cloud Platform.

Additionally, depending on your industry and country/state laws, you may have to take additional steps to ensure compliance before you can host anything on the cloud, especially user data.

Can afford downtime

Finally, in an ideal scenario, we're looking for an application without strict availability requirements that can afford downtime. That said, some methods can be employed to ensure migration can be completed without any downtime, but it is not ideal as it limits the amount of work/testing that can be done.

Choosing what application gets migrated is the most critical part of the assessment phase, so take your time when evaluating the pros and cons of each application. Ideally, we want to go all the way to optimization without changing the first mover application.

Step 2 – plan

The planning phase of cloud migration is one of the most complex parts of the entire migration. As a migration officer, you'll have to answer not just technical questions related to which migration strategy to adopt, which services to use, how many resources to provision, and more, but also make administrative decisions regarding how the cloud environment will run.

For instance, if the project involves migrating to the cloud for the first time, you'll have to address the following:

- An identity account
- Adding users, groups, projects, and so on
- Setting up billing
- Setting up a resource hierarchy, networking configuration, logging and monitoring, and security settings

We've covered some of these things in previous chapters, so we'll not be covering these here. If you are interested in learning more about how to set up fresh Google Cloud Platform accounts, you can find comprehensive, step-by-step guides at Google Cloud Platform's official link.

In this appendix, we're going to be more concerned with the technical aspects of the planning phase; that is, choosing the migration path.

Migration paths versus migration strategies

The first thing to understand about the migration path is that it is not the same as a migration strategy. Unlike a migration strategy, a migration path is specifically concerned with the landing zone of your applications in **Google Cloud Platform**. Landing zones are the pre-configured environments where your applications and workloads will run. You already know about landing zones, just by their specific names, such as **Google Kubernetes Engine** (GKE) and **Google Compute Engine** (GCE).

Here are some common examples of landing zones:

- Google Bare Metal Solution
- **Google Cloud Platform VMware Engine** (GCVE)
- GCE
- GKE
- Google App Engine

And here's a recap of the migration strategies we've discussed:

- Rehost (lift and shift)
- Replatform (move and improve)
- Refactor

That said, migration strategies and landing zones go hand in hand because certain landing zones are simply better suited to specific strategies. For instance, if your goal is just to get an app up and running quickly, you will not lift and shift the application directly to GKE – there are better landing zones for that.

Choosing the right migration path

One more thing to understand before we go any further is that Google Cloud Platform offers a wide variety of landing zones that you can use alongside the migration strategies we will discuss in *Appendix B*.

With that said, let's take a look at some examples that represent real-world scenarios you're more likely to experience.

Hybrid cloud burst

Cloud bursting usually refers to the process of setting up interconnectivity between private and public cloud environments. This configuration allows you to run applications on a private cloud but if a spike in traffic causes 100% utilization of resources, then the overflow traffic gets redirected to a public cloud – without any disruption.

However, in this scenario, because we are migrating from an on-premises infrastructure, we have the option to burst workloads from the on-premises data center.

To do this, you need to use a Google Cloud Platform feature called Cloud Interconnect and set up connectivity between on-premises and cloud infrastructures. This ensures that your workloads will run on your data center under normal load and only *burst* onto the cloud when traffic spikes.

You'll also need to choose a cloud migration strategy such as lift and shift or lift and optimize, as well as a landing zone such as **GCE**, **GKE**, **GCVE**, or Anthos.

Modernizing with Anthos

Anthos is a managed application platform that can be brought to your on-premises infrastructure for more flexible modernization. You would start by establishing interconnectivity between the on-premises data center and Google Cloud and choosing an appropriate landing zone. After that, you can do two things:

- Lift and shift applications/workloads to Google Cloud and begin modernizing on the cloud.

- Build Anthos within your on-premises data center and modernize applications before migration.

Alternatively, you can do both of these things simultaneously by moving some workloads to Google Cloud and freeing up resources that can be used toward on-premises app modernization.

Land, expand, and retire

Another common migration path is called land, expand, and retire, which means that once you have created a landing zone on Google Cloud, you should migrate *all* of your workloads through an appropriate migration strategy (usually, lift and shift or lift and optimize).

Once the migration is complete, you can retire the on-premises data center.

Step 3 – migrate

The third phase of cloud migration is the deployment phase. In this phase, we finalize a deployment process focused on transferring data, deploying workloads to the cloud, and migrating from manual deployments to automated deployments.

Once again, the deployment phase consists of hundreds of variables that influence your decisions, and discussing each variable simply isn't possible. So, to fit everything in this 400-or-so-page book, we've summarized the deployment process into three separate steps, starting with data transfer.

Transferring your data

As we discussed in *Chapter 5, Choosing the Right Database and Storage*, Google Cloud Platform primarily uses *objects*, which means before we can migrate our workloads, we need to move the information/files workloads required for running to the cloud. More importantly, we need to do this without loss of data/integrity.

And because data transfer is especially complex in cloud migrations, we need to assemble a team that can help us execute our data transfer plan and address additional factors, including (but not limited to) the following:

- Administrative decisions (such as approvals)
- Everyday operations (coordinate with internal teams to ensure no existing workloads are disrupted)
- Meeting cost, resources, and time constraints

The team you assemble should have the required authority to control IT resources, approve the movement of data, and manage the teams you are working alongside (engineering, hardware, tracking, and so on).

We also need to choose which method we're going to use for the actual data transfer. This decision is highly dependent on the resources available, especially budget and time. Some of the options that are available for data transfer include the following:

- Direct Peering
- Cloud Interconnect
- Offline transfer (physical storage hardware such as HDDs)

Google Cloud Platform also has many technologies within Google Cloud that enable you to transfer data, including the following:

- Storage Transfer Service

- The `gsutil` tool, which comes as part of the Google Cloud Platform SDK installation

- Transfer Appliance

Finally, a big amount of time needs to be given to security. Each data transfer option comes with security advantages and disadvantages. You need to evaluate these characteristics against the actual threats that you may face during transfer.

Once all the planning is done, you can begin preparing for the transfer by doing performance testing by transferring a relatively large chunk of your data (3–5%) and validating the integrity of the data once the transfer is complete. Now, just do the same process for the rest of the database.

Deploying workloads

With the data now on Google Cloud Platform, you're ready to begin migrating your first-mover application/workloads to the cloud – and there are a few ways to do this. Let's take a quick look at each:

- **Deploying manually**: Although Google Cloud has fully managed services for deployment, you still have the option to deploy your applications completely manually using tools such as Google Cloud Platform Console, Cloud Shell, Cloud APIs, and Cloud SDK.

  This can be a useful option when you are testing unique environments or when you do not have the necessary management APIs. Whatever the reason, Google Cloud gives you full control of provisioning and configuring the deployment to your requirements.

- **Using configuration management (CM) tools**: One of the biggest limitations with fully manual deployments is that it is very difficult to consistently replicate environments. That is why it is often recommended to use CM tools instead. CM tools enable you to configure the environments, provision your infrastructure, and configure your deployment the way you want.

  That said, CM tools are limited as well and do not have many features for anything beyond basic deployment and provisioning.

- **Using the Infrastructure as Code (IaC) pattern**: The **IaC** pattern allows you to provision resources in a runtime environment, just like you would treat the source code of your applications.

  Since the IaC pattern is, in essence, a provisioning tool, it's only suitable to use in the early stages of deployment and it's recommended that you still use CM tools for configuration.

  That said, deploying using the IaC pattern isn't always possible. For instance, you cannot use this method if the target environment does not offer programmatic access to provision and configure resources.

Setting up automated and containerized deployments

To make full use of the cloud environment, you want to set up automated, containerized deployments. This is because neither fully manual deployments nor CM tools are good options (or even sustainable) for long-term operations.

Ideally, you want to set up automated pipelines that can do all of the provisioning and configuring for you – and there are two ways to do this.

If you've already decided to containerize your workloads, then using a container orchestration tool will give you the functionality you need to manage infrastructure, implement deployment logic, as well as other elaborate deployment options.

To make full use of the cloud environment, you will want to set up automated deployments that use end-to-end pipelines (such as CI/CD) to standardize the process of provisioning, configuring, and deploying.

Automated deployments also reduce the risk of human error while saving valuable time that developers can use to innovate.

Step 4 – optimize

Now, with everything we need on Google Cloud we are ready to optimize our workloads and applications to make the most out of Google Cloud's services.

The first step of optimizing your applications is to set your optimization goals. Your optimizations goals can be very specific or broader and generally focused around Google Cloud's benefits, such as improving performance and scaling, making the infrastructure more resilient, increasing automation, reducing costs, and so on.

Once you have set your goals and a baseline has been established (to compare future performance to later), we can get started with optimization.

Letting internal teams takeover

As an independent developer or consultant, you're probably not going to take over your client's day-to-day operations. So, at this point in the migration, it's a good idea to start thinking about training internal or in-house teams.

Some of your main goals would be to do the following:

- Help them understand what has changed from their previous roles.
- Help them become familiar with the Google Cloud Platform ecosystem and how they can use built-in cloud-native tools and services to improve their workflow.
- Point them toward the right resources on cloud-native applications.

As a consultant, you should also take a look at internal policies and how they need to be changed to work well in a cloud-native environment. Remember, one of the most important things in cloud-native app development is a corporate environment that is flexible, open-minded, and values innovation, even if it means the occasional mistake.

Setting up monitoring

Improving is an equally backward-looking process as it is forward-looking. To continue optimizing your cloud-native environment, you need to understand your position yesterday – and you do this through monitoring.

The Google Cloud ecosystem has dozens of powerful monitoring tools that help you measure the performance and health of every individual component, as well as your overall environment – with significantly improved accuracy. On top of this, you do not have to worry about third-party licensing, integrations, or system-breaking updates.

The monitoring services you set up will most likely depend on the individual projects, but don't forget more general-purpose services such as Cloud Monitoring for real-time alerts and warnings or Data Studio for interactive dashboards.

Leveraging managed services and automation

Most of the Google Cloud services you'll come across will be fully managed, which means they can take care of many infrastructure-related operations such as provisioning and configuring resources, thereby significantly reducing your administrative workload.

In addition to these services, you'll also want to pay attention to the automation tools in Google Cloud.. Many workloads will be extremely repetitive (such as deployments) and thus great for automating. In addition to saving the developer's time and effort, you'd also reduce the possibility of human error, as well as costs.

Cost and performance

Finally, you need to find the right balance between performance and cost – which shouldn't be hard, considering Google Cloud is one of the most cost-efficient cloud vendors out there.

There are a ton of tools and services that can help you streamline usage through several different means from autoscaling to removing unnecessary versions.

Furthermore, efficient use of Google Cloud technologies isn't the only way you can reduce costs. You can also leverage the following:

- Google Cloud's comprehensive pricing options to find the right plan
- Automatic sizing recommendations for more efficient GCE instances
- Billing reports, which you can analyze to identify unnecessary expenses
- Sustained use and discounts committed use contracts for even lower GCE costs
- Flat-rate pricing for BigQuery

Appendix B
Application Modernization Solutions

Although the literature on cloud-native app development is predominantly about *new* applications, migrating existing (monolithic) applications to the cloud while enhancing their scalability, resilience, and overall performance is also an equally important part of a cloud developer's job.

In this appendix, we will briefly cover what modernization is (and why we should do it), as well as the following topics:

- How does Anthos, the primary Google Cloud service used for app modernization, work?
- The phases and steps involved in modernizing Java apps
- The six main modernization strategies available to developers

Modernizing Java apps

An overwhelming amount of applications are written in Java, and due to the value these apps provide, especially for legacy businesses, you'll likely need to modernize them without losing functionality or breaking the bank.

By modernizing old Java applications into cloud-native applications, businesses get to enjoy crucial benefits such as the following:

- Reduced time-to-market and the ability to deploy much more frequently
- Increased availability and the ability to create a seamless experience for users by reducing maintenance and scheduled downtime
- Improved resilience against unscheduled failures
- Far lower costs
- Virtually unlimited scalability without over-provisioning resources (auto-scaling)
- Hosting data in a more secure architecture

Let's take a closer look.

What is Google Anthos?

We've talked briefly about Google Anthos as a migration platform and landing zone where we can containerize different workloads, including Java applications, but there's a lot more to Anthos.

Anthos is an application management platform where you can develop and modernize applications, no matter where the applications are. It is built on popular open source technologies, including Kubernetes and Knative, and supports app development/migration in public, private, hybrid clouds, and even on-premises infrastructure.

As a result, it has a complex framework of interrelated technologies that makes it possible to achieve a lot of different goals. But today, we're going to simplify that framework to understand three of its main functions/components that make migration possible.

Key components of Anthos

The following are the key components of Anthos:

- **Anthos clusters**: Anthos clusters combine multiple Kubernetes releases for easier management and deployment of Kubernetes applications in the environment of your choice. In essence, because both main components of Kubernetes (control plane and node components) are hosted on-premises, Anthos clusters add a common orchestration layer that developers can use for easier deployment, scaling, and configuration of their Kubernetes containers.

- **Anthos Config Management**: Config Management is similar to a policy management tool; its main purpose is to allow developers to manage all of their different types of clusters using config files that are stored in a Git repository.

  In other words, with config management, you're using a Configuration as Code approach to managing clusters, similar to how you would manage applications already deployed in Google Kubernetes.

- **Anthos Service Mesh**: Anthos Service Mesh creates a network of all the applications running on Anthos clusters and includes important components such as load balancing, service-to-service authentication, and monitoring. Service Mesh is an important tool for security, monitoring, and managing services.

> **Important Note**
> There are other components to Anthos as well such as Cloud Run for Anthos, Cloud Build for Anthos, Cloud Logging, and more. Remember, Anthos does a lot of things. However, to keep our discussion focused, we're not going to explore the rest (we've already covered many of these services in previous chapters).

Now that we understand Anthos, we can continue with the next step of modernizing Java apps: planning out the process.

Preparing to modernize Java apps

Many of the steps and best practices from *Appendix A* still apply to old Java apps but the overall planning process has been narrowed down, so it should be easier to follow.

For instance, in most cases, developers choose the lift and modernize method. The entire process can be summarized in two phases:

1. The first phase is the *lift* part of the job and refers to containerizing the applications and creating CI/CD pipelines.

2. The second phase is the *modernize* part and refers to refactoring the apps to modern Java frameworks.

Some Java applications may not be suitable for the lift-and-modernize approach. In general, packaged Java apps and those running on modern Java frameworks can be containerized using Anthos. On the other hand, traditional monolithic Java apps must be run in VMs until they can be refactored into microservices, while apps with legacy backends cannot be migrated to the cloud.

With this clear, let's dive into the first phase of modernizing Java apps.

The following is a brief explanation of all the steps in phase 1.

Phase 1 – containerizing Java applications

Containers are foundational in cloud-native applications and significantly improve the development process. Each container is a package that contains everything it needs to run an application (the code, dependencies, and libraries too). This portable and lightweight package is a great alternative to VMs that is also more efficient. That's why Anthos and many other cloud services such as Google Kubernetes Engine work primarily with containers.

Step 1 – containerizing Java applications

The process of containerizing Java applications begins with building JAR files. These JAR files can then be packaged into a containerized form such as Docker files. Alternatively, Java applications can be packaged into Kubernetes resource manifests, which is another form of container.

Step 2 – deploying applications to Anthos using modern CI/CD

The next step is to modernize our applications so that they can work flawlessly in a cloud-native environment. We do this by putting them on a highly automated assembly line called CI/CD. This is an automated and reliable software delivery method that takes over repetitive deployment and testing tasks in modern applications.

Step 3 – optimizing on-premises VMs for legacy Java applications

As we mentioned earlier, not all Java apps are suitable for containerization, so some apps will have to run in VMs. There are two ways we can do this. The first option involves using **Google Compute Engine** (GCE) instances, while the second option involves using VMware as a Service to manage their VMs across multi and hybrid environments while still having VMware-specific features. Additionally, Google offers built-in tools to migrate apps to GCE instances, while setting up VMware as a Service is a bit more complex.

With these three things complete, the app modernization process can continue to phase 2 where we will begin refactoring and/or re-platforming the app.

Phase 2 – Refactoring and re-platforming

Containerizing is only one part of the job. To make old Java applications fully compatible with cloud-native technologies, we also want to refactor our apps to modern Java frameworks and turn them into microservices for more scalability, security, and resilience. Most importantly, Google Cloud already has the required services to do this in its ecosystem.

For instance, developers can use Spring Cloud GCP to simplify the process of moving old Java apps to Spring Boot, a modern Java framework. The Spring Boot programs support other Google Cloud services such as Pub/Sub, Spanner, Logging, Firestore, BigQuery, and more so that you can also expand your old Java apps' functionality.

You can also continue creating modern, containerized Java apps with a host of tools and services, including Cloud Code, Artifact Registry, and build tools such as Jib and Buildpacks.

Additionally, applications that are running on commercial Java platforms and cannot be refactored will need to be re-platformed to open source alternatives such as JBoss or Tomcat.

Finally, this leaves us with legacy applications that cannot be refactored or re-platformed. To migrate these monolithic applications, we'll have to break down the monolith into microservices.

There are different ways this can be done – six, to be exact. Each of these methods or modernization strategies will be discussed in the next section.

Modernization strategies (the 6 Rs of modernization)

We must examine the different modernization strategies available today to ensure we conduct a cost-efficient and successful cloud migration. Unfortunately, it is far too common for organizations to only see two options: *lift and shift* and *rewrite*:

- The *lift and shift* approach is used to recreate exactly what you have on-premises in the cloud, but it fails to realize the benefits of cloud architectures such as elasticity. The problems with on-premises are simply replicated to the cloud. Hence, these projects are often deemed failures.

- The *rewrite* approach is covered in the next section as the re-architect strategy. As the name suggests, this approach involves writing a cloud-native application from scratch to recreate (and enhance) the original app's functionality but in a cloud environment.

There are multiple strategies we can use to modernize our application, and while modernizing our application, we will use more than one.

In the following section, we will examine six modernization strategies, known collectively as the 6Rs.

Retire, retain, and re-architect

The **retire** strategy is when we examine the application and decide that the application is no longer needed, we have another application we can use that provides the functionality in this one, or we are going to replace the application with a new one (perhaps a Software as a Service offering). Simply put, we decide that the application is not worth modernizing and we either don't need it or can replace it.

The **retain** strategy is when we decide that, for now, we will continue to use the application in its current on-premises. There are various reasons why we may decide to do this, and we have listed a few here:

- The application could be on a language or platform that is not available in public clouds, such as IBM i (AS/400) or a mainframe.

- There may be licensing terms of components that prohibit their deployment in public clouds.

- The cost of modernization may outweigh the benefits.

- The application has a limited lifetime, so modernizing an application that will be retired shortly after modernization would be a waste of resources.

The **re-architect** strategy was mentioned earlier as the rewrite option. This is where we decide to start from scratch and architect a complete replacement for the application. We use cloud-native patterns and principles from the start to design a completely new cloud-native application that replicates the functionality of the original application.

This is the most common strategy put forward by consultants, systems integrators, and developers. It can be a valid strategy and the right thing to do. However, it does have drawbacks, some of which are as follows:

- Sunk costs in the existing application need to be written off.

- Such projects can be lengthy in duration.

- Such projects can be expensive to execute.

- The benefits are only realized after the project is completed.

- There is the risk that the expected benefits won't be realized.

We will not be using the retire, retain, or re-architect strategies in this book, but it is important to understand them and that they are valid options. When choosing strategies, it is important to assess the application in detail to decide which strategies are appropriate. Some factors to include when we assess applications are as follows:

- Business criticality

- Application lifetime

- Application complexity

- Technology/platform restrictions

- Licensing considerations

- Regulatory considerations

- Value of benefits

Assessing the application portfolio is not a one-time thing. The world changes over time, so we should schedule assessments regularly. Annual or half-yearly assessments are often used.

In the remaining sections of this chapter, we will examine three of the six strategies that are used throughout this book and are appropriate for modernizing our example application. These strategies are as follows:

- **Rehost**: Move and improve with no changes to the application and minimal changes to the infrastructure architecture.

- **Replatform**: Replace virtual machines with an *as a Service* offering from Google Cloud such as Google Cloud SQL and Google Kubernetes Engine.

- **Refactor**: To iteratively and incrementally pull out capabilities from the monolithic legacy application and make them microservices that are packaged in containers.

Let's look at these strategies in detail.

Rehost

At first glance, we may think that rehost is the same as *lift and shift*. However, rehost is actually *move and improve*. What do we mean by that? With *lift and shift*, we recreate exactly what we had on-premises. This includes all the virtual machines or physical machines that provide capabilities such as load balancing, firewalls, authentication, and so on. It also means we are not taking advantage of the cloud services provided by Google Cloud to handle those capabilities, and we do not have elasticity. The entire environment is the same as on-premises and the benefits promised by the cloud have not been realized.

With the rehost strategy, we take the core virtual machines of our application and recreate them in Google Cloud using **GCE**, replacing the non-core virtual machines with Google Cloud capabilities. As an example, some of the types of virtual machines that can be recreated in Google Cloud are as follows:

- Virtual machines that run application logic

- Virtual machines that host relational data

- Virtual machines that host caches

- Virtual machines that host unstructured data, such as images

Some of the types of virtual machines that would be replaced with Google Cloud capabilities are as follows:

- Virtual machines that host firewalls (network or application firewalls)

- Virtual machines that host load balancers

- Virtual machines that host NAT or routing capabilities

- Virtual machines that host VPNs

Mostly, the category of virtual machines that will be replaced with Google Cloud capabilities fulfill our network capabilities.

When we use the rehost strategy, we are still using the same operating systems, maybe even the same versions. We are not changing the code base of the application. We are making minor changes to the infrastructure architecture to take advantage of the capabilities provided by Google Cloud. The essence of the strategy is to make no changes to the software architecture or code base and make minimum changes to the infrastructure architecture, gaining some of the benefits provided by cloud infrastructures without making disruptive changes to our overall architecture.

The rehost strategy is not generally used alone but as a step on the path of modernization. It moves our application into the cloud and removes the responsibility of some capabilities from the application, placing them with the Google Cloud environment. After rehost, we generally move on to re-platform, which will be covered in the next section.

Re-platform

Re-platforming is where things start to get very interesting. This is where we start looking at Platform as a Service and the serverless capabilities provided by Google Cloud. We generally start by looking at the services provided to the application and ask the question, *Is there a service provided by Google Cloud that handles this?* Using these services means we no longer need to maintain a virtual machine for that capability. We no longer need to apply patches and so on. We simply configure and manage the service rather than the underlying infrastructure that supports the platform.

A typical approach we would take is to start at the data layer. Instead of managing a high availability cluster of MySQL virtual machines, for instance, and all the complexities that entail, we can choose to use Google Cloud SQL. Here, we get high availability and backups out of the box. When configuring Google Cloud SQL, we decide on the following:

- What **Relational Database Management Server** (**RDBMS**) we want to use. This could be MySQL, for instance.
- The version of the RDBMS we want to use.
- The region and zone of the primary instance.
- The private and optionally public IP addresses.
- How much CPU, RAM, and storage we need (and if the storage is SSD or HDD).
- The schedule for our backups.
- If we want HA, what zone we want to place the failover instance in.

Google Cloud SQL supports MySQL, PostgreSQL, and MS SQL. This means that there is usually no or very little change to the code base, unless, of course, the application depends on an RDBMS not listed, such as Oracle.

We continue with the other data services provided to our application and re-platform each in turn. For many such data services, as with MySQL, there will be no or very little change to the code base, as we are simply replacing the service with a managed version provided by Google Cloud. However, one area where we may need to make code changes is with unstructured data. This will depend on the decisions we make. If we don't want to make code changes to an application that accesses files, for instance, we can use Google Cloud Filestore, which provides us with Network Attached Storage as a Service. If our application is structured so that the code accessing the filesystem is well encapsulated, then we could decide to replace the filesystem code with code to access Google Cloud Storage and access Blobs rather than files.

Once we have finished re-platforming the services provided to our application, we can look at re-platforming the application itself. There are multiple options for this. We can re-platform our application with one of the following:

- Google App Engine – Standard
- Google App Engine – Flexible
- Google Kubernetes Engine
- Google Cloud Functions
- Google Cloud Run

We can categorize these options as those that are container-based and those that are not. The container-based options are Google App Engine (Flexible), Google Kubernetes Engine, and Google Cloud Run. The options that don't use containers are Google App Engine (Standard) and Google Cloud Functions. So, how do we choose between the two categories? The choice comes down to our needs:

- Do we need a microservice architecture?
- Do we need to orchestrate between components that will be deployed independently?
- Do we need cloud mobility (the ability to move the application from one public cloud to another)?
- Does the option support the language and stack we are using?

Our application may use a combination of these services. For instance, Google Cloud Functions and Google Cloud Run are very good at responding to events (triggers). It is very common to separate the code for handling events such as a file upload to cloud storage from the business logic. This separation of concerns isolates the *plumbing* code that's specific to an environment from the core of the application.

The following is a quick reference to help when making these decisions.

Simple applications that don't need containers:

- Google App Engine – Standard

Container-based applications that don't need orchestration:

- Google App Engine – Flexible

Event handling:

- Google Cloud Functions
- Google Cloud Run

Container orchestration, allowing stateful and stateless containers:

- Google Kubernetes Engine

Fully serverless stateless containers:

- Google Cloud Run

Re-platforming is not something that can be done only once. We may iterate on our re-platforming in conjunction with refactoring. So, we could do the following:

1. Re-platform the application onto Google App Engine – Standard.
2. Refactor to separate the events.
3. Re-platform the event handling of the application onto Google Cloud Functions.
4. Refactor to microservices.
5. Re-platform the microservices onto Google Kubernetes Engine.
6. Re-platform the event handling process onto Google Cloud Run.

Next, let's take a detailed look at how refactoring works.

Refactor

When using the refactor strategy, what we are doing is iteratively and incrementally taking the existing code base and restructuring it into a new architecture. This is not rewriting the business logic but changing the structure of the application so that it fits our non-functional requirements. The first step of refactoring is to separate the presentation logic from the business logic (services). These may already be logically separate in the application but they are not physically separate and often run in the same process. The approach is to have the presentation layer as a separate deployment to the business layer. Then, you can expose the business services to the presentation layer as **Representational State Transfer (REST)** services that use **JavaScript Object Notation (JSON)** to exchange information.

Once the presentation layer and the business layer are separated, we can start to refactor the business layer into microservices. The approach that's generally taken is to use the *Strangler Fig Pattern* proposed by *Martin Fowler*. In this pattern, we place a façade between the presentation layer and the business layer to hide changes to endpoint locations from the presentation layer. This façade is often implemented using an HTTP(S) load balancer with request routing.

With this in place, we can extract a specific capability we want to refactor into a microservice. This could be, for instance, a User Profile service that provides information on the logged-in user such as their preferred language, display name, contact preferences, and so on. Once separated, our microservice can be packaged into a container and deployed onto, for instance, Google Kubernetes Engine. Then, we can update the routing on the load balancer to route the URL for our User Profile capability to the new service. The presentation layer would not be aware of this change due to our facade.

This process continues until there is nothing left of the original monolithic application, and all the capabilities are now provided by microservices.

The refactor strategy allows us to gain business benefits very quickly and incrementally build on those benefits. If we had used the re-architect strategy, the benefits would come much later, and without feedback on the incremental changes delivered by the refactor strategy, decisions made early could likely have negative consequences, which will then be magnified by the time delay. The refactor strategy allows us to gather telemetry and feedback on our journey. With that information, we can implement course corrections along the way, with a minimal negative impact on our solution.

Packt>

Packt.com

Subscribe to our online digital library for full access to over 7,000 books and videos, as well as industry leading tools to help you plan your personal development and advance your career. For more information, please visit our website.

Why subscribe?

- Spend less time learning and more time coding with practical eBooks and Videos from over 4,000 industry professionals
- Improve your learning with Skill Plans built especially for you
- Get a free eBook or video every month
- Fully searchable for easy access to vital information
- Copy and paste, print, and bookmark content

Did you know that Packt offers eBook versions of every book published, with PDF and ePub files available? You can upgrade to the eBook version at packt.com and as a print book customer, you are entitled to a discount on the eBook copy. Get in touch with us at customercare@packtpub.com for more details.

At www.packt.com, you can also read a collection of free technical articles, sign up for a range of free newsletters, and receive exclusive discounts and offers on Packt books and eBooks.

Other Books You May Enjoy

If you enjoyed this book, you may be interested in these other books by Packt:

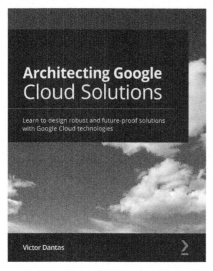

Architecting Google Cloud Solutions

Victor Dantas

ISBN: 9781800563308

- Get to grips with compute, storage, networking, data analytics, and pricing
- Discover delivery models such as IaaS, PaaS, and SaaS
- Explore the underlying technologies and economics of cloud computing
- Design for scalability, business continuity, observability, and resiliency
- Secure Google Cloud solutions and ensure compliance
- Understand operational best practices and learn how to architect a monitoring solution
- Gain insights into modern application design with Google Cloud
- Leverage big data, machine learning, and AI with Google Cloud

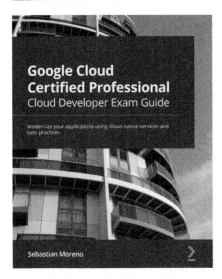

Google Cloud Certified Professional Cloud Developer Exam Guide

Sebastian Moreno

ISBN: 9781800560994

- Get to grips with the fundamentals of Google Cloud Platform development
- Discover security best practices for applications in the cloud
- Find ways to create and modernize legacy applications
- Understand how to manage data and databases in Google Cloud
- Explore best practices for site reliability engineering, monitoring, logging, and debugging
- Become well-versed with the practical implementation of GCP with the help of a case study

Packt is searching for authors like you

If you're interested in becoming an author for Packt, please visit `authors.packtpub.com` and apply today. We have worked with thousands of developers and tech professionals, just like you, to help them share their insight with the global tech community. You can make a general application, apply for a specific hot topic that we are recruiting an author for, or submit your own idea.

Share Your Thoughts

Now you've finished , we'd love to hear your thoughts! Scan the QR code below to go straight to the Amazon review page for this book and share your feedback or leave a review on the site that you purchased it from.

https://packt.link/r/1800209797

Your review is important to us and the tech community and will help us make sure we're delivering excellent quality content.

Index

U

V

W

Z

Printed in Great Britain
by Amazon

81785713R00278